RESPONDING
TO FILM

Film ← History
Literature
Social theme
in films

Benjamin Brett

RESPONDING TO FILM

A Text Guide for Students of Cinema Art

Constantine Santas
Flagler College
St. Augustine, Florida

Burnham Inc., Publishers

CHICAGO

President: Kathleen Kusta
Vice-President: Brett J. Hallongren
General Manager: Richard O. Meade
Project Editor: Sheila Whalen
Designer: Tamra Phelps
Cover Image: "White Trees #3" by Jordan
Printer: Cushing-Malloy, Inc.

All photographs used in this publication are copyrighted by © Photofest, except for the image on page 64, which is provided by the courtesy of Ronald G. Phelps, copyright © 1992.

Library of Congress Cataloging-in-Publication Data

Santas, Constantine.
  Responding to film : a text guide for students of cinema art /
Constantine Santas.
      p. cm.
Includes index.
  ISBN 0-8304-1580-7 (alk. paper)
  1. Motion pictures. I. Title.
  PN1994 .S342 2001
  791.43--dc21

                                        2001003063

Manufactured in the United States of America

10 9 8 7 6 5 4 3 2 1

 The paper used in this book meets the minimum requirements of American National Standard for Information Sciences—Permanence of Paper for Printed Library Materials, ANSI Z39.48-1984.

Contents

Acknowledgments   xi

INTRODUCTION
How to Respond to Film   1

The Individual Response   1
The Critical Response   2
All Responses Are Legitimate   3
The Experience of Viewing a Film   4
The Literary Response   9
The Aims of This Text Guide   9
Suggested Readings   10

CHAPTER 1
Responding to Film as an Art Form   11

Film as an Art   11
Film as Communication   16
The Filmmaker as an *Auteur*   18
The Screenwriter as an Artist   19
Film as a Literary Art   21

Suggested Readings and Hypertext Links   28
Suggested Films for Study   28

CHAPTER 2
Responding to Film Genre   **30**
Origins of Film Genres: Epic, Drama, and Comedy   30
The Modern Epic Film   32
Tragic Genre Derivatives: Drama and Melodrama   36
The Comic Genre: The Romantic Archetype   44
Genre Derivatives   48
Suggested Readings and Hypertext Links   51
Suggested Films for Study   52

CHAPTER 3
Responding to Film Techniques   **54**
Learning Film Techniques   54
Important Film Techniques   57
References and Suggested Readings and Hypertext Links   73
Suggested Films for Study   74

CHAPTER 4
Responding to Film Language   **75**
Definition of Film Language   75
Codes and Codification: The Semiotician's Visual Methods   76
Axes and Nodes: Reading Film Language   79
Combining Visual and Audial Nodes: Varieties of Film Discourse 85
Axes and Nodes in the Discursive Language of Comedy   87
The Soundtrack: Audial Axes and Nodes   90
Film and Music   91
The New Language of Film: Digital Technology and Hypertext   92
Suggested Readings and Hypertext Links   94
Suggested Films for Study   94

CHAPTER 5
Responding to Film as History   **96**
Placing a Film in Its Historical Context   97

More Reasons for Studying Film Historically   100

Film's Historical Settings: The New Historicism   111

History and Social Issues   112

Film Is History   113

Suggested Readings and Hypertext Links   113

Suggested Films for Study   114

CHAPTER 6
Responding to Films in Black and White   **116**

The Attraction of Color   116

The Classic Black-and-White Movies: Colorization   117

Why Movies in Black and White Endure   119

Films in Black and White Through the 1960s and Beyond   121

Black and White Today   126

Suggested Readings and Hypertext Links   128

Suggested Films for Study   128

Suggested Black-and-White Films for Study   128

CHAPTER 7
Responding to Foreign Film   **130**

The Origins of International Cinema   130

Foreign Film—Unpopular in the American Classroom   132

The Decline of Foreign Film   132

Foreign Film's Heyday   133

The Art-House Movie: Mostly Foreign   134

More Contrasts Between Foreign and Domestic Films   135

Foreign Films for Study   140

Watching a Foreign Film Today   145

Suggested Readings and Hypertext Links   145

Suggested Foreign Films for Study   145

CHAPTER 8
Responding to Film's Literary Sources   **147**

Can a Film Measure Up to Its Literary Source?   147

Film and the Literary Tradition   149

Adaptations of Merit   155

Film Equivalents of Classic Literary Works   156
Literary Derivatives   174
The Future of Literary Adaptations: A Marriage   175
Suggested Readings and Hypertext Links   175
Film Adaptations Suggested for Study   175

CHAPTER 9
Responding to Film as Film   **177**
Film's Uniqueness   177
Reality vs. Illusion: Film's Superiority   179
Film: Distinct from Literature, Matches Literature   181
Film Is Visual Reality   182
Film—Sum Total of Its Parts   183
Films and Star Power   184
Film as Film: Some Examples   187
Suggested Readings and Hypertext Links   197
Suggested Films for Study   198

CHAPTER 10
Responding to Social Themes in Film   **200**
Should a Film Contain a Moral?   200
Film Is Conscious of Moral Behavior   201
Message as Part of a Story   203
Using Film Language to Uncover Social Themes   203
Film and Gender   209
Film and Social Themes   216
Suggested Readings and Hypertext Links   221
Suggested Films for Study   221

CHAPTER 11
Responding to Film Violence   **223**
Two Facets of Film Violence   223
The Prevalence of Film Violence   224
The Historical Perspective on Film Violence   225
Dealing with Violence in Film   227
Suggested Readings and Hypertext Links   239

CHAPTER 12
Responding to Film Technology   **240**
  The Value of Commentaries   241
  Hypertext and Its Uses   242

CHAPTER THIRTEEN
A Sample Course   **245**
  The Great Dictator (1941): Information Sheet   246
  The Seventh Seal (1956): Information Sheet   248
  *Dr. Strangelove, or How I Learned to Stop Worrying and Love
      the Bomb* (1964): Information Sheet   250
  Psycho (1960): Information Sheet   252
  Amadeus (1984): Information Sheet   254
  Platoon (1986): Information Sheet   257
  Quiz Show (1994): Information Sheet   260
  2001: A Space Odyssey (1968): Information Sheet   262
  A Passage to India (1984): Information Sheet   264
  Schindler's List (1993): Information Sheet   268
  The English Patient (1996): Information Sheet   270

Index   **273**

Acknowledgements

For Instructional Design, I owe thanks to Dr. J. Peter Kincaid of the University of Central Florida and to his colleague Cindy Legg. Without their valuable assistance, *Responding to Film*, first custom-printed for my film classes last year, could not have come into existence. I would also like to thank Professor Eric Rentschler of the University of California at Irvine who discussed with me some of the concepts I use in this text guide regarding film language, and particularly concepts of social codes and codification. His syllabus of course design, which he was kind enough to send me, has become the basis for developing some of my "Film Literature" classes at Flagler College.

Many thanks go to Professor Gerasimos Santas of UCI who kindly read portions of the manuscript and offered suggestions on language and argument method. Many thanks to Professor Vince Puma of Flagler College for reading chapter 4, "Film Language," and offering suggestions from a linguist's point of view, and to Professor Chris Schroeder, who made notes on the same chapter from a semiotician's point of view. Dr. Carl Horner, Associate Professor of English, read chapter 1, giving detailed suggestions on style that have been valuable to me through the rest of the book. And many thanks go to the students of my class, "Film Literature/Media Aesthetics" at Flagler College, for making critical and very helpful comments on the manuscript in their class evaluations.

I would also like to acknowledge the contributions of Stephen Skipp of the audiovisual department at Flagler College and of Professor Todd Lidh, for

helping me with the graphic designs in this book. I also wish to thank my former student Joseph Cook for providing me with ideas, film reviews, commentaries, and extensive lists of film, some of which were included in the films
for study at the end of various chapters.

A note of thanks to Professor George Anagnostopoulos of UCSD for
sending me Greek cinema materials and to Jim Chastain, President of the
Film Society of St. Augustine, for bringing to my attention and showing films
I would not otherwise have seen. Finally, I wish to thank my daughter, Chris-
tiana Santas, for her inexhaustible supply of film books and videos over the
years, my son Telis Santas of Valdosta State University for sharing his ideas on
film social issues, and my wife Mary for countless hours of shared film viewing and opinions I might never have considered.

INTRODUCTION

How to Respond to Film

> *A film is a cooperative effort between the director and the audience. A director shows a bit of human emotion; the audience fills in the rest. The better the film, the greater the cooperation between the director and the audience.*
>
> —*D.W. Griffith*

How do I respond to film? This question has several possible answers: The first is, I respond as I want to. Whatever I think of the film when I watch it, whatever I feel, whatever meanings I gather from it after I view it—these are my individual responses, the only ones I believe in. What I've seen is what I believe is the truth; my own impressions are valid, the ones having meaning for me. To respond otherwise would be a betrayal of my own personal feelings, emotions, and thoughts.

The Individual Response

This seems a legitimate approach on the face of it and in view of recent trends in literary criticism, especially from those critics who belong to the Reader-Response camp. This view holds that meanings are not inherent in the text—whether the text is literary, or rendered in a visual medium such as film—but

1

are encapsulated in a reader's or viewer's consciousness, shaped by his or her social milieu (or range of social perceptions), and are automatically related to cultural orientations. Viewers are conditioned by the time, place, society, or institutions which they inhabit. Their responses are bound to be affected by these factors, which will influence, either consciously or unconsciously, their interpretations of what they see. Imagine, for instance, a group of people, male and female, of various ages, and varied literary backgrounds, going to see the film version of *The Great Gatsby* (1974). The responses to the film of those who have read the book will be conditioned by their knowledge of the novel, and hence by their preconceived notions of what the characters in the story ought to be. One or more of them might think the film is antifeminist or racist, or is flawed in some other way. Their interpretations are "precoded," so to speak, even preestablished, by individual status, bias, belief, or literary orientation. Thus, the argument goes, individual response is determined by factors over which one has little control. Individual response, whether conscious or unconscious, is unavoidable. Older critics, such as Rudolf Arnheim who derived his philosophical background from the theories of gestalt psychology, claimed that a reader's or viewer's mind determines the meaning of what he or she views or reads; in other words, that viewing is entirely subjective. Other critics of cinema, Sergei Eisenstein for instance, tried to balance the objectivity of filmmaking and the subjectivity of viewing (Andrew 44). All critics agree that, at least to a certain extent, film viewing is, and ought to be, first and foremost a subjective experience. Nothing can replace an individual response.

The Critical Response

But there is another possible response—let us call it the critical response: This response should be predicated on the assumption that the viewer of film searches for meanings that exist *in* the film, placed there not by some Platonic entity, but by those who made it. Such meanings can be discovered and interpreted accordingly when one studies a film using critical methods. In particular, a student should try to understand film as an art form, made during a certain historical period by a particular industry, by producers or directors who, for the most part, sought to appeal to the broadest mass audience. To respond to film critically, students must devote part of their time to trying to learn as much as possible about the film industry itself, the filmmaker's intentions, and his or her personal, social, philosophical, and artistic orientations. Study of films by Federico Fellini or John Ford, for instance—two filmmakers who were contemporaries—should take into account their backgrounds and artistic visions: John Ford was a product of the Hollywood studio system who eventually became known for his productions of western films, most of them featuring John

Wayne. Wayne's characters embodied American values such as honesty, loyalty, self-reliance, heroism. They were larger-than-life American individualist heroes of the west, and Ford's landscape was Monument Valley. Fellini had his roots in Italy's postwar Neo-Realist movement, and he concentrated on personal, self-analytical, psychological, moral tales, eventually abandoning realism for allegory. A student of either John Ford or Fellini should study not one film, but a series of films, possibly in chronological sequence, to trace the development of these directors' styles and outlooks. To study critically, a student must understand the aesthetic transaction involved: Filmmakers, whether producers or directors or companies, employ a large group of people, all of whom contribute to the making of a film. Their original materials and techniques, if understood, become part of the interpretation of a film or films. First, materials go into a film in certain ways peculiar to this art; then a student, familiar with that art form and its methods, digs up meanings inherent in the film, attempting to comprehend the reasons those meanings were placed there. This process constitutes the aesthetic transaction, that is, the transference of meanings from the maker to the object and then from the object to the viewer or student. Thus, the critical response is accomplished. There is nothing mysterious or excessively abstruse about this method; but in practical terms, the method may need to encompass a variety of responses. The critical response will require that a student go beyond his or her personal preconceptions, or even outside his or her cultural and social milieu, and seek to understand a film in the fullest possible way.

All Responses Are Legitimate

There is no such thing as responding "correctly"; no response is unique and of itself, and no response has a right to exclude another. All responses, whether spontaneous and individual or objective and study-based, are valid. The viewer's responsibility is not to cancel one response for the sake of another, but to keep all responses in a creative tension with one another. Thus, a viewer's interpretation should be a blending of personal impressions with critical analysis of the film. There is nothing wrong with retaining one's first impressions, whatever these might be. More than a century ago, Henry James, recommending a response to the novel in his "The Art of Fiction," said that nothing can take the place of "liking" (or "not liking") a story. This view still holds. How can one dismiss his or her liking a movie when first viewing it? James also said that the primary responsibility of an author is to make his work interesting. How is one, then, to discard one's own interest in and liking for a film? It is probably impossible and certainly unnecessary. It is equally important to keep searching for meanings, because that search may—and probably will—produce new meanings and new appreciation. For that reason, one has no right to exclude any approach—historical, psychological, sociological, feminist, Marxist, deconstructive, ethnic, religious, cultist, or whatever. Films have been made for many purposes, embodying the values (or disvalues) and ideas of many cultures, classes, and geographical latitudes, so their interpretation must be as free, deep, and wide-ranging as possible. Here one must truly exercise what the French critic and philosopher Derrida has called "freeplay." One must attempt to "decenter" a film—that is, to take it out of its particular cycle of epoch, culture, or mode of production; but then one must "recenter" it. New centers are created constantly, whether the new center is a classroom, the viewing circle of a film society, or the circle of one's own personal impressions. This can be done only with the addition of study to the experience of viewing. Study of film is a must.

The Experience of Viewing a Film

The *experience* of viewing a film is the first step; it must come before analysis begins. Viewing the film takes precedence over study: One does not go to a film history book to study film; one views the film itself before anything else is done. Nothing can take the place of sitting in a dark room, whether a theater or a classroom, with a group of people, all responding to images and action shown on a screen, especially if one has at one's command the latest technology and can enjoy such features as DTS or surround sound. Sound is an important element, though this does not eliminate films made in previous decades, even those of the silent era. A group response is best, since one reacts both to the action and to other people's reaction to it. Motion, space, and sound are offered simultaneously; emotions and moods change in an instant. One does not respond to film in the same way one responds to a novel, since the latter's appeal is made through printed signs, not through projected signs, visual images, motion, and sound. A response to film is, therefore, a necessarily more complex experience. Though individual viewing cannot, of course, be eliminated (and can on occasion be more reflective), the group experience is the best. That is why, despite the invention of the VCR and other viewing means (laser disc, DVD), people still prefer to go to the theaters. A class viewing should be more elaborate and analytical than that of a theater, but it is still the best approach.

Study: *L'Avventura* (1960, directed by Michelangelo Antonioni)

As noted above, there is no substitute for "liking" a work of art—whether a novel, a painting, or some other artwork. The same is true of film. "Liking it"

Sandro pursues Claudia as they both search for the missing Anna in
L'Avventura. The growing sense of their efforts' futility suggests their failed
quest for any lasting meaning in life.

or "not liking it" is the only part of study that cannot be eliminated from a
viewer's vocabulary. How, indeed, is one to study film if one sets aside one's
first duty—to find out whether one likes or does not like it? Of course, this
raises the question: Does one study a film one does not like? Yes—frequently.
In classes, for instance, instructors usually select the films they teach, and students watch them. Yet it is possible for a student—or anyone—to "like" a film
after it has been analyzed. This is the essence of our method, outlined in this
text guide, of responding to film. Study, of whatever kind or method or combination thereof, often brings out nuances, sharper observations, and knowledge of film techniques which illuminate visual imagery or aspects of plot and
action. Generally, meanings embedded in the film will become manifest or
enhanced. "Slow" foreign films, for instance, become more appealing after
analysis and commentary. Antonioni's *L'Avventura*, to use an example, has
been a trying experience for those who are used to Hollywood's fast-paced,
action-oriented, happy-ending movies. Yet the subtlety and beauty of this film's
imagery (film language) make the story not only appealing on the surface level
but even emotionally explosive: A socialite has disappeared from her group of
friends on an arid, rocky island in the Mediterranean. Despite a search by her
two closest friends, a man and woman, she is never found. This is not a typical Hollywood ending, but the viewer discovers clues, intimations, insights. A
romantic liaison has been formed between the two searchers. Anna, the lost

girl, has been replaced by Claudia. Eventually, Sandro, the lover of both, will betray Claudia too. This is a conclusion not so much of the plot, but of an emotional tie which appears to have dissolved. The viewer may need to go back to certain scenes of this film, revisit them, even view the entire film again several times. The experience of such viewing, after critical commentary, may reveal new levels of meaning, unseen at first glance. A study of this or other such films requires knowledge about what went into the film while it was being made—how a director, for instance, deals with a certain subject matter; how he or she incorporates his or her ideas in film language easily comprehended by an audience.

Study: *Eyes Wide Shut* (1999, directed by Stanley Kubrick)

Stanley Kubrick's last film, *Eyes Wide Shut,* is worthy of study as an example of critical response. It is the story of a young doctor, William Hartford (Tom Cruise) and his wife Alice (Nicole Kidman). After a lavish party where she is almost seduced by a graying, attractive Hungarian, they have an argument about Hartford's sexual drives. Alice sees her husband talking to two attractive women until he is called upstairs by his host Ziegler (Sidney Pollack) to help a female guest recover from a drug-induced coma. The girl Mandy lies naked on a couch while Pollack is putting his clothes on. Very professionally, Cruise brings her out of her torpor, saving her life but warning her that she needs help, that the next time she does this may be the last. At that party he also meets a man he knew in medical school who is now a pianist called Nick Nightingale; they renew their friendship. At home the next evening, while both of them are smoking pot, Alice starts the argument, assuming her husband was lusting after those girls. He says it was the opposite: they were coming on to him. He's innocent. She insists, and this argument lasts twenty minutes on the screen. Meanwhile, Hartford is called to see a dying patient at an old friend's. He finds the man dead, and his daughter, who is engaged to another man, makes sexual advances to him. He leaves, disturbed, and embarks on a sexual adventure. First he is allured by a prostitute, but leaves her place before making love (though he pays her fee) when he is interrupted on his cell phone by his wife. Back in the street, he is assaulted by a bunch of street punks, then goes into a bar (next to Gallespie's cafe) where Nick Nightingale is performing. The latter tells him about a place he'll be performing later that night. At Hartford's insistence, he gives him a password—Fidelio—to a high class brothel where Nightingale plays the piano blindfolded, though he has a good idea of the nature of the proceedings. Cruise rents a masked costume, is driven there in a cab, is admitted, and then is

Prolonged medium shots of an introspective Tom Cruise walking the streets in Eyes Wide Shut *induces the film's viewers to share in his process of self-examination.*

astonished to witness a ritualistic orgy. A female guest warns him to go away, but he stays until, asked for a second password, he fails and is expelled. Later that night and next day, when an ex-beauty queen's death is announced in the papers, he suspects murder. He drives to the place where the orgy occurred, but is given an envelope with a *second* warning. That night, after a visit to the morgue to verify the girl's identity, he realizes that a mysterious stranger is following him in the street. Then he receives a call from Ziegler, who was one of the masked guests at the orgy and who assures him the entire episode was a "charade," a farce. The girl, who happens to be the one who warned him to leave, was Mandy, the woman he had saved from death. She actually died of an overdose of drugs after she went home. He returns home to find beside his sleeping wife the mask he had rented but had forgotten to return. His wife knew about the orgy.

There is a reconciliation scene between them as their seven-year-old daughter shops at a mall for Christmas.

For a nearly three-hour movie (159 minutes), this may look like a thin plot line. Indeed, the pace is so deliberate it virtually comes to a standstill at times; Cruise's and Kidman's early self-confession scene takes nearly twenty minutes, unacceptable in today's fast-paced montages. The party (orgy) scene is equally lengthy and deliberate, typical of Kubrick's style, which the viewer may remember from movies like *2001: A Space Odyssey* (Keir Dullea floats endlessly through space) and *Barry Lyndon* (Redmond Barry deliberately trudges across the balcony to seduce Marisa Berenson). Kubrick's style in this movie ultimately *becomes* the meaning. One can see this in three ways: (a) the camera's relation to the character; (b) the point of view; (c) the symbolism. The camera *defines* the character(s). The angles and lighting illuminate the character's perceptions, fears, recognitions, anxieties. The camera is fixed on a character's face or body for unusually lengthy periods, until a character's emotion, thought, or feeling becomes clear to the viewer. Kubrick dwells on the face, but he also uses medium body shots, especially when Cruise wanders through the streets.

The point of view is Tom Cruise's throughout the story. There is no cross-cutting; the entire episode follows him step by step. His surprises are the viewer's surprises. This entire movie is an act of self-revelation. His wife is forcing him to look into himself, to examine his hidden motives. He is completely honest when he tells her he loves only her, that he was *not* lusting after the two girls at the party. Yet he is forced to look beneath the surface truth he believes.

The entire movie has to do with this process of self-revelation and self-knowledge. Cruise is surprised at himself, and that becomes evident in his repetition of questions—making him look a little naïve at times. He is strangely ambiguous. Throughout his odyssey, which was touted by critics as a "sex odyssey," he does not participate in any actual act of sex. In the orgy scenes, he only watches. He is not interested in the prostitute, although one assumes he would have had sex with her had it not been for his wife's phone call. His only transgression is his curiosity—which far exceeds his lust.

He is also sufficiently deluded. He genuinely believes that he is unraveling a plot and that he is being threatened. The entire movie has an air of unreality—a delusional aspect: When can one believe one's eyes? What is truth? He is told that he is the object of a farce—which is what the story turns out to be. But his point of view, faithfully followed throughout, allows the viewer to participate in his delusion.

This movie is reminiscent of Antonioni's *Blow Up* (1969), in which a young photographer thinks he has discovered a murder by blowing up a section of a picture he took at a London park. In that film, however, the outcome remains a mystery. Here, it is explained fully by Pollack's character.

Cruise's descent into a modern Hades—the participants in the palatial orgy are influential—is actually a trip into the self. Both he and his wife come to know more about themselves, their hidden desires and motives. They compromise their idealism for the sake of each other. A sadder but truer life is ahead of them. The symbolism lies in the title of the movie, which also is an oxymoron: eyes wide shut. Blindness is symbolic of Cruise's refusal to see the truth.

The Literary Response

The aim of this text guide is to suggest the various ways in which one responds to film as a literary medium, one with unique characteristics and special interests. To do so, one does not need to discard a film's entertainment value, since art, by its very nature, appeals to our sense of enjoyment. But in studying film as a unique art, one must employ some of the same tools one brings to the examination of a literary work, considering point of view, characterization, symbolism, theme, and so forth. Film, though visual, is still a form of narrative. One can study it only by viewing it, but one cannot ignore its narrative traits: a beginning and an end, an action in time, flashbacks, recognitions, reversals, and other such elements. These narrative factors must be identified and analyzed by teacher and students. Teachers will most likely adapt the critical stance they would apply to literary texts. Along with viewing, film study will be supplemented with introductory and critical material. Students will be asked to take examinations and write papers, either of the MLA kind, in the form of a periodical review, or like papers read at literary and film conferences. Students with a background in English studies may do better in that regard, while students from other disciplines—religion, social science, psychology, communication—may also apply literary methods to these works. No approach is excluded—and none should be—but a literary approach may help students understand in depth a medium that is essentially and primarily narrative. There is no reason why a student of history, for instance, cannot benefit from a literary analysis if that helps reveal the depth of a particular historical film. Conversely, a student of literature can do with some knowledge of the particular historical period in which a film is set. Take *Amadeus* (1984), for instance: Its topic is music, but its basis is literary because it was derived from a play by Peter Shaffer, who was also the film scenarist. Yet *Amadeus* requires some historical knowledge of the eighteenth century, its class distinctions, its art patronage, and some of its politics (e.g., the play by Pierre Augustin Caron de Beaumarchais on which Mozart's *The Marriage of Figaro* was based had been banned in France as revolutionary) in order to be fully understood. It also helps to know that this film uses a familiar narrative technique: the confessional flashback monologue, a means known to both Sophocles and Dostoevsky.

The Aims of This Text Guide

What is suggested above is that a response to film must be multiple, that one must study film by becoming acquainted with the many-faceted approaches to the subject.

That is why it is necessary to see film as one of the arts; to examine its literary aspects in order to see its similarities to, and differences from, literature; to learn about film techniques which help the viewer appreciate film's unique qualities; to understand film language; to understand historical backgrounds; to understand why American film can be fully appreciated only if one sees it in relation to foreign film; to understand film's relation to social trends, cultural backgrounds, and genres. That response must come not only from one's personal tastes and preferences—which are not to be discounted—but from knowledge of what a film is, of who created it, and of what the creator aimed for. Finally, one must understand recent technology and the way it has affected film studies. Today one studies film by watching it on a VCR. However, one must utilize, at least in classroom situations, wide screens or projection screens, and must use the laser disc and the DVD in addition to the VCR. DVD contains materials, such as audio commentary and analysis, which may be very helpful in film study.

This text guide examines these various responses to film, leaving the door open to interpretation from a wide variety of angles, even from opposing views. It is necessary to stress the deconstruction of film—that is, to stress differences in interpretation—but not to stop at that approach. It is also necessary to attempt to synthesize all these elements. Though interpretations may be infinite and entirely different, depending on one's point of view and the point of view of a specific approach, it is finally necessary to attempt to synthesize these views into a coherent whole. One can accept separate interpretations in a classroom, as long as these are based on actual knowledge of a film's specific circumstances: time, genre, director, and so forth. In the following chapters, we will outline these approaches in some detail, showing how each response relates to the others to make up a flexible, knowledgeable, personal, objective, yet coherent interpretation of film.

A sample course is provided as an appendix to this text guide and is intended as a *guide,* not a *prescription.* There is no *a priori* interpretation of a film. Viewing film is the first requirement. Study, which begins afterwards, is the tool of a deeper and more complete understanding of film.

Suggested Readings

Andrew, James Dudley. *The Major Film Theories.* New York: Oxford University Press, 1976.

Bazin, André. *What Is Cinema?* Berkeley and Los Angeles: University of California Press, 1967.

Mast, Gerald, and Marshall Cohen. *Film Theory and Criticism.* New York: Oxford University Press, 1979.

CHAPTER ONE

Responding to Film as an Art Form

How do I respond to film as an art form? Film is an art; therefore, one should respond to film by envisioning criteria similar to those applied to the other arts. Though film has some unique aspects, those criteria should include analysis, synthesis, appreciation of form and content, study of historical and social themes, and critical thinking in general. The history of film spans a little more than a hundred years, but film has already taken its place among the other arts—drama, fiction, poetry, music, architecture, painting, and sculpture. As a unique art form, it has borrowed from the other arts, enlarging their scope and thus becoming a superior means of communication in the twentieth century and beyond. Film has given us a reflection of life, recording in rich imagery humanity's past and present, and providing a vision for the future.

Film as an Art

As an art form, film is a derivative of photography. The word *cinema* comes from the Greek *kinesis* which means motion, thus the term "motion pictures." The recording of motion, *cinematography*, was made possible by a machine used by Auguste and Louis Lumière, the French brothers credited with producing the first cinematic images. Their sophisticated machine, the *Cinematograph*, could record, print, and project moving images on a screen—the genesis of the art of motion pictures. The name is logical. A photograph is a framed image produced on a sensitized film surface (emulsion) by the action of light. The film is developed and printed by means of chemicals, and then reveals a picture of persons, objects, or landscapes.

But how does one make moving pictures? According to André Bazin, the noted French critic, the idea of moving pictures had been in circulation since the time of Leonardo Da Vinci, and film technology might have been invented several centuries earlier, but it was in 1824 that Peter Mark Roget articulated the idea of "persistence of vision": the ability of the human brain to retain images cast upon the retina of the eye for a fraction of a second. Thus, if a series of moving photographs were projected on a screen in rapid succession, the short time lapse between them would be unobserved, thus providing the viewer with an illusion of continuity of motion. In 1912 Max Wertheimer, a gestalt psychologist, explained the idea of the "phi phenomenon," a process similar to that explained above: when one looks at the spokes of a rotating wheel on a moving automobile, for instance, one perceives a smooth surface, rather than individual moving spokes. Persistence of vision and the phi phenomenon were the principles applied to the art of filmmaking by the first inventors of film in the late nineteenth and early twentieth centuries. The first inventors—Thomas Edison, Oskar Messter, the Lumière brothers, Georges Melies—were among the pioneers of film as an art form. The inventors of cinema were also great technological geniuses, and art and technology went hand in hand.

The invention of motion pictures revolutionized our perception of the world in general. Here was a medium that could free the human imagination from the limitations of time and space which had constrained the other arts for centuries. Narrative forms such as the epic and the novel had been confined to the transmission of mental signals; film art provided both visual means and motion, at the same time retaining both spoken and written discursive language. The only arts close to film were stage production and opera, both containing dramatic representations of human events. But musical drama and stage theater were relatively static, since all action on a stage was perceived from the stationary point of view of a spectator sitting somewhere in a large chamber full of other people. Early cameras actually did the same thing, photographing moving objects from a stationary position. But soon cinematographers (camera operators) placed cameras on dollies (moving carts), cranes, or other moving objects; thus, not only could the photographed object move, but the photographing agent himself could also manipulate the photographed action by moving along with it. A great variety of shots were made possible by camera persons photographing objects from various angles and distances, and changing the lighting to enhance or create a variety of moods. Through editing and montage, this process was accelerated and gave cinema its unique ability to represent action as no narrative art had done before. These new techniques freed the spectator from both his stationary position and his perception of time, since through montage he could travel indefinitely in time and space. The viewer experienced an overwhelming sense of reality because a moving photographed image provided accuracy impossible for either painting (the predecessor of photography) or stage properties, which, compared to film's realism, seemed artificial.

Film in Relation to the Other Arts

As soon as the narrative character of film was established, its affinity with literature and many of the other arts became obvious. For one thing, film adopted and adapted many narrative forms and techniques known to literature for centuries, from the lengthy epic to melodrama to comedic episode. Like the stage, film is essentially the representation of an action, a term known since Aristotle. It was normal for it to adopt many concepts known to the literary form, such as point of view, plot, characterization, epiphany, suspense, and symbolism. Film's relationship to literature is evident from the fact that a significant number of films, not to say the majority of them, have been adaptations of novels, short stories, plays, and even poems. Ingmar Bergman's *The Virgin Spring* (1960), for instance, was derived from a medieval ballad. Many contemporary films, such as *Much Ado About Nothing* (1994), have been adaptations of Shakespeare's plays. Indeed, the works of the bard have been translated into film more than the works of any other author. Other dramatists—Euripides, Shaw, Ibsen, O'Neill, Williams, Albee, Beckett—have also enriched the cinematic repertory. Austen, Dickens, and Tolstoy, to mention only a few of the most prominent novelists, have fed the cinema rich materials for story lines which often became great popular films. Literature in general is the great foundation on which modern cinema has been built. In some cases (*Amadeus, Who's Afraid of Virginia Woolf?, A Clockwork Orange*), the film actually acquires prestige or fame equal to or greater than that of the original literary work. In some ways, film can be an extension of, a complement to, or a synthesis of various literary forms. That is one reason, at least, why a response to film ought to be thought of as a species of literary analysis, to which most of the forms of literary criticism apply. Indeed, most film critics are literary critics, aestheticians, philosophers, historians, and generally critics of the literary art.

But film has established associations (one could call them close friendships) with the other arts as well, having incorporated and adapted many of

their forms. For instance, music is part of film, both as original score written
for a film—Bernard Herrmann for *North by Northwest* (1957), *Psycho* (1960),
Taxi Driver (1976)—or as the subject of a film—*Mahler* (1974), *Amadeus*
(1984), *Immortal Beloved* (1993), and *Shine* (1996). Classical music is used
in some films to enhance visual action, as in Stanley Kubrick's *2001: A Space
Odyssey* (1967) and *Barry Lyndon* (1974) which contain music by Richard
Strauss and Franz Schubert among other composers, and Oliver Stone's *Platoon* (1986) which uses Samuel Barber's "Adagio for Strings." Of late, songs
from operas have been incorporated into films' musical scores—especially the
so-called romantic comedies. Thus, *Moonstruck* (1987) contains music from
Puccini's "La Bohème," *Pretty Woman* (1990) and *Only You* (1995) feature
arias from Verdi's "La Traviata," and in *Life Is Beautiful* (1998) the barcarole
from Offenbach's "The Tales of Hoffmann" is sung. Many filmmakers have
also borrowed ideas and images from paintings. Many directors obtain their
inspiration for film composition (*mise-en-scène*) from painters, as Kurosawa
does from Van Gogh in his *Ran* (1984) and *Dreams* (1991). Luchino Visconti, in *Death in Venice* (1971), borrows visual tableaus from the French
impressionists, and Stanley Kubrick adapts images from Flemish realism in
Barry Lyndon (1974). A modern caper, *The Thomas Crown Affair* (1999), is
set in a Manhattan museum, and has a painting by Monet as its subject.
Michelangelo Antonioni's *L'Avventura* (1960) and Alain Resnais's *Last Year
at Marienbad* (1961) are related to forms of architecture. Jean Cocteau uses
classically derived sculptures (the statue of Minerva comes to life to spear him)
in his dream sequences in *Testament of Orpheus* (1959). Charles Chaplin
employs forms of sculptural ballet in *City Lights* (1930) and *The Great Dictator* (1941). In fact, film is an amalgam of all the other arts, from which it
feeds eclectically, and some of which it expresses in a new manner. Speaking
of other arts, one has, of course, to credit costume and set designs, the
graphic arts (including computer-based), dancing and choreography, and,
above all, cinematography, the art on which the edifice of film is built. Some
of the above, costume design for instance, can be considered either derivatives
of art forms or art forms themselves. Film is a distinct medium, yet its reliance
on the other arts is unquestionably a major factor in its final synthesis.

Film as a Commercial Art

Aside from its association with the arts, film also relies on the world of technology and finance, on producers, directors, actors, stunt persons (athletes),
musicians, dancers, construction crews, photographers, art directors, and
technicians of all kinds. Because a film is the result of the combined efforts of
many such agencies, it requires a significant financial output. Such financing

has given film its distinctive social function: it is a popular art aimed at entertaining, but financial gain has become its *raison d'être*. If film cannot succeed at the box office, it will cease to exist as we now know it. The connection of film to corporate profit as part of what is called the entertainment industry must be accepted as a given before one defines it as art. Here, art is not for art's sake, despite the MGM logo. It is art for commercial success's sake. Despite the existence of independent filmmakers for whom film is a means of self-expression, film is an art used by industry and by today's giant industrial conglomerates as part of a capitalist financial venture. Film is a product which must be distributed and marketed in order to attract audiences. Outside the system, its chances of success are minimal. This is not true of many of the other arts, which usually require one person (painter, author, or musician) and his/her talents and minimal materials cost. Architecture and advertising are commercial arts, but neither of them is considered an art *per se*. Drama is certainly a commercial venture, but does not require the colossal financial output of mainstream film production. Commercial dramas are produced mainly in metropolitan areas, while drama productions on campus by amateur players (and some films of the same kind) are considered part of the curriculum and are cost effective. Symphony orchestras need financial support, but their primary aim is not profit and the realization of self-sustaining capital. Thus, film is the only art aside from pop music which can be called primarily a capitalist venture. Its success is measured with weekly charts which trace attendance per screening and dollars earned. The commercial character of film art has had a profound effect on its forms, genres, motives, and structure.

However, the popularity of film and its commercial character must not exclude it from the pantheon of the arts. Though financial support and the profitability motive influence film production, film is still an art by its very nature. Anything in narrative form is an art product, whatever its financial origin or its historical transformations, such as added sound, color, the anamorphic lens, and wide screens. Making movies is an artistic endeavor, whatever else it may be; one applies aesthetic criteria to this process. Though many arguments could be made (and have been made) for and against such categorization, film as an end product is an art form. Consider the depth of field of world filmmakers, which includes such names as Sergei Eisenstein, D. W. Griffith, Orson Welles, Alfred Hitchcock, Ingmar Bergman, Satyajit Ray, Federico Fellini, Akira Kurosawa, Louis Buñuel, Michelangelo Antonioni, and many others whose works in film have achieved a standing and fame equal to those of the twentieth-century giants of literature and art—Ernest Hemingway, Pablo Picasso, Thomas Mann, Albert Camus, Igor Stravinsky. Why indeed would Akira Kurosawa be considered a lesser genius than, let's say, Igor Stravinsky, or for that matter Albert Camus? Camus and Kurosawa are both existentialists, both have explored the futility and chaos of modern life, and both are powerful narrators. Still, one needs to be reminded that Kurosawa's art rests on a major financial output (such as it was in his time in Japan), that his art needed financing, that in the end he was expected to show some profits at the box office—which he did. Box office success or failure does not diminish art, though it may influence it. The productions of some filmmakers have arguably achieved the status of great art works, regardless of their commercial character. There are as many worldwide seminars on Hitchcock's films as there are on Picasso's or any other great artist's paintings. The productions of these film giants have also enjoyed considerable popular support from the public, from the academies of motion pictures, and from international film festivals. Such recognition is given not only to the directors but, as film is a collaborative art, also to other artists: actors, musicians, and technicians of various kinds, who are operating under the patronage of studios or other corporate entities. Commercial sponsors, as in the case of TV movies, are patrons of art though their motive is profit. The patron's motive is not the determiner of the success or failure of an art form; it is not the sponsor but the artist who is responsible for that. There is nothing new about art having patrons; it was so in the Athens of Pericles and in the Florence of Italy's Renaissance. Patrons of music have included emperors in eighteenth-century Europe. In those days it was the city-state or the pope or wealthy families who sponsored art, and their motives were only partially responsible for the artist's success.

Film as Communication

The immense popularity of film in the twentieth century may be attributed to its unique ability to communicate, and to do so far more effectively than any other medium. Though radio and television are more readily accessible to the general public, film has a greater claim to mass communication, since film—American film in particular—knows no boundaries. All world audiences watch American films, and through that medium American culture is probably better known than any other. American film's widespread popularity is unique, but films from other cultures and nations are relatively easy to access, especially now with many film societies operating throughout the United States and with the advent of video, laser, and DVD technologies. In addition, images projected on a screen are enlarged objects, overwhelming the viewer with their realism. For instance, a stage play's audience has a very indistinct impression of small objects, because they are seen at a considerable distance with a naked eye. But on a screen, objects are magnified, and a viewer sees the details. The stage viewer remains in one position which never changes in its relation to the objects viewed. But the film viewer is liberated from this static position by camera movement, angles of viewing, focusing, and tracking. The film viewer is thus liberated from the restrictions of time and space. Avenues of communication are immensely enriched as the viewer can look back in time; take in mountains and landscapes; see under water; and perceive variations of color, light, dark, stillness, or motion. Most films accurately and authentically reproduce reality, so although film is an imitation of reality, it comes closer to reality than anything else does. Plato complained that all poetic imitations are false, thrice removed from the original ideas. Coleridge, an English poet and critic of the nineteenth century, stated that the reader of a poem must suspend disbelief while reading it. Neither Plato nor Coleridge could have anticipated film's ability to reproduce objects in minutely accurate detail, nor could they have imagined what size, minuteness, speed, or slowness of film could do. With film, a copy is no longer a copy, as of a painted object or a written description. On the screen, a box of matches, a flower, a house—these are, or are made to appear, exact reproductions of actual objects. Thus, disbelief is more readily suspended in film, and the viewer is comfortable in doing so, willingly and with a sense of greater enjoyment. Because of this realism, the power of film dramatically increases the power of the stage (which is not to be underestimated). Film has become a universal visual medium which overcomes language barriers and communicates to all peoples. In the silent era, the films of Charles Chaplin, for instance, were more popular than any other form of art, and Chaplin was the most recognizable figure in the world. It is said that Hitler adopted Chaplin's mustache to achieve similar recognition. Chaplin countered by adopting Hitler's stance and oratory in *The Great Dictator* (1941). Hitler himself, quite aware of the power of film to communicate, sought the services of Germany's most talented filmmaker, Leni Riefenstahl, to film the Nazi Nuremberg convention of 1934, an effort that resulted in the best propaganda film ever made—though the activities photographed were the essence of twentieth-century evil. This is a testament to film's awesome communicative powers, for better or for worse. The recognition factor and instant celebrity (today mostly the domain of television) had their genesis in film. Many stars of the silent era—Douglas Fairbanks Sr. and Rudolph Valentino, for instance—were instantly recognized throughout the world. ("Look, I'm Douglas Fairbanks!" Dr. Aziz shouts to Adela Quested, as he hangs out of a train window, striking an athletic pose, in the film *A Passage to India* [1984], a film whose action takes place in the 1920s.) Neither musician nor poet nor painter had ever commanded such powers of recognition in the history of humankind. Frank Capra said that a filmmaker is the most powerful man in the world (taped interview broadcast, A&E, 1996). Because it depends on popular support and because its function is to reach as wide an audience as possible, film has captured the imagination of audiences throughout the world and, at least for the foreseeable future, it will continue to be the dominant popular art. Thanks to the increasingly available digital technology, many classic films—the great films of the twentieth century—now have a chance of being preserved for posterity.

The Filmmaker as an *Auteur*

An *auteur* (literally, an author) is a director who is considered the most important figure in the art of filmmaking, a creative person equivalent to the author of a novel or a play. Let us see how this term was derived and what it means today.

Though film calls for the collaboration of various agents—a producer, director, screen writer, cinematographer, costume designer, music scorer, actors, and technicians—a film can be seen as the product of a single creator, one artist—the filmmaker. Thus, a director who controls all aspects of filmmaking is called an *auteur,* a term which originated in France in the early 1950s, first used by the French critic André Bazin, who established *Cahiers du Cinema,* an influential film criticism periodical. This term gained prominence among a group of distinguished French critics and filmmakers, including François Truffaut, Jean-Luc Godard, Claude Chabrol, and Jacques Demi. The term *auteur* was subsequently introduced to American film criticism by the American critic Andrew Sarris in 1962 and in his later writings (see "Afterword: The Auteur Theory Revisited" in *The American Cinema,* 1985, pp. 269–78). Famous world directors, such as Federico Fellini, Akira Kurosawa, Satyajit Ray, Ingmar Bergman, Michelangelo Antonioni, and others, are considered *auteurs.* Consequently, many distinguished filmmakers, whether they belonged to the French New Wave school of filmmaking or not, received the designation of *auteur* to differentiate them from the Hollywood establishment of directors under the studio system. Thus an *auteur* is any director whose distinct style has left a recognizable mark on his work. Hitchcock and Chaplin, for instance, though working mainly within the parameters of the studio establishments, can be called *auteurs.* Other famous Hollywood directors with distinct directorial styles were Orson Welles, John Ford, Howard Hawks, Stanley Kramer, Billy Wilder, and, in more recent times, Francis Ford Coppola, Steven Spielberg, Martin Scorsese, Robert Altman, Stanley Kubrick, Milos Forman, Ridley Scott, Sam Mendes, and others. Most of the above are considered *auteurs.* This term has been unpopular in the Hollywood milieu, however. When great producers, during the era of the Hollywood studio system, were dominant in film production, a director's role was limited. In *Gone With the Wind* (1939), for instance, the film's producer David O. Selznick has received most of the credit. Its director Victor Fleming, who died during the production, is a less distinguished figure. The *auteur* theory has been hotly contested in Hollywood, especially by screenwriters, who, more than any other agents involved in filmmaking, resent a director's prominence in critical theory. This controversy is not likely to die soon, and in Hollywood, where film is firmly established as a collaborative art, the *auteur* theory will by and large continue to be scorned. On the other hand, it is not likely that a director such as Kurosawa will be considered in any other light, and one will continue talking of Kurosawa films, Fellini films, Louis Malle films, Satyajit Ray films, Eric Rohmer films, or Ingmar Bergman films. Even in Hollywood, the legacies of John Ford, Frank Capra, Stanley Kramer, Howard Hawks, and Alfred Hitchcock continue to bear the stamp of their directors' individuality. More recent filmmakers (some mentioned above) have also begun to build their own legends—Martin Scorsese, Steven Spielberg, Anthony Minghella, Sam Mendes, John Sayles, to mention a few.

The Screenwriter as an Artist

A student of film, however, must not forget our basic premise that film is a collaborative art. Thus, though the *auteur* theory cannot be discounted, the contributions of other agents in film production must be given full credit. Cinematographers, lighting experts, costume designers, art directors—all must be acknowledged as essential contributors to the design and production of film. Possibly the most important figure, aside from the director, is the screenwriter. Indeed, if *auteur* means author in French, why shouldn't it mean the author of the script used in making the film? To reinforce this point, think of famous directors who were also the screenwriters of their movies. These include D.W. Griffith, who adapted *The Birth of A Nation* (1915) from *The Klansman*, a novel by Thomas E. Dixon; Sergei Eisenstein, who wrote and directed *Battleship Potemkin* (1925) and *Alexander Nevsky* (1938); Charles Chaplin, who wrote his own script for *The Great Dictator* (1941) and improvised considerably as he went along in most of his movies; Joseph L. Mankiewicz, who wrote and directed *All About Eve* (1950); Elia Kazan, the director, who also wrote the script of *America, America* (1962) from his own novel; John Frankenheimer, who wrote and directed *The Manchurian Candidate* (1962); and Stanley Kubrick, who coauthored the script of *2001: A Space Odyssey* (1969) with Arthur C. Clarke and who subsequently adapted the script of *Barry Lyndon* (1974) from a novel by William Makepeace Thackeray. Kubrick also wrote the scripts for *Full Metal Jacket* (1987) and *Eyes Wide Shut* (1999). Francis Ford Coppola coauthored the script of *The Godfather* (1972) with Mario Puzo; and in more recent times, John Sayles both wrote and directed an acclaimed film, *Limbo* (1999). These few examples will suffice to show that creative directors can be authors of their films in every sense of the word.

Bette Davis confronts her nemesis Anne Baxter in All About Eve. *Female adversaries can stir audiences as strongly as do contending males.*

By and large, however, the screenwriter has his or her own distinct role and is an artist in his own right. Throughout the history of the cinema, some films of note would not have been the same without the contributions of their screen-writers. *Citizen Kane* (1941) in part owes its greatness and fame to Herman J. Mankiewicz, who coauthored the script with Orson Welles. Ben Hecht was one of Hollywood's most talented and prolific screenwriters, writing scripts for such well-known movies as *Scarface* (1932), *Gunga Din* (1939), *Gone With the Wind* (1939), *Monkey Business* (1952), and also for several Hitchcock films, including *Notorious* (1946), *Lifeboat* (1944), and *Rope* (1948). Other screen-writers of that era include John Michael Hayes, whose creative collaboration with Alfred Hitchcock produced *Rear Window* (1954); Leon M. Uris, who wrote *Battle Cry* (1955); Richard Brooks, who adapted Tennessee Williams' *Cat on a Hot Tin Roof* (1958) for the screen; and Carl Foreman, writer of *The Guns of Navarone* (1961). Some distinguished directors were blacklisted dur-ing the McCarthy era, among them Carl Foreman and Michael Wilson who did not receive credit (or the Oscar) for coauthoring the script of *The Bridge on the River Kwai* (1957); and Ring Lardner Jr., whose works were banned in 1947 and who did not produce a Hollywood movie script until 1970, when he received an Oscar for *Mash*. The list of important screenwriters is significant— and nearly as long as that of great directors. One need only mention here such distinguished names as that of Robert Bolt, the English playwright who wrote literate scripts for *Lawrence of Arabia* (1962) and *Dr. Zhivago* (1965), as well as the script of *A Man For All Seasons* from his own play; John Milius for *Dirty Harry* (1971) and *Apocalypse Now* (1979); George Lucas for *Star Wars* (1977); Sylvester Stallone for the *Rocky* series; Lawrence Kasdan for *Raiders of the Lost Ark* (1981); Paul Schrader for *Taxi Driver* (1971), *Raging Bull* (1980), and *The Last Temptation of Christ* (1988); Oliver Stone (also director) for *Platoon* (1984); Callie Khouri for *Thelma and Louise* (1991); Jane Campion (also director) for *The Piano* (1993); Joseph Stefano for *Psycho* (1960, 1998); Marc Norman and Tom Stoppard for *Shakespeare in Love* (1998); Kimberly Peirce (also director) for *Boys Don't Cry* (1999); M. Night Shyamalan (also director) for *The Sixth Sense* (1999). Prominent international filmmakers are frequently writers of their own scripts and thus *auteurs* in the fullest sense: Ingmar Bergman wrote his own scripts, which were subsequently published as novels; and such greats as Antonioni, Fellini, and Kurosawa always had a hand in the scripts of their movies.

Film as a Literary Art

Though film is a unique medium derived from photography, its narrative form invites examination from a literary point of view. Even a historian looking at film must look at it as a story first. A literary response to film requires that an *auteur*'s or filmmaker's point of view be given primary consideration, though the contributions of other agents, as noted above, must never be discounted. We talk of Fellini or Bergman or Hitchcock wanting to say this or that in this film, rather than dwelling on the fact that Humphrey Bogart or Ingrid Bergman or any other actor starred in it. The Hollywood studio system, which dominated filmmaking in the 1930s, '40s, and '50s, was synonymous with the star system, and the star (Clark Gable, Bette Davis, Ingrid Bergman, Gary Cooper, James Stewart) was the studio's most bankable commodity. In this sense, a film was often made as a vehicle for a certain star or stars. When that star's career flopped, so might the studio, not to mention a particular film. Contrarily, the success of a star meant added profits for a studio (young Deanna Durbin's popularity saved Universal from bankruptcy in the late 1930s). The value of a film was judged by its commercial or popular success, and, although many popular films have been critically acclaimed and are of enduring value, most Hollywood movies were not judged on their artistic merits or the power of their messages. However, this distinction did not always apply. Despite its commercial outlook, the studio was still dealing with an artistic and literary medium. Stories still had to be good, whether they were the products of collaboration or of the idiosyncrasies of an *auteur*-director. Many commercial Hollywood films have become great classics—witness

Gone With the Wind (1940), *Casablanca* (1942), *Double Indemnity* (1944). The list is long and significant.

As indicated earlier, film is a recognizably narrative form, having the characteristics of literature: plot, themes, symbols, ironies or contrasts. Though it has its own peculiar characteristics of visual texture, color, variety of shots, montage, cinematography, and other techniques peculiar to this form of art, film, like literature, is divided into categories or genres: epic, tragedy (drama), comedy, social satire, and so forth (see chapter 2). Film noir, western epic, biblical epic, spy thriller, and many others, are all categories derived from literary genres, and, as in literature some of those categorizations are used for commercial purposes. Like literature, a film can also be categorized by nationality (American, British, Japanese, German, French, Italian) and by school (Realist, Expressionist, New Wave, Cubist, Post-Modern, etc.), though school is a term totally ignored in commercial film production. Still, one needs to be familiar with the evolution of the historical and literary backgrounds of these terms to understand film art properly. A film course should be taken much as one undertakes a literary study of modern drama or modern fiction. Courses are offered which combine fiction and film or drama and film or general literature and film. Film is taught under the umbrella of many academic departments—as it should be. There is film and history, for instance; film and political thought; film and religion; film and philosophy; etc. But since the narrative form gives film its character as a species of literature, a course in literary criticism—along with film criticism—may be advisable for the film student. In general, the more literary background one has at one's command, the more one is familiar with analyses of literary forms, and the better able to approach a film's thematic intent. A modern student is advised to look up a film's script, if available, or a film's literary background. Commentaries by actors, directors, or scriptwriters, encoded in electronic media (laser, DVD) may prove valuable in studying a film's literary structure—a tactic that by no means precludes study of film's uniqueness as a visual art.

The Great Dictator: Classic Film as Cinema Art (1940)

The Great Dictator unites and combines most of the elements described above: it is a collaborative venture, made within the confines of the Hollywood studio system; it embodies several of the other arts; it communicates a strong message; and finally it is the product of a cinematic genius, Chaplin, a genuine *auteur.*

Let's examine each of these premises briefly.

The Great Dictator is a product of a Hollywood studio, United Artists, which Chaplin helped found in 1919. It was his sixth film for that company, and it is by all standards a collaborative effort. The total project cost $1,403,526, and it took nearly two years to complete. The script alone went through numerous revisions between November 1939 and June 1940. Chaplin agonized over details, especially the phrasing of his last speech, revising it extensively for months. He was aided by Wheeler Dryden, his assistant director, and also by Dan James and Bob Meltzer; therefore, despite Chaplin's undisputed authority, the script was a result of collaboration. The film had nine original musical segments in it, all composed by Chaplin, who wrote the music for his films, and musical director Meredith Wilson supervised the editing and performances. This was Chaplin's first talking film, and sound director Percy Townsend did a masterful job with the alternation in the tone of voice of Chaplin's dual roles. Hynkel sounded shrill and off-key while the barber spoke softly and shyly, as if afraid to offend anyone. The film premiered in October 1940, in New York and a month later in Hollywood and London, becoming an instant national and international hit. Of course, it couldn't be

The humor of Charlie Chaplin's imitation of Hitler in **The Great Dictator** *derives from his artistry in conceiving scenes that capture his character's absurd flights of megalomania.*

shown in Germany, but Hitler had the film smuggled into the country and watched it twice by himself.

The Great Dictator embodies several of the arts. It has the literary form of a plot of mistaken identity, known to literary masters since the times of the Greek Menander and the Roman Plautus who dramatized the story of a set of twins presumed to be the same person; Shakespeare in his *Love's Labor Lost* imitates Menander's plot. In modern times, doubles appear in Dostoyevsky and Mark Twain (Huck Finn and Tom Sawyer change identities). In movies this later became a well-known device in the films of such comedians as Jerry Lewis, Danny Kaye, and Peter Sellers.

Music is also an effective presence in *The Great Dictator*. Aside from Chaplin's compositions, classical music is played at two crucial moments in the film—Wagner's "Lohengrin" during Hynkel's dance with the balloon-globe, and Brahms's "Hungarian Dance" *Number Five* when the barber "dances" to a light-hearted tune while shaving a customer. The two dances—and the music—define the two contrasting personalities in the movie. Hynkel's dance is languorous, slow-paced, precise, and acrobatic, as the dictator holds the balloon globe in his hands, caressing it and tossing it in the air with fingertips or heels. The balloon floats upward, passing the double cross, the sign of Tomania, descending to be tossed again, rhythmically, to the strains of *Lohengrin*. Hynkel lightly leaps on his desk, lies there supine for a moment, content in his absolute power, and then pops the globe up again with his butt. Thus, in this rapturous but ridiculous pose, he expresses his contempt for humanity. Moments later, as he embraces it, the balloon bursts in his face, and he leans on his desk and sobs.

In contrast, the barber's dance is swift, joyous, celebratory, and communicative; he is shaving a customer while celebrating the very act of ordinary work; he is happy with life itself, and the quick tempo of the music only enhances his mood. Hynkel's dance is ballet-like; the barber's is pure mime. Both mix music with visual art. Physically, Chaplin was a skilled athlete, a dancer, skater, and one of the three or four great mimes of the century (the others being the mime Marcel Marceau, and actor-comedians and mimes Red Skelton and Danny Kaye). Besides dancing and music, there was sculpture—or a parody of that art. After his triumphant speech, Hynkel is paraded in his car along the Hynkelstrasse, "The Avenue of Culture," where the banners with the double cross are flying, past the statues of "the Venus of Today and the Thinker of Tomorrow," a mockery of two great sculptures of classical and modern times. The Thinker, a replica of Rodin's masterpiece, has his left hand raised in salute to Hynkel, himself a parody of a dictator who wears oversized hats and capes and tumbles down the stairs. Despite his ridiculous demeanor, Hynkel still attempts to appear a cultivated man who loves the arts, having conceived an artistic vision for the super-race of Tomania.

The Great Dictator communicates a powerful message. The film can be seen as a discursive dialectical process, aimed at gaining support from audiences for a certain point of view. The film's dialectic is found in the two major speeches, one near the beginning when we first encounter Hynkel in his glory, and the other at the end when the escaped barber, mistaken for Hynkel, is forced to deliver a speech in the latter's place. The speeches are juxtapositions, meant as point and counterpoint. Hynkel's maniacal nonsense, given in a gibberish resembling both German and English, is a distortion both of these languages and of rational discourse. The speech, of course, is a parody of Hitler's tirades, which had little substance, but which inspired patriotic hysteria. Here Chaplin has Hynkel deliver what appears total nonsense in a nonsensical language; yet the speech, if analyzed carefully, signals his goal: a strong Tomania where "Democratia shtunk" and "Freisprachen shtunk"—meanings that are clear enough. Through the nonsense, Hynkel demands "sacrifice" (pronounced as "office"), tightening of belts, persecution of the Jews, and peace for the rest of the world—ideas not far removed from those promulgated by Hitler in the Munich Agreement of 1938.

In contrast, the barber's speech at the end calls for a world where science works not for destruction but for the advancement of humankind. Men must love, not hate, one another. The good earth can be rich, a place where men can unite to live in freedom and democracy. The barber is transformed from a humble, lovable, but inept nobody to an inspired leader who rises to unimaginable heights and seems ready to lead, not just Tomania, but the entire world to peace, love, and prosperity. Though the transformation seems improbable, the message of the movie is unmistakable: what humanity needs is leaders for good not for evil. Chaplin, a true artist in all senses of the word—mimic, actor, musician, writer, comedian, director—has used the full extent of his talents to deliver one of the strongest messages for peace and progress in the twentieth century. Thus, Chaplin is an *auteur* in the art of cinema—but, much more than that, he is a genuine artist, philosopher, and leader of humanity. (See chapter 13, page 246, for further discussion of *The Great Dictator*.)

Life Is Beautiful (*La Vita E Bella*): Modern Film as Cinema Art (1998)

A modern sample of a film as a work of art is *Life Is Beautiful*, directed by Roberto Benigni, who also wrote and acted, and won an Oscar for his performance. The film combines mimic comedy, farce, parody, pathos, and, of course, tragedy. The film includes elements of choreography, a semioperatic musical score, and a dazzling display of dancing and architectural features in the Grand Hotel where the early action occurs. The grimness of the concentration camp settings provides a change of mood, and thus a synthesis of dramatic and cine-matic ingenuity. By all counts, *Life Is Beautiful* is both the counterpart of *The Great Dictator* and, one might say, its sequel.

Benigni plays an Italian Jew who meets a school teacher/socialite in Mus-solini's Italy in 1939. She is about to be married to a fascist aristocrat, but Guido (Benigni) wins her over, and she elopes with him from her nuptial cer-emony. He is sort of a clown, a waiter bumbling through life with no prospects, but the lady reciprocates his love, evidently won over by his hum-ble bumbling and honest humanity.

Five years later, after Mussolini is overthrown (this figure remains totally out of the picture except for the use of his name, Benito), Guido and his young son Joshua are rounded up by the Germans and taken to the concen-tration camps. His wife volunteers to go with them, and she boards the train where they are packed in with other prisoners. Guido attempts to deceive his young son, convincing him this is a game, and that if he plays along and earns a thousand points, he will win a tank. The young boy accepts the terms—and the terrible conditions of the concentration camp—and plays along, though he instinctively suspects the truth. He is game to the end, and, when the Ger-mans leave at the end of the war, he remains hidden in an iron box, obeying his father's instructions. Guido, searching for his wife, is executed, the boy emerges, and an American tank arrives to save him.

The above synopsis does not do justice to the movie's sensibilities. The evocative score is by Nicola Piovani, an Italian composer whose musical tem-perament reminds one of Nino Rota's, the composer for Fellini and Coppola movies. The score includes a fox-trot dance reminiscent of the Jazz Age, pop-ular not only in America but also in Mussolini's Italy. Most of the early action takes place at the Grand Hotel where Guido, stumbling over chairs, carrying a tray with a dog on it, abducts his future bride on a horse named *Cavallo Ebreo* (a horse that is a Jew), which belongs to his uncle and has been insult-ingly dyed green by Fascists. The sets of the Grand Hotel, in an unreal pale white, are suggestive of "racial purity," the topic discussed by a female Fascist guest. She is the principal of a school in front of whose students Guido deliv-ers his mock speech about the superior race. This speech (and Benigni's leap onto the school table) reminds viewers of Chaplin's mockery of Hitler—in fact, it seems an outright imitation of Chaplin's performance. The story has the tone of comedy, which changes to pathos in the harrowing concentration camp scenes. Even there, however, the clown Guido inserts some humor—as in the scene where he translates for his son the words of a monstrous Nazi guard who barks out instructions to the prisoners. Some critics have found this humor improper in a Holocaust story. The objection may be valid to some degree, but Benigni's comic persona displays Chaplinesque pathos, as he tries to both save his young son and deceive him as to the nature of their captivity. This could not have been done without his clowning. Chaplin did

Life Is Beautiful *can be seen both as a farcical reduction of Nazism and as a parable of individual self-sacrifice that fosters the protection of others.*

the same thing in *The Great Dictator*, when he created the bumbling Jewish barber and the demoniac but silly Hynkel (not to mention Napaloni—for Mussolini), clowning the audience did not mind because it mocked the villains. Chaplin later admitted that, out of respect for the victims, he would never have made the movie had he actually known what was happening at the Holocaust. This is perhaps an important difference, but Benigni can be justified, since Guido's aim was to show compassion for his son. The comedy here actually underscores the tragedy. Guido dies to save his son. Pathos, as an emotion fitting the scene, has fully replaced the comic elements of the earlier story. We can today watch *Life Is Beautiful* without being offended. In fact, this poignant movie reminds us all the more of the horrible persecution of the Italian Jews. The love of a parent and a wife and mother's sacrifice (which must not be forgotten) are indeed tokens of the beauty of life—regardless of the horror of circumstances. And the caricatures of the Nazis and Fascists adequately compensate for the earlier laughter. When we watch the movie, we are deeply affected. The mother's decision, the young child's eager hope, the Nazi cruelties, these are all present. Benigni's masterpiece equals Chaplin's, and in tone, music score, architectural design of sets, and pantomime—not to mention verbal patterns and sub-themes—it is an exemplary cinematic work of art.

Suggested Readings and Hypertext Links

Burt, George. *The Art of Film Music*. Boston: Northeastern University Press, 1994.

Hillier, Jim, ed. *Cahiers du Cinema: 1960–1968: New Wave, New Cinema, Reevaluating Hollywood*. Boston: Harvard University Press, 1986.

Mast, Gerald, and Marshall Cohen, eds. *Film Theory and Criticism*, 2nd ed. New York: Oxford University Press, 1979.

Sarris, Andrew, *You Ain't Heard Nothing Yet! The American Talking Film: History and Memory, 1927–1949*. New York: Oxford University Press, 1998.

Wood, Michael. *America in the Movies, or "Santa Maria, It Had Slipped My Mind."* New York: Columbia University Press, 1989.

Autumn Sonata, DVD ed. Criterion Collection, 2000. With commentary by Peter Cowie. <http://www.criterionco.com>

Chaplin: A Legacy of Laughter, Laserdisc. Side 4, chapters 19–28. CBS Fox Video, 1993.

The Orphic Trilogy, DVD ed. Criterion Collection, 2000. With commentary by Jean Cocteau. <http://www.criterionco.com>

The Passion of Joan of Arc, DVD ed. Criterion Collection, 1999. With audio essay by Casper Tybjerg. <http://www.criterionco.com>

Suggested Films for Study

Films with Literary Themes

The Virgin Spring (1960), dir. Ingmar Bergman
A Clockwork Orange (1971), dir. Stanley Kubrick
Death in Venice (1971), dir. Luchino Visconti
A Passage to India (1984), dir. David Lean
Much Ado About Nothing (1994), dir. Kenneth Branagh

Films of Hollywood Collaboration

Gone with the Wind (1940), dir. Victor Fleming
Casablanca (1942), dir. Michael Curtiz
Double Indemnity (1944), dir. Billy Wilder
Notorious (1946), dir. Alfred Hitchcock
The Big Sleep (1946), dir. Howard Hawks

Art/Auteur Films

Rules of the Game (1939), dir. Jean Renoir
Beauty and the Beast (1946), dir. Jean Cocteau
L'Avventura (1960), dir. Michelangelo Antonioni
Last Year at Marienbad (1961), dir. Alain Resnais
Eight and a Half (8½) (1962), dir. Federico Fellini
Pierrot le Fou (1965), dir. Jean-Luc Godard
Autumn Sonata (1978), dir. Ingmar Bergman
Akira Kurosawa's Dreams (1990), dir. Akira Kurosawa
Central Station (1998), dir. Walter Salles
Eternity and a Day (1998), dir. Theo Angelopoulos
The Red Violin (1999), dir. François Girard
Run, Lola, Run (1999), dir. Tom Tykwer

Films with Strong Communication/ Social Messages

The Great Dictator (1940), dir. Charles Chaplin
On the Waterfront (1954), dir. Elia Kazan
On the Beach (1959), dir. Stanley Kramer
Dr. Strangelove, or How I Learned to Stop Worrying and Love the Bomb (1964), dir. Stanley Kubrick
Platoon (1984), dir. Oliver Stone
Thelma and Louise (1991), dir. Ridley Scott
Schindler's List (1993), dir. Steven Spielberg

CHAPTER TWO

Responding to Film Genre

How do I respond to film genre? Let us outline the basic responses. The term *genre* in film was inherited from literature and from some of the other arts, such as music and painting, in which "style" (or "school") is often preferred. In literature, genre means a distinctive type of composition, having to do with both form and content, thus dictating the kind of analysis that is appropriate to it. Film genres, though literary in origin, were more or less used to identify the film industry's reaction to a popular demand for certain kinds of entertainment. When narrative film's huge market potential became evident to early producers, they began catering to the appetite of audiences for stories of adventure, romance, mystery, comedy, social satire, and other narrative forms. What was not as readily recognized was that film genre was part of the historical evolution of the subdivisions of literature that had come down to us since Aristotle's time. In his *Poetics*, written in 335 B.C.E., Aristotle defined poetry as a mode of imitation, the most important kinds of which were the epic, the tragic, and the comic. These three divisions of narrative survived through the centuries, enriched by various literary traditions, and became the basis for film genres today.

Origins of Film Genres: Epic, Drama, and Comedy

Aristotle defined the epic as a lengthy story narrated by a live voice, while the tragic and the comic were representations of actions on the stage. Out of

30

these three divisions came the main forms of the literary genre: The novel was a natural evolution of the epic; it had length, complexity of action and character, and often elements of sweeping grandeur. For instance, Leo Tolstoy's *War and Peace*, published in 1865, qualifies as a modern epic that retains the basic characteristics of the ancient epic: great length, multiplicity of plots, a style fitting its mass and dignity, reversal and recognition scenes. Likewise, tragedy has come down to us more or less unaltered since antiquity in the plays of Shakespeare, Racine, Ibsen, O'Neill, and Williams. Like the epic, tragedy has reversals and recognition scenes, and offers the audience a "catharsis of pity and fear." These characteristics are common to both genres, except that the epic is lengthier and is narrated, while tragedy (drama—from the Greek *dran*, to do or to act) is enacted on the stage. Of course, themes represented in modern drama include modern concerns: anxiety (angst), alienation, self-doubt, gender and racial issues, atomic war, globalization of economies, the effects of transmitted diseases, recognition of minorities (such as gays and lesbians) and many more. Still, constructing a good plot remains the basic requirement of good drama—or epic. Drama is an artistic expression demanding an aesthetic response from an audience, and that response is forthcoming only if a play (or a film) is well put together. (It is true that some forms of modern drama—such as the Theater of the Absurd of Ionesco, Pirandello, Beckett, and Camus—have discarded the Aristotelian formulas of plot and instead stress characterization and symbolism.) In cinema, the tragic form has been absorbed by *drama* or *melodrama*, terms that describe a story that deals with dark subjects—death, crime, catastrophic relationships, emotional or financial failure, and many other such topics. Drama remains the most dominant form of artistic expression, more capable than any other art form of embracing diverse and universal themes. Comedy, too, has undergone transformations, but to a lesser degree than epic or drama. It has more or less retained its original structure and aims, to entertain and to censure society's foibles with caustic language and amusing plot twists.

Thus, film has inherited the three main subdivisions of literary narrative forms: the epic, the tragic or dramatic, and the comic. Out of these three categories, other subdivisions have evolved, as film has adapted easily to production circumstances, historical eras, and specific audience demands. Let us consider some of these.

The epic has taken the form of biblical and historical sagas, westerns, and war or action melodramas. Epic films are known for length, wide-screen presentations, spectacular effects, "casts of thousands," and high production costs. The tragic or dramatic literary genre has evolved into the many forms of modern film melodrama: romance, crime, *film noir*, horror, war, political or psychological thriller, and so on. Quite frequently, the epic and dramatic genres overlap, especially in action or adventure films, some of which reach epic proportions in length. The comic genre in film has come to include screwball, slapstick, romantic, dance and music, satirical, and others. In its cinematic form, comedy has retained its original visual character. The mask of the ancient comic actor has been replaced by the visual styles of film comedians such as Charlie Chaplin, Buster Keaton, Laurel and Hardy, Jerry Lewis, Danny Kaye, Marcel Marceau, Red Skelton, Robin Williams, Steve Martin, Jim Carrey, and others. Comediennes with distinctive visual styles (though they are mostly TV actresses) include Lucille Ball, Carol Burnett, Ethel Merman, and Lily Tomlin. Comedy has achieved the most distinctive styles of all, mainly because it can operate under the power of star comedians, all of whom have their unique styles.

The Modern Epic Film

Thus, the genesis of film genre was the result of both literary evolution and many other factors—mainly financial—that determined the forms film production would adopt. Early film audiences, for instance, responded favorably to historical or biblical spectacles. Hence, the melodramas of D. W. Griffith about the Civil War (*Birth of a Nation*, 1915), ancient societies (*Intolerance*, 1916; *The Fall of Babylon*, 1917), and many similar topics treated in films, became huge popular successes. Other epics based on semihistorical or fictional situations were *Ben-Hur* (1907, 1926, 1959), *Napoleon* (1927), *The Ten Commandments* (1923, 1956), and many others spanning several decades, from the 1930s to the 1950s and '60s. Epic films were characterized by lengthy and episodic plots with multiple strands, huge casts, spectacular special effects, colorful landscapes, elaborate sets, and (more or less) elevated subject matter. Above all, the epic story featured a popular hero who could inspire tribal instincts. A Jewish prince, Ben-Hur, fought the injustices of the Roman system; a national leader, Napoleon, conquered Europe, inspiring his countrymen to victories; and Americans fought the Nazis and the Japanese during World War II, either as ordinary soldiers or as great generals like George Patton. The epic genre could also reveal the darker side of humanity, as in the gangster epics spawned by the Hollywood studios in the early 1930s and later revisited in epics like *The Godfather I* and *II* (1972, 1974), to mention the best known. Epic also ventured into space with *2001: A Space Odyssey* (1969) and *Star Wars* (1977).

An epic cannot be an everyday, ordinary story; hence these historical epics, most of which borrowed incidents from the Bible, from Greek and Roman mythology, and from ancient and modern history—incidents that would elicit a mass response. The key to the epic response, according to Sigmund Freud, is tribal wish fulfillment. Therefore, epics must feature heroes

The widely popular Titanic, *with its combination of spectacle and romance, testifies to the perennial vitality of the epic film genre.*

that appeal not just to elite, special, or cult interests, but to the largest possible group associated with a unified ideal: patriotism, religion, or a current social issue (freedom of speech, for instance). Moses was such a hero in the *Ten Commandments* (1956); he was both a religious and national leader, bringing his people out of exile and out of slavery into the Promised Land. Though Moses was a Jew, his appeal is broad: as a biblical figure he appeals to Christians and to all freedom-loving people, including vagabond tribes seeking refuge.

Generally, modern Hollywood preferred episodes from the Roman conquests, especially those related to the birth of Christianity and the enslavement and torture of Christians. Some of these epics were made after World War II, in the decade of the 1950s, when wide-screen productions permitted the introduction of greater spectacle. Notable among these were *The Robe* (1953), the first Cinemascope production, about the conversion of a Roman tribune who took part in the crucifixion of Christ. Another big spectacle was *Quo Vadis* (1951), which showed Christians tortured and thrown to the lions by an insane emperor. But the biggest was *Ben-Hur* (1958). This story of a noble Jew condemned to the galleys was hugely successful because of its famous chariot race. These films were followed by *Spartacus* (1960), the tale of a slave who led an unsuccessful rebellion against the Roman Empire. Rome—with its grandeur, legions, fleets, chariot races, and other pageantry— evidently appealed to Hollywood, which saw an opportunity to dazzle audiences with lavish spectacle during a time when television had made inroads into the movie industry's profits. The epic form was thus associated with entertainment and spectacle, and with advancing technological methods (Technicolor, Cinemascope, Cinerama, etc.). It was seen as a means of capturing larger audiences to stem the movie industry's decline. Other epics of that era include *The Bridge on the River Kwai* (1957), *El Cid* (1961), and *Cleopatra* (1962). A change of tone emerged with *Lawrence of Arabia* (1963), directed by David Lean. That movie led the way from the merely colorful and spectacular epic to the thoughtful literary epic. In some ways, the epics of the sixties and seventies may be considered anti-epics, with narratives stressing social conflicts, individuality, rebellion against various establishments, failure, and disillusionment. Several are worth mentioning: *The Great Escape* (1963), a tale of Allied officers who plan an elaborate escape from a Nazi prison camp but seem fated to fail; *Lord Jim* (1965), an adaptation of Joseph Conrad's tale that downgrades the image of the Western European hero; *Catch-22* (1970), a sardonic view of the military establishment; *A Bridge Too Far* (1977), the story of a disastrous attempt by Allied forces to secure a position behind enemy lines during World War II. The epic genre continued to thrive in changed form in the 1970s with the gangster epics mentioned earlier, and in the 1980s with the biography of *Gandhi* (1983) and *A Passage to India* (1984). Both of the latter used Western points of view to describe the evils of colonialism. Even a musical like *Amadeus* (1984) can be considered an epic, allowing for the biographical form as one characteristic of this genre. Contemporary epics by Steven Spielberg—*Schindler's List* (1993) and *Saving Private Ryan* (1998)—stress theme and realism, showing how the direction as well as the style and content of the war epic have changed. Whatever the changes, however, the epic has retained its basic characteristics. Between *Ben-Hur* (1958) and *Titanic* (1997), forty years passed, and yet the two films are in some ways similar. Both have appealing central stories: the loving son who returns to avenge his mother and sister, and the loving, though spoiled, rich girl who returns to a sinking ship to die with her poor but worthy lover. Both films have climactic, spectacular endings—*Ben-Hur*'s famous chariot race and *Titanic*'s sinking of the world's greatest ship. Each epic won eleven Oscars, a record. In our day, the epic continues with *The Gladiator* (2000), a modernized (and more violent) version of the traditional Roman theme. Directed by Ridley Scott, who is known for his visual style, this epic utilizes computer techniques for spectacles. It features a Roman general who is a victim of the machinations of the scheming emperor Commodus. The general loses his rank and becomes a gladiator, intending to fight his way back to Rome for revenge. To be successful, epics have to command popular attention, and spectacle (the least artistic of all the epic elements, according to Aristotle) attracts attention. Perhaps that is why some of the greatest literary epics have not been made into epic films. Film epics are basically popular fare centered on action, and they tend to discourage subtle thought. Homer's *The Iliad*, the first and greatest literary epic, has been glaringly absent from the large screen. So has Virgil's *Aeneid*, recounting the destruction of Troy and the foundation of Rome. *The Aeneid*, a popular classroom reading assignment, contains sea and monster adventures equaling Homer's and a truly engrossing love story that has long inspired both poets and musicians (Henry Purcell's opera *Dido and Aeneas* [1689] comes to mind). Here indeed is a subject for an epic film to end all epic films.

The Western

As one of the most creative of the arts of the twentieth century and beyond, film has a tendency to proliferate, splitting into genres and subgenres in response to audience preference and need. One of those forms is the western, an inheritor of the epic form. The western was born out of the insatiable appetites of audiences for horse operas, movies about good cowboys in white hats chasing black-hatted villains across open spaces that represent the mythical Old West. The western genre, a purely American invention (though it has been imitated in Japan and Italy), came into existence in the beginning of the cinematic era, but it flourished in the '30s, '40s, and '50s. During those decades, the Hollywood studio system developed the persona of the western hero, a stalwart male character who stands up for justice, guns down his opponents, and wins the girl at the end. Countless western movies were based on that formula. Most westerns featured celebrated Hollywood stars who rose to the stature of world-famous legends. Figures like Tom Mix and Buck Jones were cartoon-like characters who inflamed the imagination of youths everywhere. Hollywood stars like James Cagney, Henry Fonda, and Burt Lancaster became known as western heroes—though they played many other roles. Gary Cooper and John Wayne were admired more for their fists and fast draws than for any other quality; they personified manhood, ruggedness, individuality, invincibility, qualities associated with the open spaces and rugged terrain of the American West. In *Vera Cruz* (1954) Cooper punches a badman (Ernest Borgnine) during a saloon brawl; Borgnine staggers backwards through a swing door and tumbles into the street, to the audience's utter delight. The film, directed by Robert Aldrich, pairs Cooper with the acrobatic and fast-drawing Burt Lancaster, playing an amoral opportunist seeking Emperor Maximilian's gold. Cooper is after riches too, but no matter.

The audience expects an eventual showdown between the two. It appears that the younger and more athletic Lancaster has the advantage here. But it is Cooper—rangy, awkward, unassuming—who guns him down. Another revered western persona, John Wayne, gunned down badman Lee Marvin, twice in two movies. In *The Man Who Shot Liberty Valance* (John Ford, 1962), Valance is shot by Wayne while confronting lawyer James Stewart, a brave but inept gunman. And in *The Comancheros* (Michael Curtiz, 1961), Lee Marvin churlish, brutal, resentful, attempts to draw on Wayne after losing to him in a card game, but he is no match for the Duke. Wayne can do it with his fists too. In the *Horse Soldiers* (Ford, 1959), Wayne, a Union cavalry colonel, coolly asks for his "gauntlets" (yellow gloves) before he dispatches two southern fugitives, potential informers who could sabotage his plans to invade a southern station. He delivers a lightning blow and the first man is felled like a tree. The viewer only hears the second blow to the other man. The Duke (as Wayne was popularly known) was the most dominant figure in the western genre for several decades. Tall, imposing, broad of gesture, and somewhat stocky, he nevertheless moved lightly, as if always on tiptoe, graceful as a panther. A life-size bronze statue at the entrance of the John Wayne Airport at Orange County, California, captures his image perfectly. Seen from the side, Wayne leans forward, his left arm swinging in front of him; seen from the front, he stands at a slight angle, midriff to the left, head and feet to the right. His whole body reflects a whirlwind decisiveness; wherever he is going, nothing can stop him. The statue exudes a physical and moral presence which the screen magnified. Let the villains of the wide plains know who is in charge here, who—after a certain fancy display of gun and fist—will have the last word. Wayne of the airport, dressed in his classic cowboy form, is not Wayne the actor, but the legendary Duke, the metamorphosed image projected on the screen. No biography can reproduce that image; one has to see him in the movies to know the Duke. His statue is an archetype of western manhood, dreamed of and made real by the American screen.

Tragic Genre Derivatives: Drama and Melodrama

Just as the epic generated the modern epic film, so tragedy spawned the various forms of drama or melodrama, first on the stage—Greek, Roman, Elizabethan, modern—then in the novel (for the novel could accommodate both the epic and the tragic). Film has benefited greatly from its genre progenitors, whether narrative or stage. It can as easily take materials from a stage play (Ibsen, Shakespeare, Williams) as from a novel, and countless novels have become popular movies. The tragic form has also evolved and become what is known as melodrama, a term frequently applied to the opera from which it derives. In the modern film, a melodrama (or "soap opera") features stock characters easily recognized by the masses—a villain (man or woman) pitted against a hero or heroine who wins the sympathies of an audience. Film has the advantage here, for heroes and heroines are recognizable stars with drawing power who easily command the audience's regard. The villain also has some distinctive advantage, since he or she is usually a recognizable "heavy," an actor the audience "loves to hate." Star power, rather than plot or theme, became the staple of melodramas during the Golden Era of Hollywood (1925–1960), and star power continues to entice patrons to movie houses today. Bankable stars and star recognition are what a Hollywood movie is made of. Without those, movies run the danger of becoming "elitist" entertainment, like opera and the symphony, thus losing their mass appeal.

Some of the most memorable melodramas in Hollywood history owed their success (and drawing power) to their great stars, but also to the villains pitted against them. Let's take two examples, both from the Golden Era: *Casablanca* (1942) and *Key Largo* (1948), both featuring Humphrey Bogart, a star whose attractive persona (not always apparent in his early films) made him an audience favorite. But the villains first. *Casablanca*, directed by Michael Curtiz, features Conrad Veidt as the overbearing Nazi officer Major Strasser, who is intent on capturing Victor Laszlo, a resistance fighter who has escaped the German concentration camps. Laszlo is in Casablanca, a port in Western Africa where fugitives from Europe fled during the Nazi occupation, with his wife Ilsa Lund (Ingrid Bergman). They try to get passport visas to fly to Lisbon, then to America and freedom. But Ilsa has formed a liaison with an American, Rick Blaine (Bogart). They met in Paris before Blaine fled to escape the advancing Germans, and Ilsa then believed her husband was dead. Laszlo and Lund seek help from Rick, who now is the owner of the Café Americain, a favorite haunt of fugitives, criminals, gamblers, singers—a motley crowd. The story is complicated by Ilsa's encounter with Rick and the rekindling of their passion. Rick holds the two letters of transit (which "cannot be rescinded"), signed by none other than Charles de Gaulle himself. These are left in his keeping by Ugarte (Peter Lorre), a black-marketeer, before he is killed by the French police, who are intent on impressing the recently arrived Strasser. The film also features Claude Rains as the cynical French policeman Captain Louis Renault, who bets freely in Rick's casino and thus allows it to remain open. Renault pretends to help Strasser keep an eye on Laszlo, who claims he cannot be arrested on "free French soil." But after Laszlo provokes Strasser by singing the French national anthem, Strasser orders Renault to close Rick's café. Rick has a change of heart and helps Laszlo and Ilsa escape by handing them the letters of transit, then kills Strasser who threatens to arrest the lot of them. As Laszlo and Ilsa board a plane that will take them to Lisbon, Rick and Renault walk off, now both fugitives from the law, as Rick comments wryly on the "start of a beautiful friendship."

Such are the ingredients of a well-made melodrama that continues to attract audiences today. The good guys, Rick, Laszlo, and eventually Renault, defeat the archetypal evil Nazi (it helps that Veidt looks the part), trust between the ill-fated lovers is restored, and a new appreciation is fomented between former rivals Rick Blaine and Captain Renault. Meanwhile, Ilsa and Laszlo, the most deserving of the group, obtain the letters through Rick's generosity and fly away to freedom and safety.

Key Largo, directed by John Huston and scripted by Richard Brooks, is a grimmer and grittier tale, much more realistic in style and content than *Casablanca*. Set at a small hotel in the Florida Keys, it features two groups of characters, the sympathetic owner, played by Lionel Barrymore (in a wheelchair); his daughter Nora Temple, played by Lauren Bacall; and a drifter ex-marine major, McCloud, played by Humphrey Bogart. McCloud was in a World War II battle in which Nora's young husband was killed. The hotel is occupied by a group of gangsters headed by Johnny Rocco (Edward G. Robinson) who have chosen the hotel as the place for an exchange of counterfeit money to occur later that night. These two groups collide as a hurricane is brewing. To further complicate the plot, the local sheriff is searching for two Osceola fugitives who have been given shelter by the compassionate Barrymore. Since the plot is relatively thin, characterization is the movie's strong point. Edward G. Robinson's persona as a gangster in '30s movies establishes him as an archetypal villain, with his sharply etched, intimidating facial features—arched eyebrows; deep-sunk, narrow eyes; thick, sensuous lips. As usual, he is accompanied by an assortment of bullies, among them the potbellied, menacing Thomas Gomez, always known to audiences for his mean-spirited arrogance. The entourage includes Robinson's adoring (and drunk) ex-friend, played by Claire Trevor in a role that secured her a supporting actress Oscar.

Robinson's superficially polished manners enable him to appear to his hosts as a civilized intruder who will inconvenience them for "only a couple of hours." Despite the approaching hurricane and the unrest in the group, he remains calm, as if the hostile environment means nothing to him. He elicits some sympathy because audiences grudgingly admire unflappable villains. But his calm exterior crumbles as soon as the howling winds pick up and the bottles and glasses on the shelves shake and fall. His exterior calm gone, the cowardice of the villain is unmasked, and chaos prevails. In contrast, Bogart's image improves as events unfold. He has won Bacall's sympathies, as both she and her father expect him to join them in their hermits' existence. But when he is challenged to a gun duel by Rocco, Bogart backs down, explaining that he doesn't intend to die for someone like Rocco. "Bogie" here sounds like

Rick in *Casablanca* who "sticks his neck out for no one." It's a typical Bogart gambit. The viewer knows the real Bogart will soon stand up. Underneath his cynical exterior, Bogie possesses a soft heart, humanity, courage, and other typical Bogartian traits: tactical shrewdness, hard-nosed decision making, and the ability to stick to a mapped-out course. After their successful exchange of counterfeit currency, the gangsters intend to flee to Cuba, but their boat has sunk in the storm. In exchange for leaving everybody else alive, they propose that Bogart should steer them to Havana on the host's boat—which he agrees to do. He manages to lull them into a false sense of security, then he exterminates them in a gunfight worthy of the OK Corral. He is wounded, but naturally he returns safely to the now-admiring Bacall. Good prevails over evil.

Archetypal villains are, of course, not confined to male leads. Female villains rival their male cinematic counterparts and have populated screen dramas virtually from the start. Some well-known examples include Bette Davis as the notorious Southern belle of *Jezebel* (1938) who easily outmatches all her male counterparts in wit and cunning. Judith Anderson, playing the housekeeper Mrs. Danvers in Hitchcock's *Rebecca* (1940), remains insanely loyal to her former mistress (Rebecca), proving an iron-handed avenger in her attempts to intimidate Laurence Olivier's new bride. A beautiful but amoral Gene Tierney is brewing murderous designs (which include the drowning of a 15-year-old) in her mad jealousy of her husband in *Leave Her to Heaven* (1945). In *Notorious* (1946) Leopoldine Konstantin, playing Claude Rains' mother, coldly plots the poisoning of Ingrid Bergman, who has penetrated their Nazi stronghold in Brazil. Bergman, of course, nearly dies of both fright and poison but is rescued in the nick of time by her lover, CIA agent Cary Grant.

Women as cinematic evildoers, especially if pitted against other women leads, can evoke as strong an audience reaction as any male villain. Anne Baxter, playing upstart actress Eve Carrington in *All About Eve* (1950), makes herself perfectly hateful in the eyes of the audience as she wins first the favor and then the contempt of Bette Davis. Margot Channing (Davis), an actress whose career has peaked, discovers somewhat belatedly that her protégé Eve has been planning to replace her. It is a shock to her as well as to the audience. Eve's masterful plan is explained by archcynic and venomous critic Addison DeWitt in flashbacks on the evening Eve receives a prestigious theater award. Appearing as an admiring fan of Margot's, she waits outside the theater in a trenchcoat night after night, missing not a single performance, seeking an opportunity to be introduced. Once she manages that, she moves step by step to gain Margot's absolute trust, planning to become her understudy. She's aided by another woman's clever plot to leave Margot stranded in a car before a performance. The audience hates her—but what does it matter? Eve performs brilliantly, becomes famous, and receives her own award. That night Margot is in the audience watching the proceedings, and it is worth seeing this movie to watch Margot watch Eve's fake speech of thanks. The audience also gets a thrill from seeing Eve bested by the venomous DeWitt (George Sanders), the only one who knows her real background and can outmaneuver her. Female villains remain popular. A few examples include: Louise Fletcher playing a sadistic nurse in *One Flew Over the Cuckoo's Nest* (1975) and winning an Oscar in the process. Television villain Alexis Carrington (played by movie actress Joan Collins) dominated the early '80s. And even today, distinguished English actress Ellen Mirren plays a vengeful teacher in *Teaching Mrs. Tingle* (1999).

Villains, male or female, are essential to melodrama. Hollywood, and cinema in general, was happy to perpetuate them to the delight of audiences, who "love to hate" bad types. Without a hateful villain threatening to destroy the "good" character, there is no melodrama. The more blackhearted the villain, the greater the audience's delight when he or she is vanquished by a hero's wits or brawn. It helps when, in addition to his or her malevolence, the villain is also highly colorful. Take the James Bond series for instance—from Dr. No to Auric Goldfinger to the eye-patched Emilio Largo of *Thunderball* (who likes to throw his guests into shark-infested swimming pools) to the Elliott Carver of *Tomorrow Never Dies* (1997). Carver is a media conglomerate mogul who broadcasts distorted news, and he and the others are cold-blooded megalomaniac killers who much deserve their demise. Over a period of forty years, Bond has been the archetypal hero—having outlasted the likes of Superman and Luke Skywalker. Bond as a hero embodies enviable—and some despicable—manly qualities. He is brave, cool, resourceful, witty, dedicated to the cause of saving humanity from dangerous, paranoid villains. But he is also a flippant and remorseless killer (has a "license to kill," a title of one of his movies) and a rampant sexist, though he has lately reformed a bit in the company of female partners who can match him. Dr. Holly Goodhead in *Moonraker* (1979) has a Ph.D. and equals Bond in wit and prowess.

Villains, of course, are not always human. Some monsters such as King Kong and Godzilla qualify as villains worth exterminating with no remorse; a man-eating shark in *Jaws* (1974) and a computer HAL-9000 in *2001: A Space Odyssey* (1968) also qualify as villains that deserve their defeats.

The Tragic Genre: *Citizen Kane*

The tragic genre could be part of any kind of narrative film. Thus, a tragic film can be an epic or a drama (though not a melodrama) and a comedy can contain tragic elements. It was Shakespeare who mixed the genres he inherited from antiquity. Some of his comedies contain tragic or "dark" elements (*Much Ado About Nothing* and *The Tempest* could easily have ended tragically), and his tragedies contain scenes with fools or other comic figures (Polonius in *Hamlet* is quite comic, as are Osric and the gravedigger). Hollywood (and other film agencies) have adjusted to the Shakespearean tradition, mixing the genres when the occasion calls for it (*Catch–22* is a good example).

The basic and most characteristic requirement of the tragic genre is the delineation of the hero or heroine. He or she must be neither saintly nor a villain, but a basically good person with major character flaws that cause his or her downfall. This definition has come down from Aristotle, and it is as true now as it was then. Another characteristic of tragedy as compared to melodrama, is that it must have an unhappy ending. In fact, the unhappier the ending, the better the tragedy, said Aristotle.

The trouble with this premise—at least in commercial cinema—is that audiences do not like either flawed characters or unhappy endings. Cinema is perceived as basically an entertainment medium, and audiences go to the movies to be entertained, to have a good time. Though blood and gore are accepted as part of the action, they must appear at the expense of the bad guys. That is why dramas that end unhappily are relatively rare in Hollywood and in other movie industries around the world. Yet when everything is said and done, some of the most tragic movies have also been among the greatest.

These movies present complex characters whose motives are sometimes unclear to themselves and whose actions are self-destructive. This self-destructiveness, however, must be accompanied by a certain awareness of mistakes made, and that mistake must be acknowledged in the aftermath of that action. Consider the tragic characters of antiquity—Creon in *Antigone*, for instance. He is not so much the typical villain as a well-intentioned man trying to save his country from civil war, but he fails to see that not burying an enemy is an impiety. He cannot take the advice of his son or his future daughter-in-law, and this stubbornness costs him the virtual elimination of most of his family. A broken man at the end of the play, he admits his mistake. Arrogance, narrowness of outlook, lack of insight into the motives of others—these are fatal flaws that cause a basically decent man to fail.

The cinema has produced precious few genuine tragic heroes or heroines, but those that exist are as representative of the tragic genre as anyone in any other medium—novel, epic, or stage drama. Of the examples mentioned above, possibly the greatest is Charles Kane in *Citizen Kane* (1941), directed by Orson Welles. This movie is justly celebrated for its techniques—deep focus photography, *mise-en-scène*, montage, lighting, camera movement—which made it the model for moviemaking and cinema study for generations to come. *Citizen Kane* has consistently been regarded by international critics, as well as by the American Film Institute, as the greatest movie ever made. However, what gives this film its extraordinary status is not merely its techniques (since imitated by many others), but its subject matter, especially its classic portrayal of a tragic hero. The story is not told in the Aristotelian fashion which requires an action that covers a span of twenty-four hours. Rather, it unfolds chronologically through flashbacks which cover Kane's entire life, from his early boyhood to his death. Several narrators are involved, his close associates and friends, and they tell the story to an inquiring reporter whose face is never shown. First, Kane's entire life is capsulized in a "News on the March" newsreel, a typical news format in the early days of cinema. A reporter (Thomson) makes the rounds, interviewing several of Kane's surviving associates and his ex-wife, searching for a clue to Kane's last word—"Rosebud"—which he pronounced as he lay dying. Each narrator gives his or her version of the meaning of this word, but none seems to satisfy the investigator.

With each interview, the viewer gains another insight into Kane's life and his basic character flaw—his determination to impose his will on others. Kane is a man unable to see himself as others see him. He is unhappy despite his vast wealth. The secret of Rosebud is also the secret of his unhappiness. The viewer eventually learns that Rosebud was the name of the snow sled the boy played with before he was separated from his parents by his custodian, Thatcher. The sled was abandoned in a warehouse when his mother died and was burned with other useless possessions following Kane's funeral. Only the viewer knows the secret. Speaking this word, which he does on his deathbed at the very beginning of the movie, means Kane finally realized that his pursuit of happiness was illusory. He was never able to recapture his youthful innocence.

What the viewer learns, however, is something far more complex than that. His failure is not the inability to recapture his youth. That is only part of it. Kane is unable to connect with people—people he knows and those unknown to him. One might say—though it is only a partial truth—that wealth corrupts him. It gives him the power to buy everything he wants, including important people's services (he buys the entire staff of *The Tribune* to jump start his own fledgling paper, *The Inquirer*). He even attempts to buy people's love—the love of ordinary people—by restoring their rights. His basic flaw is egomania, self-will, the need to bend everyone to his will. This is hailed as a great American virtue ("I did it my way," crooned Frank Sinatra); it can also be self-destructive. All those interviewed by Thomson relate variations on this fatal character trait. Wall Street's Thatcher accuses Kane of using his wealth only to *buy* things, never to *invest*. This is the wrong economic use of wealth. Investing money shares it with those who seek to establish corporations or those who depend on shareholding, and it also benefits those who are employed. Thatcher is correct here, but he is frustrated by Kane's self-will. This is the reverse of the American way—or at least the ideal way—which creates wealth for the benefit not of the few but of all. Democracy creates wealth which trickles down to those who do not have it, not wealth that stays at the center with its owner to satisfy the owner's whims. Bernstein, the second person interviewed, is the ex-associate who least understands Kane. He thinks Rosebud might be a girl's name. He recollects Kane's early exuberance and dedication to the cause of the people, however, and his sympathetic portrayal reminds the viewer that Kane was not an evil man. This is perfectly Aristotelian: a man of prominence, of wealth and/or of stature, who fails because of an "error" or "frailty" (*hamaria*), not because of vice or depravity. Jed Leland's portrait of Kane is harsher and more bitter than the others. He was a friend of Kane's in school, and he feels betrayed by Kane's dismissal of the concerns expressed by those around him. He relates the failure of Kane's first marriage, his unwillingness to acknowledge defeat when running for governor, and his insistence on making an unknown and untalented woman an opera singer. Here Leland's tale merges with that of Jane Alexander, Kane's second wife. And it is that tale that reveals Kane's glaring inability to accept the harsh rules of reality. Alexander has no voice, but Kane insists she must sing. He builds a palatial opera house for her in Chicago. He rejects her voice teacher's advice and witnesses her humiliation when he is the only person in the theater to applaud her, clapping his hands futilely but persistently in a void of silence. His lonely applause despite all evidence, in spite of the boos he hears from the audience, is his most tragic moment. Later, when Alexander leaves him, he breaks her furniture in a rage, then walks stiffly through his glass corridors, a lonely man. His palace, the dome that like Kubla Khan he decreed, looms large, but it is an empty shell.

The ironies here are multiple: the dying Kane recalls his childhood happiness with the word "Rosebud," but he never knows he could have been happy as an adult. The meaning of "Rosebud" is never revealed to those who hear it spoken, but it becomes clear to the viewer.

More American Tragic Movies

Though perhaps the greatest of film tragedies, *Citizen Kane* is not the only film that qualifies as a classic tragedy in the American or international cinema. Even if comparatively few tragic movies were made, they were almost always films of distinction. Worth mentioning here are a few of the most prominent examples. In *Double Indemnity* (1944), a *film noir* directed by Billy Wilder, insurance salesman Fred McMurray is lured by prospects of sex and money to commit a murder. This film verges on melodrama (in some ways, the two genres are parallel) because he is found out and confesses his crime before he is apprehended by—of all people—Edward G. Robinson, here playing a cop. *Lawrence of Arabia* (1962), an epic story of the enigmatic Englishman T. E. Lawrence, was brought to the screen by David Lean. Lean portrays the adventurer as the vainglorious leader of an Arab rebellion, a man capable of great victories but unable to measure up to the deified image of himself. He commits suicide (shown at the beginning of the movie) when he finds out he is not a god. Perhaps the greatest American tragic movie is *Godfather II*, directed by Francis Ford Coppola, which, in conjunction with *Godfather I*, centers on the downfall of a potentially great man. The two movies have to be seen together for the fullness of this tragic fall to be comprehended. Michael Corleone (masterfully played by Al Pacino) is the son of a prominent Mafia boss, Vito Corleone, whose story begins in the second movie, so the tale is told in reverse. Don Corleone seems a man at the end of an era; he cannot escape his own criminal past, but he wants one of his sons to remain uninvolved in crime, to become someone important—a judge or a senator. Before he dies, he confesses his dream—to convert a crime family to one engaged in legitimate business. This is his version of the American Dream. But Michael takes over his father's crime dynasty when he discovers plots against him by members of his own family. As the two movies merge, Michael proceeds mercilessly to exterminate all his enemies. As he says, "I don't want to kill everybody, just my enemies." That includes his weaker brother Fredo who wanted to branch out for himself. Coming full circle, at the end of the second movie, Michael has become a monster. The movie ends with him in the yard of his home at Lake Tahoe after Fredo's murder, sitting on a bench as dry autumn leaves flutter by. He seems deep in thought. A montage flashes back to the days of his youth when the war started. He sees himself sitting around the table with his family, telling them he has enlisted as a volunteer to fight for his country. That brings a protest from his elder brother Sonny who wants him to stay inside the crime clan where he has a "future." The then-idealistic Michael opts to serve his country. The contrast is telling. The monster Michael has glimpses of what he might have been: a great man instead of a criminal. This is the momentous reversal in the story and the great tragic moment, caught in a flash of brilliant filmmaking, in perhaps the greatest tragic American movie.

Other distinguished tragic movies include another Coppola film, *Apocalypse Now* (1979). A flawed army officer has betrayed his mission in Vietnam and an assassin is being dispatched to "terminate" him. This movie was never quite exalted by critics to the lofty status of the *Godfather* saga, perhaps because it shows not individual but collective flaws of war-making. *Quiz Show* (1995) has remained relatively obscure, but it has the design of a well-made tragic plot. It depicts the fall from grace of the scion of a prominent American literary family who chooses to cheat on a TV quiz show, thus betraying his own, his family's, and his country's ideals.

Modernity has not eradicated tragic movies. It is actually amazing how, as works of art, they endure as they have, since the basics always remain the same. An error or frailty—whether an individual's or a group's—causes the downfall of an otherwise worthy individual. Here again it's not always the villain who causes the trouble. The wound is self-inflicted. Such movies portray the human condition better than the ones that reinforce an audience's self-satisfied assurance that it is always the bad guys who make us unhappy. Melodramas do that, and in that sense they may be exercises in paranoia, encouraging the practice of scapegoating which lets us avoid looking into ourselves. But it is the honest look which a tragic movie provides that tells us who we are, why we make the mistakes we make, and what it is that we can do to correct them. Tragedy is hard to take sometimes, but it teaches and cleanses— two worthwhile goals of tragic cinema.

Modernity has had some triumphs. A latecomer of a movie that nevertheless deserves all its accolades is *Boys Don't Cry* (1999). The uncompromising honesty of this film's script, together with the heroic performances, raise it to the status of a classic tragic film worthy of its predecessors. (See p. 236.)

The Comic Genre: The Romantic Archetype

Comedy in film comes in many shapes and forms, but the most popular over the years has been the romantic archetype. This film genre centers on a man-woman relationship that almost always displays the same features. A man and a woman form an attachment, a complication occurs which temporarily separates them, and then a solution brings them together again. This format has been most evident in stage presentations which basically started with the New Comedy of Menander in the third century B.C.E. (the then-bygone Old Comedy of Aristophanes featured social conflicts), continued with the plays of the Romans Plautus and Terence, then was revived and took definite shape in the comedies of Shakespeare—*Much Ado About Nothing, Two Gentlemen of Verona, Love's Labour's Lost, A Midsummer Night's Dream*—all of which are about lovers or sets of lovers who quarrel and then make up. The comic tradition continued with the stories/novels of Jane Austen, in which the archetypes developed and matured into models for the modern romantic novels and, of course, for film.

In this format, the archetypal lovers undergo an important transformation. The male, either because of his obsolete patriarchal social status or his arrogance, attempts a relationship with a woman he admires while making advances which are demeaning to her. The female, rising to the occasion, delivers an aggressive rebuttal, putting the male in his place. This sparks a character adjustment in the male, who is now scolded and remorseful and seeks to become worthy of her in manners and morals. A case in point is Mr. Darcy in Austen's *Pride and Prejudice*: When he first proposes to Elizabeth Bennett, assuming he is doing her a favor and expecting gratitude, he insults her and her family. Elizabeth, of course, responds with one of the most emphatic rejections of an arrogant suitor in all literature. Humbled, Darcy later admits that this was a reprimand he needed to deflate his selfish self-regard and allow him to become the moral equal to Elizabeth.

Modern film has favored this formula in countless movies, not only in the '30s and '40s, but continuing into the end of the twentieth century and beyond. The formula works so well that there is no end in sight. Here are synopses of several archetypal formulas, which often intermix as story patterns continue to develop in both film and literature.

1. **The Cinderella Myth**: A young woman of humble origin is elevated through her casual meeting with a man of higher social status. The story includes fairy godmother/father/hotel manager, evil stepmother and sisters, a prince, various other agents of good and evil. Film example: *Ever After* (1998), a modern version of the myth.
2. **The Pygmalion Myth or Archetype**: Pygmalion, a Greek sculptor, carves a statue of a maiden and falls in love with it. He begs the goddess Aphrodite to bring the statue to life. She does, and Galatea becomes his wife. In modern times, *Pygmalion* is a play by George Bernard Shaw, in which a phonetics professor coaches a flower girl to speak English properly, thus advancing her social status. It eventually became the musical comedy *My Fair Lady*, probably its most popular incarnation.
3. **The Beauty/Beast Archetype**: Beast is a human of high social standing, transformed into a beast through a fatal flaw in his character. Only the love of an innocent can redeem him. The transformation of the outer self, however, is only an indication of an inner change. The Beast is a double creature. At the end, through the influence of Beauty, the evil half is shed so that the good half can be brought to the surface.

These archetypal patterns often overlap, but the basic characteristics of the formula remain the same, the male-female relationship is the most important ingredient. Several films described below either conform—more or less—to one of these patterns or combine two or three.

Beauty and the Beast (1946)
Directed by Jean Cocteau, this fairy tale is of Flemish origin, based on a story by Madame Jeanne-Marie Leprince de Beaumont. The Beast lives in an impressive palace, imprisoned there by a fatal flaw in his character, but still with considerable power. He has the power, for instance, to put to death a merchant who wanders by mistake into his palace grounds and plucks a rose for his daughter. He will spare the merchant's life on one condition: Beauty must come to him, or her father dies. She must marry him, or he will die. And

then she must return to her father, who also is dying. By now, Beauty has lost her heart to Beast, whose inner kindness she is able to recognize. Her love restores him to his former self—a prince. Her compassion saves him.

Never on Sunday (1960)
Directed by Jules Dassin, it presents a dreamy, idealistic American named Homer Thrace who visits Greece. There he encounters an earthy prostitute, Ilya, whom he wishes to reform, but in the process, *he* becomes more addicted to *her* ways than she to his. The motifs are a moral tale, in which the reformer is reformed; a clash of values; and a comic reversal of fortunes. The beast submits to beauty, whose way of life (freedom from restraints) he finally appreciates. The Pygmalion myth is suggested here.

Pygmalion (1938)
Director Anthony Asquith offers the tale of a cold-hearted professor of phonetics (Henry Higgins) who teaches a Cockney flower girl (Eliza Doolittle) to speak English correctly. He has made a substantial wager that he can "pass her off as a duchess in six months" in London society. He wins the bet: Eliza speaks flawless English, but the heartless professor still treats her as a "gutter-snipe," gives her no credit for her accomplishments, and drives her to despair. Professor Higgins is humbled when she proves her surprisingly higher moral stature.

Pretty Woman (1990)
In this film directed by Garry Marshall, a powerful male mogul pulls a street-walker up the social ladder, but this encounter exposes his vulnerabilities. The film's imagery relies on motifs or archetypes: money (coins); actors' names engraved on the sidewalk; luxury car (Lotus); a luxury hotel; fashionable attire; a rented necklace; sexual gadgets; dinnerware; opera glasses; "fairy godfather"—all suggesting both the Cinderella and Pygmalion myths.

The Prince and the Showgirl (1957)
Laurence Olivier directed Marilyn Monroe in the tale of an American show-girl in London during the 1912 coronation of George V. She is romanced by the Carpathian Prince Regent (played by Olivier). Dazzled by royal splendor, the showgirl still outwits the pompous prince, teaching him a lesson or two on manners and morals in the process. Reflects the Beauty and the Beast archetype.

Notorious (1956)
Alfred Hitchcock directed this spy thriller concerning the notorious daughter of a Nazi war criminal. She accepts a mission to help expose other Nazis who

have fled to Brazil. Accompanied by Devlin, a CIA agent, she goes to Rio, where she attempts to learn Nazi atomic secrets by marrying a former colleague of her father's. Devlin, at first contemptuous of her "trade," learns to respect her—and falls in love with her—following an extremely dangerous mission that nearly costs her her life. Suggestive of Beauty/Beast archetype.

You've Got Mail (1998)
This romantic comedy concerns a powerful chain bookstore tycoon (Tom Hanks) who eradicates his opposition. One of his competitors is a children's neighborhood bookstore owned by Meg Ryan, so he puts her out of business. The twist is that the two are engaged in an e-mail romance, though they've never met. Loosely based on Austen's *Pride and Prejudice*, a book Ryan loves, the story has her character fending off Hanks' overbearing overtures. Of course, they join in the end, but not before he is humbled some. Beauty/Beast archetype.

Genre Derivatives

From the three basic categories above, numerous other subgenres have emerged in the course of twentieth-century film history. The ancient epic is the progenitor of most action movies, including war epics (see "Responding to Film as History," chapter 5); spy thrillers such as the James Bond series (which has become a genre of its own); adventures in exotic locales (*The Man Who Would Be King* [1975], *The English Patient* [1996]); and even science fiction. In fact, one of the great science fiction films, *2001: A Space Odyssey* (1968), embodies the spirit if not the boldness of Homer's epic: the movie's hero, astronaut David Bowman is the twentieth century's answer to Homer's great explorer. Striving towards a remote, even unreachable, goal (the planet Jupiter), he faces adversity, battling the demented computer HAL, crossing the borders of time and space, and arriving at a mysterious eighteenth-century mansion. There he ages, breaks a glass while having dinner, and is transformed into a newborn. If Bowman's destiny seems strange, remember Homer's Odysseus whose final mission, as foretold by Tiresias in the underworld, is to carry an oar to a strange land until it is no longer recognized for what it is. Both Odysseus and Bowman are carriers of their respective civilizations to the edges of the known cosmos—one is a mariner, the other a cosmonaut.

Proliferation, mixture, overlapping of genres—these are film constants. From the gangster epic of the 1930s to variations on love melodramas and slapstick or screwball comedies, to war movies, *film noir*, spy thrillers, horror films, adventure stories, musicals, science fiction, the list is endless. Each of these forms developed in response to social conditions and audience needs in a particular historical period. Many war movies, for instance, were created during World War II when American forces were fighting both Nazi Germany and the Japanese in the Pacific. The purpose of these films was to boost morale both at home and at the front. Even President Franklin D. Roosevelt supported the movies in the war effort by having a motion pictures bureau established in the War Department. Many units of the War Department, especially the armed forces, provided their services. Hundreds of movies were made— *Prelude to War* (1942), *Bataan* (1943), and even the popular *Casablanca* (1942), a romance which audiences of that era saw as a war movie. The success of those films at the box office remained significant until the mid-1960s when rampant antiwar sentiment diminished their popularity during the Vietnam years. When moviemakers learned to express popular antiwar messages during the 1970s and 1980s, movies such as *Coming Home* (1979), *Apocalypse Now* (1979), *Platoon* (1986), and *Full Metal Jacket* (1987)—some of them with vitriolic social messages—gained in popularity and renown. The middle and late 1990s saw a revival of nostalgic war sentiment, however, with noteworthy epic movies such as *Schindler's List* (1993), *Saving Private Ryan* (1998), and *The Thin Red Line* (1998). Gangster movies were popular during the Prohibition and Depression eras (1919–1940) when American society was experiencing the collapse of economic and moral values and found an outlet for its frustrations in hero-worshiping antisocial types. Films such as *Underworld* (1927), *Little Caesar* (1930), *Public Enemy* (1931), and *Scarface* (1932) are illustrative of this period, but the gangster film in its various transformations has remained popular throughout the twentieth century. Gangster films have given way to combinations of gangster and "action" movies in the late 1980s and 1990s—*Goodfellas* (1990), *Pulp Fiction* (1995), and *Heat* (1996). Many of these are parodies like *Pulp Fiction* (1995), and parody usually appears when a certain genre nears extinction. *True Grit* (1969) and *Blazing Saddles* (1973), for instance, were parodies of the western, one a parody of the hero (John Wayne), the other a parody of the genre itself. A genre never really dies out completely but reappears in an adapted form usually characterized by an adjustment to the mores and mindsets of different audiences in different eras. Thus, Disney's *Tombstone* (1994) is a violent remake of earlier films, such as *Gunfight at the OK Corral* (1957) and *My Darling Clementine* (1958), two movies based on the same Wyatt Earp legend. *Tombstone* retells the story of Wyatt Earp and Doc Holliday, but its violence is characteristic of the contemporary action film, rather than of the older western. The same could be said of *Last Man Standing* (1996), a remake of Kurosawa's *Yojimbo* (1961), and of Sergio Leone's *A Fistful of Dollars* (1964).

Adaptation (remake) in film genre is consistent with similar practices in literary tradition: Homer's epics were adapted by Virgil, and the plays of Menander became Roman and Shakespearean comedies. Greek tragedy resurfaced in

Racine; Aristotelian structures reappeared in Ibsen and O'Neill (not to mention Williams and Miller). Generally, tragedy, comedy, and the epic are ancestors of drama, slapstick, and the action film. Genre ramifications are extremely numerous, but the basic archetypal forms outlined above are repeated. Modern anthropologist Northrop Frye attributes the basic genre divisions to archetypal seasonal rotations: spring for comedy, summer for romance, fall and winter for epic and tragedy. Today, seasonal changes may have something to do with genre change in film. Serious drama, for instance, is reserved for the fall and winter months. New films, usually family fare, open at Christmas, and the summer is mostly reserved for romance and action films—mindless or escapist entertainment which summer vacationers seek. Steven Spielberg's *Saving Private Ryan,* a war movie about the bloodbath during the World War II invasion of Normandy, which received extremely favorable notices by critics, opened in July 1998. Not all summer movies, therefore, fall into the "mindless" category. In the summer of 1997, however, the big screen sensation was *Airforce One,* with Harrison Ford playing the President of the United States who was about to be taken hostage by terrorists aboard the most protected and safest aircraft in the world. Needless to say, being Harrison Ford as well as the President, he beat the villains with his bare fists. His plane, though riddled with bullets, did not explode. It might as well have been an armored tank. That summer's comedy was a vehicle for Julia Roberts, *My Best Friend's Wedding* (1997), witty and light-hearted as the summer breezes, though the "pretty woman" in this case played a "bad girl." But never mind. Mindlessness is at the heart of summer, and Hollywood accommodates with slick productions that do not ask the audience to think too hard. That criterion itself is the basis for a movie genre, the "mindless" genre. Audience demand usually dictates and shapes film genre, and will do so for some time to come. Mindless fare, however, is not unique to our era. Horace complained of the insouciant poetry produced by his contemporaries, some of which was meant to amuse the idle rich. The Roman historian Tacitus commented on the idle and vicious emperor Nero who sought inspiration by burning a whole city in order to compose a song. The Elizabethans were not any less shallow in their amusements. Thomas Kyd's *The Spanish Tragedy,* for instance, has the old man Hieronymo biting his tongue out in order not to betray a secret—though this play has neither the polish nor the vocabulary of Shakespeare. Film performs that function nowadays, the function of entertaining in a mindless way, and it would be fruitless to blame it for the bad taste which, among other things, is an audience demand.

From the novel, film has inherited not only the epic but the picaresque forms epitomized by *Tom Jones* (both book and film). This has spawned numerous (and heterogeneous) "road" movies: *Road to Rio, Easy Rider, Butch Cassidy and the Sundance Kid, Bonnie and Clyde, Thelma and Louise—*

all of which can be categorized as road films of one kind or another, although these involve trios and duos rather than lone wanderers like Odysseus, Gil Blas, and Tom Jones. Dual wanderers also exist in literature—Don Quixote and Sancho Panza (a story filmed many times), Dante and Virgil in *The Divine Comedy*, Huck Finn and Jim in Mark Twain's *Huckleberry Finn* (also filmed many times but never successfully).

Film genre is closely allied to literary genre, as pointed out above, but it has its own distinction and color. Film is much closer to audiences than literature and stage drama have ever been. Ancient Greeks listened to rhapsodists reciting Homer or saw plays by Euripides during festivals a few times a year. Today's audiences are much more exposed to film through multiplex outlets and video stores. Film is in our blood, so to speak, and we absorb it from our infancy. With the television set (and nowadays the "home theater"), no one can be immune to film. Therefore, the influence of the audience on the industry and on film art is far greater than it was on other arts in previous centuries—with the possible exception of music. Genre in film changes constantly, undergoing continuous transformations which are occurring as we speak. But the three main modes—epic, tragic (or dramatic), and comic—maintain their power over our collective psyche. Laughter, spectacle, and drama remain dominant as we humans journey through our present evolutionary stage.

Suggested Readings and Hypertext Links

Andrew, James Dudley. *The Major Film Theories: An Introduction*. New York: Oxford University Press, 1976.

Arnheim, Rudolf. *Visual Thinking*. Berkeley: University of California Press, 1969.

Becker, Stephen. *Comic Art in America*. New York: Simon and Schuster, 1959.

Casty, Alan. *The Dramatic Art of the Film*. New York: Harper & Row, 1971.

Frye, Northrop. "The Archetypes in Literature." In Charles Kaplan and William Anderson, eds. *Criticism: The Major Statements*, 3rd ed. New York: St. Martin's Press, 1991.

Krakauer, Siegfried. "National Types as Hollywood Presents Them." *Public Opinion Quarterly* (1949): 53–72.

Wag the Dog, DVD ed. New Line Cinema, 1998. With audio commentary by Barry Levinson and Dustin Hoffman. <http://www.newline.com>, <http://dir.yahoo.com/Entertainment/Movies_and_Film/Genres>

Suggested Films for Study

Epic Films

Birth of a Nation (1915), dir. D.W. Griffith
Intolerance (1917), dir. D.W. Griffith
The Ten Commandments (1923), dir. Cecil B. DeMille
— *Ben-Hur* (1926), dir. Alfred Raboch and Fred Niblo
—*The Seven Samurai* (1954), dir. Akira Kurosawa
Land of the Pharaohs (1955), dir. Howard Hawks
—*Once Upon a Time in America* (1984), dir. Sergio Leone
The Thin Red Line (1999), dir. Terrence Malick
The Patriot (2000), dir. Roland Emmerich

Dramas and Melodramas

— *Wuthering Heights* (1939), dir. William Wyler
Jane Eyre (1944), dir. Robert Stevenson
Magnificent Obsession (1954), dir. Douglas Sirk
The Graduate (1967), dir. Mike Nichols
Last Tango in Paris (1973), dir. Bernardo Bertolucci
Absence of Malice (1981), dir. Sydney Pollack
Cape Fear (1991), dir. Martin Scorsese
The Player (1992), dir. Robert Altman
In the Name of the Father (1993), dir. Jim Sheridan
The Insider (1999), dir. Michael Mann

Almodóvar

Tragedies

— *The Third Man* (1946), dir. Carol Reed
A Place in the Sun (1951), dir. George Stevens
The Giant (1956), dir. George Stevens
Lolita (1962), dir. Stanley Kubrick
—*Raging Bull* (1980), dir. Martin Scorsese
Ran (1985), dir. Akira Kurosawa
Quiz Show (1995), dir. Robert Redford
Affliction (1998), dir. Paul Schrader
— *American Beauty* (1999), dir. Sam Mendes
Limbo (1999), dir. John Sayles

Citizen Kane

Comic Films

Adam's Rib (1949), dir. George Cukor
Roman Holiday (1953), dir. William Wyler
Sabrina (1954), dir. Billy Wilder
Breakfast at Tiffany's (1961), dir. Blake Edwards
10 (1979), dir. Blake Edwards
Moonstruck (1987), dir. Norman Jewison
Women on the Verge of a Nervous Breakdown (1988), dir. Pedro Almodóvar
Only You (1994), dir. Norman Jewison
Emma (1996), dir. Douglas McGrath
Runaway Bride (1999), dir. Garry Marshall

CHAPTER THREE

Responding to Film Techniques

How do I respond to film techniques? Film is a medium, as dance is, music is, discursive language is. As a medium, it has its own unique means of expression, visual representation of moving objects on a screen. Filmmakers have mastered the art of this medium by employing various techniques in order to create images as a coded language to express meanings. The language of film (to be discussed more broadly in chapter 4) is dependent to a large degree on the use of various techniques that have evolved over the last hundred years—the life span of film.

Learning Film Techniques

In answer to the question of how one responds to film techniques, one must first understand what these techniques are and discover how they affect film interpretations. Film techniques are part of *film language*, that part which has a mechanical basis because it relies entirely on technical equipment: lenses, video recorders, cameras, editing equipment, tripods, cranes, dollies, lighting instruments, chemicals, the film emulsion itself, videotape, and so forth. Film techniques create effects specific only to film; they are the means by which the language of film is created. A student, consequently, needs to become familiar with their use in order to penetrate deeper into the meaning of the film viewed. Understanding film techniques is part of decoding film language, which can be extremely complicated since it relies on so many factors that affect the viewer simultaneously—classroom approaches, screen size, sound effects, individual instructor's method, textbook used, and cultural orientations of students. Although there are no standard ways of understanding that language, the knowledge *of what these terms mean,* and of what technique each term describes, is important in interpreting both directorial approaches and the meaning of a particular film or film segment. A student's first step, therefore, is to understand and appreciate what these techniques are, preferably through examples the instructor uses or through reviewing his or her own cinematic experiences. Showing segments of films relevant to each technique is a good method, although both instructor and student may improvise. Handbooks listed at the end of this chapter may help students understand the more technical aspects of filmmaking. Here we are more interested in the critical language and the concepts used to interpret film in its narrative form. But students should be on the lookout for new techniques that are constantly developing in the technology sector, because film interpretation relies on knowledge of such technical changes. Today, for instance, several directors use digital cameras to photograph action, something that can deeply affect a viewer's perceptions.

Techniques Interrelate

It must be understood at the outset that these techniques interrelate and may also overlap. The gestalt principle accepted by many film critics, such as Rudolf Arnheim's (Andrew 36) precept that the whole is greater than the sum of its parts, applies here. Everything in film is an organic whole, and all parts must work harmoniously to create that whole; no part can supersede any other or grow unhealthily at the expense of other parts (35). Techniques cooperate with each other, making up the sum total of separate parts (even if the techniques are not all used at the same time), and the whole thus created is the final product—the *film* one views. Another point to be stressed here is that not all filmmakers place the same emphasis on a given technique. For instance, in *Citizen Kane* (1941), Orson Welles made frequent use of deep-focus photography to show simultaneous group action, while Carol Reed in *The Third Man* (1949) used high and low angles to reveal distorted psychological states. Alfred Hitchcock's favorite device in many of his movies was to condense information for the sake of exposition through camera movement (*Rear Window* [1954], *Psycho* [1960]) and to relate and unify images through montage (*Psycho, The Birds* [1963]). Ingmar Bergman used lighting techniques to create mood (*The Virgin Spring* [1961]) and Federico Fellini used montage to suggest altered mental states in *8½*). But other directors, Howard Hawks or John Ford, for instance, preferred to use a minimum of elaborate camera tricks, stressing simplicity of action instead. However, the principle of whole over part applies in every kind of film, simple or complex; the student has an obligation to consider all these factors in order to achieve a better interpretation of film images.

The angle, lighting, and composition of this shot from Citizen Kane *demonstrate the effectiveness of mise-en-scène. Kane, at the top of the stairs, is diminished by his blackmailing rival descending them in the foreground. The shadows on the two men's faces accentuate the helpless anger of the former and the smugness of the latter. The ceiling encroaching upon Kane symbolizes his compromised position.*

Important Film Techniques

Some of the most important techniques discussed here are *Cinematography, Camera Movement, Deep Focus Photography, Montage, Mise-en-Scène, Camera Shots, Lighting, and Sound Effects.*

Cinematography

This all-important term in the art of film can be understood by comparing it to photography. The latter reproduces a still moment by means of a lens which records an image inside a dark chamber on film emulsion. Cinematography records a succession of images or images in motion. Photographing moving objects, then, is cinematography, but the term also implies quality of action. The cinematographer controls the tone of the photographic images through types of lighting, shooting in black and white or in color, and using various other techniques such as crane shots, close-ups, long shots, medium shots, or crosscutting. Cinematography is influenced by the director's vision of what he or she wants to accomplish at a certain moment in a given film sequence. If fast action is required, images (or whole scenes) are photographed in quick succession with a variety of shots, including dolly shots, sharp-angle shots, and rapid crosscutting, and are edited so as to suggest a quick pace. In slow scenes, the camera lingers on an object, often rendering a particular mood through close-ups and variations in lighting. Cinematography requires the skills of a director of photography (a cinematographer) and various technicians operating cameras. It is a distinct art in itself and is a special category in Oscar nominations and awards. Some of the best known cinematographers include, Gregg Toland for *Citizen Kane* (1941); Robert Krasker for *The Third Man* (1949); Edmond Richard for Franz Kafka's *The Trial* (1964), directed by Orson Welles; Sven Nykvist for *Persona* and many other Ingmar Bergman films (and late in his career many American films); Michael Ballhaus for *The Age of Innocence* (1993); and Adrian Biddle for *Thelma and Louise* (1991). Many other cinematographers are alluded to in several sections of this text guide.

Camera Movement

Another term generic to cinematography but related to a specific cinematic purpose is *camera movement.* A camera may rest on a fixed base and *seem* to move toward an object through a zoom lens, or it may *actually* move toward or away from the object on a dolly (this is called a dolly shot). It may be mounted on a crane (crane shot) or carried on a helicopter, seeming to fly through space. The camera may move ahead of an object, follow it, or move parallel to it; it may move up or down or from one certain angle; or it may pan horizontally from one object to another, thus providing a panoramic view. In the introductory sequence in *Psycho* (1960), the camera pans over Phoenix, then zooms to a window and into the room where the lovers are. In the updated version of *Psycho* (1998), an exact duplicate of the earlier one, that zoom shot was replaced by a helicopter shot which today is not distorted by vibration. Camera movement techniques are used for many purposes, primarily (as in the case just illustrated) exposition. When viewers must be given information, especially at the beginning of the action, the director may choose a variety of ways to provide it. A written introduction may be projected onto the screen as in Martin Scorsese's *The Last Temptation of Christ* (1988), which opens with a paragraph explaining the motives of the filmmaker by citing the words of the book's author, Nikos Kazantzakis. This is one of the most formal ways to introduce subject matter which may offend the viewer. Thus, clarity is of paramount importance, and speed is suspended. Disclaimers of fictional materials in a film that may resemble real events (or persons) are quite common.

But when conciseness is important, camera movement is one of the most practical ways to provide information. Hitchcock, a master of concise exposition, takes as little time as possible to give the viewer the maximum information needed to understand the essentials of the story. In his *Rear Window* (1954), the camera moves away from the window (literally exits through the window) and into the yard, surveying various scenes in the surrounding apartments. Then it returns to the room, stops at a man's perspiring face, and focuses on the thermometer which shows ninety degrees. Once again, it surveys the neighborhood where the action is to occur, returns to the man's face, moves to his broken leg in a cast with his name on it, explaining why he is immobilized. Next, the camera pans to his smashed field camera, to a negative of a girl's photo, and to the actual photo of the girl. These can also be called establishing shots. Before any action begins, we have a capsulized view of his life, environment, and habits—all in a matter of seconds. A great deal of narrative time has been saved, and an interest in the character has been created. The camera movement dramatizes exposition which would take several paragraphs of prose in a novel. The camera has functioned virtually as a voyeur—a person peering at a forbidden object—having guided the viewer through the neighborhood's secrets which are already objects of the man's curiosity. Another moment of masterful camera movement is found in *Psycho*: After the famous stabbing in the shower, the camera moves with finger-pointing accuracy from the dead woman's eye to the table where she has left the stolen money wrapped in a paper, then goes on to the window of the Bates house. The camera has provided a terse synopsis of the morality tale, succinctly giving the causes and the effects of the murder: A woman has tragically paid with her life for having stolen money and for having trusted a stranger without heeding warning signs (the stuffed birds, his weird manner when talking of his mother). The other cause of the tragedy—the window of the mad murderer—is only hinted at. The camera points to the explanation, which will be given in full detail at the end of the story.

Deep Focus Photography

The student needs to familiarize himself/herself with other photographic film techniques, such as deep focus photography in which actions in both the foreground and the background remain in focus. Deep focus is a technique associated with cinematography—in fact, it is part of it—and was introduced in the late 1930s as a substitute for the frequent cutting required by montage (see below) to ensure scene continuity. Deep focus allows an entire group of people to be photographed simultaneously, thus enabling a sequence to continue

The depth of field in this shot from Citizen Kane, *keeping all the faces in focus, emphasizes the power of Kane's influence over his table-full of admirers.*

and develop. The first to use deep focus in a significant manner were Orson Welles and William Wyler. Consider *Citizen Kane* (1941) as an example: At the *Inquirer* party, people sit around tables and watch Charles Kane, who remains the focus dancing with the chorus girls. The entire scene is one take, showing Kane's need to be the center of attention. The continuity of action within a shot replaces crosscutting, thus emphasizing the visual composition of a setting. Deep focus photography has become commonplace in modern film.

Montage

Montage, which comes from the French word for "mounting" or "putting together," is an editing technique which has both a theoretical basis and practical applications. Theories of montage abound in cinema criticism. According to the French critic André Bazin, there is *parallel montage*, in which two actions take place simultaneously—e.g., in a chase sequence. There is *accelerated montage*, in which an impression of increasing speed is given—e.g., the sight of a railroad wheel turning faster to suggest that train speed is increasing. There is also *montage by attraction*, a method evolved by Russian filmmaker and critic Sergei Eisenstein. In simple terms, he uses the fact that the human mind is capable of associating ideas or images in such a way that the senses overlap, subconsciously associating one with another to produce a unified effect (Bazin 25). The filmmaker can create an infinite number of visual associations, as a Japanese poet can string conflicting images together in the *haiku* (Andrew 52, Beaver 200). Some well-known examples of such montage include Eisenstein's own scenes at the Odessa steps in *Battleship Potemkin* (1922); the famous montage sequence in *Citizen Kane* between Charles Kane and his first wife which reveals the dissolution of their marriage; and the shower scene in *Psycho*.

As a technique, the process of montage relates to the passage of time—as, for instance, when larger time units need to be condensed. This can be indicated by revolving train wheels or flipping newspaper pages and is used to show time elapsing between the interruption of the narrative thread and the point at which it is picked up again. Chaplin uses this technique frequently. In *The Great Dictator*, for instance, Hynkel's capture of Tomania is shown through flipping newspaper headlines; and in *Monsieur Verdoux* various stages of activity are shown through revolving train wheels—as Verdoux presumably moves from one town to another for his serial killings.

Parallel montage was first used in *The Birth of a Nation* (1915). D.W. Griffith, who crosscut shots of two different activities occurring at separate locations yet converging toward the same effect. Alternating shots of a pursuer and the pursued person, for instance—one on a vehicle, the other on a horse—if shown in a parallel fashion, can create suspense. The viewer expects the pursued person to escape the pursuer, especially if the latter is evil. The opposite is true if the pursued is a villain whom the pursuer, an agent of the law, is expected to capture. This technique of parallel editing was used with great success in western films whose narrative structure called for these situations. Examples can be found in John Ford's *Stagecoach* (1939) and in numerous feature films and TV westerns of the '50s and '60s, and even in the '70s, when car chases (*Bullitt* [1968]) replaced horses and trains. In *Bullitt*, Steve McQueen is pursuing two villains in a speeding car. The camera cuts from the streets down which the cars speed to their screeching tires and flying hubcaps to the faces of the two villains and to McQueen—until the chase comes to an end when the villains' car hits a gas station and bursts into flames. More examples of parallel montage can be found in Hitchcock's *Strangers on a Train* (1951) when distraught murderer Bruno Anthony (Robert Wagner) is trying to recover a lighter he dropped into a sewer. The lighter is to be left at an amusement park where Anthony has murdered a woman; it will implicate her husband (Farley Granger), a tennis player. The suspense is created by crosscutting: While Bruno's fingers reach desperately for the lighter at the bottom of the sewer, an equally anxious Granger tries to finish an important tennis match and get to the amusement park before Wagner does. Another very impressive example of parallel editing is found in *The Godfather I*. A scene of baptism, a sacred ritual, is juxtaposed with equally ritualistic scenes of mobster killings ordered by Michael Corleone (Al Pacino), whose child is being baptized. Aside from the suspense, parallel editing here conveys the huge irony of the juxtapositions of sacred and profane images, the simultaneity of divine and monstrous actions shown in clipping, nearly identical shots.

Accelerated montage is a technique that enables the filmmaker to speed up action, thus concluding a particular scene by combining similar shots. A train, for instance, is approaching a station in *High Noon*, and three villains are expecting their leader, Miller, to arrive. The images of the train get progressively larger in a much shorter time span than the real approach would have taken. Thus, the element of suspense is sustained and reinforced until the climax of the confrontation between four united villains and the lone Gary Cooper. One of the best-known sequences of accelerated montage is in *Citizen Kane's* famous scene between Charles Kane and his wife Emily. They are sitting at the breakfast table. In successive shots seamed together, the couple is shown at different stages of their marriage. As they get older, their alienation from each other is revealed in their hairstyles, speech patterns, distance from each other (always increasing), and general body language.

Montage by attraction is basically conceptual. The image here has no meaning in itself until it is juxtaposed with other images. Viewers are exposed to a quickly alternating set of shots that direct their attention in an extremely manipulative manner to produce a particular association of ideas. An inference is drawn and emotion is invoked—fear, pity, compassion, indignation, or some other response. The filmmaker is urging viewers to at least *see* a certain point of view, even if they do not accept it. In *Schindler's List*, for instance, the filmmaker (Spielberg) seeks to influence his audience through montage by underscoring such Nazi atrocities as the confiscation of the possessions of the captive Jews— piles of extracted gold teeth, jewelry, photographs of victims. He juxtaposes images like inkpots, stamps, and a clicking typewriter, printing the names of rounded-up Jews. Montage also is important in determining a film's pacing.

Mise-en-Scène

Mise-en-scène is a term used for both a film technique and an approach to filmmaking. It was first used in the '40s and '50s when French filmmakers reacted against Russian theories of montage which placed emphasis on individual shots and their juxtaposition to create a psychological effect on the mind of the viewer. Shots placed in contrast to each other to create an association necessary for one unified meaning do not allow the continuity of a single shot that includes an entire scene without crosscutting. By contrast, the *mise-en-scène* approach not only allows a shot to continue but, more importantly, enables the filmmaker to arrange the objects within a shot to give them special meanings, visually speaking. These meanings then need to be decoded. The *mise-en-scène* technique itself was, of course, not invented by the French. Orson Welles uses it to great effect in *Citizen Kane* when Thatcher, the banker, comes to the Colorado ranch where Kane's family still lives, to pick up young Charles and bring him up like a young tycoon in the big city. The scene starts with Charles's parents and the lawyer at a table in the ranchhouse, signing the papers. The father is reluctant to sign and protests weakly, but when he's told he will receive fifty thousand dollars a year, he gives in: "Maybe it's for the best," he mutters. While this is going on with no cutting, we can see in deep focus through the window frame young Charles playing outside. Two stories are told here: the story of what is going on inside and also the "framing" of the carefree child playing outside. It is done seamlessly. The camera moves away; there is just a single cut to the mother at the window calling Charles. The one single shot continues from there to the snow-covered yard outside where the three adults tell the boy the news: this gentleman will be taking him to the city. Charles, holding the now-famous sled Rosebud protests, even attacks Thatcher. This scene changes angles to accommodate the various stances of the group, but it is one single shot, each moment of it—if one freezes the frame—a composition.

Another film, this one French, lays emphasis on *mise-en-scène*; Jean Cocteau's *Beauty and the Beast*. Several scenes—in fact, most of those that juxtapose *Beauty and the Beast*—were designed as *mise-en-scène*. When both stand in the garden, for instance, Beauty is on one side and Beast on the other, with the statue of a stag between them. This suggests the nature of the beast, that which separates him from common humanity. In another scene Beast carries Beauty up the stairs to his palace after she faints at the sight of him. They pass various animal statues (one of a huge stag) that suggest the beastly nature of the hero. This kind of crowded frame is characteristic of French filmmaking, which stresses the compositional aspects of a single shot by placing various items within the frame of that shot, just as a photographer creates aesthetic effects with his camera by including background items in his framed image. The *mise-en-scène* approach was enhanced in the 1950s when wide cinema screens became prevalent, altering the aspect ratio (the width of the frame divided by its height) from the original film frame of 1.33:1 to 1.86:1. The even wider Cinemascope screen altered that ratio to an incredible 2.35:1. A screen of that width could not be left empty. In spectacles, the problem was solved by filling the scene with extras—armies in formation around a hill, troops converging on battlefields, sweeping landscapes, or combatants dueling, like the gladiators in *Spartacus*. Needless to say, modern spectacular films (*Titanic, Gladiator, The Patriot*) welcome this added screen space, although budget-wise, the bigger screens are the least cost effective.

Shots (Camera Shots)

A shot is the basic unit of film, the briefest recording of film action. It begins when the camera starts rolling and concludes when it stops. Combined and edited, these shots comprise a film in its entirety. A medium-length film (two hours or less) contains anywhere from 1,000 to 1,500 shots. Hitchcock's *The Birds* (1963) contained 1,400 shots, a little over the average.

There is a great variety of camera shots, but we will consider these commonly used types:

a. The *long shot* is shot from a distance which can vary from a hundred feet to several miles. In *Rear Window*, long shots predominate because we see people and objects across the yard from the viewpoint of Jimmy Stewart, who is confined to a wheelchair. The only medium and close-up shots in this film are taken as if through the telelenses of his camera and his binoculars. *Stagecoach* (1939), on the other hand, was photographed mostly in Monument Valley, so its long shots take in the entire valley, allowing the scope of the viewer (and the camera) to cover

1.33:1—Full Frame/Pan and Scan

1.86:1—Wide Screen, Letterbox

2.35:—Cinemascope

distances of several miles. A film like *Thelma & Louise* (1991), part of which was photographed in western locales including Monument Valley and the Grand Canyon, gives viewers long shots of landscapes, sometimes with objects moving through them. Kurosawa's *Dreams* (1991) features stunning long shots of Van Gogh painting in the midst of a wheat field. In a famous scene from *Lawrence of Arabia* (1963), Omar Sharif approaches on his camel, appearing first as a dot, then gradually growing larger—exactly as the human eye would perceive an object/person coming out of the hazy desert.

Long shots may alternate with close-ups to alternate points of view: Spielberg's *Duel* (1971) switches from subjective shot (man in car) to long shot once the car emerges from the city onto the open road. This alternation suggests changes of points of view from the subjective to the objective.

b. The *close-up* is the most frequently used technique of the cinema, the feature that distinguishes cinema from stage production. It is nearly impossible to see clearly the facial changes of a person on the stage, unless one sits very close or watches the action through magnifying lenses. The lens, on the other hand, can dwell on the human face—the subject of most close-ups—and focus on its expressions, providing intimate knowledge of or insight into this person's feelings, emotions, or state of mind. Of course, close-ups of objects (like the newspaper with the money in *Psycho*) are also employed. In this sense, the invention of the close-up technique is one of cinema's most telling achievements. The close-up is the primary cinematic means of expressing point of view. Close-ups can vary: medium (from the waist up), an entire head, a face or portions of the face, or two faces (as in Antonioni's *L'Avventura* or Bergman's *Persona*). In one instance worth mentioning, Adela (Judy Davis) ventures into the ruined Indian temples where she sees erotic statues in David Lean's *A Passage to India* (1984). Her face reveals shock, amazement, fascination, and sexual awakening. The moment when her face is captured is the culminating moment of this film.

c. The *medium shot*, the *reaction shot*, and the *jump shot* serve different purposes. The medium shot shows the human frame from the waist up, but the face is still the most important aspect of this shot. For example, Saito in *The Bridge on the River Kwai* looks through his binoculars at the British troops building the bridge. Zhivago in *Doctor Zhivago* watches from his balcony as communist troops massacre civilians. Sometimes this shot (and also the close-up) is called a *reaction shot*, which means that the audience must gather what is happening in the field of action from the reaction seen in a character's face. Zhivago is horrified by the massacre of peaceful protesters by armed dragoons which takes place

Figure 3.1
Reaction Shot

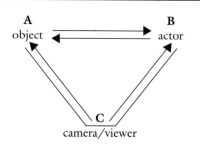

beneath his window. Not a word is spoken nor is the massacre fully shown, but the audience knows what is happening from the expression on the actor's face. Lean specializes in such shots (medium close-ups), and they are found throughout his films. In *The Bridge on the River Kwai*, Japanese commander Saito looks on amazed when the British colonel Nicholson empties the hospital of its patients to help finish his bridge. Reaction shots are very common when the object that the actor sees is also shown to the audience. The camera cuts to that object (A) and then back to the actor's face (B). The viewer's (and the camera's) point of view is C. In Hitchcock's *The Birds*, Jessica Tandy enters a neighbor's house the day after an attack by the birds. She advances towards the kitchen, sees no one at first, then suddenly catches sight of the neighbor who has been blinded and torn by the birds. The camera cuts to her face as she gasps in horror, covering her mouth with her hand. The camera/audience follows B, then cuts to A, then back to B.

A jump shot is a frequently used type of medium shot, a cut in the sequence of photographing a particular person. In Spielberg's *Duel* (1971), for instance, Dennis Weaver's face is shown from medium to close-up in three quick, successive shots indicating a moment of resolution when he accepts the challenge offered to him by the truck driver. Woody Allen uses quick editing cuts (technically jump cuts) in *Deconstructing Harry* (1997) while some of his characters (mostly Woody/Harry himself) converse, thus disrupting the flow of the character's thoughts—part of the attempted "deconstruction" of Harry's life. Here, aesthetic effects, technique, and meaning interrelate. Abrupt time change, disconnectedness in the social milieu, fragmentation—such themes, especially in French filmmaking, favored the technique of the jump cut.

d. The *master shot*, or *establishing shot*, frequently consists of a sequence of long shots followed by medium shots or close-ups. Its purpose is exposition, to go from the general to the specific. In *All About Eve* (1950), the camera establishes the general view of the awards banquet then moves on to several shots of the protagonists whose stories the film will tell, and finally follows up with medium shots of these individuals. In an establishing shot, the camera may pan from one object to another, providing useful information to the viewer as in the opening shots of *Rear Window*. Such shots are also useful in revealing the location: The opening shots of *Psycho* give a general panoramic view of Phoenix, Arizona, then close in on the apartment where the lovers are. The opening shots of Hollywood Boulevard in *Pretty Woman* (1991) serve the same function.

e. The *hand-held camera action shot* is used, for example, in Kubrick's *Barry Lyndon*, a film often studied for the variety and richness of its film techniques. Near the beginning of this film, Redmond Barry, a picaresque Irish character, finds himself in straitened circumstances after losing his money to a band of robbers, so he enlists in the army. There, a burly fellow taunts him and he responds by hurling back an insult. The man challenges Barry to a boxing match, sure he can pulverize him since he is twice Barry's size. But Barry, however small his fists, can dodge. He repeatedly escapes the burly man's vicious swings, then floors him with a series of left hooks. The scene is masterfully filmed with a hand-held camera which gets so close to the combatants' faces, fists, and other moving bodily parts as to achieve realism of a high order, a realism that would be impossible with a static camera. Thus, dynamic tension is created which, among other things, enables the viewer to stay engaged and enjoy the spectacle. One must never forget that viewers need to be engaged and to enjoy what they see. Viewing is, above all, an experience, and as such it must be enjoyed as actual experience is. Action shots are the most enjoyable of all, for the human spirit is engaged in adventure. Hand-held camera action shots are commonly used today, especially in movies that require the constant motion of some object and thus require a moving camera to establish point of view. In *Rosetta* (1999), a Belgian movie directed by Jean-Pierre Dardenne and Luc Dardenne, the camera follows a fast-moving young girl, mostly in over-the-shoulder shots, never leaving her for a single moment throughout the movie. The girl's grim determination to survive a series of setbacks and her vast energy are established by closely following behind her; the camera angles jerkily, pushing through space to move forward. Her face is not shown directly, only her neck and the curling hair at the back of her neck. Viewers are somewhat alienated by this technique, but they are rewarded at the end, when a lucky turn shows the smile on her face.

f. The *static shot* has its own visual power. Consider *High Noon* (1951), a film by Fred Zinnemann: U.S. Marshal Will Kane (Gary Cooper) awaits his archenemy Frank Miller, who will arrive by train at high noon. Three members of Miller's gang are already in town, waiting at the railroad depot. The camera shifts from them to shots of Cooper as he walks through town vainly trying to round up deputies to help him confront the villains. No one else is on the streets; the town is desolate, abandoned. Everyone is behind closed doors, fearing both the villains who will probably take over the town, and the impending gunfight itself. They do not want to get involved. This shedding of responsibility by the citizens is one of the film's major themes. The camera then shifts to a long shot of the railroad tracks, which recede at a sharp angle created by the perspective. The camera lingers on this shot for several seconds, allowing viewers time to absorb its purpose: the static shot creates a contrast with the moving head of Cooper, who seconds earlier was seen walking the empty streets. It also creates suspense, making viewers visually aware of the imminent arrival of the feared Miller.

   The student, here and elsewhere, is invited to give his/her own interpretation of these shots, which are the visual media of film. The shot, provided by the creative filmmaker, does not speak for itself. It needs attention and interpretation; it invites comment. The viewer's mind can be as creative as the filmmaker's. And interpreting shots of various kinds becomes the most intriguing part of film viewing. A filmmaker constantly experiments with a range of shots which are invented and reinvented as variations of the above. The viewer has an obligation to stop and consider. The pause/still button on the DVD remote thus becomes an instrument of interpretation.

g. The *crane shot* (or overhead shot) is photographed from a height, achieving objectivity and a panoramic view. The camera on a crane, with a zoom lens, can be raised or lowered to look at an object from increasing or decreasing distance. One of the best examples of this shot is in Hitchcock's *Notorious*. A scaffold was built to mount the camera at the point where the top of the stairs would be. From there, the viewer watches the scene below, where a large party is in full swing. The crane shot's intention is to show viewers, with increasing subjectivity, Alicia hiding the key to the cellar, which she must hand over to Devlin. From the top of the stairs, the shot "descends" to her closed fist, which opens briefly to show the key. Only Alicia and the viewer share this secret. Thus the crane shot achieves the ultimate in subjectivity.

h. *Overhead shots* are seen at the beginning of the film *Elizabeth* (1998) when heretics are burned at the stake. In his DVD film commentary, the film's director Shekhar Kapur explains that overhead shots are used to establish objectivity, to show horrible events and individuals' actions from a distance to eliminate the empathy a close-up would create. Elizabeth becomes likable when viewers see her hair floating in the wind or observe her radiant face as she dances. She becomes a pawn of fate when she strides in panic along the stone walls of her palace after an assassination attempt. The objective overhead shot replaces viewers' empathy with distanced, objective observation of a moving object. Overhead shots are also long shots, whose purpose is to establish a given spatial relationship between the viewer and the object viewed—usually one or more persons whose behavior can be analyzed rationally without the interference of emotion which a close-up creates.

i. *The multicamera action shot* places cameras in strategic positions to film an extremely complicated action sequence that needs to be photographed from many angles simultaneously. In the scene that shows the blowing up of the bridge in *The Bridge on the River Kwai*, cameras are placed in at least two locations on the bridge itself. There Japanese troops prepare to celebrate the arrival of a train carrying a VIP. Saito (Sessue Hayakawa) cuts the tape as Nicholson (Alec Guinness) struts proudly on the bridge and Warden (Jack Hawkins) watches from above, ready to take a few potshots at the train with mortar shells. Meanwhile, Joyce (Geoffrey Horne), from his position downstream, clutches a detonator device, ready to compress it when the train starts across the bridge. Across the stream, Shears, the American commando, is waiting with his Siamese partner to cover Joyce (William Holden) when he swims across the stream after the detonation. Nicholson warns Saito, and the two descend the ladder to the bottom of the river. Tension grows.

To create this tension, Lean's cinematographer Jack Hildyard set up five cameras, one on the bridge on a dolly; two on each side of the river to show Joyce and Shears; one over to the side where Clipton, the uninvolved medical officer, watches the action; and one on a spot along the riverbank. Montage is used to crosscut to the faces of those watching the action, but most of these are long shots, making the action panoramic and thus a unified narrative.

Lighting

Lighting is the most essential element of cinematography and one of the most important elements of moviemaking in general. Control of lighting to produce certain effects is as essential to cinematography as it is to photography and painting. Lighting helps us understand where the action takes place, roughly what time of day it is, and what mood the filmmaker is trying to establish. Before photography was invented, painters understood the importance of light in their works, especially in the rendering of landscapes. Impressionist and postimpressionist painters (Monet, Cezanne, Renoir, Van Gogh) made it a priority to capture with utmost precision the different times of day through light variations. Many filmmakers—Bergman, Visconti, Kurosawa (especially the last)—tried to imitate painting's techniques of rendering color and light. Bergman used strong black-and-white contrasts of light and shadow to etch tragic human figures and faces (*The Virgin Spring*), Visconti invented *tableaux-vivants* of women/fates strolling in the sun with parasols (*Death in Venice*), and Kurosawa boldly reproduced sunlit Van Gogh–like canvases for his student/artist to ramble through (*Dreams*). Like painters, filmmakers understand the value of light and lighting in rendering meaning and mood. For them, lighting is a tool, and part of the language of film.

Photography—and filming—can be done outside, in which case the light is natural, or indoors where the light has to be artificial. A filmmaker will use both approaches in the vast majority of cases, for very few films are shot entirely outdoors or indoors. A combination of both types of lighting is usually called for. Even in outdoor shooting, artificial lighting is sometimes used, as in a late evening or night scene. Indoor shooting can also allow for natural light coming through windows and doors. The source of light is very important in both cases. The sun outside and lens light or focused lamps inside pro-

Special ultra-sensitive lenses were developed to shoot this interior from **Barry Lyndon** *with nothing but natural candlelight. The result is a ghoulish representation of gambling as a civilized machination for gaining dominance.*

vide most of the natural and artificial lighting. Of course, inside lighting can come from a great variety of sources—light bulbs, kerosene lamps, even candlelight—when a film attempts to reproduce the atmosphere of times gone by when electric light was not available. In *Barry Lyndon* (1974) Kubrick used candlelight for interior shots, striving to accurately reproduce human images as they would have appeared when lit with the means available in the eighteenth century. Many adaptations of Jane Austen novels in the 1990s (*Emma, Sense and Sensibility, Mansfield Park*) followed the same technique to present natural imagery and realism. Candlelight produces what is called *diffuse* light or *soft* light, which means that the source of light does not hit the surface directly. The surface lit appears smooth and, in the case of a human face, unwrinkled. *Hard* light, direct light from either the sun or an artificial source, shows a surface more clearly and in greater detail. In *Lawrence of Arabia* (1962), David Lean shows the face of Peter O'Toole as he rides his camel across a desert. He is sand-covered, sweaty, and wrinkled, these details enhanced by the bright sunlight. This film was almost entirely shot in the desert on actual location in Jordan, practically without the aid of artificial light. The hard sunlight brightly reflected on the desert accounts to a large degree for its success. By contrast, in northern climates—Alaska, Ireland, Norway—where the sun hits the surface of the earth at sharp angles, filmmakers take advantage of the diffuse light to create images softer in tone and, in some cases, of greater beauty. In *The Secret of Roan Inish* (1993), made in Northern Ireland, John Sayles (who also filmed *Limbo* [1999] in Alaska) uses overcast skies, alternations of mist and dim sunlight, and a leaden sea surface to create an aura of mystery as a young girl searches for her missing brother on the mythical Island of Seals. In this film, "cold" (blue, gray) colors predominate, although there are a few contrasting shots of "warm" (red) colors when the action is transferred to the village. Color, in both the above cases, is a manipulation of available light—natural or artificial—to create or suggest meanings the filmmaker wants to express.

For more detailed discussions of the effects of lighting on color and image, see the suggested sources below.

Sound Effects

Sound is one of the most important elements of film. Sound in film is provided by heard dialogue, composed music (or *score*), source music, and natural sounds added to create special effects. Even during the silent era (1902–1927), music was performed by musicians at the theater while the film was shown. Later, sound was encoded in the film itself, on the magnetic (or optical) strip opposite the sprocket holes that advance the film. Today, placing sound in film is a complicated procedure involving synchronous or separate recordings on a number of tracks that eventually become the "mix" in the film's soundtrack. Over the years, especially during the 1980s and 1990s, the film soundtrack has become extremely sophisticated, capable of reproducing sounds from various sources minutely and accurately, thus providing the viewer with astonishing realism not only visually but also in sound. Such phrases as Surround Sound™, Dolby™ Prologic, and Dolby Digital have become commonplace for theatergoers everywhere. Home theater systems are capable of providing *imaging*, the discreet separation of sounds that come from various points on the screen: If, for instance, a not-yet-visible horse is approaching from the left of the screen, a correctly positioned viewer will hear the horse's hoofs on his left side. A passing car can be heard from the rear left to the rear right or diagonally towards the center. In the film *Fargo* (1996) viewers hear footsteps crunching the snow. In *Saving Private Ryan* (1998), recorded in DTS soundtrack, bullets are flying in all directions during the invasion of Normandy, placing viewers and listeners in the middle of the action. With the right kind of equipment (which is very expensive), sound systems like Dolby™ Digital 5.1, or DTS 6.1 can deliver sounds encoded in the film with astonishing accuracy, not to mention quality. Most DVD players today can deliver decoded sounds to five separate speakers (two front, two rear, one center) plus a subwoofer for low frequencies. Though most viewers (for obvious reasons) still watch movies on small TV screens, with minimal acoustic systems, it is worthwhile to watch a movie the way it was intended to be viewed, at the proper aspect ratio and with full sound. Otherwise, viewers are not being quite fair to the movie and will not get all it has to offer. Of course, the theater experience is preferred above all, but for the busy film student, home experience is a worthwhile substitute. (For more on the soundtrack, see chapter 4.)

Technology and the Film Viewer

The technical terms discussed above represent only a small portion of what a student of film eventually has to learn to become adept at film analysis and interpretation. These descriptions are basic and are intended for the viewer only. Actual film production requires much more knowledge of technical equipment, not to mention the necessary skills acquired through on-the-job training. However, critical analysis and use of technology are not mutually exclusive practices. A student of film may end up doing lots of things: film criticism, teaching, script writing, production, operation of machinery, costume design, art direction (set design), cinematography, directing, or acting. There is no limit to the complex endeavors of filmmaking and film interpretation. Many actors and directors appear on television channels like BRAVO to discuss their careers, their techniques, the process of directing, and their experiences with filmmaking in general. Commentators on the DVD and laser formats reveal a great many specific circumstances under which a film was made and also discuss their intentions and specific techniques. Filmmaking is an evolving art, so experimentation is both encouraged and pursued, especially in our technologically fast-advancing age. Many more choices are available to the viewers today. In the early 1950s, technology changed the viewing experience for the theatergoer with the advent of the anamorphic lens, the wide screen, and stereophonic sound (in theaters). Today, in the 2000s, viewers can have the option of seeing a movie on the large screen (which is still recommended), but they can also watch it at home (only a few months after its release) on a VCR, laser, or DVD. As large TV screens and electronic equipment become more cost effective, the experience of viewing movies at home becomes fuller and more sophisticated. Portable DVDs and laptop computers even allow viewing while traveling. Videos and DVDs can be obtained over the Internet, and international sales help to advance the knowledge of foreign films. Web sites for film festivals also help viewers find out where films are shown and discussed at film society meetings. Names of film periodicals, dates of events, and other information are easily available on the Internet. None of these options can be excluded if they are satisfactory to viewers. Indeed, serious students of film must take full advantage (within practical limitations) of the great number of choices available to them in their pursuit of knowledge of the technologically greatest art medium of the twentieth century—and beyond.

References and Suggested Readings and Hypertext Links

Andrew, James Dudley. *The Major Film Theories: An Introduction.* New York: Oxford University Press, 1976.
Ascher, Steven, and Edward Pincus. *The Filmmaker's Handbook: A Comprehensive Guide for the Digital Age.* New York: Plume Books, 1999.
Bazin, André. *What Is Cinema?* Vol. 1. Los Angeles: University of California Press, 1967.
Beaver, Frank E. *Dictionary of Film Terms: The Aesthetic Companion to Film Analysis.* New York: McGraw-Hill Company, 1983.
Sherman, Eric, and Tom Schnabel. *Frame by Frame: A Handbook for Creative Filmmaking.* Los Angeles: Acrobat Books, 1987.

Suggested Films for Study

The Birds, DVD ed. Universal, 2000. With production notes from Alfred
    Hitchcock.
Citizen Kane, Laserdisc ed. Criterion Collection, Janus Films, 1984. With a
    visual essay by Robert Carringer.
The Lumière Brothers' First Films, DVD and laserdisc. King Video, Image
    Entertainment, 1996. With commentary by Bernard Tavernier.
The Secret of Roan Inish, DVD ed. Columbia Tristar, 2000. With director's
    commentary by John Sayles.
Senses of Cinema. Online reviews from the 49th Melbourne International
    Film Festival. <http://www.sensesofcinema.com>

CHAPTER FOUR

Responding to Film Language

How do I respond to film language? Film language is part of human language. Human language is generally discursive—that is, it uses words, whether written or oral, as a system of symbols and signs with which humans communicate. Art in general has expanded this system to include pictures (images), movement (rhythm), and sound. Aristotle dealt with this topic in his *Poetics* (335 B.C.E.) when he said that all kinds of poetry are modes of imitation, differing only in the medium of imitation: prose and poetry have language (or meter), dancing has rhythm, painting has color and design, music has song, and so forth. In our day, film has evolved its own language. Let us see how it can be defined and what it is.

Definition of Film Language

In the progress of the evolution of the arts, the medium for film has become the screen on which moving images are projected and from which sounds are heard. Thus, film language is a combination of visual imagery, written or oral discourse, and natural or artificial sound. However, film language must be primarily understood as a visual medium: We see moving pictures and images on a screen, and we interpret them as signs and symbols. The power of film to communicate comes mostly from its visual character. But film also uses oral and written discourse through dialogue, narrative voice-over, and words or letters projected on the screen (including credits and subtitles). Still, the force of film language resides in its visual character, the photographed imagery which includes a vast number of objects: faces, bodies, groups of people, masses of people, buildings, streets, landscapes, and pictorial reality in general, conveyed through the lenses and projected onto a screen. The soundtrack of a film is also part of its language, contributing to the establishment of mood and emphasis on key dramatic moments. Other aspects of film language are the exploration of the time and space dimensions—contracting or expanding time through montage, or creating space through wide-screen ratios and *mise-en-scène*. Whatever is communicated through film becomes part of its language. Some of these elements we have already examined in the previous chapter on film techniques. All the techniques that have evolved through technical means—photography, montage, editing—are part of the syntax of film language and comprise what has been called "the *grammar*" of film. There is, however, another dimension to film language, a less systematic part of its grammar. It has to do with visual imagery, the presentation of which changes from film to film and from filmmaker to filmmaker. This broader concept of film language includes visual images, discursive language, and the language of sound. In this chater we will explore the visual aspects of film language, adding a segment on discursive language and one on the soundtrack.

Codes and Codification: The Semiotician's Visual Methods

Visual reality in film is imagery in motion. Images that enter our consciousness in the spatio-temporal dimensions of film are captured by the eye and automatically decoded in our brains as the film progresses. Codes, however, may also be read consciously after a film has been viewed. In that case, the process becomes a learning experience, an interpretation of film language. Students who concentrate on the reading of codes gain perspective on film meanings and become adept in the process of interpretation. They must keep in mind that reading encoded film messages is a deliberate process, related to the complexity of filmmaking, but also to many other factors such as the cultural and historical orientations of viewers, their linguistic competence, and the conditions of viewing. Viewers need a good command of specific film terminology, some of which has been provided in other chapters of this text guide. Everything said in the previous chapter is germane to the process of reading film's coded messages.

Let us concentrate here on the words *code* and *codification* as they are related to film language. In the language of semiotics, a sign or signifier is something that stands for something else; what is signified may be a letter, a gesture, a sound, a natural object like smoke or water, or even a sound. Codification, however, is by and large a cultural and social phenomenon. Along with their intuitive interpretations of a sign, readers or viewers are affected by their cultural orientations. An American passing a barbershop, for instance, may recognize the establishment by the revolving pole outside the shop. Literary orientations also determine the meanings of signs or codes. For readers of F. Scott Fitzgerald's *The Great Gatsby,* a green light acquires a series of symbolic meanings (lost hope, disillusionment, failure) different from those of an ordinary pedestrian or driver who sees a green light only as a traffic sign. Code in film, the key term in interpretation, means a logical relationship between an object on the screen and an idea, usually an idea already formed in viewers' heads by their cultural backgrounds. Codification can be seamless, as it is in most mainstream films. Viewers assume, for instance, that a moving train translates into the image of an object carrying passengers or freight from one place to another. Here, the signifier has a direct relationship to the narrative flow on the screen. Thus, the signified (the idea represented) is clear.

However, this relationship may not always be so direct or logical. Filmmakers often introduce an extratextual technique to signify something intrusive in the narrative. In *Breathless* (1959) and *Pierrot le Fou* (1965), Jean-Luc Godard often interrupts his linear story with montages of famous paintings (Picassos, Renoirs) with voice-over comments on the meaning of narrative, or with a character who speaks directly to the audience (Jean Seberg in *Breathless*). Similar techniques are used by Woody Allen in *Annie Hall* (1977) when Allen steps out of his fictional character several times to make literary observations to the audience. In *Deconstructing Harry* (1997), accelerated shooting (jump shots) condenses the temporal duration of a scene. To students of film, a specific code may be affected by their knowledge of the filmmaker's techniques and practices. In studying Hitchcock's films, for instance, the term MacGuffin, according to Hitchcock, referred to an object or plot device that the filmmaker has selected to drive the action. Therefore, it needs to be understood in that specific context. In this sense, the language of a Hitchcock film is codified; interpretation is the process of decodification. Consider the bottle in the film *Notorious* (1946): Viewers see a bottle of champagne left in an office at the beginning of the action. Later they learn that similar bottles in the cellar contain uranium, and in this particular environment that is considered subversive and dangerous to the protagonists. In this case, students easily infer that the bottle is a signifier of Alicia's (Ingrid Bergman) dipsomania and Devlin's (Cary Grant) irrational passion for her, but it is also a means of uncovering a plot that begins to unravel when one of the bottles in Alex Sebastian's cellar is found to contain uranium. Here, the relation of signifier

This scene from **The Seven Samurai,** *with the dangling swords as the main axis in the story, speaks dramatically of the vulnerability of life in the midst of war.*

and signified is seamless, and the decodification process is relatively easy. More examples of MacGuffins may be found in the crisscrossing of railroad track at the beginning of *Strangers on a Train* (1951), which indicates the crisscrossing paths (and fates) of the two main characters, psychopathic killer Bruno Anthony and well-known tennis player Guy Haines who meet on the train. The mirrors in *Psycho* (1960) suggest self-reflection and self-discovery by Marion Crane, a secretary who has run away with $40,000 entrusted to her by her boss. She finds herself in the restroom of a car dealership, where she has gone for privacy. She needs to take the money out of the envelope to buy a car. Guilt, fear, and nervousness are reflected on her face as she looks in the restroom mirror. Later on, as she drives, she looks at herself in the rear-view mirror and, through a voice-over she creates in her imagination a scene in which her boss discovers her theft. Numerous other filmmakers also use signs or signifiers in which meaning is encoded. Antonioni uses architectural settings in *L'Avventura* (1961) when two persons of different generations (a father and a daughter) are set against contrasting (old/modern) architectural patterns that reveal these characters' inner tensions. Kurosawa's fluid shots of warriors clashing in *The Seven Samurai* (1955), their swords dangling at different angles, suggest continuous movement as a symbol of life against death, the major theme of this film. To understand film codification, the relationship between the signifier and the signified, the viewer must understand social and cultural codes and a filmmaker's intentions, techniques, and practices. Some critics use the term "synecdoche" (the part used to stand for the whole) to indicate a sign (signified) with broader thematic meanings. In a recent film, *Snow Falling on Cedars* (1999), a lantern becomes a synecdoche, a means of illumination, "shedding light" on an obscure sequence of events that lead to suspicion of murder, according to the DVD commentary of director Scott Hicks.

Axes and Nodes: Reading Film Language

In a broader sense, one reads film as one reads a written text, following the process of translating signifiers (images or words) into signifieds (ideas or meanings). Visual imagery—bottles, train tracks, mirrors—as we have seen above, can just as well be described in words. Therefore, the decodification of film becomes a process similar to the decodification of language in general, whether visual, discursive, or auditory. Let us follow a specific procedure to see how this can be done.

When a film critic describes a means of visual expression, he or she provides the viewer with necessary analytical tools for the thematic decoding of a film, an activity comparable to reading a text. In his essay "How to Read?" noted French semiotician Tzvetan Todorov defines reading as a process in which the reader seeks meanings through the text, attributing equal importance to every part of a sentence (635). Instead of reading "syntagmatically"—that is, in temporal or sequential order—we search for points of focalization, *axes* and *nodes*, which strategically dominate the rest. Every reading is fresh, yielding new results. The reader seeks axes and nodes, parts of the text that stand out and give a variety of interpretations. A reading is "rich," rather than "true or false" (635). Certain images, then, achieve prominence in a text, either because they have certain characteristics in common, because they are identical, or because they call for our attention as we read. Their placement in the text is strategic, meaning that they are intended to invite the reader to discover and group together images related to general ideas or themes in the text. Todorov speaks of rich readings, rather than true or false ones. A subsequent reading may supersede a previous one. A student of film can use intuition, perception, and/or logical relationships between images. There are no specific rules for this reading. It is free, requiring only that images—axes and nodes—explain the film's meanings and that such explanations make sense. Let's look at these terms a little more closely:

An axis is literally defined as a straight line around which a sphere (or another shape such as a cube) rotates; thus, it serves as a unifying reference. The axis of a sphere has two poles. On a sphere like the earth, the two poles are at the north and the south; the earth rotates on the axis (figure 4.1A). But if one imagines these two poles to be elsewhere—if, for instance, one situated one pole in Africa, the other will be exactly across from it. Thus, the earth could have an infinite number of axes and could rotate in any number of different directions (figure 4.1B). Likewise, if one imagines a text as having dimensions—as Todorov does—it too could have an infinite number of axes. An image that runs through a text, then, can be imagined as an axis. This axis might be an idea or a theme that runs through the text. As an axis can be anywhere in a sphere, a theme can be found at any place in a text and a meaning can be discovered by seeking the other point of the axis.

A node also has a mathematical meaning: It is either of two points which intercept the path of an ellipsis, as in the case of the orbit of a planet or the path of a comet. A node also has other meanings: a swelling of an arthritic

Figure 4.1
Axes

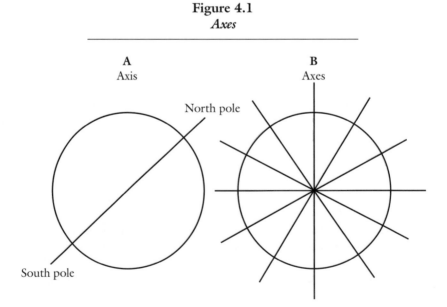

A
Axis

B
Axes

North pole

South pole

Figure 4.2
Nodes

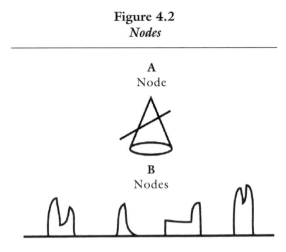

A
Node

B
Nodes

joint, a protuberance of any kind on a surface, and the place on a plant's stem where a leaf grows (figure 4.2). Here, nodes are the points in a text which call for a reader's attention. Readers can connect in any way they wish. Axes and nodes are also markers or synecdoches, and can be interpreted as codes for certain signals. Since codes are often limited to cultural orientations, signs and signals (signifiers and signifieds) may be limited to a specific audience. No such limitations exist in identifying axes and nodes. Any reader can offer a sociological, psychological, literary, cultural, or other reading, provided he or she (figure 4.2) engages, in Todorov's terms, in a "rich" (rather than true or false) reading. Students of film are, of course, free to follow the same guidelines as students of literature, and they frequently do. They read a film as one reads a text, seeking meaning through axes and nodes. Some examples will clarify the procedure.

Axes and Nodes in *Goldfinger*

Seeking a rich reading, let us see what happens when we look for axes and nodes in *Goldfinger* (1964), a film known for both its discursive inventiveness and its visual imagery. To begin with, Goldfinger is a dealer in gold bullion, a paranoid villain whose madness is visually expressed in the golden-hued jackets and sweaters he wears, in his gold-plated car, and in the golden shades and hues used in the decor of his residences. Thus gold and its color variations are the primary visual and verbal metaphors of this movie. It is both an axis and a node, strategically placed throughout the movie. Goldfinger enterprises are called Auric,

from the Latin *aurum*, gold, and Auric is also Goldfinger's first name. He plans
to contaminate the Fort Knox gold deposits by detonating an atomic bomb he
obtained from a Third-World country, thus rendering U.S. gold useless for 58
years. During that time, Goldfinger's considerable gold holdings will quadruple
in value and he will corner the market. As an axis and a node, gold provides
viewers with an image suggestive of modern civilization and its discontents.
Greed, power, and the acquisition of wealth may drive mankind to nuclear detonation and death. Most of the film's ideas are encoded in its imagery: Goldfinger even uses gold paint to suffocate his victims. Equally suggestive on the other
side of the spectrum are the gadgets used by British secret agent 007, who is
charged with thwarting the plans of the villainous Goldfinger. These axes and
nodes are also indicative of a civilization gone haywire in its attempts to defend
itself from mad terrorists by inventing diabolical gadgets. Q's lab, through
which James Bond is paraded in order to observe its function, includes displays
of an exploding, fog-producing parking meter, a bulletproof raincoat, and an
Aston Martin DB-5 with various "modifications." Coolly, the gadgets' field
expert Q (also a node) describes to Bond the car's bulletproof windscreen; the
revolving number plate ("valid in all nations"); the cigarette lighter–like tracer,
a transmitting device, and its smaller model (which "fits into the heel of your
shoe"); the "defense mechanism controls" concealed in an arm next to the driver's seat, which include a smoke screen, an oil slick, a rear bullet-proof screen,
left/right front wheel machine-gun, and a red button which activates the ejection of the passenger seat. "A passenger ejection seat! You're joking!" Bond
exclaims, astonished. "I never joke about my work, 007," Q condescendingly
replies.

   Bond is expected to use these devices and does so later in the film, but
the main axis or node—the key metaphor for his persona—is the laser beam
used by Goldfinger to "execute" his opponent. Bond has been caught by the
villains after a chase, and his Aston Martin is wrecked and lying useless. Fit-
tingly, 007 is now lying stretched out with his legs tied open on a bed-like
gold plate while a laser beam, suspended at an angle from above, begins to
zing through the gold plate. The awesome beam moves slowly and agoniz-
ingly, aimed between Bond's open legs. Soon it will cut him in half, severing
his genitals. The symbolism here is obvious, but telling. Bond is famous for
casual sex, pursuing numerous glamorous women to gratify his insatiable sex
drive. ("Pussy Galore" is Goldfinger's mistress who will become allied to
Bond later in the film.) Goldfinger, mad though he is, chooses a fit punishment for the archetypal sexual renegade of twentieth-century western civilization, death by castration. Bond, a modern, amoral Odysseus, uses his wit
to escape this peril (as Odysseus escaped Charybdis) and later defeats Goldfinger to save Fort Knox and the world. For several decades, James Bond films
have continued to use gadgetry significant of each era in the villains' arsenals
or in Bond's special armory. These include extension-wire watches, stinging

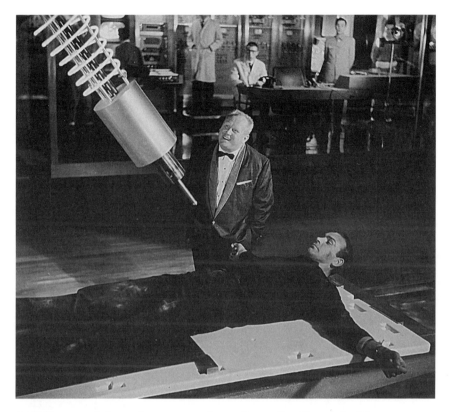

Goldfinger positions a laser to zero in on James Bond's crotch. The symbolism of this node is excruciatingly ironic: Bond, the captivator of women, is now captive and subject to punishment by castration.

baleen umbrellas, blade-equipped shoes, and numerous others, including automobiles. One of the latest cars is the BMW-750 that replaces the Aston Martin of yesteryear in *The World Is Not Enough* (1998). The gadget-master Desmond Llewlyn, perhaps ironically, died in a car crash in 1999, but we have not seen the end of gadgetry nor of the axes and nodes of technology in the modern age.

Axes and Nodes in Kubrick's *Lolita*

Classic filmmakers leave their distinctive marks on their films, one of which is each individual's way of manipulating imagery. Here, the decodification process through use of axes and nodes yields rich results. Let us look at one scene in Stanley Kubrick's *Lolita* (1963) in which Kubrick uses nearly all the forms of film language—visual, auditory, and discursive axes and nodes. This scene, lasting thirty minutes—nearly one fifth of the movie (the length is significant in itself)—deserves our attention.

Early one morning during Humbert Humbert and Charlotte Haze's postnuptial season, Lolita's mother Charlotte wakes up to find that Humbert has left their bed. She finds him in the bathroom, where he has locked himself in in order to write in his diary. Charlotte stands outside the closed door whining that she's being ignored. Eventually Humbert comes out, and tries to conceal the diary in his desk, but Charlotte storms in and embraces him, preventing him from locking it in his drawer as he has always done. They go into their bedroom and he sits on the bed while she takes a gun from a drawer beneath her dead husband's picture and the urn with his ashes. She holds the gun and when Humbert protests that it might be loaded, she assures him it isn't. "That's what they always say," he retorts sardonically.

"This is a sacred weapon," she intones melodramatically. "It's a tragic treasure." She explains that Mr. Haze purchased it when he found out he was ill, intending to spare her the sight of his suffering. Luckily (or unluckily) he was hospitalized before he could use it. Charlotte holds the gun before Humbert's face, but when he tells her to put it down, she does—on the bedside table next to him. They embrace on the bed, and he kisses her while he looks at a picture of Lolita. Charlotte tells him a French servant girl will be occupying Lolita's room because the latter is going to a boarding school abroad, and then on to college, never to come back. Humbert turns away, stunned at the news (and at the fact that he has been outfoxed by what he considers an addlebrained woman) but telling Charlotte he is following "a train of thought." The *mise-en-scène* positions the gun in the foreground, Humbert's face in the middle, and Charlotte's just above him. He looks at the gun, but she cannot see his face.

The gun here is the node. The viewer already knows it. This is the gun with which Humbert kills Clare Quilty at the beginning of the movie. It is already a murder weapon and was potentially a suicide weapon. Its anachronistic reappearance at this point in the action explains its existence, and at the same time it becomes the means of furthering the plot. The phone rings; it is Lolita. She tells Charlotte to thank Humbert for sending her candy; instead, Charlotte berates Humbert severely for doing so against her wishes. He explodes (the first time he loses his cool), pointing out that he is the man in the house, not her lapdog. She leaves the room enraged. A storm breaks outside, and we hear thunder. There is a close-up of the gun; Humbert looks at it; no words are spoken, but the viewer knows what Humbert is thinking: he could kill her (or commit suicide?). He checks the gun and bullets fall out of it. It *is* loaded. Now Humbert's voice-over begins. The viewer clearly hears this train of thought: He will kill Charlotte, and explain to the police that it was all a joke. She had just told him the gun wasn't loaded and "naturally," he believed her. She dies; he is free of his tyrannical wife, free to see Lolita. Here is a perfect murder. He grabs the gun and proceeds toward the bathroom where he believes she has gone. Now in another voice-over; he decides he cannot kill her, despite his resolution. He is talking to the audience, potentially to his jury, saying he couldn't quite bring himself to do it. He finds her in his study, reading his diary. She knows and she raves at him in a hysterical outburst, calls him a monster, flees the study. Moments later, we see him downstairs fixing her a drink, imploring her to understand that the diary is part of a novel he is writing. No answer. The phone rings and he is informed that his wife has been hit by a car. He is astonished, still believing she is upstairs. He goes to the window and sees a crowd gathering. Rushing outside in the storm, he finds Charlotte dead. This is a classic reversal: the gun, which would have been his means of killing her, has not been used. When we see him next in his bathtub, complacently sipping the drink he had fixed for Charlotte, a look of utter relief is on his face, and the gun lies next to him on a small stand. Voices are heard, and a friendly neighborhood couple appears to console him in his "loss" with the usual platitudes. Concern shows on their faces when they see the gun and suppose he is about to commit suicide. The presence of the gun photographically inside the *mise-en-scène*, underscores the final irony/reversal in the scene. The gun which could have been used to kill Charlotte has now become a means of allaying any suspicion that he might not have loved her, that they might have quarreled, that she might have run out in desperation. In that case, he could have been accused of indirectly causing her death. Instead, Charlotte's friends assume he loved her too much and is contemplating suicide. Humbert Humbert is now free to see Lolita; his goal has been achieved without the necessity of murder, and the gun has done its job in terms of film language. It has become the axis and node of a subtheme: The story is as much about murder as it is about pedophilia. The gun itself tells a story within a story: Purchased for suicide, it is a reminder to Charlotte of the "sacredness" of her bond with Harold. Then it is used by Humbert in his contemplation of Charlotte's murder and eventually becomes the means by which Quilty is executed. It is also a potential sexual symbol for Charlotte, lying unused (and loaded) in a drawer beneath the urn with Mr. Haze's ashes, the urn which Charlotte clutches tightly to her chest in a fit of neurasthenic ecstasy just before she rushes out to be killed by an oncoming car.

Combining Visual and Audial Nodes:
Varieties of Film Discourse

To show the variety of means and the inventiveness employed by filmmakers to find prose equivalents in film language, let us take a scene from the adaptation of Jane Austen's *Pride and Prejudice* in the 1985 BBC production. This scene involves the reading of a long letter which Darcy delivers in person to Elizabeth Bennett after she has rejected his proposal of marriage. The problem is the letter itself; it is lengthy, but it is essential that the audience know its contents, otherwise the plot (the plot of a psychological novel can be difficult to convey on the screen) would not be advanced. This is how this scene is managed by the director: Elizabeth sits on a fallen treetrunk (not shown) and begins reading the letter. The audience hears a Darcy voice-over while Darcy himself turns away and stiffly and formally walks in the opposite direction, a piece of acting performed perfectly by British actor David Rintoul. He remains with his back to her through this entire scene, while she faces in his direction as she reads. He continues to draw further and further away while the narration is delivered in Rintoul's voice, an intoning, undulating, slow-paced articulation that matches his deliberate step. The camera cuts from Elizabeth's face, its paleness expressive of her utter seriousness and shock, to Darcy's back as he walks away. Thus she learns Darcy's explanations of his behavior to her sister and to Wickham. She reads on, turning the pages of the long letter, while he continues his stately pacing over a hillside, past a tree, his figure gradually diminishing to a dot, but still visible. This long shot is several times interrupted by a side medium close-up of his face, which remains calm, grave, expressionless, self-assured. Elizabeth's own voice is heard several times as she acknowledges that she has wronged him. This scene juxtaposes long shots, motion, stillness, close-ups, and voice-over. It is a symmetrical combination of the means used by the filmmaker to convey, in a dramatic and totally filmic fashion, a scene originally presented in prose. How can one "do" a letter on the screen? The prose must be communicated audially and visually. Here, the medium of imitation, which is verbal, is adapted to include the many ways that film can express itself.

As seen in the above example, film language can be simultaneously imagistic, audial (the soundtrack), and discursive. Discursive elements in film can employ dialogue, voice-over narrative, or anything in the visual frame. Billboards, labels on wine bottles, traffic signs, and stoplights can all be part of film language. Thematic nuances can be expressed this way. The fateful roadside cafe where the women stop for refreshments in *Thelma & Louise* (1991) is called the Silver Bullet. Before they leave its parking lot, Louise shoots a man, so the "bullet" may refer to his sexual organ, the male penetrating symbol, and also to the means of his undoing. Thus, the road sign becomes a means of expressing irony and the movie's phallic theme is underscored. Discursive language in film can be decoded or broken down in any number of ways, even anagrammatically, to express or suggest a meaning: HAL, the 9000-Series computer that runs Discovery I on its flight to Jupiter in Kubrick's *2001: A Space Odyssey* stands for *H*euristically-programmed *AL*gorithmic Computer (Clarke), but many viewers interpreted the name as an acronym for IBM (H=I, A=B, L=M) because of the film's satiric slant on the communications conglomerate. In *Dr. Strangelove, or How I Learned to Stop Worrying and Love the Bomb* (1964), the names of the characters themselves carry a wealth of double entendres: the mad general Jack D. Ripper is a double for the notorious sex killer Jack the Ripper. He is paranoid beyond belief, claiming the Soviets have been polluting our water since 1946 and destroying "our precious bodily fluids." The grotesque-looking Soviet ambassador is De Sadesky (de Sade). There are more examples throughout the film: The R in Wind Attack Plan R stands for Romeo, a lover (of the bomb). The Texas pilot of the attacking bomber is nicknamed "King-Kong"—is he after a girl? To be sure, one of his bombs is decorated with the words, "Hi, there!" and its primary target is Laputa, an ironic parallel to the flight of Laputa, the floating island in Swift's *Gulliver's Travels* (to which this film frequently alludes). Just as Swift's Laputa ("the Whore") rained rocks on the Irish inhabitants disloyal to the English king, so America can drop bombs on those it doesn't like.

Axes and Nodes in the Discursive Language of Comedy

Comedy also thrives on decodified discursive language such as is found in clever puns, elliptical comments, non sequiturs, and generally in expressions that defy logic. Todorov describes this decodification as *intratextual superposition,* the goal of which is "the establishment not only of classes of equivalence but of any describable relation: whether of resemblance (in the strict sense), opposition, gradation, or even of causality, conjunction, disjunction, exclusion" (637). No example of verbal discourse could fit this definition better than a scene in the Marx Brothers' *A Night at the Opera.* Anarchic language or disjunction (which includes language of signs) is employed in almost all Marx Brothers' scenes, and that language is part of their anarchic behavior—which creates a chaos destructive of social order and of language itself. Groucho, as agent Otis B. Driftwood, is sitting at table with rich widow Mrs. Claypool, a potential donor to the New York Opera Company. After an abortive effort to convince her he loves her ("I was having dinner with a woman at the next table because she reminded me of you!" and "Everything about you reminds me of you, except you!"), he points to a man eating a few tables away:

> "You see the man over there eating spaghetti?"
> "No. . . ." (a forkful of spaghetti is shielding the man's face)

"But you see the spaghetti, don't you? Now, behind the spaghetti is
   Hyman Gottlieb, director of the New York Opera Company. Do
   you follow me?"
"Yes. . . ."
"Well, stop following me or I'll have you arrested!"

There is a visual "node" here, the spaghetti that conceals Gottlieb's face
and points up his grotesque manners. But the verbal node is the pun on "following"; Groucho—tired of Claypool's attachment to him which prevents
him from courting other women—disrupts the logical progression of the
argument. He is verbally abusing her without suffering any consequences,
because Claypool doesn't understand his pun. This is his harmless (to him)
revenge for her enslavement of him, and it continues throughout the film.
Later in a scene where Chico and Groucho are negotiating a contract for a
tenor whom Chico represents, both men hold a copy of the contract. It's a
con game they are playing: Groucho buys the tenor's services for pennies
($10) instead of his full salary ($1000 a night), which he intends to pocket.
Groucho also intends to cheat Chico, who is both inexperienced and suspicious. He can do that by manipulating language and in the process destroying the "order" represented by a legal document:

Groucho: Now, here are the contracts. You put his name at the top, and
   you sign at the bottom. There's no need you reading it, because
   these are duplicates.
Chico (hesitatingly): Yes, duplicates . . . duplicate.
Groucho: I say, these are duplicates. Don't you know what duplicates
   are?
Chico: Sure, there's five kids up in Canada. . . .
Groucho (not grasping malapropism): I wouldn't know about that. I
   haven't been in Canada for years. Well, go ahead and read it.
Chico (obviously unable to read): What does it say?
Groucho: Go ahead and read it.
Chico: You read it.
Groucho: OK, I'll read it (reads silently). Can you hear?
Chico: I haven't heard anything yet. Did you say anything?
Groucho: Well, I haven't said anything worth hearing.
Chico: That's why I didn't hear anything.
Groucho: Well, that's why I didn't say anything.

The point here, of course, is that Groucho is careful *not* to read—if he
did, his con game would be up. But he pretends to read, which he actually

can do, since reading can be done both silently and aloud. Thus, he convinces Chico he has read the contract without needing tell him *what* he has read. Chico is naïve about contracts, but he's not dumb. He says he didn't hear anything—stating the obvious—but also reminding Groucho that he is onto the con game and is staying alert. At this point Groucho gives up: he didn't "say anything"—the equivalent of "Touché!" in fencing. He concedes to Chico, his equal in verbal play and conmanship. Here we have the destruction of the order of language and the recreation of that order.

There is also language play in the films of Laurel and Hardy. Laurel is known for his incapacity to "hear" correctly; in their case, language is not anarchic, not illogical, but antilogical. In their short *Be Big*, the boys are preparing to go to a club to cheat on their wives. Hardy has put Laurel's boots on by mistake. They're too tight, and he is trying in vain to remove them. As he struggles, Laurel stands by, hands in his pockets, totally oblivious to his companion's frustration. Finally, Hardy begs, "Don't just stand there. Give me a hand." Of course, Laurel takes his hand out of his pocket and shows it to his pal. It does not occur to him that "hand" is a metaphor (metonymy) for "help." In another instance (*Helpmates*), the two are conversing on the phone. Hardy had a wild party on the previous night, his house is a mess, his wife is coming back from vacation at noon, and he needs Laurel's help:

Hardy: Say, what are you doing?
Laurel: What do you mean? Now?
Hardy (impatiently): Yes, now. What are you doing?
Laurel: Why, I'm talking to you.

Here, the problem is the logic of language itself. Strictly speaking, Laurel is correct, though stupid. He *is* talking to Hardy. Here, Stanley Fish (in his, "Is There a Text in This Class?") would claim that both meanings are determinate and therefore legitimate. Still, the answer is nonsense, though clever. Laurel should understand that his friend is asking about his general plans for that morning—what he is doing, whether or not he is busy—not about what he is "doing" at that moment. But Laurel is an expert at these non sequiturs. To Hardy's exasperation, Laurel chooses to answer precisely, responding to the literal question. *Now* he is talking to Hardy, so that is the logical answer to the question. Here, verbal comedy shows what a fragile instrument of communication logic can be. The logic of language depends on the audience's perception of it. If one chooses to be stupid, one can be stupidly logical—outrageously stupid and completely logical at the same time—so, logic becomes anti-logic. The audial node is discursive, and the visual is the telephone—the medium which makes this perversion of meaning possible.

The Soundtrack: Audial Axes and Nodes

The soundtrack is part of film language and includes all sound materials in a film, from dialogue to natural sounds of the film action's environment to music and to all sounds organically related to film, which become part of what is called the mix. The mix is the final product of all the sounds contained in a film as they are synchronized with the images on the screen. Most references to film sound refer to musical content, so *soundtrack* usually means the music either composed or borrowed from other sources which has become part of a film's sound system. The vast majority of films contain music, mostly music conceived and composed for those films, though existing music is also used (e.g., Ravel's "Bolero" in *10*). Music usually enhances the emotional content of a movie, accompanies variations in modes of action, or is used as an indicator or sign to be decoded by the audience as described earlier. In fact, all sounds in a film are signals that contain meanings; to use the language of Todorov, they are axes and nodes. Music is only *part* of a film's sound system, albeit a significant part. However, in a commercial sense, as for instance on a soundtrack CD edition, the soundtrack is only the music, usually in its original form rather than as contained in the film. When we talk of a soundtrack in film criticism, however, we mean the entire sound system—the mix.

Pure Sound Without Music

A good example of a film in which sound is important, but which contains no music, is Hitchcock's *The Birds* (1961). On the soundtrack of that movie, the sounds of the attacking birds are essential to the subject matter. The soundtrack was composed electronically and supervised by Bernard Herrmann, the composer for many Hitchcock films, including *Psycho* and *Vertigo*. In a way, the soundtrack of *The Birds is* a sort of musical composition, because it basically performs the same function that music would: signification of the emotions and psychological states expressed by the actors—fear and anxiety. Viewers are projected into an apocalyptic world that is enveloping the small community of Bodega Bay, where the action is set. An actual musical score would distract the audience's attention from the main subject matter by sending mixed signals. Any musical sound, no matter how intense or suggestive, would lessen the effect of fear and anxiety generated by the sound of fluttering gull wings at the moment when protagonist Melanie Daniels is trapped inside a telephone booth and the audience hears only the hollow thumps of birds smashing against the glass. No music could produce an effect equivalent to that sound. Another moment of pure and effective sound occurs in the attic scene when the viewer hears the whistle of scissoring wings and nothing else. Meanwhile, viewers see Melanie's hands covering her face, as it is gradually disfigured by bird scratches and bites. Here, the visual and audial elements complement each other, and pure sound is undisturbed by the distraction of music. The whistling wings and the screeching of birds as they attack become the axes and nodes of this film and, needless to say, the basis for its thematic decodification. They represent the fear the viewers experience as they witness the apparent disintegration of an ordered universe.

Film and Music

For the vast majority of films, music has become a vital element, an irreplaceable way of enhancing and producing emotion. Aristotle said that the end of tragedy is to produce pity and fear. Since that time, audiences of dramas—including all forms of drama and of comedy—expect their emotions to be stirred by the dramatic situations they experience when watching a stage or screen play. Hence, it follows that the production of emotion is the business of moviemaking. This is a broad point, but let us limit it in this discussion by asserting that an "intellectual" movie or drama—something like a Platonic dialogue—is not possible. That is a different species of rhetorical composition, a form of discourse that depends primarily on logic alone, although rhetoric based on logic can also produce emotion. Plato himself rejected poetry on the grounds that stirring up emotions is harmful to humans. "Poetry stirs emotions," he said in *The Republic*, "instead of drying them up" (14). St. Augustine in his *Confessions* wondered why humans go to the theater and enjoy seeing someone suffer calamities. He thought theater-going sinful. St. Augustine and Plato notwithstanding, people have overwhelmingly encouraged the production of—and paid large amounts of money to witness—emotion-evoking action on stage or screen. In movies, music has been a primary means of producing and enhancing emotion, and the business of movie criticism is the decoding of emotion, whatever the means used to achieve it.

Music in movies has taken many forms and has been included for many reasons. In the average drama—including melodrama, comedy, adventure, and many other subgenres, that is: in the vast majority of films—music is used routinely. Composers of scores, such as Bernard Herrmann and Patrick Doyle (*Sense and Sensibility* [1994])—have become well-known. Many musicians in the old days were at the service of studios; others independently contracted to write scores for movies. Today it is almost inconceivable to make a movie without a musical score, *The Birds* notwithstanding. Some directors try to limit musical content, thinking it an impediment to dramatic effect. Antonioni, for instance, said that music cluttered the furniture in a movie (his *L'Avventura* contains minimal music). In the audio commentary on the DVD edition of

The Apostle (1997), Robert Duvall explains that he limits music to a minimum so that it will not interfere with dramatic action. Some movies are indeed over-loaded or cluttered, depending on one's view of what a movie should do. A movie like *Much Ado About Nothing* (1995) contains so much music as to be practically a musical. Emma Thompson sings iambic verses, there are voice ensembles throughout, and all of this blends with Doyle's score. The poetry of Shakespeare is sung in a polyphonic composition. The term *musical* today means something different from what it meant forty or fifty years ago in the 1930s, '40s, and '50s. Then, its purpose was to exhibit the musical talents of singers, dancers, and musicians, e.g., Gene Kelly and Fred Astaire. A musical was also a stage production such as *Oklahoma*, *South Pacific*, and *Camelot*. The stage musical *My Fair Lady* became a film with identical music and dance num-bers, though with some different actors. *Amadeus* and *Immortal Beloved*, movies of the '80s and '90s, can be considered modern musicals, though the subject of those movies is the music itself. The drama tags along to help Mozart's and Beethoven's music. It is hard to imagine those movies without music or with a musical score composed *for* them.

The New Language of Film:
Digital Technology and Hypertext

Over the last few decades, not only has film itself changed, but so have the critical means of expression. The advent of the computer; digital montage; digital photography; and the encoding of film on VHS tape, laserdisc, and DVD adds to the constant intrusion of online reviews and commentaries on a viewer's critical apparatus. This is called "hypertext," any comment (includ-ing visuals) that comes to the viewer through electronic means. The language of film is constantly affected by advances in technology, both in terms of film making and of film commentary and information. A few examples will suffice: When Howard Hawks directed *The Land of the Pharaohs* (1955), he needed the thousands of extras that populated most epics of that era (*The Ten Com-mandments, Ben-Hur, The Fall of the Roman Empire*). Such films would be impossible to make today because of the enormous cost of hiring casts of such magnitude, building elaborate sets, and filming on location. Since the 1970s, starting with the first film of George Lucas's *Star Wars* trilogy, massive sets and large casts have been replaced by digital processes which can duplicate and triplicate *ad infinitum* the numbers of people involved in action. One recent example is *Titanic* (1997), in which both the floating liner and its pas-sengers were computerized in several important crowd scenes. This affects even relatively small films like *Run Lola Run* (1999), directed by Tom Tyk-wer. That movie begins with a montage of a seemingly huge crowd moving in all directions. In fact, digital technology simulates a large cast (usually only two hundred people). *Lola* also uses animation, rapid cuts, flashbacks, and hypothetical flash-forwards, to show projections of the stories of several characters. The entire movie resembles a video game played and directed at will on a computer. Viewers who watch the film on DVD have interactive menus allowing them to listen to the voice of the director as he comments on the action. Such an audience *watches while listening*, engaging in two levels of activity, one visual, the other audial and interpretive. The DVD commentary (or anything else on the interactive menu) becomes the hypertext. Students can read two texts—at the same time or separately. Hypertext can be added because it is any written or heard commentary, or any extra information encapsulated on DVD, laser, database, CD-ROM, or cyberspace in general. A new dimension, a multivocality, is added to language, so modern students can be sensitive to all forms of film language, whether in the film text itself or in spaces adjacent to it.

The new and constantly evolving language of film does not invalidate any of the older ones. The relationship of the signifier to the signified is fluid, involving both a director's vision and the alteration of that vision through the accident of progress. One can trace axes and nodes in Tykwer as one can in Hitchcock and the earlier Kubrick. Tykwer's animated scenes of Lola running are part of the fantasy viewers create by imagining the manipulation of the action in a video game; everything in the computer age is interactive. Here the node may be the mouse that clicks to change an image on a computer. Watching the film, one imagines that Lola can be saved. She is running to help her boyfriend who will be killed if she does not find 100,000 marks in time. She has twenty minutes. The viewer watches her breathless trot and imagines helping her along by interacting with the image on the screen. The signifier, the node, is her run; the signified is an infinity of possibilities, as the film suggests, and is subject to the will and disposition of the viewer. It's only a question (hypothetically) of clicking the mouse in a viewer's hand.

What we have discussed in this chapter is the complex medium of film language, and the fact that the reading of film is a complicated and ever-changing process. It is most important to remember that film language requires not a *correct* reading but a *rich* one. Viewers need to understand film techniques in general, to look for a filmmaker's use of specific techniques and cultural codes, and above all to understand that film language combines oral and written discourse, visual imagery, sounds on the film's soundtrack, and digital technology. Viewers constantly adapt to evolving mediums and to the new techniques offered by digital technology, hypertext, and interaction. Todorov's concept of axes and nodes can be used to interpret all the language modes and mediums. Here it is a specific method for decoding film imagery, whether audial, visual, discursive, or digital. It is not the only method, but in this text guide it can help students understand and interpret film for their own satisfaction and enjoyment.

Suggested Readings and Hypertext Links

Aristotle. *Poetics*. The Loeb Classical Library, vol. 23. London: Harvard University Press, 1927.

Kagan, Norman. *The Cinema of Stanley Kubrick*, 3rd ed. New York: Continuum, 2000.

Kindem, Gorham. "Sound Editing." In *The Moving Image: Production Principles and Practices*. Glenview, IL: Scott, Foresman & Company, 1986.

Monaco, James. *How to Read a Film: The Art, Technology, Language, History, and Theory of Film and Media*, 2nd ed. New York and Oxford: Oxford University Press, 1981.

Todorov, Tzvetan. "How to Read." In *Criticism: Major Statements*, 3rd ed. Charles Kaplan and William Anderson, eds. St. Martin's Press, 1991.

2001: A Space Odyssey, MGM DVD ed., 1998. With interview with co-screenwriter Arthur C. Clarke and an eight-page booklet featuring production notes and details of the making of the film. <http://www.mgm.com/dvd>

Goldfinger, Deluxe Collectors' ed., THX laserdisc. T. Wine Entertainment, P.O. Box 152, Dunellen, NJ 08812. Distributed by MGM Home Video, 1995. With left analog commentary by director and cast.

The Last Temptation of Christ, Criterion Collection laserdisc ed. Universal, Janus Films, 1997. With commentary by Martin Scorsese, Paul Schroeder, and Willem Dafoe. A good example of reading hypertext, language of film on two levels at once. A significant portion of this commentary offers insights into why, for example, Scorsese chose to have biblical characters speaking with Brooklyn accents. Also available on DVD.

Lolita, Deluxe Letterbox ed., extended-play laserdisc. MGM/UA Home Video, 1991.

Suggested Films for Study

Fort Apache (1948), dir. John Ford. Search for nodes in the magnificent setting of Monument Valley.

8½ (1963), dir. Federico Fellini. Note the musical score by Nino Rota with music from Wagner and the American popular tune "Blue Moon."

The Godfather I (1972) and *II* (1974), dir. Francis Ford Coppola. Search for nodes in the religious imagery juxtaposed to scenes of murder—holy baptism in *I*, religious procession in *II*.

Barry Lyndon (1974), dir. Stanley Kubrick. Observe how visual movement corresponds to classical compositions from Schubert, Vivaldi, and Mozart.

Akira Kurosawa's Dreams (1991), dir. Akira Kurosawa. Search for audial nodes in the eastern/western musical compositions and for visual nodes in the paintings of Van Gogh.

Much Ado About Nothing (1994), dir. Kenneth Branagh. Note the musical/discursive mix.

Quiz Show (1995), dir. Robert Redford. Watch for discursive nodes such as the several quotes from Shakespeare and other verbal exchanges between Charles Van Doren, his father, and the NBC executives.

The English Patient (1996), dir. Anthony Minghella. Notice the musical score and nodes in desert scenes.

You've Got Mail (1998), dir. Nora Ephron. Students may want to explore the film's hypertext—that is, the double language within the film's action.

The Loss of Sexual Innocence (1999), dir. Mike Figgis. Note this film's innovative techniques: dream sequences, nonlinear narrative, absence of dialogue, and symbolic representations in general; its richness in axes and nodes; and its classical musical score.

CHAPTER FIVE

Responding to Film as History

How do I respond to film as history? To respond to film as a part of history does not require viewers to know the entire history of film nor to consult history texts before seeing a movie. In fact, that's a bad idea because it makes a viewer conscious of the subject matter in a way that can interfere with spontaneous enjoyment and understanding of the movie. Responding to film is a natural act, an experience which should be similar to the experience of any other work of art. As discussed in our previous chapter, students become skillful in "reading" film language. That is why it is not necessary to read a history book in whatever field of art before visiting a museum, admiring a piece of sculpture, reading a poem, or viewing a film. Like the experience itself a film's pure aesthetic impression should not be tampered with. Even a historical film can be viewed spontaneously and without preparation, though if viewers have previous knowledge of the subject matter, that knowledge certainly does not need to be suspended. In most cases the spontaneous act of viewing is what most audiences engage in anyway. They don't go to the movies armed with a history book or an encyclopedia, though they may have read reviewers' comments that influence them one way or the other. Students may have the comments and introduction materials of a professor in mind, but on the whole they view on their own (although a group viewing may influence their reactions in a class), understand what they can, and enjoy a film accordingly. That experience is like a first impression of a very young child which nothing can replace.

Placing a Film in Its Historical Context

That said, the critical viewer knows that a film is not created in a vacuum. Sooner or later, preferably *after* one has viewed a film, the question arises of relating film to its historical context. Here one must make a distinction. There is a difference between a film that has historical subject matter, but was made after the event it describes, and a film made during the period it describes. Often, students of film confront both questions. For instance, they can study a film about the Dust Bowl and the Great Depression, *Grapes of Wrath* (1939), which was made during the period it depicts. Today, a film made about the Depression would have a different historical perspective, one which would include the new and/or revised view of that decade. The Great Depression would be "deconstructed," to use the critical term: that is, it would be looked at from a number of angles allowed by historical distances. No one today can be free of these perspectives on previous historical eras. Consider Oliver Stone's *Platoon* (1984), a film about the Vietnam War made while that war is very much in living memory. As recent as that film is it is difficult to fully understand it unless viewers have some knowledge of that war. *Platoon* was shot in the Philippines and follows the actions of American soldiers subjected to psychological traumas that leave them permanently scarred. Their actions relate indirectly to actual episodes such as the so-called My-Lai massacre. Stone was himself a soldier in Vietnam, and his film's action is carefully and painstakingly documented. Despite the controversy they evoked, the episodes about the destruction of a Vietnamese village are convincing and authentic. Stone went to great lengths to train the thirty or so actors at a boot camp in the Philippines where conditions were similar to those in Vietnam. Here history was not fictionalized, as it frequently is in Hollywood movies, but was reproduced as accurately as conditions allowed. Even counting the filmmaker's biases (which are inevitable), this film carefully documented facts and reproduced reality with minute fidelity.

In both cases above, students need neither the entire history of the movies, the entire history of America, nor the whole history of war or economics to understand the historical situation. But having background knowledge of the war, and recognizing the efforts of its director to represent his own vision of it can be extremely helpful. Viewers must place a historic film—any film, in fact—in its historical context. How much knowledge is necessary depends on the specific conditions set out in the movie and on

Painstaking efforts were taken in the making of **Platoon** *to be as accurate as possible in depicting the destruction of Vietnamese villages by soldiers.*

their connection to a contemporary viewer's historical interests. A viewer equipped with the critical tools suggested in this chapter can become a good judge of whether a film's special historical interests have been achieved. Some films invest heavily in the concerns of their eras, and they cry out for recognition. Chaplin's *The Great Dictator* (1941), for instance, makes special historical demands on contemporary students who know little or nothing about Hitler's Nazi henchmen Göering and Goebbels, or about the confinement of European Jews in city ghettoes. Without a historical background on both Chaplin and Hitler—two of the most recognizable figures in the world between 1930 and 1940—it is impossible to understand Chaplin's intentions in creating the double character of Hynkel and the Jewish barber. Both were figures that evolved from Chaplin's earlier film persona, the Little Tramp.

Both were clowns, with their jerky movements, ill-fitting garments (Hynkel's cape always slipped off his shoulders and his cap sank to his ears), and acrobatic dancing. Both wore characteristic toothbrush mustaches. If Hitler adopted Chaplin's mustache, Chaplin retaliated by imitating Hitler's hyperbolic oratorical style, rendering it verbal rubbish. Hynkel's speech retains recognizable phonetic structures ("democratia schtunk") that allow Chaplin to expose Hitler's vulgarity, his contempt for democratic values, his ignorance of freedom, his hatred of Jews, and his absurd glorification of the Aryan race. The speech makes sense, at least in terms of the filmmaker's intentions. One need only contrast this speech to Hitler's actual speeches (available in many documentary videos) to recognize the fierceness and effectiveness of Chaplin's attack on the "great dictator." In 1939, not many (including FDR) had the courage to launch such an assault on the most powerful man in the world, a man who would soon plunge the planet into its bloodiest war. Only an artist of Chaplin's stature and world recognition would dare to do that. Humanity owes a debt to Chaplin for his courage and service to a cause. The historical approach to this film (discussed more fully in chapter 1) makes the viewer realize that.

Similarly, a film as recent as *Schindler's List* (1993) is better understood with the history of the Holocaust in mind. Spielberg's attempt to achieve an all-important authenticity in his historical background must be taken into account if this film's significance is to be grasped. Spielberg, of course, had historical distance from which to view events, and thus he could give it to viewers in its historical completeness. Both movies focus on the same historical phenomenon—the Nazi attempt to exterminate the Jews—and by contrasting them students can learn as much from one as from the other. In the Spielberg movie, for instance, Hitler does not appear except as a picture hanging on a wall, but if practically ignored as a character, his actions are abundantly and horrifyingly illustrated. Viewers can go back to Chaplin and listen to Hynkel's speeches, then return to Spielberg to see where they led. If these two films are studied sequentially, students can understand these changes in historical perspective. Today, we know of Hitler's actual evil acts which Chaplin's film could only foreshadow. Chaplin was aware of Hitler's persecution of the Jews, but he did not know about the Holocaust at the time he made the film. Had he known, he said later, he would never have made a comic film about such a subject. Indeed, Roberto Benigni's *Life Is Beautiful* (1998) offended some viewers with its comic antics. Many saw it as ill-advised to set comedy amid the horrors of the concentration camps. Other viewers believed that by replicating Chaplin's humor, Benigni succeeded in evoking pathos. By inserting sadness into comedy, he portrayed comedy as part of life. These are questions for students to ponder, questions on which the historical approach to film can shed light.

More Reasons for Studying Film Historically

A student interested in gaining knowledge of the historical origins of film in general is encouraged to take at least one introductory course in the history of film before attempting the advanced courses concerned with criticism and interpretation. Titles of several books on film history are found in the Suggested Readings at the end of this chapter. Film students are urged to scan the reference sections of their libraries for film dictionaries and encyclopedias, and to search for web sites (hypertext) containing materials on contemporary movies, DVD releases and reviews, and past and current commentaries by directors, actors, screenwriters, or critics. This text guide provides a sample course in its final chapter, which contains samples of class materials to be distributed to students before a film is shown. These include historical references and facts where these are pertinent, and there is no harm in scanning these briefly before a showing begins. But the real study of a historical era in which a film is set must begin afterward.

Many instructors treat film courses as a species of history course. Whether that is appropriate or not—and no matter what the specific class approach— the historical component of a film always comes to play in a film analysis course. Naturally, students can dig deep if they become interested in, let's say, Queen Elizabeth I after seeing the film *Elizabeth* (discussed below). That film's attempts to recreate a historical context won it an Academy Award for costume design. Ideally, *every* history-based film should emulate this effort. A movie has the power to stir students' historical consciousness to such a degree that they may begin to study a historical period. That is a good development. After the film *Titanic* was released in 1997, there was a resurgence of interest in an event that had stirred the imaginations of previous generations. Film and history coexist. Many great films borrow incidents from history and dramatize them, often taking liberties with the original facts to make the drama more appealing. Students have a certain responsibility to check on these discrepancies, not in order to condemn the film but because they need to know whether a filmmaker consciously altered history to express certain personal ideas. One example is Bergman's *The Seventh Seal* (1957), which is set in the Middle Ages. It depicts the return of a knight (Antonius Block) and his squire from the Crusades. The Great Plague (or Black Death) has been ravaging Europe, and populations have resorted to religious rituals (including torture, witch-burning, and self-flagellation) to placate the wrath of God. In his film, however, Bergman stresses the search for God and meaning not as a particularly medieval pursuit but as a universal and twentieth-century phenomenon. Made at the height of the Cold War, the film expressed humanity's fear of impending disaster, doubts about the existence of a "divinity to shape our ends," and doubts about human justice raised by the McCarthy purges. Thus,

Allegory and history combine in **The Seventh Seal**'s *portrayal of medieval Europe. Here the Knight, an Everyman figure, plays chess with Death, an embodiment of The Great Plague. By metaphorical extension, the Knight's trials become universal and the turbulence of the middle ages mirrors the fears and uncertainties of contemporary times.*

Bergman seems to transcend topical and chronological history in order to make a value judgment on his contemporary world. The apocalyptic sub-themes of this film match the period of the 1950s when the nuclear threat was at its peak and the possibility of atomic blasts threatened human existence. Many other films of that time had similar messages: *On the Beach* (1959), directed by Stanley Kramer, presented a group of survivors of an atomic holocaust, waiting to die of radioactivity. They live on a remote part of the planet (Australia), coping as best they can with a pointless *carpe diem* existence.

Film as History: *Elizabeth* (1998)

Though practically every historical film contains fictional elements, some do establish a historical basis for their narrative. A historical film has no obligation to represent an entire period in all its details. Given a film's limitations of time and space, this would be impossible. What a film can do, and do well, is focus on an incident and let that incident be as representative as possible of its

era. *Elizabeth,* directed by Shekhar Kapur, captures a slice of the early life of
Queen Elizabeth I, a mere episode in a period of complex and prolonged historical conflicts. It begins with the reign of Queen Mary, elder daughter of
the notorious King Henry VIII, who is dying of cancer. A Catholic, she has
undertaken a systematic purging of Protestants, including her relatively free-
thinking (and free-playing) younger sister Elizabeth, Henry's daughter by
Anne Boleyn. Mary accuses her sister of treason and imprisons her in the
Tower of London, but before she dies, Mary relents and allows her sister to
live—and to become queen.

From that point on, the movie focuses on young Elizabeth's struggles to
survive and to exert control over her male-dominated and divided court. Two
groups soon emerge: the members of Parliament, including Catholic prelates,
who pressure her to choose a husband among the French and Spanish suitors
to secure allies and to produce a Catholic heir; and a smaller faction of four
individuals, all of whom will play distinctive roles in her life: Sir Francis Walsingham, Sir William Cecil, Elizabeth's lover Lord Robert Dudley, and her
archenemy Lord Norfolk. Each influences her life decisively, but in very different ways. Dudley (Ralph Fiennes), the love of her youth, cannot reconcile
himself to the fact that she has grown up. He calls her "my Elizabeth" in public, and her rejection of him after her coronation stuns him. Sir William Cecil
(Richard Attenborough) patronizes her, convinced she will not survive without a husband. Lord Norfolk (Christopher Eccleston) plans her overthrow.
Only Walsingham keeps a respectful distance, recognizes her intellect, and
thus is able to influence her actions.

For Shekhar Kapur, a mainstream Indian director with very few credits in
western cinema, it was somewhat of a challenge to handle English actors, but
he managed admirably. As a director he stresses characterization and photography as against dialogue. He follows history and historical fact closely, especially in costume design and setting. But in his own words, he "deconstructs"
certain scenes: though accurately rendered, for instance, an Elizabethan
dance—when Elizabeth dances with Dudley—is photographed so as to suggest modern sexuality. He uses overhead (crane) shots, for the burning of the
"heretic" Protestants at the beginning of the film, thereby creating distance.
The camera becomes an objective eye overseeing the folly of these atrocities,
rather like a Homeric deity overlooking the slaughter of the Trojan War in
Homer's *Iliad.* The gods pity the humans but usually leave them to their own
foolish devices.

These shots establish the tone in *Elizabeth.* Many times figures move
through vast cathedrals or palaces whose stone columns represent permanence
in contrast to the fleeting hostilities, barbarities, and absurd behavior of human
beings. Most of what happens in this movie is consistent with an absence of
logic that reduces conflicts to absurdity. During the reign of Queen Mary,
Catholics slaughter Protestants. When Elizabeth comes to power, she holds on

to her fragile regime by sending boys to fight a war against her opponent, Mary of Guise. Child soldiers die horribly, though Kapur shows only the aftermath of the battle. The camera surveys the horror accomplished rather than the action, like a Greek messenger (here replaced by the camera) keeping the audience informed. The absurdities continue: When the roles are reversed, and Elizabeth has consolidated her power, it is the Catholics' heads that (literally) fall. The severed heads (including Norfolk's), are impaled on spears like shish kebabs, but the actual decapitations are suggested by a movement of the axe. Other moviemakers (especially today) might have made this scene much more gory. But one of the points of the movie is clearly made: Religious fanaticism will drive men (and women) to extinction. It will also drive them to bravery (as in Norfolk's case) when they unflinchingly face death for their beliefs. Religious war is utter and total war with no gray areas. To stay in power, Elizabeth becomes as ruthless as her opponents. A degree of barbarity is involved in preserving and holding power, and she has to learn that game. Viewers admire her mettle when she does, but also deplore the way she distances herself from her humanity. She becomes the "virgin" queen in the political sense at a somewhat overt point in the movie when she looks up at a statue of the Virgin and wonders why men will die for her.

Of the many comments made by Shekhar Kapur in his DVD commentary, two are worth mentioning. Quite aware of the controversy his film sparked by showing Dudley and Elizabeth in bed, Kapur contends that Dudley, a sincere lover, fails to realize that the young girl he knew has grown into a queen. This failure is responsible for his downfall. The second point concerns the role of Walsingham, admirably portrayed by Geoffrey Rush. He survives to become her loyal confidant by addressing her respectfully and not arguing with her as most of the other advisers do. Unlike Robert Dudley, who demands sexual favors (and thus power over her), Walsingham exercises the self-control and wisdom needed to serve and counsel a queen. He understands Elizabeth's genius and greatness, he knows that she needs only some gentle nudging here and there, and he steers her a straight course (even if that means decapitating her enemies).

This is a superior movie overall, serious and reflective, respecting history but interpreting it in a modern metaphor for the game of power and its destructive (or constructive) effects on humanity.

The War Movie as History: *Midway* and *A Bridge Too Far*

Two war films produced in close chronological sequence—*Midway* (1974) and *A Bridge Too Far* (1976)—took thoughtful looks at operations of World War II. Though based on entirely different premises, they both depict significant turning points in the war, one in the Pacific and the other in Europe. They differ in that one film focuses on a great victory, the other on a great defeat. Both are almost totally preoccupied with the planning and the execution of the plans, one defensive and the other offensive. Both films have almost entirely male casts with only minor female roles. Both cast distinguished actors in relatively minor parts. *Midway* features such worthies as Henry Fonda, Charlton Heston, Glenn Ford, Robert Mitchum, and the distinguished Japanese actor Toshiro Mifune. Mifune plays the commander of the Japanese fleet, Admiral Yamamoto, who defeated the Americans at Pearl Harbor. *A Bridge Too Far* mounts an impressive ensemble of veteran British, American, and one or two German actors: Dirk Bogarde, James Caan, Ryan O'Neal, Sean Connery, Edward Fox, Elliott Gould, Gene Hackman (playing a Russian), Anthony Hopkins, Hardy Kruger, Laurence Olivier, Robert Redford, Maximilian Schell, and a lone female star, Swedish actress Liv Ullmann. These films differ in outlook and conclusion, but they are fairly accurate documentations of significant historical events. They are, however, meant not as documentaries but as real dramas, which employ a minimum of the fictional elements inevitable in film to show the human drama of war in poignant and realistic ways. Both contain objective views of the adversaries (which was impossible during the war years), and both illustrate the tragedy of war from both sides.

Midway (1976), produced by the Walter Mirisch Corporation and directed by Jack Smight, is a war epic that details the greatest American naval victory in the Pacific during World War II. It is based on real events, contains actual footage from the battle, and could be described as a docudrama. It is in some ways a continuation of *Tora, Tora, Tora,* another war movie about the Japanese attack on Pearl Harbor. *Midway* works on the same premise in that it shows both the Japanese and American sides, though in this case the Japanese speak English. It is not jingoistic, as were so many American movies made during and immediately after the War. However, it is a patriotic movie, objectively but clearly highlighting American bravery and attempting to make amends for the defeat at Pearl Harbor. The Japanese themselves acknowledge defeat at the end of the battle, and the American admiral modestly admits that the American victory was in some ways a matter of luck.

Midway focuses not so much on the battle itself, as most war movies do, but on the crucial strategic planning of the Americans. Admiral Nimitz (played by Henry Fonda) and Admiral Yamamoto (Mifune) who both play the war game somewhat blindly. The latter feels that this is the right moment to launch another attack like Pearl Harbor. This, he believes, will finish off the Americans, who have established a stronghold on Midway, a pair of tiny islands about 1300 miles northwest of Honolulu. The Japanese are uncertain how many aircraft carriers the Americans have left after the massive destruction of their fleet at Pearl. They think the U.S. Yorktown is out of commission and that the U.S. Enterprise cannot defend the island. The massive Japanese force, which includes four heavy carriers, three light ones, and eleven destroyers, is set in motion. The Japanese high command, however, cannot agree on the plan of attack. Some argue for launching a decisive blow to wipe out the air base at Midway, thus destroying American defenses in the Pacific and forcing the Americans to sue for peace. In fact, had they won this battle, the Japanese might well have won the war.

A Bridge Too Far, produced by Joseph E. Levine and directed by Richard Attenborough, is set three months after the D-Day invasion of Normandy. Allied forces have liberated Paris, advanced through Belgium, and are nearing the border of Holland four hundred miles into enemy territory. But the Allies were running short of supplies due to the haste of the retreating German army. An army moving faster than it should cannot be supplied adequately since supply units (trucks, etc.) move more slowly. The Allies, therefore, had to slow down their advance into Germany. Now they are looking to strike a decisive blow, finish off the Germans quickly, and bring the boys home for Christmas. A female narrator introduces these facts to the audience while a reduced black-and-white square on the screen shows scenes of battle. General Eisenhower—reluctantly, we are told—assigns operation "Market Garden" to General Montgomery rather than to his rival General Patton who is not popular with the British. The plan calls for dropping 35,000 paratroopers behind enemy lines, the largest such drop ever. They will occupy several bridges and hold them until reinforcements arrive, thus cutting off the enemy's retreat. Germany will then surrender. Of course, things do not quite work out that way. The Germans recoup, organize resistance at Arnhem, the last bridge, in Holland, and the Allies fail to hold off a superior German force, despite their valiant resistance and the nearly total destruction of that city. It is not lack of courage, but bad planning and a miscalculation of German resolve that prove fatal for this operation. This was one of the darkest days of the war, proving that the final Allied victory was not without setbacks. The film tells this story honestly and with painstaking accuracy, using authentic weapons borrowed from war museums, real locales, and a distinguished cast of actors who bring credibility to these roles. (For further information, look for the MGM DVD edition, 1998, with eight-page booklet and production notes.)

The War Movie as Biography: *Patton* (1970)

Patton is probably the most historically accurate war movie made during the 1960s and 1970s. Directed by Franklin J. Schaffner and produced by Frank McCarthy with a screenplay by Francis Ford Coppola and Edmund H. North, the movie, filmed in Spain, is based on authentic materials and on biographies of General George Patton (1885–1945), especially *Patton: Ordeal and Triumph* by Ladislas Farago. *Patton* is by far the most successful war movie in terms of box office proceeds and awards won. It is also one of the most carefully produced war movies made in an era that had already seen scores of good movies about World War II.

George C. Scott's landmark performance as General George Patton is memorable for its psychological complexity and ambiguity as well as for its historical authenticity.

Everything about the movie looks and sounds authentic. George C. Scott plays General George Patton to perfection, striving along with the director and producers to render a piece of American history as accurately as a film possibly can. The result is a compelling movie that has drawn the attention of movie buffs interested in the war, but also of anyone interested in a great American personality.

The film concentrates on only one portion of Patton's career, the time when he was made a two-star general and assigned the extremely difficult task of defeating Germany's Field Marshal Erwin Rommel. Rommel has devastated the Allied forces (mostly the English) on the African front, but Patton defeats Rommel. Then the campaign moves to the invasion of Italy, and Patton plays a vital role in the occupation of Sicily, disobeying orders in order to occupy Messina in the north. His unorthodox behavior, which includes slapping a soldier for showing "cowardice," exposes him to army reprimands and costs him promotion. Later, after the invasion of Germany, Patton becomes instrumental in the war in Europe. He is killed in a car accident in Germany at the conclusion of the war.

Basically, *Patton* is a character study, but it is also an antiwar movie though it does not directly or indirectly condemn World War II. This film is a vehicle for showing that movies do not have to exaggerate or glamorize to make truth acceptable or enjoyable. Shot in dimension-150, a wide nonanamorphic lens, the movie achieves a panoramic "flat" screen effect that allows for a wider *mise-en-scène*, realism, and a broader spectrum to represent the many battle scenes and other spectacular events. The battle scenes seem authentic because the producers (Twentieth Century Fox) essentially rented large portions of the Spanish army, which was equipped with World War II materiel sold to the Spanish by the Americans after the war.

In the midst of this spectacle and all the action of the war, the center of attention remains Patton himself. To his contemporaries, fellow generals and soldiers alike, he was an enigma. Arrogant and tough, he believed the best soldier was the one prepared to give his life for his country—no matter what the circumstances. He hated war for killing the best men, but he loved war because he saw it as a great field for human achievement. He believed only in attack, not in defense. A considerable historian, he thought himself a reincarnation of the great generals of antiquity. Walking with General Omar Bradley through the ancient ruins where the Romans defeated the Carthaginians, he quotes poetry and then reveals he has written it himself.

He is bold, intemperate, and decisive, and he will not tolerate weakness in anyone. He is brilliant to the point of thinking everyone else a fool. When he takes Palermo against orders in Sicily, both the German commander and General Montgomery—Patton's rival British general—say "Damn." Neither can figure him out.

Above all, General George Patton typifies American individualism at its best and its worst. He sees a course of action, that which is dictated by his own mind. He is not a team player—a contrasting American virtue—and can ignore his military commitment to obey orders. His attitudes apply to both generals and foot soldiers. Patton likes to *give* orders. He has a centuries-old understanding of the role of an army commander, though the Romans, Persians, and Carthaginians he reveres all had absolute rulers. Patton is living in the past, an anachronism with no political instincts and no sense of compromise. He is not like other war heroes who adjust to civilian life and even aspire to political office. After the collapse of Germany, Patton wants to go on with the war and push the Russians out of Western Europe. "We have the army now," he tells Bradley. "Why not do it now, rather than having to do it later?"

Above all, he was a purist. He believed a soldier should carry out his duties under any conditions—heat, cold, utter privation, whether healthy or wounded. When paying tribute to a young captain killed doing his duty, he says the man was brave, good, and had no vices. To him, there is such a thing as a perfect human: good, brave, spotless in every way. This is patriotism. This is America. This is what Patton had in mind, and it comes through in an uncompromising film that is worth all its Oscars.

Saving Private Ryan (1998)

Directed by Steven Spielberg, *Saving Private Ryan* is a three-hour movie about the D-Day invasion of Normandy on June 6, 1944. That decisive Allied victory eventually defeated the Nazis and ended that war. Students conscious of the great historical moments of that war can ill afford to ignore this film. In this powerful, haunting, and harrowing movie, virtually every scene is a masterpiece of moviemaking, instantly etched deep in the mind if not the memory. Based on a historical person, tank driver Jim Ryan, the movie proves that film need not always rely on fictional events and characters. *Private Ryan* is for anyone with even a vague idea what World War II was like. It is not a pretentious movie, as many war movies are, but a simple, straightforward story.

It is also refreshing to find a war movie that is not an antiwar movie. After a series of antiwar movies in the 1970s and 1980s—e.g., *Apocalypse Now* (1979) and *Platoon* (1984)—this was almost a revelation. Of course, *Saving Private Ryan* is not a *pro*war movie either. It shows the horrors of war in a harsh light and with a stoic detachment that is almost Homeric. But this movie also has a philosophic point of view and—if one dares use the word—a patriotic one. It goes back to the good guys/bad guys syndrome. Spielberg, as in *Schindler's List*, makes no bones about who is fighting for the right cause. *Private Ryan*, though, is more objective than *Schindler's List*, which unequivocally condemned Nazi atrocities. *Saving Private Ryan* concentrates instead on the task at hand: the search for a soldier whose brothers have been killed.

Much has been made of this movie's brutal violence. The opening sequence on Omaha Beach is probably the most sustained scene of violent action ever filmed. The point, though, is not to show violence for its own sake (See chapter 11, on violence). The film slowly develops a theme: Is war ever, under any circumstances, justified? Is killing? The answer is yes, if by killing some—even your own men—you can save the lives of ten or twenty times more. But sending eight men to save one does not seem to make sense. It goes against logic. The film deals with, and solves, that dilemma. When the right Private Ryan is found, he refuses to abandon his post. His rescuers stay to fight with him, holding a point where German tanks are to pass. Almost all of them except Ryan are killed. The two missions have merged: Ryan is saved, and the sacrifice of the others has contributed to victory—the object of this war. That is heroism. The film makes that statement without the pretense or pomposity that has undone so many war movies.

A Historical Movie? *Gladiator* (2000)

Directed by Ridley Scott, *Gladiator* is violent, sick, and brutal, but is somewhat redeemed by its spectacular visuals, direction, montage, and *mise-en-scène*.

Gladiator is supposedly based on actual Roman history, but is only marginally historical. Commodus, the Roman emperor played (well) by Joaquin Phoenix, lived from 161 C.E. to 192 C.E. He was strangled in his bed by his mistress Marcia, not killed in a gladiatorial duel by Maximus, an ex-general sold into slavery who turned gladiator and returned to Rome to avenge the deaths of his wife and son. Commodus did not strangle his father, the Roman emperor Marcus Aurelius, as the movie contends. Marcus Aurelius died fighting German tribes during an expedition to the Danube, though history does not record the manner of his death. Commodus was indeed a corrupt and inept emperor who dressed as Hercules, wanted to rename Rome after himself, and preferred gladiator spectacles to managing a city ravaged by the plague. In the film he "played" gladiator in the arena, a role he enjoyed playing in real life. There is no real evidence that he had an incestuous desire for his sister—here played with distinction by Connie Nielsen—though he was notorious for other perversions which the movie mercifully spares us. Maximus himself (played by Russell Crowe) is a total fabrication, though gladiators like him did exist, and the reality of fighting on the Roman fronts was more brutal than a movie can show. Commodus did reign for twelve years (180–192), and he was as corrupt a madman as Nero or Caligula, though less notorious (in part because cinema has up to now ignored him). The movie shows him as a character beneath contempt, someone with no redeeming qualities whatsoever, an utter villain richly deserving of his spectacular death in a gladiatorial duel.

The movie creates a great deal of tension and some suspense, since viewers anticipate the prospect of Maximus returning to battle his archenemy. These expectations are fulfilled, but, shockingly, Maximus himself dies at the end (the treacherous Commodus stabs him prior to their fight, expecting an easy kill).

This is the stuff Hollywood is made for. It is in some ways reminiscent of *Ben-Hur*, since that movie too concerned an innocent man wronged. Judah Ben-Hur survives the galleys and returns to search for and avenge his mother and sister. He too has a worthy (or unworthy) opponent, Messala. There is a confrontation between these adversaries, the climactic chariot race. Messala loses and is killed, and justice prevails. However, an enormous gap separates these two epics, and it lies in the tension created and in the levels of violence. *Ben-Hur* runs four hours (*Gladiator*, two-and-a-half), and it moves at a leisurely pace, taking long moments for reflection and thoughtful exchanges between characters. It also has religious overtones, since Ben-Hur's story runs parallel to the life of Jesus Christ. *Ben-Hur* contains only two violent episodes, the naval battle, and the chariot race. The latter is an enduring masterpiece of realistic staging of a spectacle and of great stunt work (reduced to a minimum because Heston himself did most of the chariot driving). *Gladiator*, on the other hand, features battles. One occupies the first fifteen minutes of the movie, offering viewers mutilation, decapitation, slicing of body parts, and unbelievable cruelty graphically depicted. Ridley Scott, a director known for his visual style, gives this movie the full treatment, providing some breathtaking vistas of northern landscapes and of Africa. The word violence (*violentia*) is inscribed on the wall outside the Roman Coliseum. The movie, though, takes violence beyond the graphic to the conceptual. This is not just violence as an aesthetic necessity in a movie (showing gladiators means showing how they fight), but violence as part of the moral subtext of the story. In a way, Maximus is no less a killer than Commodus—in fact, he commits many more violent acts. Training to be a gladiator in Africa under the tutelage of Oliver Reed, he kills numerous opponents with lightning speed and without the slightest remorse, demonstrating his mettle and unsurpassed skill as a swordsman. As a general, he is used to killing, since in those days generals fought on the battlefield. Maximus is a killing machine. He has right on his side, but by the time he's finished righting a wrong, he has killed hundreds with his own hands. His ruthlessness has a stoic resignation to it, but that does not alter his monstrous deeds. Of course, a gladiator kills; Maximus even attains certain nobility in wanting to rid the world of a murderous monster like Commodus, but being in the killing business himself tarnishes his image irreparably.

Though Russell Crowe does a creditable job of portraying Maximus and keeping him sympathetic, no one capable of brutal killings of this magnitude can remain unaffected by them. A compassionate killer is a contradiction in terms. The Rambo movies of the 1980s showed us Sylvester Stallone as Rambo returning to Vietnam to save one MIA, but gunning down dozens, if not hundreds, in the process. Is he an admirable man—a hero—after that? Good question.

A word on the moral of the story: Why do movies like *Gladiator* have such mass appeal? Are Americans or other societies so obsessed with violence? Are not violent sports—football, ice hockey, pro wrestling—indications of a mindset that allows moviemakers and sports executives to go for excessively violent shows? Certainly, we protest loudly when real-life shootings occur. We are caught in a contradiction: we abhor and denounce real violence, but we condone it when it appears as entertainment. *Gladiator* is as much about our historical/social context as it is about Roman society. It is more American than Roman, a means of using Roman history to depict contemporary social phenomena.

One could think of Maximus not as a killer, but as what he might have been—a philosopher like Marcus Aurelius (refreshingly played by Richard Harris). Could he have gone to Africa or Spain, like his compatriot Seneca, and written a *book* about Commodus? That would have left a better legacy, though not a subject for a moneymaking picture. After all, Roman writers who detailed atrocities—Suetonius, Tacitus, Livius—left us something to think about, but they are not household words. Maximus is (at least this year).

Film's Historical Settings: The New Historicism

In addition to brushing up on the history of film, students should be familiar with the basic points of the so-called new historical approach which this text guide advocates. Many literary critics, especially those of the school called Neo-Historicism, maintain that each film should be studied against both its historical milieu—the period in which it was made—and the period it represents. For instance, films made in the 1950s during the McCarthy era, are sometimes covert attempts by filmmakers to state their independence or to express disapprobation, or resentment of the blacklisting of many distinguished authors and screenwriters. Such films as *High Noon* (1952), *Paths of Glory* (1957), *The Wrong Man* (1957), and particularly *The Manchurian Candidate* (1962) can be seen as metaphorical diatribes against McCarthy repression of Hollywood. Films of the 1960s can be studied in the context of profound social changes in American society, as youth rebellion, antiwar demonstrations, and conflicts brought about by the Civil Rights movement and the Vietnam War. In the 1970s, films unleashed screen violence with *The Wild Bunch* (1969), *Death Wish* (1973), and the *Godfather* series. The 1980s also glorified violence in Sylvester Stallone's Rambo films (not to mention *Rocky* and its many sequels) as a backlash against the defeatism of the Nixon and Vietnam years. In the 1990s, *Goodfellas* (1991), *Natural Born Killers* (1994), *Pulp Fiction* (1994), and *Die Hard with a Vengeance* (1995) can be seen as ultimate convulsions of violence in the American psyche. The paradox of violence and moral thrust in *Schindler's List* (1993) is presented in a film too complex to be easily understood or broadly popular. This is time for reconsideration, in the aftermath of the Oklahoma City bombing or the 1998 high school shootings in Arkansas and Colorado, of the effects of violence in film on our society. Historically, film can illuminate the dilemmas of a society that wishes to perpetuate ownership of assault weapons and curb violence at the same time. Historical films by thoughtful filmmakers, such as those mentioned above, call for self-examination where violence and its evils in our society are concerned. (See chapter 11, "Film Violence.")

History and Social Issues

Historical film is viewed seriously in our time. In film we may see social progress or retrogression and may observe what happened when serious social conflicts arose. The Great Depression, Prohibition, World War II, the McCarthy era, all are well-documented in film, both fictional and historical. Today we wonder how to control and eliminate violence in our society. Will this lead to another McCarthy Era or to a genuine reevaluation of social mores? Students of film, in any case, must always place these ideas in a historical perspective. *Public Enemy* (1932) started the process of self-examination when the rise of gangsterism was threatening the safety and security of society. Hollywood had a hand in this self-examination then, and it has a hand in it now. A film like *Quiz Show* (1993) is an objective description of TV's game show scandals in the late '50s and early '60s, which forced America to look within. To judge the film properly and gauge its value, the viewers must recall the period in which the film was made. Having done so, viewers also realize the relevance of the social commentary on today's materialistic world, on corruption in high places, and on the erosion of values. Historicism, properly understood, calls for an examination of the value system of a society, and any film whose message is presented in subtle film language can be a devastating commentator. It can take the place of the Roman *satura*, the Juvenalian and Horatian satire intended to cleanse Roman society of its excesses. Whether a film expresses itself satirically or not, whether it is taken as seriously as some other film, historical film is a commentary on a society's mores. Take

Wag the Dog (1998), for instance, a film about waging of war on a small country to divert attention from a U.S. presidential scandal. In August 1998 the United States attacked terrorist bases in Afghanistan. Some TV commentators, suspicious politicians, and ordinary people suggested that President Clinton was launching the attack to divert attention from Monica Lewinsky's Grand Jury testimony the same day. Whether the charges were true or not (who really knows?), this caustic historical film actually preceded and even forecast the real-life events. The premise that life imitates art which had imitated life was assumed and remarked on by several commentators.

Film Is History

Film is history, just as the novel is, and the filmmaker is also a historian of sorts, even if the events depicted in the story are fictional or highly exaggerated. Henry James said the novelist acts like a historian, and Aristotle said poetry is "more philosophical" than history. Both are correct. James meant that, although the plot of a story is made up, the *context* of the story must be researched and presented in a historical manner, so the novelist must proceed authoritatively, like the historian. The novelist is the last person to tell us that his story is false, or he does not take his art as seriously as he should. Aristotle is also right: he meant that poetry (film, in this case) concentrates on the universal (not the particular) aspects of human action—that is, by expressing permanent truths and ideas distilled in an invented or represented story (*mimesis*). A historical film—or a film cast in historical context—forces the audience to face a truth. In that sense, narrative film is a form of history, a tale with a moral.

Suggested Readings and Hypertext Links

Cook, David. *A History of Narrative Film.* New York: W.W. Norton, 1989.
Earley, Stephen A. *An Introduction to American Movies.* New York: Mentor, 1979.
Frank, E. *On Film: A History of Film*, 2nd ed. New York: McGraw-Hill, 1983.
Giannetti, Louis, and Scott Eyman. *Flashback: A Brief History of Film*, 2nd ed. Beaver, 1991.
Landy, Marcia, ed. *The Historical Film: History and Memory in Media.* New Brunswick, NJ: Rutgers University Press, 2000.

A Bridge Too Far, DVD ed. MGM, 1998. With production notes and revealing look at the making of the film. <http://www.mgm.com/dvd>

Elizabeth, DVD ed. PolyGram, 1999. With director's commentary. <http://www.PolyGram.com>

The Manchurian Candidate, DVD ed. MGM, 1998. With audio commentary by director John Frankenheimer.

Midway, DVD ed. Image Entertainment, 1998.

Patton, DVD ed. Twentieth Century Fox, 1998. With bonus features: documentary on the making of *Patton* and audio essay on the historical Patton. <http://www.Foxhome.com>

Saving Private Ryan, DVD ed. Dreamworks, 1999. With exclusive message from Steven Spielberg.

Suggested Films for Study

Gone With the Wind (1939), dir. Victor Fleming. Realistic description of the North's invasion of the South during the Civil War, with the burning of Atlanta as the highlight. Good documentation of the aftermath of the war and the period of Reconstruction.

The Grapes of Wrath (1940), dir. John Ford. Loosely based on John Steinbeck's novel, the film captures the desperate flight of Okies to California during America's Dust Bowl and Great Depression. Realistic view of the hardest economic conditions in twentieth-century American society.

For Whom the Bell Tolls (1943), dir. Sam Woods. Based on the novel by Ernest Hemingway, the film depicts guerrilla warfare against Franco during Spain's Civil War in the 1930s. Depicts war conditions in a country not directly touched by World War II.

Spartacus (1960), dir. Stanley Kubrick. Screenplay by Dalton Trumbo (one of the blacklisted Hollywood authors during the McCarthy era). Though almost altogether fictional, this movie provides a view of ancient Rome at the peak of its power. Focuses on the efforts of a group of slaves, led by the historical figure Spartacus, to rebel against the mighty empire. Depicts Roman leaders as decidedly evil, enjoying the staged showdowns between trained killers called gladiators.

Lawrence of Arabia (1963), dir. David Lean. Based on T. E. Lawrence's *The Seven Pillars of Wisdom*, this film depicts the struggles of various Arab tribes to unite and, with the support of Western powers (Britain, in particular) to overthrow Turkish domination. Establishes criteria for an outsider's look at a foreign culture within historical parameters shaped by the policies of the British Empire, which treated these tribes as pawns in its colonial game.

Doctor Zhivago (1965), dir. David Lean. Based on the novel by Boris Pasternak, this film provides a panoramic view of an older order, Czarist society, in dissolution during and after World War I, and the emergence of the Bolshevik state. Plenty of colorful episodes, good battle scenes, and literate dialogue enable students to glimpse that society's conflicts.

A Man for All Seasons (1966), dir. Fred Zinnemann. Written by Robert Bolt (who also wrote the stage play), this film, a richer movie than *Elizabeth,* examines sixteenth-century religious conflicts and conflicts of conscience in a time of the king's absolute power (Sir Thomas More vs. King Henry VIII).

Z (1968), dir. Constantin Costa-Gavras. This political thriller details the assassination of a Greek political leader during the dictatorship of the "Colonels," 1967–1974. Though naming no specific country, the film (made in France), captures the turbulent spirit of that period of Cold War tensions in Europe.

Easy Rider (1969), dir. Dennis Hopper. To the modern student, *Easy Rider* offers a retrospective of a bygone era, the 1960s. In a torn American society, alienated youths run away from established order via typical escapist options—drugs, sex, rootlessness—that end in death. Cross-country motorcycle trek of two drifters features a splendidly photographed west-to-east geographic tour.

Gandhi (1982), dir. Richard Attenborough. Based on the real life of one of the most celebrated personalities of the twentieth century, Mohandas Gandhi, the Mahatma, who instigated a program of "passive resistance" in India in order to liberate his country from British colonial rule.

CHAPTER SIX

Responding to Black and White

How do I respond to black-and-white film? Contemporary students, having viewed color both on television and in film throughout their entire lifetimes, are habitually inimical to viewing films photographed in black and white. Clearly, color film is more realistic, offering a fuller representation of life, whereas black-and-white film, especially when viewed on small television screens, seems grainy, faded, and gloomy. One misses both the details, which are more visible in color, and the cheerfulness of tone associated with colorful and live things. There are natural reasons why viewers prefer color.

The Attraction of Color

Color enhances the representation of atmosphere, time, place, and landscape; color lightens the mood of a film and gives pleasure. Black-and-white film, of course, has its own beauty, enhancing contrast, creating luminosity of image, sharpness of definition, and intensity of lighting. But, like still photography itself, black and white fell out of fashion and was replaced by color as technology brought in larger screens (including for televisions, on which most films are viewed today), the anamorphic lens, Cinemascope, Cinerama, and other wide-screen formats. Color, which had been used sporadically in Hollywood films (*The Ten Commandments* [1923], *Hell's Angels* [1930]), suited the spectacular film epic far better and found new life in the late 1940s and early 1950s when filmmakers decided to use superior (and more expensive) technology to counteract the impact of television. Color was here to stay. The same was later true of television. About a decade later, in the early to mid sixties, color prevailed.

The Classic Black-and-White Movies: Colorization

Today, more than 99 percent of movies are made in color. Black and white is used only for compelling reasons; generally, it is considered anachronistic. However, a great many classic films, including nearly all those made before 1935 and most made before the 1950s, were photographed in black and white. For that reason alone, film students must view black-and-white movies.

The luminous, captivating presence of Ingrid Bergman in Casablanca *would have been lost if the film had been made in color.*

But there is an even more substantial reason: some of the great classic films would be unimaginable in color. John Ford's *The Informer* (1935), for instance, a film about an Irish rebel who betrays a friend for a reward, is worth watching today. The story takes place within a twelve-hour period, during a single night. The same is true of Orson Welles's *Citizen Kane* (1941), which would be much different, and possibly not as great, if it had been shot in color. The heavy expressionism of scenes such as the one when the reporter Thomson enters Thatcher's vaults is enhanced by the contrasts in lighting that suggest the shadowy character of Kane and the inscrutable nature of the search itself. In color, this effect would be lost or altered. In Jean Cocteau's *Beauty and the Beast*, black-and-white photography is equally expressionistic: In one scene Beast carries Beauty, inert in his arms, into his palace. As he climbs the stairs, shafts of light contrast with the shadows enveloping him. Many *films noir*, prevalent in the 1940s and even in the 50s, would have had less effect on audiences if they had been photographed in color. Their subjects were crime, mystery, and deception; and the action occurred in dark alleys, saloons, or dimly lit streets. It was important for the lighting to be low to enhance the contrasts between blacks and shades of gray. All the famous *film noir* movies of that era—*The Maltese Falcon* (1941), *The Big Sleep* (1946), *Double Indemnity* (1944), *The Killers* (1947), *A Touch of Evil* (1958)—might have lost their impact or have had a different one if they'd been photographed in color. This is readily evident when one watches these films colorized. Colorization of black-and-white films through a computer process became possible in the late 1970s when distributors, especially of films shown on television, attempted to capture the attention of younger audiences. For one thing, the color looks faded and unnatural, and for anyone familiar with the original black-and-white versions, it is destructive of a film's appeal. The luminosity of an actress's face is lost. Take one example: Ingrid Bergman's face in a series of films made in the 1940s (e.g., *Dr. Jekyll and Mr. Hyde*, *Casablanca*, *Notorious*) is never captured with the same intensity and brilliance in the films she later made in color (e.g., *Anastasia*). Part of the credit for the facial luminosity achieved in the black-and-white medium goes to cinematographers like Arthur Edeson, who photographed both *Casablanca* and *The Maltese Falcon*. Ted Tetzlaff, the director of photography in *Notorious*, was also responsible for capturing the expressive pallor of Bergman's face in that movie. Colorization was discredited, at least with older viewers, when many actors and directors protested against this change, claiming that it diminished the artistic value of their works. When a colorized version of *Casablanca* came out, it was apparent that the ambiance, tone, and luminosity of the film were destroyed. On the other hand, *Casablanca*'s contemporary, *Gone With the Wind* (1939), could hardly be imagined in black and white. Those muted tones would not have captured its antebellum settings, spectacular war scenes, and its great romantic story, all of which call for vividness and color. *Gone With the Wind*, rereleased in the summer of 1998, continues to draw audiences today. Color is the appropriate means here, the "medium of imitation," as Aristotle would have put it. But black and white has no peer when it comes to its own distinct qualities. Films in black and white are still alive and must be watched as their creators intended.

Why Movies in Black and White Endure

Black-and-white films have stood the test of time for other reasons. There is no better medium than black and white for evoking psychological moods, mostly in interior or intimate settings, especially when contrasts of shadow and light are important in the interpretation of a specific shot. Light and shadow, black and gray, shape the image to evoke a specific response, a mood of irony, a tone of seriousness, anguish, despair, or some other tragic feeling. Comedy can also benefit from black-and-white photography, but with comedy, tone is not the issue. Everything in comic action, especially the physical action of early comedians, is straightforward, depending on movement, whereas tragedy and the dark subjects in general depend on tone. That is why comedy had an easier time adapting to color than did tragedy. There are such things as dark or "black" comedies such as Billy Wilder's *One, Two, Three* (1961) and Stanley Kubrick's *Dr. Strangelove* (1964), both of which ridiculed mores and attitudes prevailing in the Cold War years. About a decade later, dark comedy readily adjusted to color with *Catch-22* (1970), and *MASH* (1970), both outrageous burlesques of military life. Another contemporary movie in that satirical tradition is Woody Allen's *Celebrity* (1998), shot in black-and-white as a showcase of the medium's enduring value (see page 126).

Because black-and-white film renders graver moods, it is more suitable than color for stories with dark themes, and no era is better known for black-and-white movies with tragic themes than the decade of the 1940s. *Double Indemnity* (Billy Wilder [1944]), photographed in "glorious black and white," is the story of an insurance salesman (Fred MacMurray) who plots with a blond *femme fatale* (Barbara Stanwyck) to murder her husband and is subsequently caught by a shrewd investigator. This movie could hardly be imagined in color. An international thriller, *The Third Man* (1949), directed by Carol Reed, is photographed in black and white by Robert Krasker, who won an Oscar for cinematography. It is a classic example of a dark topic—the betrayal of friendship, country, and conscience amid the ruins of a decadent post–World War II Europe. In the next decade, the black-and-white medium prevailed again in the movies of Swedish director Ingmar Bergman whose *The Virgin Spring*

(1959) epitomizes the darkest of tragic plots, a father avenging the rape and death of his young daughter. Bergman employed the services of superb cinematographer Gunnar Fischer in some of his earlier movies, and of the equally masterful Sven Nykvist who photographed most of the Swedish filmmaker's movies beginning with *The Virgin Spring*. Motion, fluidity, and painting-like frames are some of the characteristics of Nykvist's photographic art, but per-

The high-contrast shadows of Double Indemnity *endow this classic film noir with a striking darkness of mood.*

haps his greatest triumph lies in his lighting. Often hard light is focused on a subject—e.g., the face of a boy—to show intense feeling. The boy is the young brother of the two shepherds who have raped and killed a farmer's daughter and who, without realizing it, have sought shelter for the night at the farmer's house. The farmer has discovered the identity of the killers and is determined to kill all of them. As the boy senses the truth and awakens in terror, a flood of light covers his face in a close-up shot that fills the screen. Later, the girl's father (Max Von Syow) strives mightily to uproot a young sapling in his yard, clutching it against his chest, leaning and falling on it in a moonlit exterior scene. He realizes who his guests of the previous evening were, and he will use the sapling in a steamy bath scene photographed in stark contrasts, lashing his body in preparation for the expiatory killing of the murderers. The dimly lit interior scene fits the mood of this action. The killing is graphic, even by today's standards. One of the murderers is knifed; the other is choked to death, his face dropping against the fire, the flames devouring it. Even the frightened boy—innocent as he is—is hurled against the wall and dies. Von Sydow looks at his bloodied hands in a medium shot under hard light, the camera panning to show his face. No medium other than black and white could have captured his expression of horror so perfectly. Nor is this effect lost on contemporary audiences. Black and white endures.

Films in Black and White Through the 1960s and Beyond

The necessity of choosing between color and black and white based on the theme of a film's story emerged in the 1950s when color film had already made inroads, particularly because of the attention paid to the musical genre—eminently suited to color—and the spectacular epic. Color had made rapid advances, and the big Hollywood studios realized that audiences were reluctant to go back to black and white. As with everything else in business-motivated Hollywood, commercial considerations came first, but some film-makers continued to shoot some films in black and white. Hitchcock, for instance, had already used color in several of his films (*Dial M For Murder* [1955], *Rear Window* [1954], *To Catch a Thief* [1955], *The Trouble With Harry* [1956], and *The Man Who Knew Too Much* [1956]). He reverted to black and white for *The Wrong Man* (1957), largely because of its subject matter. Based on a true story, *The Wrong Man* is filmed in a documentary style, and contrasts of black, gray, and light are used adroitly to render the mental state of a man disintegrating under the stress of wrongful incarceration. When viewers see him in his prison cell, his face contorted in fear, his hands clutching the bars of his cell, they feel a high tension which color photography might have diminished. The Kafka-like tone of this film, its dark subject matter, its somber narrative (which includes the wife's mental breakdown), and the fact that it centers on a nightclub musician (played by Henry Fonda) and its action takes place at night—all these call for black-and-white photography.

Black-and-white film was no longer the prevalent medium by the mid-1960s. Color had prevailed, and only rarely was a film produced in black and white after that time. Nevertheless, throughout the 1960s and 1970s, and even into the '80s and '90s, several filmmakers continued to make movies in black and white when their subject matter called for this medium. In addition to the movies listed above, there was *Franz Kafka's The Trial* (1963), an Italian-French-German film based on Kafka's famous novel and directed by Orson Welles. The story concerns an innocent man arrested and lost in a maze of legal proceedings and labyrinthine corridors and halls, which lead nowhere but to his execution. Edmond Richard's cinematography perfectly captures the mysterious tone and mood of the story in a visually stunning film. Other examples from that decade include *Dr. Strangelove, or How I Learned to Stop Worrying and Love the Bomb* (1964), Stanley Kubrick's dark comedy about the paranoia of the Cold War. Color would have introduced a tone of cheerfulness not fitting to a film that abounds in "black" humor. *Zorba the Greek* (1964), a black-and-white film by Michael Coacoyannis (discussed in chapter 9), features Anthony Quinn as Zorba, a moody peasant with a pessimistic outlook. Some other black-and-white films made in the 1970s, '80s, and '90s include *The Last Picture Show* (1971), by Peter Bogdanovich; *Young Frankenstein* (1974), by Mel Brooks; *Manhattan* (1979), by Woody Allen; *Raging Bull* (1980), by Martin Scorsese; and most notably *Schindler's List* (1993), by Steven Spielberg. *Raging Bull* and *Schindler's List* have color inserted at certain spots: in *Raging Bull* during the double weddings of Jake La Motta and his brother Joey, and in shots of happy occasions recorded on home video; in *Schindler's List* when a lost little girl is observed during the evacuation of the ghetto, her red coat may represent hope—though this point has been debated. Most of these films have had a considerable popular following, which suggests that black-and-white film remains viable when the subject matter calls for it. Some filmmakers feel that such use of black-and-white is pretentious, but others are concerned about the rapid deterioration of color films from the 1950s and '60s. Scorsese decided to photograph *Raging Bull* (1980) in black and white for a number of reasons (e.g., that bright colors would be distracting in bloody scenes in the ring), but he also expressed concern about Kodak color film deterioration over time (see page 000). Some famous color films had to go through a vigorous restoration process before they could be rereleased. Hitchcock's *Vertigo* (1958) had its original color hues restored in 1996 (see page 000) and was shown in selected theaters around the country that year. *Psycho* (1960), on the other hand, was released on DVD Universal Home Video in 1988 (in a wide-screen Collector's Edition), and it had suffered no such deterioration because black-and-white film holds up much better than color. *The Manchurian Candidate* (1962), rereleased in 1987, suffered no substantial deterioration, and the DVD version (1998) is of exceptional quality. This film, incidentally, was made in black and white because the fears, prevalent in the early 1960s, of communist infiltration could be better expressed in black and white. The anxiety the film expresses about a Red takeover of the U.S. government and the assassination of key presidential candidates proved oddly prophetic: it was released one year before the assassination of President Kennedy.

Psycho (1960, 1998): Contrasting Color with Black and White

Perhaps the best example of contrast between color and black-and-white is a comparison and contrast between the versions of *Psycho*. The first was made by the classic master Alfred Hitchcock in 1960, the remake by Gus Van Sant in 1998, nearly forty years later. The first *Psycho* was not filmed in color, because, according to Hitchcock, the image in its violent shower scene when blood gurgles into a bathtub drain would be too disturbing for the audiences. Today, filmmakers no longer have compunctions about splashing blood all over the screen. Times have changed, color film has prevailed, and scenes of blood have become ordinary screen fare. In his latter-day version of *Psycho*, Van Sant renders the identical shower scene in full color. Critics have argued that his movie is not as effective as the earlier version. Indeed, critics and audiences alike wondered what the purpose of it all was. Some felt downright insulted, even outraged, by the result, and, judging from the box-office figures, the remake did not cash in on its predecessor's fame. Two years after its release, Van Sant's movie is nearly forgotten, while the original Hitchcock *Psycho* is still circulating regularly on the home cable channels—not to mention in film class syllabi. Van Sant did not recreate the original in the usual fashion of remakes—that is, by keeping the plot but changing character motivations and settings. He offered as exact a replica as possible, shot for shot, used the same music by Bernard Herrmann, and enlisted the services of original scriptwriter Joseph Stefano to supervise and up-date the script. The only significant change was that the new *Psycho* was shot in color using different actors.

Hitchcock's original still holds our attention and its continuing appeal may in part be attributed to the fact that it was shot in black and white. Violence, of course, existed in film (see chapter 11), but not in today's graphic terms. Blood did not spurt from wounds; swords flashed in myriad duels between Basil Rathbone and Errol Flynn in the swashbuckling 1930s and '40s, but they did not slash faces; and knives were not shown penetrating human skin. *Psycho* changed all this in the shower scene, and in 1960 such violence was a total shock—which was Hitchcock's aim. He wanted the audience caught by surprise, but not revolted, so black-and-white photography suited his purpose. It also suited the atmosphere and tone of the movie by enhancing the symbolism of certain scenes where contrast was more natural. Marion Crane's attire, for instance, in the opening shots at the hotel with her lover Loomis, includes strikingly white underwear. Then she wears a black slip and bra when she heads home the same afternoon with the stolen money. The viewer sees this— and in the 1960s this was a shock in itself—and also sees her undressing at the Bates motel before taking a shower, while Norman peeps at her through a hole in his office wall. The darkness of tone has already been established by Marion's escape through the night in the rain, her arrival in darkness, the gloomy motel off the main road, and the gothic structure that looms in the background with a ghost-like figure at the window. The setting is also perfect for the demeanor and appearance of Anthony Perkins as motel owner Norman Bates. Tall, thin, and handsome, with a winning smile and an occasional stutter ("fal-fal-falsity," he says when speaking of birds' eating habits), Bates assumes a fiendish look and his dark eyes shrink to the size of pinheads when he watches the car containing Marion's dead body, suitcase, and money slowly sink into the nearby morass.

Meanwhile, Van Sant's movie, precise and accurate in reproducing most of the original details, abandons the one factor most essential to the original— black-and-white film. In his DVD commentary, he explains that he imagined that shooting in color was the best way to make the famous film accessible to young modern audiences. The objection here, however, is not merely to color itself, but to the use of particular colors in specific sets and scenes. Consider the opening scene, which is identical to that in the original. Anne Heche as Marion Crane appears in pink underwear, and later wears a green slip. When she flees from Phoenix and from her pursuers, she wears an orange dress, carries a light-colored umbrella, and even wears shell-shaped pink earrings. When Heche arrives at the Bates motel light colors—orange, pink, light or medium brown—predominate. The sign she spots through the blinding rain says MOTEL (the name "Bates" remains inconspicuously on the side), and it is orange, as are the walls of Bates's office, and the umbrella he holds as he trots down the steps from his house is pink! The blood in the shower scene leaves orange patches on the tub surface and on the floor. This pink/orange deluge continues: After the murder, the scene changes to the Loomis store, and the walls of Loomis's back room are orange! Practically the entire movie is photographed, not just in color, but in orange and pink. There are a few greens and blues—Arbogast's suit is dark blue, but his tie is pink-flowered, Julianne Moore's hair is chestnut red, fitting the colorful composition of the scene as she arrives seeking her missing sister. What was the point of filming an identical *Psycho* yet changing the colors so radically from the original? Since the second *Psycho* is a literal repetition of the first, this contrast between black and white and "candy" colors seems to make its own statement. The tone seems alien to the idea. The color choice must be deliberate. Is it there to suggest the shocking reality of murder? Did the black or black-gray of Hitchcock conceal the plain horrid truth of bloodshed? Certainly, modern movies make a point of showing as much blood as possible. Occasionally the orange deepens to brown, as on the walnut surfaces in the motel (desks or chests of drawers). Does the monotony of these tints (pink, orange, brown, blue) suggest a human darkness somehow similar to what black and white suggests? There is no telling what the psychological effect of these prevalent tints might be, but even after one screening, the viewer cannot fail to notice it. The light colors certainly suggest sexuality, effortlessly projected by Heche, although the psychologically traumatized Marion of the Hitchcock film is generally missing from the lighter image projected by Heche's dress, movements, and demeanor.

Despite having stolen $400,000, Heche's Marion Crane does not seem as overwhelmed by her action as Janet Leigh's did. Heche seems instead to be toying with the idea of a weekend caper, even seeming amused when she flirts with the salesman at the car lot. In the DVD commentary, Heche talks to Van Sant and suggests that the orange color of her dress, designed by costume designer Beatrix Aruna Pasztor, reflects her understanding of her role in contemporary terms. The green slip she wears before she leaves her apartment—in contrast to Leigh's stark black—is expressive of her adventurous mood, of her desire for flight and romance. Leigh, in the same scene, is grave, deeply troubled by her action, fearful, and nervous. Van Sant explains this as an "existential" mindset, typical of the Hitchcock era. The decision to film a "dark" movie in black and white was not unusual for Hitchcock. (One is reminded of *The Wrong Man*, filmed in black and white only two years before.) For Leigh's Marion, stealing $40,000 and running away is shattering. Joseph Stefano, also a participant in the 1998 DVD commentary, finds this the major difference between Leigh's and Heche's portrayals. With Leigh, Marion's guilt is essential, though it is washed away by her decision to return to Phoenix and give back the stolen money—a decision ironically and tragically interrupted by her murder. If her murder is shocking, her decision nevertheless precedes it and provides a moral resolution. Heche's Marion, by her own admission, is a "daft" person, not quite conscious of the enormity of her act, doing something crazy on a whim. This is not bad acting; it is simply Heche's contemporary understanding of the character of Marion. To Heche, no contemporary woman in her right mind would steal $400,000 (even the inflated number seems preposterous) for someone whom she meets at a motel room every two weeks. To contemporary audiences, Leigh's Marion may seem hopelessly naïve or neurotic. And the mention of stealing $40,000 fails to stun an audience as it did in 1960. These differences in themselves argue against the possibility of making an "exact" copy of a movie made so long ago. Either a new *Psycho* in totally different terms should be made, or the attempt should not be made at all.

Black and White Today

Of course, the most famous example of black-and-white filming in the 1990s is Steven Spielberg's *Schindler's List* (1993), a film that won numerous awards and was also an international box office triumph. Not only was black and white not an impediment to *Schindler's List*'s popularity, it probably enhanced its box-office status. It was entirely appropriate for viewers to see the horrid events of the Holocaust in the darkest possible photographic context. The Nazi troops marching into the streets of Krakow, the crowds yelling at the ghetto dwellers during the evacuation ("Good-bye, Jews!"), the horrid conditions of the ghettoes, the concentration camps, the soot in the ovens at Auschwitz, Goeth casually shooting prisoners from his balcony—these images invoke horrible feelings, pity and fear if you will, intensified by the brilliant and stark black-and-white photography. If black and white serve an ulterior thematic purpose, Janusz Kaminsky achieved it in the photographing of this film.

Black and white still has value and will continue to be used in film, but only selectively when the subject matter requires it and when the conditions allow. The era of its general use has passed, but its value is still appreciated by those who uphold film's aesthetic values.

A Light-Hearted Review of
Woody Allen's *Celebrity* (1998)

Saving the best for last? After thirty-odd years of filmmaking, is Woody Allen getting better? Hmm. . . . Not so sure. He is not getting worse, though. Neither better nor worse—just about the same as always—still a hugely neurotic male, usually played by Allen himself. This time the role is relinquished to Kenneth Branagh, who comes out of nowhere to deliver an Allen smoother than Allen himself.

And so on. The hugely neurotic male is outmatched by a hugely neurotic female—this time Judy Davis, replacing yesteryear's Mia Farrow, Diane Keaton, etc. Judy Davis is more neurotic than the rest of them. David Lean, her former boss in that admirable *A Passage to India*, would not have recognized her. Here, she is a foul-mouthed, hysterical, insecure, sex-crazed, infantile woman, who has nothing to say but screams it anyway. She is, of course, on the verge of divorce (why not?) from Branagh, an insecure, down-on-his-luck, inept novelist, who remains a celebrity in New York, for who knows what reason. Davis finds a new boyfriend, a celebrity TV producer, who lures her into abandoning her job (Guess what? She teaches English literature) and becoming a gossip TV hostess who interviews (what else?) New York celebrities. Of course, she becomes an instant hit and a celebrity herself. Branagh, meanwhile, picks up new girlfriends (the supermodel tops them all), or they pick him up, while he tries to "finish" his latest novel. The manuscript is tossed into the Hudson by one of these women whom he has left for Wynona Ryder—who also happens to be in this mess.

Nevertheless, Branagh as an actor is matchless. Rather stocky in this one—it took me a minute or two to recognize him—and with a flawless American accent, he hardly reminds you of the fluent Benedict of *Much Ado* or the hapless Hamlet he played only a few years back. I think Allen did himself a favor by letting someone else take his usual role, and I hope he does it again. Branagh is more convincing as a failed lover—flat nose, curly hair, loose pants and shirt, run-down appearance—but he has *some* looks that might attract the opposite sex, while Allen is always a stretch as a lover—even a failed one. Of course, the ladies have always fallen for the latter's wit, indomitable intellectualism, angst, and existential shtick which is stuck in reverse every time he opens his mouth. In Europe they adore him for that; in America he is just a third-rate director, too self-absorbed to entice Main Street.

This switch is a lucky change. Branagh carries the whole thing admirably, if somewhat boringly. After all, he lacks Allen's quizzical facial expressions and irrelevant gestures (who doesn't?). Branagh is both a success and a demotion. The movie compensates, though, with a brief appearance by Leonardo DiCaprio as an amoral young actor, an enraged beast who beats up his girlfriend (Elizabeth Shue, lately an Allen regular), then takes her and Branagh to a getaway where they attend a major orgy, including a lesbian tit-for-tat, before DiCaprio flies to Africa for his next movie. Allen manages to film this as a PG-13 movie. Sheets cover the action. No harm done.

All this is insane, but offered with Allenesque gusto and absence of malice (not that anything is forgiven for that reason). His point is that celebrities—any of them—live pointless, shallow, kinetic, decadent lives, with no regard for anything other than themselves. They are the cream of New York's corrupt crop. This recalls Fellini's *La Dolce Vita*, in which Marcello Mastroianni scours the Roman underground in search of a woman with madonna-like purity. A waitress beckons to him from across a beach, but Marcello, gorged by an all night orgy and blinded by morning sunlight, fails to see her. Similarly, Branagh confesses to the supermodel that she's the loveliest thing in the universe. She thinks he's super and offers to sleep with him right away. Seek and ye shall find.

By the way, T. S. Eliot, a regular Allen footnote, is mentioned too. Branagh, who lives the life of a crab, quotes Prufrock: "I have measured out my life with coffee spoons." Better be "a pair of ragged claws, scuttling across silent seas." Never forget that this movie is intended as literature.

The choice of black and white as a medium for this movie, stunningly photographed by the great Swedish cinematographer Sven Nykvist, remains somewhat of a mystery. To show the darker side of New York City? Maybe. Celebrities, after all, live in a topsy-turvy world. They should be, and are, at the bottom. Human decency belongs at a different altitude.

See you next time, Woody. You're good. You can still make heartless but innocent movies with lots of laughs.

Suggested Readings and Hypertext Links

Beaver, Frank E. *Dictionary of Film Terms: The Aesthetic Companion to Film Analysis*. New York: McGraw-Hill, 1983.

Nelson, Thomas Allen. *Kubrick: Inside a Film Artist's Maze*, expanded ed. Bloomington: Indiana University Press, 2000.

Spoto, Donald. *The Dark Side of Genius: The Life of Alfred Hitchcock*. New York: Econo-Clads Books, 1999.

———. *The Art of Alfred Hitchcock: Fifty Years of Motion Pictures*. New York: Doubleday, 1976.

Scorsese, Martin, and Michael Henry Wilson. *A Personal Journey with Martin Scorsese Through American Movies*. London: Cappa Production, Inc., 1997.

Suggested Films for Study

Psycho (Alfred Hitchcock), DVD Collector's ed. Universal, 1998.

Psycho (Gus Van Sant), DVD Collector's ed. Universal, 1998. With feature commentary by Gus Van Sant, Anne Heche, and Vince Vaughn.

Suggested Black-and-White Films for Study

The Passion of Joan of Arc (1928), dir. Carl T. Dreyer
L'Atalante (1934), dir. Jean Vigo
Top Hat (1935), dir. Mark Sandrich
Wuthering Heights (1939), dir. William Wyler
The Magnificent Ambersons (1942), dir. Orson Welles

Rashomon (1951), dir. Akira Kurosawa
La Strada (1954), dir. Federico Fellini
The Seven Samurai (1956), dir. Akira Kurosawa
Touch of Evil (1958), dir. Orson Welles
The World of Apu (1959), dir. Satyajit Ray
La Dolce Vita (1960), dir. Federico Fellini
Last Year at Marienbad (1961), dir. Alan Resnais
The Testament of Orpheus (1962), dir. Jean Cocteau
Winter Light (1962), dir. Ingmar Bergman
8½ (1963), dir. Federico Fellini
The Trial (1963), dir. Orson Welles
Alphaville (1965), dir. Jean-Luc Godard
Persona (1966), dir. Ingmar Bergman
Manhattan (1979), dir. Woody Allen
Raging Bull (1980), dir. Martin Scorsese

CHAPTER SEVEN

Responding to Foreign Film

How do I respond to foreign film? One should respond to foreign film as one responds to any other film. Viewers can study it as a work of art; for its historical, social, or literary significance; and for various other reasons.

However, certain characteristic approaches to the study of foreign film can help American students understand it better. Film is a single phenomenon, utilizing the same visual means understood by all cultures, all nations, regardless of geographical and historical origin. In the silent era, the films of Charlie Chaplin, Buster Keaton, Douglas Fairbanks Sr., and other well-known actors and directors of that era, whether domestic or foreign, were accessible to audiences throughout the world. Today, lines are drawn mainly on the grounds of language, and thus boundaries divide the films of various nations—whether these be Indian, European, or South American movies. This boundary separates American and non-American movies according to the organization of video store shelves, rental movie catalogs, computer web sites, and newspaper ads. Most movies other than American are dubbed "foreign." Should viewers treat them differently? Before we attempt to answer this and similar questions, let us take a quick glance at the origins of foreign film.

The Origins of International Cinema

Film is international in origin, though many American students, conditioned by the constant influx of Hollywood movies, fail to see this. Though the first man to use a moving camera, the Kinetograph, was Thomas Edison in 1891, the first film was actually shot by the French brothers, Auguste and Louis Lumière. It was called *Workers Leaving the Lumière Factory* and was shown to an audience in Paris, on December 28, 1895. Between 1895 and 1905, the Lumière brothers shot thousands of short subjects on film, using the *Cinematographe*, a combination of motion camera, printer, and projector. Another Frenchman, Georges Méliès, shot *A Trip to the Moon* in 1902, the first film in narrative form. A year later another American, Edwin S. Porter, shot *The Great Train Robbery*, a movie that caused audiences to flee the theater from what they thought was an oncoming train.

The first film studios and companies—Biograph, Mack Sennett, Keystone—were American, but many international companies also originated between 1910 and 1930, such as *Film d' Art* in France. Famous German directors, such as Friedrich Murnau (*Nosferatu* [1922]) and Erich Von Stroheim (*Greed* [1924]), established what came to be known as the school of German Expressionism. The great Russian director and aesthetician Sergei Eisenstein produced *Battleship Potemkin* in 1925. These pioneer filmmakers, including the American D.W. Griffith (*The Birth of a Nation* [1915]), laid the foundations for the development of filmmaking techniques such as lighting, deep focus photography, and montage/editing. Hollywood enjoyed its greatest creative period during the 1930s, '40s, and '50s, the era dominated by the great studios—Paramount, Universal, MGM, and Warner Brothers. During those decades, cinema in other countries was developing along parallel lines, though its development was subject to external factors, such as World War II, which inhibited normal production in France, Italy, and Germany. In fact, international cinema enjoyed a renaissance during the postwar years. French cinema, vibrant in the 1930s with productions such as Jean Renoir's *The Grand Illusion* (1937) and *The Rules of the Game* (1939), came back in the late 1940s with Jean Cocteau's *Beauty and the Beast* (1946) and the productions of such New Wave directors as François Truffaut, Alan Resnais, and Claude Chabrol, along with major cinema theorists like André Bazin. Italian cinema flourished with Neo-Realist directors such as Vittorio De Sica (*Bicycle Thief* [1947]), Roberto Rossellini, and Federico Fellini, whose movies became international hits. Japan gave international cinema Akira Kurosawa (*Rashomon* [1954]) and Kenji Mizoguchi (*Ugetsu*, 1953), India brought us Satyajit Ray (*Pather Panchali* [1955] and *Aparujito* [1956]), Swedish cinema produced Ingmar Bergman (*The Seventh Seal* [1957], *Wild Strawberries* [1958]), and there were significant developments in Polish, Czech, and German cinema in the 1960s. Today, international cinema extends beyond the boundaries of Europe and Japan to Brazil, Argentina, Mexico, Africa, Iran, Greece, China, Australia, and many other countries. International cinema is designated by its production values and film title. International films are listed as "foreign film" in video stores, and the most prominent factor is the film's title, not its director or the nation from which it came. Credits on the back of videocassettes serve as advertisements and do not usually highlight either the director or the film's nationality. American students have to work hard at learning to like foreign film; it is usually an acquired taste. Helpful links on the Internet (see below) will help students locate useful sites and names of film periodicals, international film institutes, and other organizations.

Foreign Film—Unpopular in the American Classroom

By and large, for the reasons outlined above, the response of American students to foreign film has been negative. Again, the main reason is their lack of exposure to foreign film in mainstream movie theaters in the United States. Distributors do not consider foreign films marketable for any number of reasons: European films, especially, are known for their lack of fast action and sometimes for poor production values compared to those in American film. Most foreign films emphasize character rather than plot, and American students may be unfamiliar with exotic locales and foreign customs and may find subtitles tiring. As a result, films from around the world, especially those from Third World countries, do not reach American screens on a regular basis. They are accessible mostly on cable TV (the Bravo channel, for instance), if at all, and some of them arrive with their reputations tarnished. Adrian Lyne's *Lolita* (1998), for example, did not find its way into any U.S. theaters due to its subject matter. It was available only on cable channels and later in video stores. In a less notorious case, Theo Angelopoulos's *Ulysses' Gaze* (1993), a critically acclaimed Greek film tracing conflict in the Balkans, was totally ignored in both theaters and video stores, though it has been released as VHS video. Scores of other neglected foreign films can be cited, for many more films are made in other countries than in the United States: in India alone seven hundred movies are produced every year. It is hard to make a case for a foreign film in the mainstream domestic market these days. The heyday of foreign films in the United States, for the time being at least, is past.

The Decline of Foreign Film

Foreign films were much more accessible to American markets in the 1950s and '60s, mostly because foreign film was considered more daring in matters of sex or graphic violence, and American films were still subject to various U.S. censorship agencies which inhibited the normal artistic evolution of

movies produced by the Hollywood studio system. These agencies, in operation virtually from the film industry's inception, were:

1. The National Association of the Motion Picture Industry (NAMPI),
   which operated from 1916 to 1922
2. The Motion Picture Producers and Distributors of America (MPPDA),
   in operation from 1922 to 1930
3. The Hays Production Code, in force from the 1930s to the early 1960s
4. The Production Code Administration (PCA), operating from 1930 to
   1961

In addition to the above, the Catholic-sponsored Legion of Decency,
which was effective in barring films with such controversial topics as suicide,
adultery, homosexuality, and blasphemy, was also in force until the mid-
1960s. Not until 1968, when the self-regulating system of the Motion Picture Association of America (MPAA) came into existence, did the influx of
foreign movies into mainstream theaters rather than art houses come to a virtual stop. With the advent of sex and violence in R-rated and X-rated U.S.
movies, the movie-going public turned its attention to American-produced
movies. Foreign movies seeped in occasionally, and the most distinguished
ones continued to do so, but they were no longer in the mainstream.

Foreign Film's Heyday

When and how did foreign movies flourish in America? A few instances will
suffice to explain *how*. In 1951 under Chief Justice Tom C. Clark, the United
States Supreme Court ruled that Roberto Rossellini's controversial film *The
Miracle* (the subject of which was a virgin birth) could be exhibited in the
United States. This court decision opened the floodgates for foreign films
with daring subjects to be shown in this country. Roger Vadim's *And God
Created Woman* (1957) with Brigitte Bardot became a hit due to its sexual
content. When Federico Fellini's *La Dolce Vita* premiered in New York City
in 1960, it was a major cinematic event, capturing audiences everywhere, due
partly to its sexual orgy scene (mild by today's standards). Its reputed decadence became its main drawing card. *Never On Sunday* (1961), directed by
Jules Dassin with Melina Mercouri in a mildly ecdysiastic scene, broke attendance records. The films of Ingmar Bergman, less daring in terms of nudity,
dealt with such subjects as rape, incest, and masturbation by female characters
and were avidly attended by a small but devoted group of viewers, especially
on university campuses. Henri-Georges Clouzot's *The Wages of Fear* (1954)

and *Diabolique* (1955) and Jean-Luc Godard's *Breathless* (1959) achieved cult status in the United States. Michael Cacoyannis's *Zorba the Greek* (1964) left fond memories with American viewers for decades. This is not to mention many British movies, from the Otto Rank productions of the late 1940s and early '50s to the so-called New Cinema of Karel Reisz' *Saturday Night and Sunday Morning* (1960) and Tony Richardon's *A Taste of Honey* (1961), *The Loneliness of the Long Distance Runner* (1962), and *Billy Liar* (1963)—all extremely popular in the United States. Regardless of their artistic merits, these foreign films and numerous others remained near enough to the American mainstream until the late 1960s when the various codes were lifted and the rating system supplied a guide to what constituted "adult" movies. Interest in foreign films began to decline drastically, and foreign movies were relegated to the art houses.

The Art-House Movie: Mostly Foreign

In fact *art-house movie* and *art movie* today refer more or less to films of foreign origin, even though some domestic or English movies (Merchant/Ivory productions, for instance) are considered art-house films. More often than not, a foreign movie is shown at an art house movie theater. In the United States, this gives them limited distribution ("selected theaters") in both time and location. The rerelease of the restored Fellini masterpiece, *Nights of Cabiria* (1957), was shown in select cities in select locations for a limited time (summer of 1998), and was attended only by small, though devoted, groups of cineastes. Limited engagements restrict attendance. If one cannot find a film in the neighborhood video store, one cannot see it. These same factors inhibit production and production values. Art-house filmmakers know that their movies are made on small budgets and without big box-office names. Martin Scorsese's *Taxi-Driver* (1976) was made on a shoestring budget, but, despite low expectations, it had a good run at the box office. Such exceptions do happen, but by and large, art-house movies—including most foreign movies—do poorly at the box office despite carefully written and thoughtful scripts and fine characterization. Today's audiences, conditioned by explosions, bloodbaths, and provocative sexual content, refuse to watch the quieter and slower narratives typical of most foreign movies. Aside from Bravo, classic cable TV channels like TCM (Turner Classic Movies) and AMC (American Movie Classics) specialize in older American movies. Pay channels like HBO and Cinemax will show foreign movies occasionally (and some good ones too), but most of them are buried in the middle of the night and are usually heavy in sexual content. Thus the distinction between American and foreign film is preserved on cable TV.

More Contrasts Between Foreign
and Domestic Films

There are other reasons for foreign film's decline in recent decades: intellectual content, perceived or real, has become a disadvantage for foreign film. The principle of "immediate gratification" became prevalent in the 1980s and continues today to motivate the average moviegoer, whether at the theater or in the video store. Movies are entertainment—they always have been—and, indeed, the cheapest and most available form of it. For about $3.79, viewers can rent their favorite movies, and the whole family can enjoy them. One rarely sees family groups renting foreign movies. Who wants to read subtitles? American movies offer fast action, special effects, plot twists, happy endings, and glossy stars. Julia Roberts (*Notting Hill* [1999]), Leonardo DiCaprio

Nights of Cabiria *is a poignant portrayal of the dashing of a spirited soul's dreams. Rooted in World-War II neo-realism, the film draws on disturbing post-war images of Italian society to express the ravaged feelings of its protagonist.*

(*Titanic* [1997]), and Tom Cruise (*Magnolia* [1999]) are familiar names. Victor Banerjee (*A Passage to India* [1984]), Fernanda Montenegro (*Central Station* [1998]), and Franka Potente (*Run, Lola, Run* [1999]) are not. Most American films provide lively entertainment. The producers know what their customers want and are happy to oblige, as most Hollywood fare is escapist, designed for mass appeal and mass consumption. It must not be too serious, must not challenge the audience's intellectual powers. It aims to make the audience "feel good." With honorable exceptions, this has been the film industry's goal from the outset. A French film like *My Favorite Season* (1997) with Catherine Deneuve and Daniel Auteuil was the Official Selection of the Cannes Film Festival and got favorable notices from American critics (*Entertainment Weekly*, Siskel & Ebert). But it made no dent in either domestic distribution or video stores (though it has been picked up by Fox Lorber for a DVD edition). On the other hand, the film *Ever After* (1998), with such bankable stars as Drew Barrymore and Angelica Huston, tells a typical Cinderella story, so you know the servant girl will marry the prince despite the wicked stepmother's plotting. It has done well at both the box office and the video store. One need not go too far into the past to make this comparison: Biblical and historical epics such as the *Ten Commandments* (1956), *Ben-Hur* (1958), and *Spartacus* (1960) were far greater box office successes here and abroad than Antonioni's *L'Avventura* (1960), which has frequently been cited by international critics' polls as one of the ten best movies of all time. The aforementioned epics contain war scenes, a massive biblical exodus, a famous chariot race, naval battles, and other spectacular events that display Hollywood's superior technical achievements in moviemaking. These films and dozens of their kind are epics not only because of their subject matter, but also because of the spectacles they provide. Epics, as defined by Hollywood, are not thinking movies. A movie like *L'Avventura*, made on a tiny budget and with an enigmatic plot resolution, challenges the audience to ponder the collapse of human relationships among a small circle of people. Another meritorious foreign movie, Satyajit Ray's *Ghare Babire* (*The Home and the World* [1984]) is a sensitive story about woman's liberation in Indian's caste-conscious society, and it has disappeared from the video stores. Late Fellini movies like *Roma* (1972), *Amarcord* (1974), and *Intervista* (1987) have not enjoyed mainstream distribution either in theaters or in video stores, and the distinguished movies of Lina Wertmüller (*Swept Away* [1975], *Seven Beauties* [1976]), made in the 1970s, can be seen only in chopped up versions on Bravo (and, luckily, in some recently restored DVD versions). In fact, with Fox Lorber's recent transfers of Jean-Luc Godard's *Alphaville* (1964) and *Pierrot Le Fou* (1965), it seems that contemporary viewers may have found at least one new, though limited, avenue of approach to foreign film on laser and DVD.

A Distinguished Foreign Film: *Claire's Knee*

By Hollywood and box office standards, foreign films are slow-paced and talky. Let us look at one example, the critically honored *Claire's Knee* (*Le Genou de Claire* [1969], directed by Eric Rohmer), one of this filmmaker's six "moral tales" (*contes moraux*). The movie received the "Best Picture of the Year" award from the National Society of Film Critics. The subject matter of the six tales (which include *A Night at Maud's* [1970] and *Chloe in the Afternoon* [1976]) is the same: an amoral man crosses certain boundaries, mostly involving fidelity to the opposite sex, and faces the consequences. The theme is Gidean and existential. What matters in this case is Rohmer's technique and narrative method. The story has the barest of plots and is based on a single episode: Jerome is a writer vacationing at a lakeshore resort he hasn't visited in years. He meets an old flame, Aurora, also a writer, and begins a series of conversations with her, mostly about his love adventures. He tells her he is about to be married to Lucinde, a woman he has known for six years (and who never enters the story). Aurora introduces him to a family also vacationing there, a mother with two teenaged daughters by two different husbands. While verbally flirting with Aurora, Jerome has a brief affair with Laura, the older daughter, who is sixteen but looks younger. Then he moves on to Claire, her stepsister, who is blond, prettier, and less communicative. Jerome develops an obsession for Claire, but has only one wish—to touch her knee. His wish is fulfilled during a rainstorm on a sheltered spot on the lake, where he cruelly reveals to Claire her boyfriend's infidelities. As she breaks down and becomes vulnerable, he refrains from assaulting her (which he assumes she expects) and only touches her knee with his hand. His gesture is not resisted, and that's all that happens. All this he confesses to Aurora, who serves as his moral counterpoint, in a series of casual conversations. The story, which takes place in the month of July, is presented in diary form with a date flashed on the screen to preface each episode. He explains that his behavior was an act of will—he had to be "heroic" to do what he did. He believes Claire accepted his gesture as a caress meant to comfort her in her distress. He claims something good will come out of this, even for Claire who from now on will know better about choosing boyfriends. His vacation ends and he leaves, saying goodbye to Aurora. Claire's boyfriend comes along, and he and Claire reconcile.

The film bears an uncanny similarity to Kubrick's (and Lyne's) *Lolita*, at least in its subject matter (a middle-aged man's obsession with a teenaged girl) and could in fact be a French version of *Lolita*. A middle-aged man, a writer (like Humbert Humbert), develops an obsession for a teenaged siren— or two. His obsession overwhelms him and makes him seek a connection—in this case, the touching of her knee. However, here the similarities end. The French movie is subtler. Though it is called a "moral tale," there is no overt moral tagged on to the story. The story just wraps itself up in an open-ended fashion. There is no moralizing by Jerome or Aurora, and whether anyone learned anything from these events remains a question. Nor is there the emphatic categorization of the young girl(s) as a nymphet, a "demonic" child, made by Nabokov and subsequently implied on film by both Kubrick and Lyne. The latters' Lolitas are destructive and self-destructive, while both Humberts are weak-willed perverts with minor redeeming qualities here and there. On the other hand, both young girls in the Rohmer movie are normal, well-bred teenaged girls behaving according to the mores of their era and class. Laura is extravagantly intellectual and experimental, while Claire is ordinary (even a little banal) and is concerned only about her relationship with her boyfriend. Jerome may be characterized as amoral in the sense that he explores the trickier boundaries of permissiveness, but he does what he does in broad daylight, and all his "experiments" have been confessed in advance to Aurora his mentor, the definer of his moral perimeters, and his amused commentator. Aurora is somewhat bewildered by Jerome's eccentric behavior, but she does not fail to tell him the truth to his face each time. The morality tale lies not in the moralistic tone of the story—there is none—but in the dialectic of the story, in its nuances, in Jerome's perpetual re-evaluation of his perilous actions. Jerome could have been jailed for touching Claire's knee or even for moving a little further toward her. He knows how close to real danger he has come, and he leaves congratulating himself. Whether this is success or not, the story leaves to the viewer's speculation. The dialectic is carried on through extensive dialogue, hence the "slowness" of the movie. No real aesthete of movie art would mind, though; the movie is dazzlingly photographed and exquisitely edited, and its moral is delicately balanced between the extremes of amorality and overt moralizing.

Another French Film of Merit: *Pierrot le Fou*

Pierrot le Fou (1965), directed by Jean-Luc Godard, is another case in point. The title means Pierrot the Fool. It's a film one rarely hears of, and if one has, that is now forgotten. Viewers are mainly attracted by two names, Jean-Paul Belmondo and Jean-Luc Godard, two gods of the French cinema. They remember *Breathless* (1959), a film that broke new ground because of its techniques, had a substantial international run, and was an art-house hit in the United States. Its American remake with Richard Gere (1983), an excellent movie in itself, carries its existential pathos to an extreme but does not have the innovative technical superiority of the original. In many ways *Pierrot Le Fou* is a continuation of the themes and techniques used in *Breathless*. The same abrupt cuts, the same intrusion into the narrative by an extraneous voice, the same disruption between the signifier and the signified, usually so seamless in mainstream cinema. For instance, in *Pierrot Le Fou* the voice of the protagonist reads his diary notes of his adventure, thus distancing viewers from the immediate action, forcing them to think of fate, freedom, and other themes superimposed on the narrative structure. Other means are used, all of them cinematic: paintings of modern masters—Picasso, Renoir, and others—intrude on the screen, adding visual dimension to the themes of disruption and the chaos of life, although the art itself is beautiful and meaningful. Politics is introduced in images of burning Vietnamese villages. Montage breaks the continuity of time and space. Add the voice of the protagonist Marianne (Anna Carina), who sings and dances some of her thoughts. The name Pierrot is itself artificial; the man's name is Ferdinand (Belmondo), but she calls him Pierrot (Little Peter, a clown's name) the fool or madman. Nothing in the film is exactly real or literal, but the action occurs on the realistic level, though it is also dreamlike and surrealistic. Dino de Laurentis's lush photography adds to the impressionism of the movie. This innovative film combines painting and color, and an extra dimension possible only in film, which is comprised of many voices: painting, sound and music, movement, discursive language (many axes and nodes), and philosophic tone. To this, add an element of surrealism, for one feels that a dream is unfolding. This is a movie nobody in America could make or has made. Some audiences would find it deadly boring and would run out of the theater halfway through, but to the connoisseur of cinematic art, this is a little treasure of delights, both visual and contemplative.

Pierrot le Fou has been compared to Bonnie and Clyde, which was made three years later, but it has a rather meager storyline. A young man in his early thirties is married to a rich but indifferent wife. He runs off with the babysitter, who is an old flame, leaving his wife at a decadent party. Ferdinand knew Marianne, years ago, and now they meet again, accidentally. She's mixed up with gangsters, but he doesn't know that, nor would it matter. They go on a spree in the "south of France" and live by stealing cars, robbing, and living like castaways on a deserted beach. Each time she calls him Pierrot, he corrects her. He is a fool, though she does not call him *that*. She's as beautiful as a movie actress and everybody notices her, so she wants to escape from him when his company begins to tire her. Several dubious characters appear, claiming she has stolen a sum of money from them. She presumably kills one of them, and the rest of the action is both complicated and terribly unrealistic. The sets are exquisite, the beaches glorious, the Mediterranean as azure as in an expressionist painting. These castaways never eat, of course, and they are constantly doing meaningless things—dancing, singing, or just looking at each other, bored.

What makes this picture so attractive, despite its incoherence and seeming lack of aim? Aside from De Laurentis's exquisite cinematography, the movie is watchable for a couple of reasons: as a study in the New Wave cinema of Godard, or as a commentary on existentialism, a philosophy/way of life which in France and elsewhere has been widely accepted. As in *Breathless*, two young people run away because they are tired of bourgeois existence that offers little to the existentialist. The two castaways have freedom, and *joi de vivre*, but their adventure seems empty. They hang around on beaches and mix with gangsters, but Pierre doesn't seem to want anything. Marianne really wants the stolen 20,000 dollars, and she runs away with it. Pierrot tracks her down and kills her and her male companion, then blows himself up with explosives.

Existentialism presents a choice which offers freedom, but freedom in itself is useless and even dangerous. The American movie *Bonnie and Clyde* is careful to say that all this—the tragic ending—is a result of a bad system. Wasn't Bonnie a poet? Had the system been better, she might have been teaching at a university instead of robbing banks. Ah, there's the rub! Establish social justice, as they say, and none of this would happen. In France, though, social justice wouldn't mean a thing. People would run from it too. Existentialism—nihilism—is there a difference?

Philosophy aside, *Pierrot Le Fou* is a triumph of cinematic art: it combines painting, sound, montage, camera movement, voice-over, allegory and symbolism, abstractions and myths—not to mention war imagery—all of which provide a cinematic challenge to discerning viewers. On top of this, it is said that Godard shot the movie *without a script*.

Foreign Films for Study

Whether students opt to study foreign film by chance, on purpose, or because they are obliged to watch them in a class, there are many good choices. Students can select films by searching web sites, or they can pick films that have won prizes in international film festivals—the Cannes Film Festival, Sundance Film Festival, Venice Film Festival, Toronto Film Festival, Australian Film Institute—or films nominated for Golden Globe Awards or Oscars. Histories and encyclopedias of foreign film (see Suggested Readings) will give students a chronological and historical orientation. In fact, a historical study of international film may be the best beginning, and some films discussed in this chapter would be suitable. Keeping tabs on films one wishes to see, in some order of importance, is a good approach. Background information, even what appears in the most basic movie and video guides, helps make some distinctions and get things started. Taking a class in foreign film is bound to help an eager learner. The language may be a problem, but with multiple audio tracks in DVD, audiences can hear a French or Brazilian movie in English, and conversely, an American movie in French or another language. Technology will eventually demolish the linguistic barrier, though it is a good idea to listen, for instance, to *Life Is Beautiful* in Italian and read its subtitles. Students of English in other countries often confess to having learned English by watching American movies, which may be an incentive to American students to imitate the process. Film teaches in more ways than one.

Students might select:

- Jean-Luc Godard's *Breathless* (1950)
- Ingmar Bergman's *Wild Strawberries* (1959) and several of his subsequent films
- Alain Resnais' *Hiroshima, Mon Amour* (1960) and *Last Year at Marienbad* (1961)
- François Truffaut's *Jules and Jim* (1961), which shows the failed relationship between two men and a woman, stressing film sensibility, an arty disposition, and character development
- Federico Fellini's *8½*, the first major movie to "deconstruct" the artist's self-projection (Woody Allen's Deconstructing Harry [1997] is its modern counterpart) is frequently mentioned as one of the ten greatest movies ever made
- Louis Bunuel's *Belle de Jour*, Ingmar Bergman's *Persona*, and Eric Rohmer's *Chloe in the Afternoon* (1978)—all favorites with film classes and available in most video stores
- Lina Wertmüller's *Seven Beauties* (1976), a stunning film that outlines the adventures of a macho Italian man surviving in a German concentration camp
- Ingmar Bergman's *Autumn Sonata* (1978) and Claude Sautet's *Un Coeur en Hiver* (1993), both stories of unusual intensity and profound characterization
- Claude Berri's *Jean de Florette* (1985) and *Manon of the Spring* (1986), an outstanding narrative and its sequel that struck gold in mainstream American movie houses
- Akira Kurosawa's *Ran* (1986) and *Dreams* (1991), perhaps the outstanding last testaments of this great director and deserving of much attention
- Bernardo Bertolucci's *The Last Emperor* (1988) and Chen Kaige's *Farewell, My Concubine* (1995)—both popular with American audiences
- Roberto Benigni's *Johnny Stecchino* (1995)
- Theo Angelopoulos' *Eternity and a Day* (1998) from Greece
- Serbo-Croatian Emir Kusturica's *Black Cat, White Cat* (1998)
- Abbas Kiarostami's *Taste of Cherry* (1998) from Iran
- Jean-Pierre and Luc Dardennes' *Rosetta* (1999) from Belgium
- François Girard's *The Red Violin* (1998) from Canada

Film for Study: *Eternity and a Day* (1998)

Directed and written by Theo Angelopoulos
Music by Eleni Karaindrou
Cinematography by Yiorgos Arvanitis

Background: The Greek film industry flourished after World War II until the mid-1960s, producing films that won international acclaim, such as *Stella* (1956) with Melina Mercouri, directed by Michael Cacoyannis; *Never on Sunday* (1960), directed by Jules Dassin; *Guns of Navarone* (1960); and *Zorba the Greek* (1964). It was silenced under the dictatorship (1967–1974), but was revived in the 1970s, mainly through the leadership of Theo Angelopoulos, who was a newspaper critic in the 1960s and indirectly denounced the Greek dictatorship of the colonels with his first film. His major films are: *Reconstruction (Anaparastasi* [1970]), a critique of the military junta that ruled Greece from 1967 to 1974; *Traveling Players (O Thiassos* [1975]), which follows a group of itinerants around Greece, reconstructing Greek history from 1939 to 1950; *The Hunters (I Kynigi* [1977]), which recounts the years of Greek Civil War (1947–1951); *Alexander the Great (Magalexandros)*, which won the Venice Film Festival's Golden Lion, in 1980; *Taxidi sta Kithira (Trip to Kythira)*, which won Best Screenplay at Cannes in 1984; and *The Beekeeper (O Mielissocomos* [1986]); *Landscape in the Mist (Topeio Stin Omixli* [1988]); *Ulysses' Gaze (To Vlema Tou Odyssea* [1995]), which concerns a Greek American who returns to the Balkans during the war in Bosnia in search of a film documentary made about the Balkan conflicts earlier in the century, only to encounter the disintegration of communism and the tragic chaos in Bosnia.

Angelopoulos' films are characterized by *length*, slow pace, poetic language (long shots, smooth sequences), and utter seriousness. His themes are the geopolitics of the Balkans, revisionist Greek history, the influence of the past on the present, and perceiving the past through the present. In *Ulysses' Gaze*, he expresses hope that one day the Balkans will be united in spirit and brotherhood.

Eternity and a Day (Mia Aeoniotita kai mia Mera) runs about two-and-a-half hours. It is a visually impressive film with an unusual number of long shots and startling images: crowds with umbrellas, wide views of damp streets, a green bus photographed from the side and occupying the entire screen, beaches where blue water beckons, a magnificent rock, a rain storm (in which people actually get wet from the rain, not doused by sprinkler water!). Credit goes to Yiorgos Arvanitis for the magnificent photography and kudos to Eleni Karaindrou, who once again (as in *Ulysses' Gaze*) comes up with a hypnotic and energizing score. The movie is visual and musical—a grand aesthetic treat, a feast for the senses.

The story is somewhat unusual, since nothing much happens. Alexandros, a writer dying of an incurable disease, leaves his house to enter a hospital where he encounters a young boy. They begin a life together. The boy is a parentless Albanian refugee expatriated to Greece during the 1990s, living on the streets. The film does not focus on the boy's background (we never know where he came from) but rather on the appeal he has for Alexandros. The boy is not of Greek-Albanian descent, but he does speak good Greek which he evidently picked up from his neighbors in an Albanian Greek village. He knows some unusual words—*korfoula, xenitis, argini*—which remind Alexandros of Greece's national poet Dionysios Solomos. Solomos, who lived and studied in Italy until he was twenty, tried to learn Greek by paying the villagers of Zante (Zakynthos) to gather words for him. Solomos wanted to learn the language as quickly as possible so he could write Greek poetry dedicated to the cause of Greece's liberation. His "The Hymn to Liberty," a poem modeled after Shelley's "Hellas," became Greece's national anthem.

In the movie, Solomos is a pivotal metaphor for Alexandros himself. Solomos was an artist/poet of the highest caliber, equal—at his best—to any other Greek poet or to any of his Romantic contemporaries (Byron, Shelley, Hugo, Lamartine, Foscolo) in Italy, France, and England. Solomos not only learned Greek, he became a great wordsmith, chiseling verses of unsurpassed classic harmony balanced by romantic feeling. His greatest poem, which the movie dwells on extensively, is "The Free Besieged" (*Eleftheroi Poliorkimenoi*), which remains unfinished. Only fragments—exquisite pieces of yearning verses juxtaposing death to life—have come down to posterity. The "besieged" were the inhabitants of Missolonghi (a town in western Greece where Byron died), who preferred to starve rather than give up to the Turks who had surrounded their city. They ate corpses, cats, and dogs rather than surrender. In what survives of his lyric poem Solomos expressed his yearning for life among the ruins of death. Angelopoulos seizes upon this literary and human tragedy to infuse the spirit of Alexandros, who aspires to finish Solomos' poem. He is seen boarding a bus in a black hat and coat or sauntering in his garden, reciting his verses. Both Alexandros and Solomos are emblems of Greece's past and present, of a country that has remained "unfinished" despite centuries of existence. "Greece is through," a taxi driver in *Ulysses' Gaze* remarks to Harvey Keitel. Endless wars—Balkan wars, World Wars, a civil war, occupations, dictatorships, border disputes, a deluge of refugees— are the signs of natural and moral disintegration of a geographical area never stable to begin with. Always on the verge of a renaissance, modern Greece never quite makes it. Alexandros himself is an expression of Greek pessimism: he will die before he finishes an unfinished masterpiece by a fellow poet. He leaves behind an alienated daughter and an elderly, bedridden mother, and his visions of his dead wife are little more than alluring specters on an enchanted beach. However, his life gains some momentum when he befriends the abandoned

Albanian boy. Here is Angelopoulos' vision: A poem is metaphorically "finished," and a border has been crossed at the same time. Greeks have lived in southern Albania (*Voreios Epiros*) for many centuries. Some of them, as well as other Albanians, crossed the borders after the disintegration of the communist regime in the mid 1990s. Their situation is analogous to that of Cuban exiles in southern Florida. Most crossed illegally, but many have been accepted and now live productive and decent lives. But many tragedies occurred too. The film shows groups of refugees seized and deported. Some died. The Albanian boy is an Elian Gonzalez to Alexandros, and he becomes joyous in his recollections and musical fantasies, his dreams mixing with relentless reality. In a sense, he "finishes" his poem by meeting the boy.

The lengthy film meanders through landscape, recollection, and musical extravaganza for nearly two-and-a-half hours. With all his poetic imagery, all the armor of dazzling cinematography, Angelopoulos does not altogether avoid the pitfalls of sentimentality. Alexandros is played by Italian actor Bruno Ganz, who is obviously not very fluent in Greek (nor is Harvey Keitel, who stumbles mutely through *Ulysses' Gaze*, a good actor unable to express himself). Ganz's whole performance lacks spark. He is literally dying. Though he sees a doctor, his death is never attributed to a cause, so it seems metaphorical, like everything else in this movie. Many viewers complained about the film's slow pace, but slow pace can be accepted, as it is in Antonioni's and Kurosawa's films. The problem is that Alexandros seems to lack purpose as a real, live person. His dream world is shown to us by the camera, telling us what to think and feel. But Alexandros is himself a specter, unable to escape his atrophied screen presence for lack of anything to *do*. He is real when, for instance, he buys the boy a sandwich. He comes to life when the rain pours down and he tries to help others find shelter in a cave, but on the whole he is catatonic, wandering about listlessly in his heavy dark overcoat, oblivious to the weather and everything else.

His individual story lacks an "objective correlative," a "chain of events" to arouse our emotions and awaken our interest in him. There is beauty in his vision, but there is no pity and no fear at the end. Aristotle's and T. S. Eliot's formulas still work and are indications of an artist's ability to create a living story. This may be unfair to Angelopoulos, who has a great vision of reality, but his reality is offered in segments in the individual vignettes of this and some previous movies. Many small stories, brilliant as they may be, do not necessarily add up to a large story.

Much beauty here, though. And that should not be neglected.

Watching a Foreign Film Today

The list of outstanding foreign films of the last several decades is extremely long, and only touched upon here. The slow pace of foreign movies does not generally appeal to audiences used to Hollywood's fast tempo. Foreign films are often more complex, and, in the long run, more rewarding. This is not to underestimate the power of American movies, which have always produced film giants, but foreign film easily wins the day when it comes to quality and quantity of significant films. If film belongs in a college curriculum, foreign film must certainly be a part of it.

Suggested Readings and Hypertext Links

Elert, Nicole V., James Vinson, Nicholas Thomas, et al., eds. *International Dictionary of Films and Filmmakers*.: St. James Press, 1990–1996.
Paris, James Reid. *Classic Foreign Films: From 1960 to Today*. New York: Citadel Press, 1993.
Sarris, Andrew, ed. *The St. James Film Directors Encyclopedia*. New York: Visible Ink Press, 1997.

Australian Film Commission News. <http://www.afc.gov.au/news/summary>
British Film Institute—Sight & Sound. <http://www.bfi.org.uk/s&s>
Canadian Journal of Film Studies. <http://www.film.queensu.ca/FSAC/CJFS.html>
FILM International (Iranian film journal). <http://www.neda.net/film/>
Film Journal International: <http://smartdev.com/titlesq.htm>
Filmkultura (Hungarian/English journal). <http://www.filmkultura.iif.hu:8080/contents.en.html>
The Lumière Brothers First Films, laserdisc ed. King Video, 1997.

Suggested Foreign Films for Study

Battleship Potemkin (1925), dir. Sergei Eisenstein
The Rules of the Game (1939), dir. Jean Renoir
Black Orpheus (1958), dir. Marcel Camus
Breathless (1961), dir. Jean-Luc Godard
La Notte (1961), dir. Michelangelo Antonioni
Through a Glass Darkly (1961), dir. Ingmar Bergman
Viridiana (1961), dir. Luis Buñuel
Jules and Jim (1962), dir. François Truffaut

Knife in the Water (1962), dir. Roman Polanski
The Leopard (1963), dir. Luchino Visconti
Gertrud (1964), dir. Carl Theodor Dreyer
The Gospel According to St. Matthew (1964), dir. Pier Paolo Pasolini
Woman in the Dunes (1964), dir. Hiroshi Teshigahara
Loves of a Blonde (1966), dir. Milos Forman
La Guerre Est Finie (1966), dir. Alain Resnais
The Garden of the Finzi-Continis (1970), dir. Vittorio De Sica
Il Conformista (1971), dir. Bernardo Bertolucci
Aguirre, the Wrath of God (1973), dir. Werner Herzog
Picnic at Hanging Rock (1975), dir. Peter Weir
Seven Beauties (1976), dir. Lina Wertmüller
The Marriage of Maria Braun (1978), dir. Rainer Werner Fassbinder
Confidence (1979), dir. Istvan Szabo
Mephisto (1981), dir. Istvan Szabo
Das Boot (1982), dir. Wolfgang Petersen
The Gods Must Be Crazy (1984), dir. Jamie Uys
Ran (1985), dir. Akira Kurosawa
Babette's Feast (1987), dir. Gabriel Axel
Pelle the Conqueror (1988), dir. Bille August
Wings of Desire (1988), dir. Wim Wenders
The Vanishing (1993), dir. George Sluizer
Vanya on 42nd Street (1994), dir. Louis Malle
Insomnia (1997), dir. Erik Skjoldbjaerg
Eternity and a Day (1998), dir. Theo Angelopoulos
Taste of Cherry (1998), dir. Abbas Kiarostami
All About My Mother (1999), dir. Pedro Almodóvar

CHAPTER EIGHT

Responding to Film's Literary Sources

How do I respond to a film's literary sources? To deal with this important question, one must deal first with a series of smaller ones:

- What is the relation of a film to its literary source?
- What are the origins of literary adaptations?
- Why does film often fail to measure up to its literary master source?

Literature has held a dominant position in western and world cultures for thousands of years, so it is natural for it to frown upon newcomers and on usurpers of the art of narrative. Film *is* a relative newcomer, but in the short span of a hundred years it has achieved both glamour and unmatched popularity. Cinema art seems almost inconceivable without the literary predecessor on which it has depended and from which it has borrowed the narrative form. It seemed like a courtship, this meeting of the younger with the older art. But when a conjugal relationship was attempted, the strain of that union threatened to snap the connection. Will this marriage continue to thrive? Or is it doomed to tension and divorce?

Can a Film Measure Up to Its Literary Source?

Knowing that films have frequently been derived from literary works such as novels, plays, poems, etc., one has to make a distinction between a film and its original source, if there is one. In the case of well-known literary works, the question often arises of whether the film measures up to the merits of the work from which it was adapted. This point is frequently debated, and answers are often far from unanimous or satisfactory.

Generally, many viewers and critics agree that films fail to rise to the level of the literary works they imitate. This opinion has created a bias against film vis-à-vis literature, a bias which is hard to shake. To achieve objectivity on this topic is of utmost importance. Viewers must consider many factors, some of which will be examined in this chapter. It would be presumptuous to assume that genius is granted abundantly to novelists and playwrights whose works are translated into films, but is denied to filmmakers who make literary adaptations. Many masters—E. M. Forster, for instance—stubbornly refused to allow their works to be made into films. Not until the death of this author in 1971 did his famous novels *Room with a View* (1985), *A Passage to India* (1984), *Maurice* (1987), and *Howard's End* (1994) become distinguished films.

Origins and Limitations of Literary Adaptations

When and how did film begin to borrow from literary works?

Since its inception at the beginning of the twentieth century, film has borrowed stories from the stage and the novel. When early filmmakers Georges Méliès in France and Edwin S. Porter in America decided to replace Kinetoscope's shows—dances, prize-fighting, target-shooting—with narratives, the motion picture industry found itself in dire need of suitable subject matter, stories that could be readily adapted to film. Stage plays were already in place, ready to provide stories for dramatic performance, but moviemakers preferred to use the great nineteenth-century novels. Among these were Jules Verne's novel *Trip to the Moon* (1902), *Uncle Tom's Cabin* (1903), *Ben-Hur* (1907), *The Scarlet Letter* (1909), *Vanity Fair* (1911), and *The Count of Monte Cristo* (1913). The novels of Dickens, in particular, were in great demand during those early days of moviemaking, though most of them were filmed as speedy, popular one-reelers. The process of turning fiction into movies had begun, and it was routine for filmmakers to use novels as the primary material for a film throughout the twentieth century. Some of the greatest films ever made were based on novels, usually novels of the popular variety: *Ben-Hur* (1907, 1926, and 1957), *The Three Musketeers* (1946, 1974), *Frankenstein* (1931, 1973, 1984), *Gone With the Wind* (1939), *The Great Gatsby* (1946, 1974), and *Dracula* (1931, 1973, 1979), to mention some of the best known examples. This practice has continued into modern times, and the novels of best-selling authors Stephen King, John Grisham, Tom Clancy, and many others, have become popular films. The works of modern literary masters Kurt Vonnegut Jr. (*Slaughterhouse Five* [1972]) and Flannery O'Connor (*Wise Blood* [1979]) have also turned into worthwhile literary films.

Sometimes, however, film adaptations of great literary works make mediocre or disappointing films. There has never been an adaptation of Thomas Mann's *The Magic Mountain*, no satisfactory version of Homer's *The Odyssey*, and until the 1990s no good adaptations of Jane Austen's novels. There have been no worthwhile film versions of Cervantes' *Don Quixote*, Dante's *The Inferno*, or Jonathan Swift's *Gulliver's Travels*, though several below-par television miniseries have been produced. To its credit, British television—the BBC, often in conjunction with the American A&E Channel—has produced works of Tolstoy, Dickens, Thackeray, George Eliot, and many other novelists whose works demand a longer treatment than feature film can give. What has prevented some literary works, especially some great classics, from becoming films of equivalent merit? This question is complex, and answers are bound to differ. It is necessary to deal with it piecemeal as we progress through this chapter. The simplest and most direct explanation is that film is a visual medium and most of the problems arise in translating discursive language signals into moving images that require different spatiotemporal relationships. The translators—that is, the screenwriters and moviemakers—must know the language of both mediums and must be adept at transferring one language form into the other. A novel is not restricted by temporal limits; it has much more space and time for details and offers a larger span than film does for story complications and descriptive passages. Failure or omission to include these may have an adverse effect—thinner plot, elimination of characters—on film. Such omissions, though occasionally turned to advantage, often work against the visual medium, especially since film requires a running time of about two hours, often not enough time to dramatize a massive novel. Viewers feel cheated by these omissions, especially if they are familiar with the original work.

Film and the Literary Tradition

Another problem difficult to ignore is that literature enjoys a three-thousand-year-old tradition which includes embedded critical commentary and various schools of interpretation. A filmmaker who attempts his own version of a literary work is bound to run into intense critical scrutiny when, for instance, he films Shakespeare's *Hamlet*. Countless screen and TV versions of it, including several good ones, have fallen short of the original stage play in stature. The same is true of Homer's *The Odyssey:* The 1956 version, with Kirk Douglas and Sylvana Mangano, is a parody of the original; and the 1997 TV version relies more on spectacle than on fidelity or quality. Filmmakers have not been able to deal successfully with such classics as *The Scarlet Letter, Moby Dick, Tom Sawyer,* or *Huckleberry Finn* despite numerous TV and film versions (especially of the last two, which are usually perceived as unambitious family fare). Generally, as unfavorable comparisons come to bear on the new medium, a film based on a classic novel, play, or epic is bound to suffer by comparison. Classical literature commands respect, even awe. Film, a century old, has yet to win such respect despite its undeniable popularity. Thus, the literary tradition itself works against the establishment of a critical canon for film comparable in size and reputation to that of literature. Insufficient time has passed to prove the durability of film as an art form. Though the French critic André Bazin (19) says that film has affected and been affected by painting, film has not yet acquired the status painting enjoys. No great art monuments—no Parthenons, no pyramids, no Davids, no Mona Lisas, no *Iliads,* no *Divine Comedys,* no *Macbeths*—exist, Oscar night notwithstanding. Of course, film viewers (though they may be discriminating) know this. Consequently, they do not accord film the respect due to an art. Movies were conceived as popular entertainment, not art. Art is elitist; one must go to a museum to see it. Movies are, to paraphrase, "the opium of the masses," available at the neighborhood movie house. The coming of the VCR and the video store may have accelerated this tendency to see film as non-art or inferior art, for viewers are unlikely to lavish respectful attention on a tape rented for three dollars to pass two idle hours on a rainy night. The classic book or art work demands more attention, possibly even more concentration, and that alone elevates its stature. Nor have schools accorded film studies sufficient space in the curriculum. Studies in the humanities, where film mostly belongs, are filled with courses in literature but not in film. Luckily this is changing. For one thing, film studies are now found in categories such as history, communications, social studies, religion, philosophy, etc. But until recently, film was hurt by its categorization as entertainment (the "entertainment industry"), reduced to the status of "popular" art—not serious art. The fact that film can teach as well as any other medium is not sufficiently stressed. Chaplin's *The Great Dictator* and Roberto Benigni's *Life Is Beautiful,* for instance, can teach as much about the history of World War II and the persecution of the Jews as any literary work of the twentieth century. These contributions have not been sufficiently recognized. When *Schindler's List* (an adaptation of Thomas Keneally's book) appeared in 1993, critics and audiences alike realized that film had achieved its potential both as a powerful medium on its own and as a legitimate translator of literary works. When this recognition is fully achieved by both critics and college curriculum committees, film will take its rightful place in the pantheon of great arts. A great literary work may even gain new readers when its screen version appears. This has actually happened with works of Shakespeare, Austen, and Dickens. In fact, today a reversal is occurring: a film can and does spark interest in the written form, and many a popular film has ben "novelized," published as a novel based on the script of a successful film—e.g., novelizations of *The Patriot* and *Gladiator*, two recent blockbuster films. A few years ago, when *Sense and Sensibility* was adapted by Emma Thompson from Jane Austen's literary masterpiece and became a popular movie, she was asked to "novelize" her own script. She rejected the idea with horror.

Hollywood Adaptations: Mediocre Productions

The cause of literary adaptations has not been helped by the numerous poorly made film versions of great literary works produced during the early and middle twentieth century. Most of the blame for this goes to the Hollywood studio system whose main concerns were popular entertainment and box office returns, not the production of accurate or complex versions of demanding literary works. Hollywood projected star power, simplified story lines, added fast action, and inserted happy endings (for the most part). Thus, literary works such as *The Scarlet Letter* (1926, 1934, 1945), *Wuthering Heights* (1939), *Jane Eyre* (1934, 1944, 1971, 1996), *The Great Gatsby* (1949, 1974), and others became average melodramas, some worthy of attention (and quite popular), but none equal in stature to the original. Of course, there were notable exceptions, mostly made outside Hollywood: Anthony Asquith's *Pygmalion* (1938) was in every way worthy of the original George Bernard Shaw play; David Lean's adaptations of *Great Expectations* (1947) and *Oliver Twist* (1948) were movies of merit, corresponding at least in spirit to the original Dickens works. But by and large, the golden era of the Hollywood studio system, which lasted for several decades (1930s–1950s), took little interest in first-rate or accurate literary adaptations. Literature was merely fodder for entertaining movies, and movies were made to bring in the highest possible gross returns. A few more examples illustrate the point: Hemingway's novels have never become equivalent masterpieces on film. *A Farewell to Arms* was filmed in 1931 and in 1957, and both films are inferior to the novel, despite the presence of Gary Cooper and Lillian Gish in the earlier version and despite the fact that this film helped launch Hemingway's literary career. *For Whom the Bell Tolls* (1942), again with Gary Cooper, seems overlong and uneventful today, even with Katina Paxinou and Ingrid Bergman on the screen. The 1949 version of F. Scott Fitzgerald's *The Great Gatsby* failed because Alan Ladd was identified by audiences as a tough persona, not a romantic lead. (Today, Ladd's performance is considered quite good, though the film failed.) The later version (1974), directed by Jack Clayton with a

A film adaptation of a classic novel, such as David Lean's version of **Great Expectations,** *can visually convey the original's atmosphere, characters, and themes.*

script by Francis Ford Coppola, hardly fared better with either critics or audiences. This lavish film, which does indeed capture some of the color and tone of the twenties and features some excellent minor characters—especially Sam Waterston as Nick and Bruce Dern as Tom—is generally considered a failure because of the two leads, Mia Farrow and Robert Redford, who seem miscast according to many critics. While the film is interesting as a panorama of the Jazz Age, it lacks depth and misses the ironies in the famed Fitzgerald work.

Hollywood is, of course, not the only place where literary adaptations fail. Claude Chabrol's 1993 version of Gustave Flaubert's *Madame Bovary* (which has been adapted for the screen several times) is surprisingly mediocre. Chabrol is a member of the celebrated group of French filmmakers known as the New Wave directors, which includes François Truffaut and Jean-Luc Godard among others. Most of these are original filmmakers who almost never adapt literary material. Perhaps Chabrol's poor version of *Madame*

Bovary can be attributed to its literalness. The story is exactly the same: Emma Bovary indulges in a series of adulterous affairs and reckless spending, and ends up ruining both herself and her family. She finally commits suicide. The details of the plot are all there, but the film lacks emotional depth, and the misfortunes of the protagonist fail to gain viewers' sympathy. This may be attributed to actress Isabelle Hupert's persona (though she does a creditable job in the suicide scene), but it is not primarily a question of actors or acting. The film's failure lies in the absence of the overwhelmingly rich detail of Flaubert's novel.

Length and Complexity: Problems of Literary Adaptations

There are other reasons why many adaptations have not worked. Some producers focus on a film's box office potential and lack sufficient interest in all the literary dimensions of a classic, so they truncate the original to meet mainstream film demands. In general, the greater the length of a novel, the more it is a burden to a filmmaker with a limited amount of running time for his film. Works of novelists who won Nobel Prizes, such as the novels of William Faulkner and John Steinbeck, have not as a rule fared well in Hollywood, mainly because producers or directors have failed to render the complexity of plot and character. *The Long Hot Summer* (1957), based on several works by Faulkner, has a certain sultry quality that suggests a Southern atmosphere, but the film lacks depth and dimension. *The Sound and the Fury* (1959) is almost unrecognizable to viewers familiar with the original complex masterwork. *The Reivers* (1969), with Steve McQueen, enjoyed a favorable critical response but it is a forgettable movie. With the exception of *Grapes of Wrath* (1939), directed by John Ford, Steinbeck has also been unlucky in the film adaptations of his works.

These are all major American authors of the twentieth century, but major novelists of the nineteenth century have fared no better. Though many movies (some of them made for television) have been made of Hawthorne's *The Scarlet Letter* and of Theodore Dreiser's *Sister Carrie* (two women's movies *par excellence*), these adaptations failed, and their failure can be attributed to the shallowness of approach that is typical of many Hollywood productions. Despite many attempts, probably no film has been able to capture the major novels of Dostoevsky (Joseph von Sternberg's *Crime and Punishment* [1935] may be an exception) or Dickens. Tolstoy's *War and Peace* (first published in 1865) is another case of failed film equivalents: The 1957 Hollywood movie, featuring major stars Henry Fonda and Audrey Hepburn, offered nothing more than an ordinary spectacular epic of the 1950s.

The Russian version (1968) is lavish, well mounted, and faithful, but its flaw lies in its length (eight hours) which is overwhelming to the average spectator. Who can sit and watch one movie for an entire day? Such lengthy movies as *Lawrence of Arabia*, *Cleopatra*, *The Godfather II*, *Dr. Zhivago*, and *Schindler's List* approach or slightly exceed four hours, which seems the maximum time viewers can endure. Three hours is better yet, and movies that tell their stories in two hours or less are best of all. All movies, whether literary adaptations or not, need to be well paced and to tell their stories in snappy details, even if they lavish extra attention on some of these details. Most Hitchcock movies focus on a central plot line: *Psycho* (1960), *Dial M For Murder* (1954), and *Rear Window* (1955). *North by Northwest* (1958) and *The Birds* (1963) are somewhat longer and more episodic, though both have tense climaxes. Today's movies run an average of two hours, and that time limit can be exceeded only for compelling reasons. A long but fast-paced movie like *Schindler's Lit* (1993) gives viewers plenty of reasons to stay seated for three-plus hours. A lengthy western like *Wyatt Earp* (1994) does not.

Length, on the whole, is a major stumbling block to successful adaptations. The adapter of a novel must deal with extraordinarily complex problems, a great many of which arise from a novel's wealth of material that must be condensed into two or three hours. Scenes must be cut, minor and even major characters sometimes eliminated. Thus, subtle shades of relationships are lost. In this transition from one medium to another, what is often tarnished is the reputation of the film because of its sacrifice of significant detail. The novel's message is simplified and diminished, so the film cannot rise to the status of the classic novel. Most movie adaptations examined below owe their success or failure, in some measure, to questions of the length and complexity of the original versus the simplified film versions.

There are also other factors, one of which concerns the era during which an adaptation was made. As a rule, before 1960 most adaptations conformed to commercial standards applied to all mainstream films, aside from rare exceptions (*A Streetcar Named Desire* [1950], for instance). Starting in the early 1960s, and continuing into the 1990s, significant film adaptations of literary works have commanded the respect of both film critics and students of the literary canon. Filmmakers of distinction—Luchino Visconti, David Lean, Fred Zinnemann, Francis Ford Coppola, Stanley Kubrick, Kenneth Branagh, Martin Scorsese, James Ivory, Anthony Minghella, Mike Figgis—have produced films expressive of their own personal visions, and also meticulously crafted visual correlatives of prose masterpieces. They did so despite potential drawbacks at the box office, for mainstream audiences are generally suspicious or neglectful of literary adaptations if they are advertised as such. What follows is not an exhaustive list of successful adaptations made during the past several decades, and it does not intend to slight those not mentioned.

Adaptations of Merit

Kubrick's *Lolita* (1962) vs. Adrien Lyne's (1998), and *A Clockwork Orange* (1971)

Let us look closely at two films made from the same literary source during two different eras.

Based on the controversial 1955 novel by Vladimir Nabokov, Stanley Kubrick's *Lolita* (1962) marks a turning point in the art of literary adaptations. *Lolita* broke new ground on a taboo subject—a relationship between a middle-aged man and a twelve-year-old girl. Movies with explicit sexual content had been shunned by Hollywood ever since the Hays Production Code came into effect in the 1930s. In the early 1960s, censorship agencies still had a firm grip on Hollywood productions, and so the film was made under protest by both the Hays Code and the Catholic-sponsored Legion of Decency. That induced Kubrick and producer James. B. Harris to film *Lolita* in England. Even there, Kubrick had to abandon the novel's explicit sexual scenes, and at least the first half of *Lolita* became a social satire. Interestingly, more than three decades later in the late 1990s, Nabokov's novel was filmed again by Adrien Lyne, and its sexual content was still an impediment to its release. This time, censorship was exercised by U.S. film distributors who refused to release the film and forced the producers to show it on the cable TV channel *Showtime* on August 2, 1998. Even so, Lyne's film is clearly indicative of contemporary changes in the degree of sexuality allowed on screens, large or small. Decades have passed, and audiences today are ready to accept increased levels of sexual content. That fact alone makes for interesting comparisons. Though the two films share the same literary source, they take different approaches to the same story. Kubrick, forced to give more space to Charlotte Haze's story, creates a different organic whole, placing his film in a setting of multiple relationships—mother-child, wife-husband, mother-lover, adult-illicit sex. As in the novel more than one relationship is explored, proving that film can explore the depths of a literary work more fully if it chooses to. Kubrick's version of the Nabokov novel is a more complex work than Lyne's. James Mason, though a good choice as the novel's tormented protagonist Humbert Humbert, is balanced by Peter Sellers' brilliant rendering of the twisted Clare Quilty. In the Lyne version, Jeremy Irons proves as good a choice for Humbert Humbert, coming across as even more intense and obsessed than James Mason, and Dominique Swain seems a more natural Lolita than Sue Lyon. She is closer to Lolita's actual age ($12^1/_2$). Adrian Lyne is able to use today's looser standards of sexuality to show sexual encounters on screen, though his film's sexual content is restrained and avoids a soft-core explicitness. But the main difference between the two films is one of focus: The Lyne film centers on the relationship of Humbert Humbert with Lolita. Quilty, played here by Frank Langella, remains a background figure, a secondary and even shadowy character, despite his bloody murder at the end. The Lyne film, then, centers on Humbert Humbert's obsession with Lolita's demonic nature. It sacrifices some satiric elements—e.g., Melanie Griffith does not match the sardonic tone of Shelley Winters—but that is compensated for by the emphasis on Humbert's passion for his young stepdaughter. Jeremy Irons conveys a character much more obsessed with a teenaged nymph than the elegantly European and rather distant Mason. Nevertheless, overall Kubrick's work remains the classic. In the older movie, Lolita and Quilty are two demons—the obsession and the avenging fury. Still, Lyne's sensuality is more attractive to a modern audience used to sexual explicitness. Visually, both are stunning films, with color giving the Lyne version a decided advantage.

But Kubrick has made his share of brilliant literary adaptations. His *A Clockwork Orange* (1971), for instance, caused author Anthony Burgess a pang of resentment when a film based on his book attained greater success than the novel itself—or any of his other works (see "Preface" to *A Clockwork Orange*). Kubrick's adaptation of William Makepeace Thackeray's 1844 novel *Barry Lyndon* was far less successful with modern audiences than with critics, despite Kubrick's meticulous depiction of authentic eighteenth-century English locales, costumes, and mores. More recent critics have "rediscovered" *Barry Lyndon* (1975). Martin Scorsese, in a recently broadcast commentary on the Turner Classic Movie channel (see "A Personal Journey"), praised the film's deliberate pace which combines music with visual style to chronicle the theme of a man's rise and fall: Redmond Barry, an Irish fortune-hunter, has the skills needed to *achieve* wealth and status, but not those needed to *retain* them. This film is a work of art on its own terms as well as an equivalent worthy of, or surpassing, the original.

Film Equivalents of Classic Literary Works

Luchino Visconti's *Death in Venice* (1971)

In the annals of literary adaptations, Luchino Visconti's *Death in Venice* (1971), based on the 1912 novella by Thomas Mann, stands out as one of the most individualistic and perhaps the most intriguing of film adaptations. Even here there are significant differences of approach to the subject matter between the author Mann and the filmmaker Visconti. Visconti, a Marxist ideologue, was more preoccupied with depicting a decadent society—the declining aristocracy of twentieth-century Europe—than with the Platonic/Freudian questions raised by Mann about the relationship of art to sexuality. Some critics believe the selection of Dick Bogarde, a youthful-looking British actor, to play Gustav von Aschenbach is the film's major drawback (Boyum 213–31). The artist's metier itself was changed from novelist to musician with Aschenbach representing the composer/conductor Gustav Mahler whom Bogarde remarkably resembles. The relationship is not platonic as in Mann's story, but overtly homosexual. The music of Mahler in the score (from Mahler's symphonies No. 3 and No. 5) overwhelms the viewer who is swept by the film's romantic overtones and existential/Nietzschean despair. Questions about art and morality are played out in flashbacks between Aschenbach and his mentor Albert in shrill dialogues which somewhat interfere with the film's narrative flow. These are no match for the yearning, Platonic/Socratic ruminations of Mann's protagonist. However, Visconti, an opera director, creates a complex semioperatic work, visually stunning and musically compelling, though the music is borrowed from preexisting

Luschino Visconti's **Death in Venice** *is remarkable for its retelling of the Thomas Mann story primarily through imagery, with sparse use of dialogue.*

sources. The success of the film (admittedly not for all tastes) lies not in faithful rendering of the novella, but in the originality and perception of its subject matter. Both novella and film are marked by Aristotle's *spoudaiotes* (Matthew Arnold's "high seriousness"), and there is nothing gross or vulgar in either of these creations. Their outlooks are different, even contradictory: Mann concentrates on the Germanic will power (*Durchhalten*) versus the Bohemian *laissez aller* (sweet idleness, dissipation). Visconti explores the psychic make-up of the homosexual urge, whose lure his hero cannot resist. Ultimately, both tell the same story: a middle-aged man of artistic inclination, civilized and kind, succumbs to the demonic urges inside him and falls prey to his yearning for forbidden fruit.

David Lean's *A Passage to India* (1984)

David Lean's *A Passage to India* (1984), based on E. M. Forster's 1924 novel, is another successful film adaptation of a great book. Some critics have called it "splendid" and "restrained" (Cook 600), though others found flaws in the movie's upbeat ending and in the portrayals of the characters of Mrs. Moore (Dame Peggy Ashcroft, who won an Oscar) and of the farcically rendered Professor Godbole (Sir Alec Guinness). This adaptation suffers somewhat from reduction in length and complexity: Some of Forster's minor characters are eliminated—Nawab Bahadur, the hospitable Indian rajah, with his car and Eurasian chauffeur; Ralph Moore, Mrs. Moore's other son; and Aziz's third child. So is almost the entire third part of the book which covers the Krishna birth, Aziz's long recognition of Ralph, and the final scene at Mau when Aziz and Fielding, riding their horses, despair of a reconciliation between their races. Some critics (Pauline Kael, for instance) feel that Forster's pessimistic resolution of the book is lost, to the detriment of the movie. Lean, however, fully aware of the greatness of the literary work he was adapting, was very stubborn about making "his own" movie. Rejecting a script composed by Santha Rama Rau (who had written a play from the novel) as "too wordy and literary," he wrote his own script (Brownlow 313–14), making notable changes in the story. He actually lengthened certain scenes such as the adventure at the caves and Aziz's trial, which was orchestrated by crowds outside and a raging storm above. And he added the entire scene in which Adela ventures into the ruined temple and sees statues of Hindu deities in erotic embraces. Lean made this film Adela's story, a modern epic of a woman in search of her identity, rather than Forster's condemnation of Britain's imperialistic occupation of India. Lean also added visual splendor to the whole: The actuality of India is emphasized much more in the film than in the novel, as are themes of man's and woman's lack of empathy, of a mother and son's lack of mutual understanding, and of people's inability to "only connect." This is also the theme of the book. This is not a question of disloyalty to the original. The purpose of a film is not merely to be loyal, but also to play different notes in the same key. Literary and cinema critics often find that films made from great books do just that.

Martin Scorsese's *The Last Temptation of Christ* (1988)

Perhaps no modern adaptation of a novel into film has caused more controversy than Martin Scorsese's version of Nikos Kazantzakis's novel *The Last Temptation of Christ*. The film, released in 1988, was hailed as a cinematic landmark by some while condemned as blasphemy by others. It met with emphatic rejections by Christian fundamentalists and many other Christian groups, including officials of the Greek Orthodox and Catholic Churches. The uproar reached frenetic dimensions when various religious groups protested outside theaters where the movie was shown, holding signs asserting that the movie denied the divine nature of Christ. The film is banned from some video stores even today. Though Scorsese did not intend to make a blasphemous film, he was unprepared for such vehemently negative reactions. He had wanted to make a movie of the Kazantzakis novel for many years, but had been thwarted by lack of financial backing. With a script written by Paul Schrader, a collaborator on many of his movies, he strove to adhere faithfully to the novel, not straying from the original in letter or spirit. The author's intent to depict the dual nature of Christ, as stated in his preface to the book, and his reverence for Christ's struggle to follow his divinity are repeated verbatim in the film's opening credits. The Kazantzakis plot is followed loyally and conscientiously, Scorsese having gone to considerable lengths to reproduce the crucifixion scenes from medieval paintings and to obtain authentic-looking locations for filming the exteriors. There are, of course, differences in outlook and degree of modernity. Scorsese was faithful to Kazantzakis's novel, but he was interested in "western" ideas, incorporating his Catholic background, while Kazantzakis was influenced by his Eastern Orthodox background. The filmmaker sought to reconstruct the image of Christ, stressing his human side, and dwelling on the enigmatic content of the phrase "fully human and fully divine." He did not want the film to look like a traditional Hollywood epic with characters speaking in British accents (as for instance, in *The Robe*). Instead, his characters speak in American idioms, plain language, some even with Brooklyn accents, stressing the earthiness of both Jesus and his disciples. Taking a clue from Kazantzakis, but making an even stronger point, he makes Judas the only apostle who is a *thinking* friend and who understands Jesus' human dilemmas. This was a shock to those who thought of Judas only as a traitor.

If there are flaws in this movie, they are not flaws of intention or of doctrine but of performance. The flaws of the film are the flaws of the novel: Neither Kazantzakis nor Scorsese, it seems, could decide whether or not Jesus was to be presented as fully divine. In the early parts of both novel and film, Jesus wanders about undecided and doubting his own nature, and seems dangerously assailed by the temptation to become a happily married family man with a wife and children. But in the middle of both the book and the film, after successfully facing the Tempter in the desert, Jesus appears sure of himself, having overcome his doubts about his divinity and performing miracles like the Jesus of the Gospels. The film has other problems: the mixture of Brooklyn and foreign accents does not always work, and much of the visual sorcery—especially in the desert scenes (lions, circles, flames, etc.)—looks fake. In his disc commentary, Scorsese states that he stressed simplicity to avoid the look of Hollywood special effects which would detract from the picture look even more. On the positive side, the film's soundtrack, composed by Peter Gabriel, adds to the story's evocativeness. The last scene, the one about which controversy raged, shows Jesus descending from the cross in a dream. It is admirably staged and completely loyal to the book. Scorsese succeeds in rendering the Kazantzakis hero, a Christ-like figure who embarks on a spiritual quest, modern man's search for the divinity inside man. Here, both reader and viewer are overwhelmed, forgetting the story's inconsistency. This is a well-intentioned, daring film, whatever its faults.

James Ivory's *Howard's End* (1993)

A perfect adaptation comprises all the basic elements found in a book—plot, characterization, and ideas. Such adaptations are rare, and they deserve special notice. In a perfect adaptation (or a literal adaptation, which may or may not be the same thing), do the adapters simply transfer materials from one narrative medium to another? While doing a good job of imitating the original work, do they lack a vision of their own? This raises the question of what is the most desirable adaptation? Is it an exact copy, the transfer of a story from one medium to another? Or is it a reshaping and remolding of one artist's vision into that of another, perhaps even more powerful? Filmmakers like Luchino Visconti, Stanley Kubrick, David Lean, and Martin Scorsese were never one-hundred-percent adapters. They were original filmmakers who respected an original source, but had distinct ideas of their own. Some adapters—like producer Ismail Merchant and director James Ivory who always collaborated with each other and with screenwriter Ruth Prawer Jhab-

vala were known for their more or less faithful translations of several works—
novels of E. M. Forster, and Kazoo Ishiguro's *The Remains of the Day* (1994),
for instance. The literalness of their approach and their high standards of
accuracy have pitted them against moviemakers who take a looser approach.
Let us take the example of *Howard's End* (1992) to illustrate the point.

E. M. Forster's famous work, published in 1921, describes the cultural
clash between three families—the Wilcoxes, the Schlegels, and the Basts—
who represent three English classes: the money-making Wilcoxes, obtuse
about personal relations; the intellectual and humane (and German-origi-
nated) Schegel sisters; and Leonard Bast, an unsung hero of the masses. The
tragic liaisons among these people, the contours of an almost invisible plot,
march on like a Greek tragedy. Shadings of character, the general commentary on class struggle, and the omniscient point of view all contribute to the
making of a superbly readable book, which has not generally been accorded
the recognition given to its sister, *A Passage to India*. Luckily, the film came
along late in the twentieth century to reawaken interest in the book, which
stands on its own. Unlike *A Passage to India*, with its numerous lovable characters (who can forget Aziz, Richard Fielding, Adela Quested, and especially
Mrs. Moore and Godbole?), *Howard's End* has hardly a body to love. All the
Wilcoxes, except the gentle family matriarch Ruth, are self-centered boors.
Ruth dies early, after setting the plot in motion. Readers are struck by the fact
that the sympathetic and intelligent Margaret falls in love with the egotistical
Henry Wilcox, who is blind to the feelings of anyone outside his family and
who is unable to follow the book's motto: "only connect. . . ." He does connect in the end when his son, Charles, is about to be arrested for manslaugh-
ter. Even though Henry fully feels the pain of seeing his family about to be
destroyed, he is still not likable. The always humane and heroic Margaret forgives him for the second time and he does repent when he leaves Howard's
End. The house was bequeathed to Margaret in a handwritten note by Ruth
before she died. It belongs to her and her sister's son. But why does she love
Henry in the first place? She likes the solid businessman in him, the money-
making and enterprising tycoon whose kind have helped erect the pillars of
the British empire. She likes him from the beginning, despite her sister
Helen's aversion to him. Perhaps she yearns for a virile type like him, a patri-
arch of a large but spiritually sterile family. In some ways, the
Margaret/Henry liaison reminds us of the Darcy/Elizabeth Bennett connection in Jane Austen's *Pride and Prejudice*. Elizabeth castigates Darcy at the
moment he proposes to her and thus helps correct his egotism, as he himself
later tells her. But Darcy is not a bad guy—he has enviable qualities of character: "understanding" (translate, "intelligence"), a sense of fairness, generosity, and above all an ability to search into himself. These qualities are hidden from Elizabeth because of her prejudice. Margaret, on the other hand,

sees through Henry immediately. She has no illusions about his formidable limitations (e.g., his closed mind). Still, she cannot comprehend that Henry will not allow a pregnant Helen to spend one night at Howard's End. She rejects him and is ready to leave him, but she relents after his son is incarcerated. They connect, but just barely. Perhaps that is enough. Forster gives us a more realistic view of human nature, and his world is a far cry from Austen's Age of Enlightenment universe.

The film loyally follows all these lines of action and characterizations. It is an intelligent, polished movie which can stand on its own with viewers who have never read or known anything about the book. Indeed, it might be best received by just such an audience. When Anthony Hopkins, who plays Henry Wilcox, was interviewed by Larry King (after winning the Oscar for *Silence of the Lambs*), King seemed to have no knowledge that a book called *Howard's End* existed. Hopkins had simply dropped the name of the next picture he was to appear in, and perhaps he did not want to embarrass his host, or perhaps he did not think the book mattered enough to be mentioned (Hopkins is known for his laconic answers both on and off screen). However, the book cannot be forgotten. To the literary reader, the source material cries out for recognition. A classic novel brought to the screen has its birthrights. A call for a comparison is both inevitable and reasonable. But when this book and this film are placed side by side—as they should be—neither wins. The stories and characters are identical. One might even object that the film adds nothing to what the book gives us. Despite the film's fidelity to the original, some critics might consider this a drawback. Viewers have little opportunity to look at some of the things the book deals with at length. Nothing much is said about the clash of cultures—German/English or Teutonic/Anglo-Saxon—that the book dwells on at great depth. In the book Margaret's point of view is frequently interrupted by the story of the Basts and by the thread of the Wilcoxes. The book elaborates on three universes: the lower class, deprived and undernourished, with mind and body in a state of perpetual weakness because of lack of adequate income; this lower class has nowhere to go. Only the socialism that the Wilcoxes distrust addresses its problems. The upper class is split in two: those with the means to live a life of leisure (the two sisters and their aunt), who therefore turn to art, literature, and culture; and those who strive to build the basis of material security—money, commerce, industry—on which the Empire rests. The Wilcoxes only draw looks of contempt from Helen, the more emotional of the two sisters, who sees them as nothing but moneyed boors. Margaret, on the other hand, is attracted by Henry from the start and accepts his offer of marriage soon after his wife dies. This connection plays up the dramatic irony of the "only connect" opening epigram of the book. Margaret likes Henry, but they do not connect intellectually or in any other way, except perhaps purely physically, something neither the book nor the film elaborates on. Neither book nor film satisfactorily answers the question of why she is romantically inclined toward him. Only dramatic necessity brings them together: she must be the avenger, having brought Mrs. Wilcox's humanity to Henry at last through a second wife. The book has the advantage here. For one thing, it explains the character of Ruth Wilcox who, despite her short-lived appearance in the book, enables Henry and Margaret to connect at last. She is somewhat like Mrs. Moore of *A Passage to India*, possessing insight, humanism, compassion, and vision. Like Mrs. Moore, Ruth Wilcox dies but leaves a legacy that will enrich the lives of the survivors (at least of those who count—for the Wilcoxes are on the whole an unreformable lot). That is why Ruth is the great exception: not only does she enable the plot to jell, but she also elevates the action in the midst of mediocre personalities and gives it depth. As the owner of Howard's End, she sees with transcendent insight that her house must go to Margaret because Margaret is losing Wickham Place. Ruth recognizes this necessity and leaves the handwritten note that is destroyed by the Wilcoxes.

The film offers some unexpected advantages in its choice of actors: Vanessa Redgrave plays Ruth Wilcox, as in *A Passage to India* Dame Peggy Ashcroft plays Mrs. Moore. The two great actresses bring life to these roles with consummate skill. In fact, they so dominate the characters they portray it is hard to imagine anyone else playing them. Likewise, Emma Thompson is a perfect Margaret, and Helena Bonham Carter is an ideal Helen. Anthony Hopkins makes a solid Henry Wilcox, square-jawed, obtuse, yet coming up with unexpected moments of tenderness and insight, for he loves his Margaret. The film's advantage is its superb photography, its pace, its music, and its synthesis of plot and character elements. It contains no great amount of dialogue—nor does the book—and that turns out to be an advantage because the action remains mostly visual. In Margaret's first visit to Howard's End, she walks into the parlor and is taken by Mrs. Avery, the housekeeper, for the ghost of Mrs. Wilcox. Many other scenes are memorable because of their visual gloss and aesthetic nuance.

This film is a literal translation, a repetition, of the story told in the novel. What it lacks, speaking from a rather demanding point of view, is inventiveness. In *A Passage to India*, for instance, Lean, who is more of a filmmaker than an adapter, creates his own version of the novel. He believed the novel was great, an immortal masterpiece of English literature, but the film was his film and would be made in his way—by liberally dropping characters, by adding new scenes, and by omitting most of the book's ending (altering it so significantly as to make some critics uncomfortable—i.e., Pauline Kael). In the process he altered the message. *Howard's End* is different. Whatever one thinks of the merits and drawbacks of the literal approach, *Howard's End* is as perfect a movie as they come. It is difficult to choose between the novel and the film.

Anthony Minghella's *The English Patient* (1996)

Generally, there is good news about adaptations in the last few decades. Francis Ford Coppola's *Apocalypse Now* (1979), a film based on Joseph Conrad's 1899 novel *Heart of Darkness*, succeeds as an adaptation without adhering literally to a text. Coppola replaces the British Marlow's river journey into the Congo in search of the mysterious trader Kurtz with a similar story set during the Vietnam War. Here the American Captain Willard (Martin Sheen) travels upriver to locate and remove a renegade—and possibly insane—American colonel (Marlon Brando). John Milius's script is as inventive as Conrad's novel itself. By contrast, Merchant/Ivory productions are generally the most meticulous and literal of all movie adaptations: *A Room With a View* (1987) and *Maurice* (1991) are excellent examples of this producer/director group. Their other important adaptation is Kazuo Ishiguro's complex novel *The Remains of the Day* (1994), probably one of the most meticulously loyal and totally successful adaptations of a literary work ever made.

Anthony Minghella's *The English Patient* (1996) is worth special mention. It is based on the Michael Ondaatje novel, an impressive and at times difficult book made up of flashbacks to World War II action, scenes of Count Almasy's expeditions in the desert, passages from Herodotus, descriptions of Lord Suffolk's teaching the mine experts. The book excels as an essay/novel on loss of identity; lost civilizations and their rediscovery; themes of betrayal, death, Platonism, the Renaissance, and the destruction of humanism by the likes of Savonarola. These great crisscrossing themes—which some critics have labeled "labyrinthine"—are mostly thinned out in the film, although it is still overwrought with themes and images, so much so that a single viewing is insufficient to capture all of them. Yet the film is impressive too. It offers exquisite photography; multilayered meanings embedded in desert imagery that symbolizes femininity, aridity, mystery, elusiveness, and passion. The love between Katherine Clifton and the Hungarian Count Almasy dominates the film, giving it a coherent narrative structure missing in the book. The film dwells on the human and personal elements of the story: guilt, angst, betrayal, desperation, the "tragic march of doom"—to borrow Francis Ferguson's term. While the book is rich, erudite, and impressionistic in its sketches of character and vision, the film raises the book's enigmatic and shadowy characters to the level of breathing, passionate, romantic, and tragic heroes. This film won nine Academy Awards (including Best Picture), but comparing it with great film masterpieces of the past or with other great films of the 1990s (such as *Howard's End* and *Schindler's List*), a viewer may well ask: Is it a great masterpiece or not? No doubt it is a cut above the ordinary "good" entertainment film. It is even literary. The photography of the desert and the music score are both exquisite. So why hesitate to call it great?

Somehow the film, by comparison with the book, lacks something. The story of Hana, the nurse who cares for a burned and dying man, is very vague. Why is she so dedicated to this patient? Her motivation for staying behind with him is strained, even ethereal, so the relationship seems unreal. Her attachment to the Indian mine expert Kip is also odd—not at all romantic, and thus a burden to the film. The long and the short of it is that watching a mutilated, half-burned ghost tell a story is not very interesting and is even slightly repugnant. Nor is Carravagio's persona compelling, aside from the scene in Cairo when the sadistic Nazi officer cuts off his thumbs.

Viewers of Hana's humdrum story grew impatient for the film to get back to Count Almasy (Ralph Fiennes) and his love affair with Katherine Clifton (Kristin Scott Thomas). Their ill-starred romance may rank with the great love stories of all time, reminiscent of the novel *Anna Karenina* and the film *Dr. Zhivago*. Both Almasy and Katherine render the fierceness and desperation of their impossible love, which will sweep them to destruction, becoming both passionate lovers and passive observers of their own obsession. The incidents in their story are linked in logical succession: Katherine's husband Jeffrey Clifton, played with quiet intensity by Colin Firth, is a British cartographer who leaves his sophisticated and lovely wife to go on an expedition into the desert with a band of men led by Almasy, while he undertakes a spying mission for the British in Ethiopia. She quotes to him from Herodotus' story of Gyges and King Candaules: The king exposed his wife to Gyges, who then murdered the king, married his lady, and succeeded to the throne to rule for 28 years. Unconscious of the paradigm/allegory, Clifton remains unaware of the risk and entrusts his wife to the cartographers (believing they are afraid of her). Among them is the alluring and amoral Almasy. The sandstorm in the desert, the illicit love affair, and the betrayal by Almasy are events of dramatic impact, though the film takes its time telling of Almasy's ties to the Nazis. Clifton becomes aware of Almasy's liaison with his wife and tries to murder him (in a scene reminiscent of the cornfield in *North by Northwest*) in a murder/suicide plane crash intended to kill him, his wife, and her lover. As he is flying low toward Almasy, his plane crashes, he is killed, and Katherine is injured. Almasy escapes, leaving Katherine to await his return in the Cave of the Swimmers where antique drawings were discovered. He is arrested, escapes, and then surrenders secret maps to the Nazis who agree to help him. They arrive at the cave to find Katherine dead and Almasy is burned when his plane explodes as he leaves with Katherine's body. This is where we come in—with Hana and the burnt Almasy, who dies at the hands of Hana after he has confessed his secrets. Caravaggio has meanwhile revealed who he is, and Hana takes off for the North with Caravaggio (who has found an Italian girlfriend named Goya).

Ondaatje's book is an impressive mixture of stream of consciousness narrative, arcane geographical data, and philosophical reflections. The historical material from Herodotus is a powerful commentary on the relationship of western civilization to the African desert: lost civilizations, lost identities; the shaping of tribal identities by the forces of the desert. The book says much more about the relationship of Hana to Caravaggio and about Kip, whose story occupies larger portions here. Lord Suffolk's teaching of the mine experts is a fascinating aside on World War II—perhaps the theme of the book, which several other themes crisscross, some of them barely touched upon in the book. For instance, the description of Poliziano's Renaissance villa is a brilliant aside, revealing Almasy's (and the author's) passionate lament for the destruction of humanism by the religious fanatic Savonarola, whose persona is intended as a parallel to Hitler's. The book is rich in ideas, in-depth characterization, and philosophical commentary, only marginally touched upon in the film. Yet the film, focusing on the betrayal of love and friendship, is powerful too. The film's triumph is the portrayal of Almasy himself. The enigmatic character of the book becomes the romantic/tragic hero of the film.

Ang Lee's *Sense and Sensibility* (1994) and Douglas McGrath's *Emma* (1995)

The works of Jane Austen have enjoyed a tremendous revival, mostly because of the many adaptations produced for both television and film since 1980. One very good recent adaptation is *Emma*. Written for the screen and directed by Douglas McGrath, it stars Gwyneth Paltrow as Emma, Jeremy Northam as Mr. Knightley, and Greta Scacchi as Mrs. Weston. A BBC adaptation followed, the second production in a year of Jane Austen's novel. What's more, *Clueless* (1994) was a modernized version of *Emma* which did well on the screen a couple of years earlier. In terms of fidelity to the original, McGrath's *Emma* is probably the best of the Austen adaptations for screen or television made in the mid-1990s. It is technically superior to *Persuasion* (1995) and a closer rendering than Emma Thompson's (script) and Ang Lee's *Sense and Sensibility* (1995), which cut significant characters, diminished the satirical thrust of the book, and made it a romantic story instead of an antiromantic comedy of manners. *Emma* is caustic where foolish and showy characters are concerned (Mrs. Elton, Frank Churchill), and it fully explores its heroine's character flaws. In that regard, the movie is helped by Gwyneth Paltrow's fine performance. She is the perfect Emma: slightly vain, a bit spoiled, meddlesome, unflirtatious, unromantic (without realizing it), a busybody, and a charmer in her immediate environment—protected by her wealth, beauty, and position. Herself unattached, she makes it her business to marry off everyone else, and Harriet Smith is her first victim. From then on, mistaken love interests and misconceptions abound: Emma thinks Mr. Elton is in love with Harriet when he is really in love with Emma herself. When Frank Churchill comes along, people assume he will marry Emma, though he is secretly engaged to Miss Fairfax. Learning that, Emma thinks Harriet loves Mr. Knightley, who of course loves Emma. She considers him like a brother (his brother is married to her sister) since he is the only one who clearly sees her flaws and corrects her—severely reprimanding her when she insults the garrulous but harmless Miss Bates. Emma realizes she loves him, but believes he is in love with Harriet. Emma is like most heroines in Jane Austen's novels: the plot is an opportunity for the heroine's self-discovery. The novel's premise is, "Know thyself," a precept embedded in eighteenth-century enlightenment and going all the way back to the Greeks. Gwyneth Paltrow's performance is equal to the task. Her performance has the charm, sweetness, winsomeness, and antiromantic/romantic tension that make Austen's stories delightful. It is a rare union of emotion and reason.

Kenneth Branagh's *Hamlet*

Kenneth Branagh's extraordinary efforts to produce his mammoth, four-hour *Hamlet* (1996) with such dull results deserves special attention in the chronicles of literary adaptations. This film is admittedly very impressive in parts: Derek Jacobi's Claudius in the palace scenes, for instance; Charlton Heston's unexpectedly excellent player king; and Billy Crystal's gravedigger—these practically steal the show. But on the whole, this translation of Shakespeare's great play into a movie doesn't work for several reasons. Shakespeare as a whole is not cinematic; the bard's plays are theatrical, written for the stage and requiring attention to the written word; in short, the poetry is the thing, whereas cinema is a visual medium. The words of the play have to be spoken, but often the action becomes static, stopping until the speech is delivered, as for instance in the famous soliloquies. Branagh, who also directs, sometimes found ways around this difficulty by adding action and movement to the recitations. Hamlet moves from room to room while delivering his lengthy dissertation on Denmark's corruption just before the ghost appears. This movement/recitation technique sometimes works, but at other times it falls flat or seems ludicrous—as when the ghost, shouting through a mask, is followed into a forest of bare branches. The verbal exchange is lost amid the not-very-impressive special effects. In other words, the director beefs up the action while the lengthy passages are gotten out of the way. Hamlet's famous third-act soliloquy is delivered before a mirror, which works only because of Branagh's almost heroic performace.

In other respects, however, Branagh's performance itself detracts. He is dynamic, a consummate actor with perfectly honed language skills and a good understanding of the text, but he has physical limitations. His voice grows shrill at critical moments when he strains for effect, and the result is overacting. His tension is so great at times that his Hamlet seems more like a hysterical middle-aged man than a melancholy and philosophical youth. Branagh is best at conveying irony and sarcasm, especially during his exchanges with Polonius and some of his scenes with Ophelia. Played by a weepy Kate Winslet (who was an excellent Marianne in *Sense and Sensibility*), she is overemotional. The actress is clearly overawed by the role of Ophelia.

This four-hour movie strives conscientiously not to omit a word of the original script, but surely some scenes could be hurried up and others shortened or omitted. Take the scene in which Polonius sends Reynaldo (Gerard Depardieu, of all people) to France. It could easily be cut or shortened, but Branagh fails to understand that a movie depends on action, and plot flow— even in *Hamlet*—must be continuous. Instead, he produces an aggregation of scenes—some bad, some good, a few excellent—which do not add up to a great movie. Here the parts, in other words, are greater than the whole.

To make the unavoidable comparison, Branagh is not Laurence Olivier (*Hamlet* [1948]); he does not have the latter's depth, reach, polish, smoothness, voice, or wisdom. Just as Shakespeare put to shame all subsequent poets, so has Olivier's *Hamlet* obliterated subsequent performances. There is nothing wrong with trying again, and trying in different ways. But difference is not the issue. Branagh's *Hamlet* is a good try, awesome in some dimensions and wonderful in particular scenes; it is certainly worth seeing. But even this talented man has not yet created the truly cinematic *Hamlet*—if such a thing exists.

Mike Figgis's *Miss Julie* (1999)

Directed by Mike Figgis, a British director known for his literary themes (*The Browning Version* [1994]), *Miss Julie* is an example of a modern filmmaker's undertaking challenging projects by adapting works of literary merit. Set in northern Sweden in 1894, *Miss Julie* is based on the well-known (and much performed) play by August Strindberg, a contemporary of Henrik Ibsen. Here, it is rendered in English with English actors Saffron Burrows, Peter Mullan, and Maria Doyle Kennedy, and with British director Figgis, who films in the manner of a New Wave French auteur. Mullan is considerably shorter than Burrows, which makes him a perfect match for her since, as her father's footman, he is supposed to be her inferior in social status. She is his master— and his mistress—for a night.

The play/movie is set at a time when class distinctions mattered. Miss Julie is the daughter of a count, though her mother was a commoner. She is cultured, beautiful, inaccessible, haughty, condescending, rude, and dominating—the only member of her family or her class who appears in the movie. Mullan, used to polishing his master's boots, is engaged to Christine, a servant and a very religious girl who nevertheless has a physical passion for him. When he comes to work, Mullan is served his dinner while Christine watches and does dishes. He behaves like *her* master and drinks wine from his master's cellar. He speaks well (above his class), shows common sense, and has the will to rise above his lot.

It is a midsummer night, one of these endless evenings in northern Sweden when the sun shines brightly at midnight, and the servants and neighbors are preparing for a dance. The celebration looks like a northern *Walpurgisnacht*, a fertility rite and a bacchanal. The film opens with an elaborate montage of the preparations for the event by the numerous servants, including some young maids.

Miss Julie comes into the spacious kitchen where Christine has fallen asleep on a chair, exhausted from the chores of the day. The young mistress makes advances to Jean who, surprised at first, takes advantage of her desire and seduces her while the party goes on outside. He later proposes that they run away, asking her to go upstairs and take money from her father's safe. Emboldened by her passion, he says he will buy a hotel, become manager, change his name, even buy a title for himself if she likes, and thus become "gentry" like her. She loathes both his conceit and his plan, but does as he says, and goes upstairs to take the money. Meanwhile, Christine awakens, guesses what has happened, and asks him to repent and take her to mass—it's St. John the Baptist's Day. Maybe God will forgive him. After all, the Lord said the last will be first.

Miss Julie comes down with the money, dressed and ready to go. She wants to take her caged bird with her, but she can't catch it so he does it for her—then cuts off its head. He tells her she can't take a bird with her because it will give them away. As he calmly shaves—having decided to stay where he is—she goes outside to a fountain and slices her wrist with his razor. Her suicide occurs outside the viewer's range, and the viewer sees only the fountain's spurting water turn to red.

Figgis is known for his innovative photographic style (photography by Benoit Delhomme) and unorthodox characterizations (*Leaving Las Vegas* [1995]). This is a masterful transfer of a stage play into a movie, a transfer which seems effortless because the staginess and rigidity apparent in too many filmed plays—the sense of too much talk—is absent. It is a visually remarkable film, though its stage origins are apparent to the discerning viewer. Basically, only three characters appear, and for the greater part of the movie, only two— Julie and Jean. Figgis does not give the viewer the usual teasers: abundance of lush landscapes, crosscutting of outside and inside scenes, large get-togethers in similar English movies derived from literary works (*Jane Eyre*, for instance). We never see Julie's father, who is sleeping upstairs. The camera leaves the kitchen area only twice, briefly, for a few shots of people dancing and when Julie confesses to Jean. We guess what is going on outside when a drunk, bald-headed suitor barges in in search of Julie. That is the moment when Jean pulls her aside behind a parapet and makes love to her. The camera always focuses on these two principal participants; if a third is there (e.g., Christine), she is asleep or out of focus.

This makes for enormous concentration, cinematically speaking. It is a stage device, but with Figgis it becomes totally cinematic; his method is the close-up shot. He photographs faces, Jean's or Julie's, almost never both. We see Julie's ravaging passion in her facial contractions. Jean's contempt for her, but also his lust, is painted on his face. Fish-lens is used to distort some shots, the *mise-en-scène* alternates between close-ups and contextual shots containing a covered birdcage (the bird remains blind to the unholy union), a cross on the wall, or the master's hat and coat. During the love scene, the camera splits the screen, and we have two simultaneous shots of the same action from different angles and distances while the sound is the same (this cannot, of course, work in a dialogue scene).

The entire episode is told chronologically. There are no flashbacks except in speech. Julie speaks of her mother, Jean of his downtrodden past and his plans for the future. The episode lasts from early evening to early morning, and is almost filmed in real time, a feat few films have achieved (see *High Noon* and Hitchcock's *Rope*).

The themes remain Strindbergian, but the movie is very modern. Strindberg's Miss Julie is a young woman who strives to be liberated, much like Ibsen's heroines. Her mother taught her to consider herself equal with men. She has been trained by her father to ride, shoot, and play in the same manner men do. She has even been taken to a slaughterhouse to see how animals are killed. Figgis makes her liberation much more sexual in nature; and that is also the cause of her self-loathing and eventual destruction. She is shocked to discover that, after making love to her, Jean only wants to use her to run away. To him, she was a means to an end. She despises him, but submits to his leadership because he can lead her away from her shackled existence. He also misjudges her. He supposes she will comply with his wishes and be a means of escape for him. In a visual sequence outside the narrative, she falls from the top of a tree into an open pit, a metaphor for her desire to descend to his level, and for her the drop is an unbearable ordeal. She does not have the strength to be what she wants to be—and he guesses wrong. In its lines, this is a classic tragedy; liberation is accompanied by degradation and is an unattainable goal. Like the bird in the cage and John the Baptist, she is metaphorically beheaded.

A Glorious Adaptation: Anthony Quinn as
Zorba the Greek (1964)

When the late Anthony Quinn was interviewed by various television hosts (including Larry King), he discussed many of the roles he had played, including his famous Zorba. Quinn was asked the usual questions about his career, and much he said is revealing. Many critics have ambivalent feelings about this actor. Here's the Quinn of *La Strada* and of *Zorba the Greek*, and there the Quinn of a heterogeneous mixture of melodramatic roles—Latin bad guys, regular bad guys, Marlon Brando's partner in *Viva Zapata*. He's won a couple of Oscars on the way. He played an Arab leader in *Lawrence of Arabia*, a pope in *The Shoes of the Fisherman*, and myriad other types, good, bad, or indifferent. Quinn said he enjoyed being the French painter Gauguin in *Lust for Life* as much as he enjoyed playing Zorba; he thinks he was better in *Lust*, which seems absurd.

Zorba in shirt and tie dancing on the beach in Zorba the Greek *communicates an infectious* joie de vivre *that is waning in modern culture, including his own.*

Quinn would be nowhere near where he is without *La Strada* and *Zorba*, especially the latter. That role created a special mystique for him and immortalized both him and the character he played. Zorba has become an English word. It is the name of restaurants, and not only Greek ones; it refers to a certain type of dance—the syrtaki—associated with the character and it suggests a particular attitude towards life. There has even been a movie called *Zorba the Girl*. When the late Mike Royko of Chicago's *Daily News, Sun-Times*, and (finally) *Tribune* was dwelling on the shortcomings of presidential candidate Michael Dukakis, who was of Greek extraction, he complained that Dukakis did not remind him of Zorba. "Zorba," Royko said, "had fire in his belly. Dukakis has vanilla yogurt in his. . . ." This is a tribute to the type Zorba personifies. To many, he has become mythic, an archetype, someone unique and unusual with an approach to life that many people yearn for. He is an inspiration and a passion—maybe even salvation.

Why was *Zorba* so successful (or inspiring) as a movie? It had everything, all the unique ingredients of a perfect work of art, though the movie does have flaws. A great script derived from the novel of Nikos Kazantzakis, who has never been given enough credit for the creation of this character he based on a real Greek called Alexis Zorba. The direction of Michael Cacoyannis made the story a visual treat in alternately stark and brilliant black and white. Walter Lassally's Oscar winning photography captured the rhythms of a tragic Greek chorus. Add the music of Mikis Theodorakis, so ingrained in the movie that one cannot think of the one without the other: the Cretan beaches and slopes; the local people; and the other actors, especially Irene Pappas, Giorgos Foundas, and the Oscar winner Lila Kedrova as Madame Hortense, the French coquette. Finally, the quiet brilliance of Alan Bates, the perfect foil for Quinn.

Great ingredients, though, do not by themselves make a great movie; it is the blending, the synthesis, and something else. That something else here may be the role itself, which inspired Quinn to almost entirely finance a failing project, since producers had never heard of Zorba *or* Kazantzakis. To his credit, Quinn discovered the role, imagined how it should be played, understood it, and then created it with a zest and exuberance equaled only by Kazantzakis's original creation, Zorba the true sage, the modern visionary who penetrates through appearances to reality. The original Zorba is informed by a duality in Kazantzakis himself: here is a modern intellectual, reading Buddha, trying to understand existence through books; Zorba is a plain peasant who laughs at all this. One side of Kazantzakis is an ascetic, seeking freedom through self-discipline and contemplation. As Zorba says of his Englishman, "He thinks too much." Zorba preaches a different freedom: from jobs, marriage, social responsibility, wealth, and ambition. One must be liberated from fear, and one must be liberated from hope. One of the fables Zorba tells in the novel is the story of the worm that eats the leaves of a tree.

At last the worm climbs to the last leaf and sees the chaos underneath. At that moment, the worm discovers, poetry and beauty begin.

Zorba's happiness, however, is a facade. He has often met with failure. He has seen war and dissent, done ugly deeds (some for his country), lost his child, found disaster every time he connected with someone. His despair surfaces from beneath his jovial manner. Zorba laughs at everything western civilization values—house, wife, children, "the full catastrophe." He scoffs at success, scorns the villagers for their infatuation with the inaccessible widow, and bamboozles the monks to bargain for their timber. He drinks "to the devil too." He knows that he, like everyone else, "is food, for worms."

The movie oversimplifies the ideas in the book, and even the character of Zorba. But the character himself develops with the movie, a fact that is rarely acknowledged. Many readers are disdainful of motion pictures that come from books. They see them as acts of rapine, the stealing of a master's work just for the sake of a movie—that is, just to make money. What they don't acknowledge is that a well-made movie *has* to add depth to the original tale, though this may be done visually, through images rather than words. This is a way of adding to the role. Walter Lassally's photographic sketches of Zorba capture him with a bottle of wine lifted to his lips, his eyes suddenly flashing as he looks at the mountainside and sees the abundant timber he needs. In another scene, the camera finds Zorba stretched on the ground after his exhausting dance, muttering to Bates, "When my boy Dimitri died, I got up and danced." One dances when one is full to bursting, whether with joy or despair.

Zorba makes taunting remarks about anything and anyone. He is verbally abusive to women and abandons Hortense after making love to her. He is far from politically correct on any subject. He sees the monks as fools and the Cretan villagers as a lynch mob (which did not earn the movie a medal in Crete or any other part of Greece). On the surface, Zorba seems totally amoral: his boss's money can be used to buy the services of a prostitute for several days. But while living in "paradise with the female sex," Zorba is doing some creative thinking about the boss's business. Now, he announces to his infuriated boss, his mind is clear. The boss reads his letter pacing up and down. "Her name is Lola," he adds sardonically.

Yet this same Zorba attempts to save the widow (Irene Pappas) from a village mob, valiantly though futilely coming to her rescue. He is no coward. He rises to the occasion in a crisis, and he is the only one with compassion enough to stand at the bedside of the dying Madame Hortense, holding her in his arms as she expires. Following her death, as her house is being looted by rapacious old hags, he walks away holding the one thing left in her house: the cage with the parrot she named after the admiral she had loved, Canavaro. Hortense, too, had lived in a dream world, happy with her fantasies, unhappy with reality. There will be no burial for the foreigner who was Catholic and crossed herself with four fingers. What does it matter? Zorba asks the anguished Bates, "She's dead; it makes no difference." Zorba is above nationalities and artificial partitions, ethnic or religious. "What do I care if a man is Greek or Turk? I only ask if a man is good or bad."

Zorba is a crossroads character. Like Kazantzakis himself he's a mixture of various Cretan bloods: Oriental, Greek, European. Kazantzakis merged the strands of Cretan civilization, "Greek" only in the movie's name (the original work is titled "Alexis Zorba"). Homer, Christ, Buddha, Nietzsche—a strange combination—were the figures Kazantzakis worshiped as his true masters. But above them all was Nietzsche, his Zarathustra, the archetypal Kazantzakis. The dance of Zorba is the dance of Zarathustra.

Anthony Quinn was also a mixture, born of a Mexican mother and an Irish father. Here is a triangular infusion: a Mexican-Irish man playing a Greek who is actually Cretan, which means he is a mixture of several civilizations. Quinn's intuitiveness was astonishing. With one giant step, he rose to true stardom, demolishing his own previous persona as a Hollywood hack and, with one giant blow, became this unique, heartbreaking, glorious, sad, exuberant character.

With him in top form, his true self at last, audiences heard the eternal *No*, but also the eternal *Yes*—Nietzsche's, Camus's, and Derrida's. In the middle of the chaotic twentieth century, one hears the affirmation. *Zorba*, the movie, deconstructs western civilization, but Zorba and Bates dance as an affirmation. It is the god Dionysos, drunk again, coming from Thrace to invade civilized Thebes, which is ruled by a pompous king. Dionysos unleashes his fury, then laughs above the ruins.

The two men are left alone on the beach after the scaffold built to carry the timber from the mountain collapses, and the crowds flee. "Teach me how to dance," says Bates to Zorba. "Did you say dance?" Zorba tosses off his jacket, and pounds his chest. "Come on, my boy." Moments later: "I have lots of things to tell you: I never loved a man more than you."

The camera lingers a few moments on a long shot of the two men dancing and laughing, drunk in Dionysian ecstasy.

Literary Derivatives

Many films have been derived not from adaptations of actual stories but from themes, incidents, symbols, or subtexts in literary works. *Citizen Kane* features themes from Coleridge's "Kubla Khan"; *The Seventh Seal*, from the *Book of Revelations*; Fellini's *Satyricon*, from Petronius (though this may be considered an adaptation); *Don Juan de Marco*, from Byron's *Don Juan*; *Out of Africa* alludes to Coleridge's "The Rime of the Ancient Mariner" and A.E. Housman's "To An Athlete Dying Young"; *Shakespeare in Love* makes numerous literary references to Christopher Marlowe's poetry and stages a portion of *Romeo and Juliet*, *You've Got Mail*'s plot derives from Austen's *Pride and Prejudice*. In *Love and Death* Woody Allen quotes both T. S. Eliot and Dostoyevsky. Mike Figgis's *The Browning Version* (1994) concerns an elderly professor teaching classics who reads from Aeschylus's *Agamemnon*. The story of Agamemnon's betrayal by his wife parallels the professor's own tragedy. Examples abound and students are encouraged to discover more. If nothing else, this practice will demonstrate film's close affinity to literature.

The Future of Literary Adaptations: A Marriage

Major literary works will continue to be adapted into films because the literary and cinematic arts are inextricably bound together. Some observers contend that cinema will never reach the status of an art equal to literature. Literature is older, wiser, and surer of itself. Film is still young, in some ways still in an experimental stage, still seeking to establish itself. The younger art courts the older, depends on it, and hangs on its narrative superiority. After the flirtation a steadier bond is sought, and finally there is a marriage. But a successful marriage requires that both partners have equivalent merits. If one of the partners fails or weakens the marriage will break up.

Suggested Readings and Hypertext Links

Boyum, Joy Gould. *Double Exposure: Fiction into Film*. New York: Mentor Books, 1985.
Brownlow, Kevin. *David Lean*. New York: St. Martin's Press, 1996.
Giannetti, Louis, John W. Langdon, and Edward H. Judge. *Understanding Movies*. Englewood Hills, N.J.: Prentice-Hall, 1988.
Kagan, Norman. *The Cinema of Stanley Kubrick*. New York: Continuum, 1993.
Keyser, Lester. *Martin Scorsese*. New York: Twayne Publishers, 1992.

Film Adaptations Suggested for Study

Greed (1925), dir. Erich von Stroheim, based on the novel *McTeague* by Frank Norris
The Grapes of Wrath (1940), dir. John Ford, based on the novel by John Steinbeck

Madame Bovary (1949), dir. Vincente Minnelli, based on the novel by Gustave Flaubert

The Sun Also Rises (1957), dir. Henry King, based on the novel by Ernest Hemingway

The Old Man and the Sea (1958), dir. Henry King and Fred Zinnemann, based on the novel by Ernest Hemingway

Catch-22 (1970), dir. Mike Nichols, based on the novel by Joseph Heller

Slaughterhouse Five (1972), dir. George Roy Hill, based on the novel by Kurt Vonnegut Jr.

Amadeus (1984), dir. Milos Forman, based on the play by Peter Shaffer

A Room With a View (1985), dir. James Ivory, based on the novel by E. M. Forster.

The Last Temptation of Christ, (1988) laserdisc issue, 1998. With audio commentary by Martin Scorsese, Paul Schrader, Willem Dafoe, and Jay Cocks.

The Remains of the Day (1993), dir. James Ivory, based on the novel by Kazuo Ishiguro

Much Ado About Nothing (1993), dir. Kenneth Branagh, based on the play by William Shakespeare

Persuasion (1995), dir. Roger Michell, based on the novel by Jane Austen

Vanity Fair (1999), BBC/A&E miniseries, dir. Marc Munden, based on the novel by William Makepeace Thackeray

Miss Julie (1999), dir. Mike Figgis, based on the play by August Strindberg

CHAPTER NINE

Responding to Film as Film

How do I respond to film as film? Despite film's similarities to the literary genres—novel, epic, stage play—a student responding to film must regard it primarily as a distinct art with unique characteristics. Its uniqueness arises mainly from its visual character. To be properly and effectively analyzed, film must be seen as a visual medium. Unlike the radio, for example, which appeals only to the sense of hearing, film uses vision to create a sense of space, of time, and of the auditory elements of discourse, natural sound, and/or musical composition. Though the visual aspect of film predominates, other elements contribute to its uniqueness, so it is a *synthesis* of elements, of which imagery projected on a screen is the most important. Though never dissociated from its social and historical foundations, film employs its visual character and special film techniques to deliver its message in a way that no other art does.

Film's Uniqueness

Film is like nothing else that went before it, mainly because it became possible only after certain technological advances were made in the nineteenth century. Some critics, like André Bazin, maintain that such advances were possible as far back as the sixteenth century and that film as an art could have developed then. Indeed, some film historians insist that the "persistence of vision" phenomenon, the principle on which filmmaking is based, was known to Ptolemy in Alexandria in 130 A.D. (Monaco 497)! But those are moot points. In fact, before the end of the nineteenth century, film not only did not exist, it had scarcely been imagined in its present form. Had it originated earlier, it might have taken a different art form, perhaps more akin to painting or to opera or to private entertainments for courts. That film emerged toward the end of the Industrial Revolution contributes to its uniqueness. It appeared during an era when the mass audiences essential to the development and expansion of narrative film were able to attend its showings, thus becoming its principal patrons. Attending film was cheap, so nearly everybody could afford to go to the movies, and movies are still widely attended today. Before the Industrial Revolution, mass audiences couldn't afford to attend operas or symphonies. In America, patrons could obtain movie tickets for a nickel— hence, the name nickelodeon was given to the converted storehouses that became the first cinema halls. Film as an art form is about one hundred years old, counting from the year 1902 when several feature films in more or less their present form appeared. The youth of film—the art of the twentieth century, as it has been called—along with its easy availability are offered as the main argument against it by its detractors who resist calling it a legitimate art form. Compared to the other arts (literature, painting, dance, architecture, music), film is still in its historical and chronological infancy. True, it may not live as long as the other arts and have time enough to grow, thrive, and be recognized. By its very nature, film is the most fragile of the arts. Its material existence lies in photographed shadows chemically printed on celluloid emulsion, a perishable substance that is subject to rapid deterioration. Indeed, half of all films made before 1935 have already been lost, and efforts to restore old films (e.g., by the American Movie Classics TV channel, Turner Classic Movies, and other film agencies) have been hampered by high cost and the deterioration of materials. Besides, such efforts are aimed at the preservation of great classics, not average films. Of course, the other arts have also been subject to the ravages of time, but most of them can be preserved in ways not accessible to film. Models of sculpture and architecture, for instance, can survive for thousands of years. Music and paintings can last for hundreds. Books have faced no survival problems since the invention of the printing press. Digital technology, not available earlier in the century, may likewise ensure film's longevity. Today digital technology is being used for filming, editing, and creating the soundtrack, and celluloid film may eventually be entirely abandoned. Older films must first be restored before they can be transferred to a digital form—videotape, laser, DVD. Film must also be preserved in its original format, since its signals, screen ratios, etc., are subjected to alteration and deterioration.

Reality vs. Illusion: Film's Superiority

An important characteristic of film that has boosted its popularity, especially vis-à-vis its literary counterparts, is its ability to manipulate space and time. To a certain degree, film shares that characteristic with the novel and the stage play, both of which can transport the mind of the reader or viewer from one location to another and from one period of time to another. However, only film can achieve these effects with overwhelming visual realism. In a novel or any other written narrative form, readers must imagine what a character or a landscape looks like, what a specific location consists of, no matter how well these are described by the author. If there are musical elements in a novel (e.g., Tolstoy's *Kreutzer Sonata,* based on a Beethoven composition), these are lost to the reader, who can hear the music only separately. A stage play has significant limitations, such as the distance between viewers and the objects on a stage, most of which are perceived from a fixed position. Sounds on the stage (viz., the human voice) are not usually amplified, so viewers may miss them or miss spoken exchanges. But film offers a sense of liberation from these limitations. Viewers can see a face in close-up, so enlarged that it is clearer than in real life. They can hear all sounds loudly enough (too loudly sometimes), no matter how far back they sit or how large the auditorium is. Action is—or can be made to seem—entirely believable in a film, whereas the stage cannot overcome the audience's awareness of illusion. On stage, for instance, viewers cannot see a person or object fall from a great height. Because technology allows this through stunt work, montage, and other techniques, film can achieve a degree of realism unimaginable on stage. Some directors (Stanley Kubrick in *Barry Lyndon* [1974], Oliver Stone in *Platoon* [1984], and Steven Spielberg in *Saving Private Ryan* [1988]) sought authentic locales and costumes, or shot scenes in natural lighting to not only create an illusion of reality but, in a restricted sense, to approach *being* reality. So-called docudramas (movies based on or imitating real events) do that as well. Of course, through special effects, film can also go to great lengths to enhance the illusion of reality. Though cinema is illusion, the practical business of photographing and representing screen action aims to eliminate the illusion. The filmmaker invites viewers to visit a dark chamber and see shadows on a screen, which viewers know are illusory. And yet the filmmaker at the same time invites viewers to obliterate awareness of the illusion. By its very nature, film is the only art that strives mightily to appear real (as painting did until the advent of expressionism and cubism). A box of matches on the screen *must be* a box of matches, whereas on the stage any small box will do. Filmmakers go to great lengths to create as true a picture of reality as possible, though tricks may be used. Director James Cameron constructed a model of the

Titanic for his movie *Titanic* (1997). In design and size, it was as close as possible to the original. The interiors of the ship were minutely duplicated, compelling viewers to suspend disbelief. This high degree of verisimilitude is what gives film its uniqueness and separates it from the other arts. Photography is the precursor of the movies, creating an accurate but static representation. Paintings and novels are imitations of reality in the Platonic sense—twice removed from the original idea or form. Plato believed that the painter imitates the carpenter who makes a table or a bed, but not the *idea* of the table; the novelist imitates but also invents, thus being closer to the painter than to the photographer. The photographer, of course, is also an imitator of sorts, despite the fact that he strives for accuracy in reproduction. Moviemaking is the art of creating an illusion of reality while striving to eliminate awareness of the illusion. Film is a form of fiction. Homer, Aristotle says, taught all the other poets how to lie skillfully. Henry James in "The Art of Fiction," published in 1887, asserts that it is essential for the novelist to have the tone of the historian, to be as meticulous in his search for factual data as the historian is. To do otherwise is to betray his craft. What is true of the novelist in this

Conceived as the epitome of pure image and sound, The Birds *is replete with scenes like this one that are uniquely suited to film.*

case is *a fortiori* (for the stronger reason) even more true for the filmmaker whose lapses of accuracy will be magnified on the screen. Consider Hitchcock's *The Birds*, for instance. How believable is it that a flock of birds will launch massive attacks on humans with malice aforethought and uncanny intelligence? And yet the situations in that film are entirely believable and therefore frightening. The action was photographed in Bodega Bay north of San Francisco, in a real community. Hitchcock used actual town locations for the sets. Through trick shots, he created the illusion of reality in scenes where a flock of birds attacks a group of schoolchildren. By using the best technology available to him in 1960, he stove continually for—and achieved—the illusion of reality. Special effects, montage, trick photography, wide-angle and zoom lenses, and lighting are some of the means by which film appeals to the eye and ear to establish credibility and a sense of reality. Belief indeed is more readily suspended in film than in any other medium—though radio may come close. Large audiences can empathize with characters on the screen and feel themselves liberated from restrictions of time and space. Of course, any audience is aware of the fabrication, aware that they are witnessing a technological deception, an illusion of action. These very factors attract audiences to film. Viewers are knowingly and willingly deceived but they require the highest possible authenticity of representation. Though they are not fooled, audiences crave illusions that are as real as life itself. Their pleasure is greater when the likeness is greater. In that sense, innovations in technology enhance the illusion and work to film's advantage. This enhancing of illusion gives film its superiority and establishes its uniqueness in the pantheon of twentieth-century arts.

Film: Distinct from Literature, Matches Literature

The greatest uniqueness of film lies in its demonstrated ability to exist apart from literature. Specifically, film is not a corollary to the literary text. Though it has coexisted with the literary narrative form (plot, for instance, is an element it shares with epics, plays, short stories, and novels) and has creatively collaborated with it, it can be created without a literary precursor. For instance, a film can be adapted from a novel, play, or short story, but it does not *need* such models. Many screenwriters write scripts directly for film or adapt them creatively to suit film's needs. A screenplay, the most protean of artistic forms, can be manipulated by a creative director. French New Wave directors like François Truffaut and Jean-Luc Godard, who sometimes directed *without* scripts, frequently improvised or included scenes not present in their scripts. A creative director treats a script as a literary form if he chooses (Bergman published his scripts as literature afterwards) but the script is not a film. The film can exist without much of a script, as in the case of Chaplin's *City Lights* (1931). Chaplin held up the production of this film for months until he could visually perfect the tramp's first encounter with the blind flower girl. He felt that the actress's facial expressions did not correspond to the emotional state the scene was supposed to communicate ("The Unknown Chaplin" document by narrative tape). Scenes in many films which are purely visual require this treatment even today when scripts provide the smallest possible detail in written form (Lyne, in *Lolita*, allows Dominique Swain to drop her dentures into Humbert's glass—a detail not in the script). As in sculpture, this involves visual intuition. The cameraman and director imagine and render a scene visually, a process that has little correspondence in words. Even if all the words are there, the director must see action in visual terms. One example will suffice: Jean Cocteau in *Beauty and the Beast* (1947) borrowed photographic inspiration from such Flemish painters as Vermeer for the *mise-en-scène* when the two main characters are juxtaposed—when Beast visits Beauty every evening at seven and proposes marriage while she dines. As Beauty glides in balletic steps through the Beast's labyrinthine corridors, disembodied arms hold candelabra. Here imagination revels in the visual, creating imagery that rivals the verbally poetic: Think of Coleridge's Christabel gliding through the mysterious, moonlit forest, carrying the evil spirit Geraldine to the turret. Film imagery can match literature's best, and the filmmaker's invention parallels the poet's mastery of words. Cocteau is as much a poet and dramatist as he is a film director. Why should one grant him genius in one medium but deny it to him in the other?

Film Is Visual Reality

The reason film is an independent art even when it relies on or adapts a literary source is that film as a medium is basically a continuous translation of materials into visual reality. Imagination is captured by the visual reality rather than by a written text. Because visual reality presents different dimensions of time and space, changes in a text may be necessary when the written script is inadequate, or inappropriate to the creation of a particular mood. David Lean added the scene in which Adela Quested ventures into the ruined Indian temple and sees the erotic statuary. That scene might not have been imaginable in 1924 when E. M. Forster wrote *A Passage to India*. This scene is fraught with so many clues to Adela's real identity and is so visually subtle (not a word is spoken) that it staggers the viewer and resonates throughout the rest of the film. In fact, it alters the entire content of the story so that it becomes much more Adela's story, whereas in the book it is Fielding's and Aziz's story. In this sense, the film adds a dimension to the book which does not make it superior or equal as work of art, but which does make it *independent*. There is no need to go back to Forster after seeing the film. The film speaks for itself; it speaks visually.

Thus visual reality dictates the fashion of narrative in film and makes film an independent art form. Because directors have to deal with photographing scenes, using various sized lenses, mounted cameras, lengths of shots, and other such techniques, their concept of reality is governed and constantly modified by the technical means at their disposal. They cannot be tied down to different standards of conceptualization. This is what Aristotle meant when he said that, although all the arts are modes of imitation, they differ in medium, objects, and manner of imitation. The manner here is not stage or narrative, but screen. The medium is not language, but photography—magnified as in no other photographic medium and rendered not in stills but in motion. Unless a director is cognizant of the properties and potentialities of this medium—its potential and its limitations—a third possible dimension is lost. The director will not be able to use it to full effect. The medium defines both the advantages and the limits of creativity. To put the matter differently, a filmmaker does not need to be a novelist any more than a novelist needs to be a filmmaker. The two arts are distinct. Film is creative in its own way.

Film—Sum Total of Its Parts

Film is the sum total of its component parts, but in the gestalt sense, the whole is greater than the sum of its parts. To follow the precepts of Coleridge's organic theory, a film is a total concept of which the script (or any other component) is only a part. All the other parts "must be consonant with it." (*Biographia Literaria*, chapter xiv). All the elements required to make a film—set designs, costume, camerawork, special effects, music score, acting, directing, editing—give it its distinct form and make it unique, though some of these elements also belong to other arts.

The fact that film is related to other arts—music, dance, literature—does not signify either a superiority or a subordination to those arts. Film is not inferior to the novel or play, although the "movie verson" is often regarded as an imperfect imitation. At its best (*Citizen Kane, L'Avventura, The Seventh Seal, Schindler's List*), film can compete with any of the other arts. It need not compete with older arts.

Film, however, though in some ways an imitator of other arts has time and opportunity, because of its immense popularity, to perfect its form. The films of Orson Welles, Ingmar Bergman, Akira Kurosawa, Federico Fellini, Charlie Chaplin, Stanley Kubrick, Alfred Hitchcock, Francis Ford Coppola, and Steven Spielberg among others, have reached consummate narrative and aesthetic standards, measurable against the other arts—despite the stubborn resistance of certain critics and art ideologues.

The main obstacle to film's acceptance as an art is its commercialism.

Studios such as MGM (notwithstanding its "ars gratia artis" logo), Paramount, RKO, Warner Brothers, and others, were industrial units operating on the principle of the assembly line, developing stars and typecasting them in particular genres to guarantee box office success. In the studio era, such great stars as Douglas Fairbanks Sr. and Jr., Greta Garbo, Gary Cooper, Barbara Stanwyck, Joan Crawford, Bette Davis, Ingrid Bergman, Myrna Loy, Errol Flynn, Tyrone Power, Rita Hayworth, and many others emerged on screen. Film art has been somewhat awkwardly termed the "entertainment industry." The fact that it is part of the capitalistic system has, in certain circles, diminished its value as an art form. But why? Many filmmakers from noncapitalist countries (notably Sergei Eisenstein and Vsevolod Pudovkin from the former Soviet Union) and independent filmmakers subsidized by the state (Ingmar Bergman in Sweden) have proven that film can flourish and prosper regardless of its patronage or business connections.

One must respond to film *as film*, an independent art which may combine other arts but has achieved a status and identity of its own. As an art, it arose, succeeded, and thrived in one century, the twentieth, making it the unique art of that century and its most popular art. The Renaissance fostered and made popular its art—painting. The eighteenth, the century of Mozart and Haydn, enhanced music as a popular art. And the twentieth century produced film.

Film and Star Power

The distinctiveness of film as an art is due to a large measure to its ability to project the human form in a powerful and glamorous light. Through manipulation and projection, cinema art brightens, polishes, and enlarges the human image to a degree impossible in any other art. This projected image can inspire audiences to virtual worship of their heroes and heroines, to an admiration that transcends national boundaries and makes film stars—especially Hollywood stars—recognizable everywhere. In Hollywood the star and the film by and large developed together. Many films were and are star vehicles for Gary Cooper, John Wayne, Marilyn Monroe, Cary Grant, Audrey Hepburn; later for Meryl Streep, Jane Fonda, Barbra Streisand; and currently for Harrison Ford, Michael Douglas, Gwyneth Paltrow, and Julia Roberts. These stars are often what attracts audiences to a film. This star power has become an important component of film as a unique work of art, from the audience's point of view perhaps the *most* important. Of course most other arts have concentrated on the human form. Sculpture gave us the Hermes of Praxiteles, the Venus de Milo, Michelangelo's David, and Rodin's Thinker. Painting gave us the Mona Lisa, the naked Maja, and Botticelli's Madonna.

Photography introduced countless fashion models who adorn our magazines and set standards of taste, style, and demeanor. Weekly television programs rely on the magnetism of their stars, and many popular TV actors transcend their roles and rise to cinema stardom—Steve McQueen, John Travolta, Robin Williams, Clint Eastwood, and George Clooney. But no art (except perhaps opera) has given more prominence to the human persona.

Since its early days, feature film has relied on the screen appeal of actors and actresses for its popularity, and, naturally, for its financial success. During the early days of the studio system in the twenties, thirties, and forties when the great Hollywood studios dominated the industry, actors were under contract to studios for prolonged periods of time and were obligated to comply with certain practices established by their studio. They could not work for another company unless they were "rented out." Like screenwriters, directors, or technicians, actors received regular paychecks whether they worked or not, and their images—appearance, speech, make-up, hairstyle—were carefully manipulated to appeal to devoted fans. During that time, males had to appear heroic, masculine, handsome, and athletic, while females were as luminous beauties, remote goddesses worshiped by mass audiences. Such actors as Errol Flynn, Tyrone Power, Gary Cooper, and Clark Gable typified the male ideal, while Mary Pickford, Greta Garbo, Ingrid Bergman, Barbara Stanwyck, Gene Tierney, and Lana Turner were their female counterparts in glamor, talent, and star power. Very talented actors with less glamorous images—Spencer Tracy, Ronald Colman, Henry Fonda, Bette Davis, Katharine Hepburn—won audiences with their brilliant performances and sheer force of character.

Screen dominance by great stars was not a phenomenon confined to the early days of cinema. It continued into the second half of the twentieth century. In the late fifties and early sixties, however, actors broke loose from studio constraints. Especially after the McCarthy era when actors, directors, and screenwriters found themselves in great jeopardy, they began to work independently, forming movie companies of their own or working abroad for international or Hollywood-based filmmakers: William Holden worked for English producer Sam Spiegel in *The Bridge on the River Kwai* (1957); Gregory Peck participated in an English-sponsored war adventure, *The Guns of Navarone* (1960); Burt Lancaster joined an international cast in *The Train* (1964); Frank Sinatra owned the rights to, and starred in, *The Manchurian Candidate* (1962); Clint Eastwood worked with Italian director Sergio Leone in *A Fistful of Dollars* (1964) and *For a Few Dollars More* (1965), two popular non-Hollywood westerns. Among female stars, Ingrid Bergman was brought to Hollywood from Sweden by the legendary American producer David O. Selznick, and she remained captive to the studio system for a decade, making some of her greatest movies: *Casablanca* (1942), *Spellbound* (1945), and *Notorious* (1946) among others. She then moved to Europe following her affair with Italian director Roberto Rossellini, and came back to Hollywood for *Anastasia* (1956), for which she won an Oscar. Toward the end of her career, she returned to Sweden to make *Autumn Sonata* (1979) with noted director Ingmar Bergman. In the aftermath of the Hollywood studio breakup, European actors and actresses—especially those fluent in English—crossed international boundaries to star in independent productions. English actors were particularly successful in America: Stewart Granger and James Mason in *The Prisoner of Zenda* (1952); Peter Sellers in *The Pink Panther* (1964); Vanessa Redgrave in *Camelot* (1968); Julie Cristie in *Dr. Zhivago* (1965); Michael Caine and Sean Connery in *The Man Who Would Be King* (1975); Anthony Hopkins in *The Silence of the Lambs* (1991); and Hugh Grant in *Nine Months* (1995).

It was not only the Hollywood system that developed and relied on star power. Most major international filmmakers had their own casts or companies comprised of distinguished actors. Ingmar Bergman had Max von Sydow in *The Seventh Seal* (1957), and *The Virgin Spring* (1960). Von Sydow made the leap to America later and played Jesus Christ in *The Greatest Story Ever Told* (1965). Bergman also introduced Liv Ullmann in *Persona* (1965). Federico Fellini relied on his wife, the distinguished actress Gulietta Massina, for significant roles in *La Strada* (1954) and *Nights of Cabiria* (1956); and on Marcello Mastroianni in *La Dolce Vita* (1959) and *8½* (1962), films that made him an international star much admired in America. Japan's Akira Kurosawa employed Toshiro Mifune in *Rashomon* (1951), *Seven Samurai* (1955), *Yojimbo* (1961), *Sanjuro* (1964), and several other movies. Mifune later appeared in the American production *Hell in the Pacific* (1968) with Lee Marvin and in the American television miniseries, *Shogun*. His persona as a Japanese samurai warrior, highly skilled in the use of the sword, helped mold Clint Eastwood's fast-drawing, gun-slinging character in Leone's "spaghetti westerns." Both of these actors established the image of an imperturbable, alienated, monosyllabic individual, better with weapons than with words. They were the opposite of, for instance, Errol Flynn and Ronald Colman, who were equally adept with swords and discourse (rather like the wisecracking James Bond actors, Sean Connery and Roger Moore, always ready with a sharp remark to put down an enemy). On the whole, the macho actors of the mid-sixties reflected a popular admiration for the loner, the man who was cornered and fighting numerous adversaries but would win against all odds. This type of actor was an outgrowth of both the American western hero (Gary Cooper in *High Noon*, for instance) and the superspy (James Bond). The thriller genre, very popular today, has its roots in both the western and the superspy formula. Current heroes include Michael Douglas in *The China Syndrome* (1979), Mel Gibson in *Lethal Weapon* (1987), Arnold Schwarzenegger in *The Terminator* (1987, 1991), Bruce Willis in *Die Hard* (1988, 1991),

Harrison Ford in *Air Force One* (1997), and Tom Cruise in *Mission Impossible* (1996, 2000)—not to mention Pierce Brosnan, the current Bond. Most of these heroes fight terrorists—elusive, hardened, and highly sophisticated villains adept at functioning in cyberspace. The heroes' purpose is to save humanity from these villains.

The modern female screen persona is more complex and intricate than her male counterpart. Her contexts range from socially oriented drama to adventure to romantic comedy. Meryl Streep, perhaps the most talented actress of our time, has starred in such worthy films as *Kramer vs. Kramer* (1979), *The French Lieutenant's Woman* (1981), *Sophie's Choice* (1982), *Out of Africa* (1985), and many others. Ms. Streep is distinguished for versatile style, emotional depth, and ability to portray a wide variety of women and to master their idiosyncrasies of speech (i.e., accents and dialects). Other talented actresses include Gwyneth Paltrow, at home as both seventeenth- and nineteenth-century Englishwomen in *Shakespeare in Love* (1998) and *Emma* (1996), and as twentieth-century Americans in *A Perfect Murder* (1997), *Great Expectations* (1998), and *The Talented Mr. Ripley* (1999). Julia Roberts is an American icon after her great success as a golden-hearted prostitute in *Pretty Woman* (1991). Roberts has the distinction of having earned around $20 million for her latest screen venture, *Erin Brockovich* (2000), a salary level usually reserved for male stars like Tom Cruise, Bruce Willis, and Brad Pitt.

Film as Film: Some Examples

The Passion of Joan of Arc (1928)

Directed by the legendary Danish filmmaker Carl Theodor Dreyer, *Joan of Arc* stands as the definitive rendition of the much-filmed story of St. Joan. What makes this film so distinct is the total visual experience. In the Criterion Edition on DVD (1999), viewers can watch it without any sound whatsoever (a soundtrack with *Voices of Light*, an oratorio composed for this film by Richard Einhorn, is available on the same disk). Only a few essential subtitles convey dialogue; actually, none seems needed. The face of Maria Falconetti as Joan, eloquently photographed by cinematographer Rudolph Maté, expresses so wide a range of emotions—mystical joy, surprise, horror, pain—that words seem to have no place. The movie is the epitome of montage as the camera cuts from Joan's agonized face to the grim faces of her inquisitors and back to her, creating a seamless photographic narrative. The entire story is told in one day (the actual trial lasted for months), thus conforming to the three unities—of time, place, and action—required of Greek tragedy, which Dreyer consciously imitated. The only exterior shots are of the graphic burning of Joan and of the popular riots that followed. Both the trial and the burning are based on meticulously researched medieval transcripts, so this film belongs to the category of historical film examined in chapter 5. However, history aside, this is a prime example of film as film and a must for the serious student of cinema art.

The Testament of Orpheus (1959)

Jean Cocteau's last film is the last in his *Orphic Trilogy* (after *The Blood of the Poet* [1930] and *Orpheus* [1949]). As in the two previous films (and also in *Beauty and the Beast*), Cocteau follows a strain of surrealism ("realism of the unreal") which ran through French art in painting and poetry during that era. In fact, surrealism (better known to Americans through the paintings of Salvador Dali) has never left French cinema, resurfacing in the films of Alain Resnais (*Last Year at Marienbad*) and Jean-Luc Godard (*Pierrot le Fou*). Surrealism in cinema is mostly expressed in non-chronological episodes and dreamlike states. The technique was known to other directors, of course—to Hitchcock, for instance, who used surrealistic imagery in several films, including *Spellbound* (1945) and *Vertigo* (1959). In the *Testament of Orpheus*, an eighteenth-century poet (played by Cocteau himself) travels through time and space, encountering mysterious contemporary and historical personages who bring about his death and resurrection. The artist becomes his own creations, interfering in their lives, so to speak, but also being interfered with, a technique used with a lighter touch by Woody Allen in *Deconstructing Harry* (1997).

Citizen Kane (1941)

This is a much discussed film (often referred to in this text guide) and possibly one of the most overscreened. Yet, if any American film is worth studying it is *Citizen Kane*. The lines are blurred between mainstream or art film in this case: it was shown in mainstream theaters but was never the enormous popular success that its contemporary, *Gone With the Wind,* was. There has never, however, been any doubt of its greatness and of the high esteem it enjoys among critics. Whatever else it might be, *Citizen Kane* is a work of great cinematic art, a landmark and a prototype of moviemaking, combining technique (deep focus, montage), narrative tension (flashbacks), and a great tragic story of human reach and failure. *Citizen Kane* could have been a play, could have been a novel, but probably no transformation into those literary forms could have improved it. It is the paradigm of nearly perfect film art.

The World of Apu (1959)

Directed by Satyajit Ray, this film is set in India during the postwar era. *The World of Apu* is the last part of the celebrated director's "Apu Trilogy," which included *Pather Panchali* (1955) and *Aparajito* (1957), all three based on a novel by the Bengali author Bibhutibhushan Banerji. In this simple story of rare emotional depth and human interest, a dreamy young man lives in a run-down apartment, composing verses and writing his first novel. He is so poor he showers and washes his underwear in the rain. His landlord threatens to throw him out unless he pays several months rent that is past due. Apu is saved temporarily by his friend Pulu, who bemoans his condition and urges him to find a job. Apu tries unsuccessfully but eventually has some luck: his short story is accepted by a magazine. Then Apu is invited to the wedding of a female relative of Pulu. But the bridegroom suddenly goes insane, and that means the bride will be cursed—unless she marries someone else. Pressured by Pulu, Apu agrees to marry her. Aparna is perfectly brought up, shy, and intelligent, and Apu is soon madly in love with her. Though poor, they're happy. Apu stops smoking regularly, plays his flute, and works on his novel. They live on his minimal salary, and she is happy to have him home early. This idyllic interval does not last, however, because Aparna has to go back to her parents when it is time for their child to be born, and she dies during childbirth. The news crushes Apu, who wanders off, grows a beard, and tosses his novel to the wind. Five years pass, and Apu is working at a coal mine when he encounters his loyal friend Pulu. Pulu tries to convince him to visit his child, who is being brought up by Aparna's parents. Apu has never wanted lasting responsibilities, so he refuses at first but finally agrees to go. He loves the child at first sight, as he did his wife. To Kajal, though, he is a stranger, and the boy does not want to go with him. Apu prepares to leave without the child, though the grandfather urges him to take Kajal away by force. Apu cannot do that and walks away alone. The child follows him from a distance, then runs toward him, asking him if he will take him to his father. Apu says yes. Kajal asks who Apu is, and Apu says, a friend. The two go off together, Kajal riding on Apu's shoulders.

There is no evil in the world of Apu, except that brought about by accident. In his world, happiness is only a brief interval to be relished as long as possible, but not expected to last. Apu tastes the honey of unexpected marital bliss, then is engulfed in grief after his wife's death. His life revolves around two choices, both of which he makes reluctantly: one to marry a strange woman on the spur of the moment, the other to find the son he has never met and for whom he feels nothing. Twice he is saved from his desolate, lonely existence, and good fortune is brought into his life almost by accident.

The movie's appeal is enhanced by silk-smooth camera work and by strikingly beautiful Indian music composed by Ravi Shankar. The *mise-en-scène* is inclusive, almost always containing more than one subject: smokestacks in the distance suggest the paltriness of working-class Indian society as Apu aimlessly crosses the train tracks after Aparna's death. Most of the action is set in plain domestic interiors, suggesting Ray's debt to Italian neorealism which transcends the mundane by revealing intensity of feeling in photographed faces. There is minimal camera movement and full reliance on the contents of the frame, almost always shown in deep focus. Thus, two characters at a considerable distance from each other appear together. In a close-up, Apu leaves his father-in-law's house, but as he turns the camera looks over his shoulder at a dot in the distance—his young son Kajal who has decided to follow him. The two characters are still separated because the close-up shot is also a long shot. When the young boy dashes towards his father, the camera unites them in a close-up of both.

Butch Cassidy and the Sundance Kid (1969)

Directed by George Roy Hill and written by William Goldman with a score by Burt Bacharach, this is clearly an "entertainment," but it also has claims as a classic film mainly because, as a postmodern Western, it defines the end of an era. Based on actual characters, it shows no reverence for the heroes played by Paul Newman (Butch, a train robber and notorious outlaw) and Robert Redford (the "kid," a ruthless gunslinger and killer). Both are based on actual villains—outlaws—of the late nineteenth and early twentieth centuries. It was an end of an era, with outlaws going out of business as fast as they were tracked down, killed, or otherwise eliminated by efficient posses and by the establishment of law and order in the western territories.

Following a ruthless manhunt after their botched train robbery of the Union Pacific Railroad, the two outlaws flee to New York then to Bolivia. There, they continue to ply their trade, but after robbing several banks and becoming notorious again, they decide to go straight. Circumstances conspire to force them to kill and they revert to being bandits. Eventually, in a showdown with the Bolivian army, they are killed.

As a film, *Butch Cassidy and the Sundance Kid* comes close to being the opposite of a classic Western film. Western heroes usually win, and the villains fall. Here, the heroes *are* the villains, but they are very likeable, and that poses a problem for the film's ending. One of them (Cassidy) is not even a killer; indeed, he never killed anyone until he was forced to defend his lawful property. The other (Sundance) is adept with the gun, but even he does not kill unless he believes he's absolutely forced to. The character of Sundance, however, is based on a real person who was actually a vile killer.

The film is also postmodern in its music and editing. The music is not the classic Western score (e.g., Elmer Bernstein's score for *The Magnificent Seven*). It is a series of songs/lyrics inserted into the movie's action at critical moments to establish characterization in non-dialogue scenes. The other techniques used are montage, the freeze-frame, and transition scenes photographed in sepia (a brown tint). These combine to give the movie its unusual look.

The film has charm, a new look for its time, and entertainment values, but it is hard to decide whether or not to take it seriously. George Roy Hill, in DVD commentary on "The Making of *Butch Cassidy and the Sundance Kid*" explains that he wanted to make the characters and situations "real" by making them funny occasionally. But being real and being "light" are two different things. *Bonnie and Clyde*, made only a year or two earlier, also innovates: it uses suggestive cinematography, features charismatic actors as villains, and introduces graphic violence to a much greater degree than does *Butch Cassidy and the Sundance Kid*. But there is never a question of whether *Bonnie and Clyde* is anything but a tragedy. Its moments of humor are few and far-between, and those flawed characters are never (and never seem) happy, whereas Newman and Redford never seem to take their lives or actions seriously; they joke to the end. They are loners, outcasts as much as outlaws, who never seem capable of confronting their inner selves (as Bonnie and Clyde do) or the gravity of their crimes. They remain affable children, living in illusion and fabricating one illusion after another. The West collapses ("them days is over" is the movie's favorite dictum) and they move on to Bolivia as if Bolivia were paradise. They even plan to go to Australia as they are dying. These characters are light-hearted existentialists, care-for-nothings living in a dream world even as they play with other people's lives. Even acts of brutal violence (the sudden shooting and death of the man who hires them) don't seem to shake their eternal joviality. Affable actors like Newman and Redford do exist, but do actual people, like Butch and Sundance?

Quiz Show (1995)

Directed by Robert Redford, *Quiz Show* is based on the 1950s TV scandals which ended in Congressional hearings and destroyed the career of one of the most prominent literary men in America. One is impressed by the movie's tough moral fiber. It could be categorized as a docudrama because it is based on a historical event—exposure of cheating on a TV game show. That era may be virtually forgotten and its scandals seem mere peccadilloes compared to Watergate, Iran-Contra, Whitewater, and what have you. But the movie oddly reminds us of those later, greater scandals. It is an echo of recent events.

Whatever spin is given to these facts, the movie is unyielding in its lofty tone and moral certitude. A scandal is a scandal; wrongdoing is wrongdoing; lies are lies; and the effects of such corruption are devastating whenever it arises. The movie is fearless. Top TV executives at NBC, in collusion with the head of a giant pharmaceutical corporation (Geritol), wash their hands and claim total innocence of the fraud that goes on just below them. Unlike real-life scandals which have to be unraveled bit by bit by investigators and journalists, a movie has the luxury of telling the truth, the whole truth, and nothing but the truth (as the movie sees it). At the end you know that the top TV executive, a crass liar and hypocrite, oversaw and directed the whole scenario. You know that the top men pulled the strings for every move to replace contestants who no longer "drew." You witness the depths of shame and humiliation that young Charles van Doren brought on his family.

The movie never budges from its position. It judges the participants harshly, shows the total cynicism and crass deceptions of *all* the players from the producers to the host and all the way up the ladder. They are all guilty. The movie never forgives them, nor attempts to show them in any favorable light. They are corrupt, and Dante would have placed all of them without exception in the lower circles of Hell. Even some members of the U.S. Congress's Oversight Committee are suspected of sympathy toward young Van Doren at the moment of his confession, though a few are honorably repelled by him.

Of course, the movie is also cynical for reasons inherent in its premises: TV has had us and will continue to have us. It is an omnipotent, unassailable giant, and so are the conglomerate giants that sponsor it. But the movie has some sympathy for the industry's pawns. Two are highlighted sharply, played by two diametrically different actors: John Turturro's Herb Stempel is a moral clone of Willie Loman, driven by his inordinate and ridiculous desire for success. His ambition is a corruption of the American Dream which tempts him to do a rigged quiz show. He resents being dumped for the more glamorous and literate Van Doren and plunges into hysteria, clownish resentment, buffoonery, jealousy, and despair. He thinks he will be vindicated if he tells the truth, so he betrays after he is betrayed and ends up (in the movie) a bitter man. His successor, Charles Van Doren, is played by Ralph Fiennes in an astonishing tour de force performance on the heels of his monstrous Goeth in *Schindler's List* (to be followed a year later by the amoral Almasy in *The English Patient*). His face shows the subtler nuances and ambiguities of the errant scion of a famous family, sure to rise to fame as a "mere" literature professor but struggling to conceal his moral compromise and corruption. He is seduced by the easy lure of money and instant fame which beckon at him into this moral muddle that he only vaguely perceives. He is lionized by the TV audience and his students, all of whom think he is a demigod of learning and culture. He is also self-deceived, believing that he is promoting literature—

which he is—which exonerates him in his own flawed conscience. Lying becomes a way of life; to cheat or not to cheat is no longer an ethical question but a practical means to an end. He is cocky even to his venerable dad, Mark Van Doren, a distinguished scholar and professor portrayed superbly by Paul Scofield. Charles refers to his "level" of income, flaunting his new social status. He finds his nemesis, the man who reluctantly brings him down, in congressional investigator Dick Goodwin (Rob Morrow). Goodwin uncovers these unholy alliances but aims only to get the TV executives. He does not want to destroy the name of an honorable family. Indeed, he sees Charles's inner struggle and would let him go scot free, though Goodwin's wife (Mira Sorvino) accuses him of being the "Uncle Tom of the Jews."

Stempel testifies buffoonishly to the scorn and laughter of the audience, and so does Charles as he falls from grace. NBC fires him from a position reading poetry on the Today Show, and the Columbia board of trustees fires him from his teaching position.

Both Stempel and Van Doren come off as stooges of the system. They're the fall guys, so they fall and live the rest of their lives in mediocrity. The film does a good job with its final ironies: the camera lingers tellingly on the colonnades of the Capitol while Al Freedman (one of the producers) is heard as he testifies: "Here, we're not exactly hardened criminals . . . This the entertainment business. . . ." That may involve a little cheating, a little fraudulence. . . . But for heavens' sakes, the public loves it. . . .

Robert Redford deserves congratulations for his honesty and consistency and for his refusal to lower the moral tone of this movie for box office considerations. The movie barely made it with the critics and wasn't a box office success, but as for conscience checking? Give it another try.

The Loss of Sexual Innocence (1999)

Written and directed by Mike Figgis and photographed by Benoit Delhomme, this film achieved some notoriety because of its innovative techniques: dream sequences, nonlinear narrative, ensemble casting, and absence of dialogue/reliance on visual action. Because of its silent sequences, *The Loss of Sexual Innocence* can almost qualify as a silent film. It has a minimal script—about sixty pages—unlike the typical hundred-page Hollywood screenplay. Lushly photographed in northern England (Figgis's birthplace is Carlyle), it moves on to northern Italy and Rome, and to a dried salt lake in Tunisia near where *The English Patient* was filmed. A group of native Tunisian women were used in the film's last sequences with one or two local actors.

The film follows two storylines: one, obviously symbolic, telling of Adam and Eve in the garden, was actually shot on an abandoned English estate. The

With minimal dialogue and a script less than two-thirds the length of a typical Hollywood screenplay, The Loss of Sexual Innocence *seems like a silent film. Its concentration on atmosphere and mood rather than plot and character opened the eyes of many viewers to exciting possibilities of the medium overlooked since its infancy.*

man and woman emerge from the calm waters of a lake in brilliantly photographed sequences shot in octachrome. Adam is African, Eve a white blonde. She is tempted by the snake, both eat the fruit, succumb to stomach convulsions (fruit poisoning?), make love in something like an abandoned barn, and are expelled from the estate. As an iron gate closes behind them, they are mobbed by a crowd while they hastily put on clothes. The other story is told in flashbacks and dream sequences, covering Figgis's reminiscences of growing up in Kenya, East Africa. His vivid memories intertwine with vivid cinematic images of a boy who witnesses several sexual encounters—one between his parents—and loses his innocence, as the title promises. As a grown man called Nick, played by Julian Sands, he is married with a wife and child (both go through sexual dream sequences), but gets involved with a girl in a group of topographers. The mapmakers are unlike those in *Patient*, much more amateurish. The girl is Saffron Burrows, who has a twin sister from whom she has been separated since birth, and the two girls meet casually in an airport. They just look at each other but never exchange a word or show recognition.

Some have made light of this movie. Its innovativeness is not so new: Fellini mixed consciousness with dream states in *8½*, a movie this movie consciously imitates, in my opinion; Truffaut merged dreams and reality in *Jules and Jim*. In his DVD commentary, Figgis says he borrowed ideas from Jean-Luc Godard. He innovates on innovations. He does not think the age of experimentation is over or that Hollywood has wiped out all opposition from those who make movies on extremely low budgets (*Loss* cost three million dollars, one-sixth of Julia Roberts' salary). Figgis obviously contributes to the genre of individualistic, experimental, noncommercial films. He tells simultaneous stories on practically split screens.

Figgis uses an interesting soundtrack mixture: Chopin piano music, Beethoven and Mozart sonatas, some pop music, and a composition of his own to substitute for a Charles Ives piece that he could not afford to use. Does this work? In a purely aesthetic sense, yes; the visuals are beautiful and Benoit Delhomme's photography breathtaking. The whole movie was shot with a super 16mm camera then blown up to 35mm. This enables the photographer to crowd his equipment into a very small space (a car, for instance) and to handhold for special scenes which require quick movement. The overall absence of a linear story and of dialogue (what there is is soft-spoken and barely heard) forces viewers to concentrate on the image rather than the word. This is purely cinematic, but the confusions it produces for ordinary viewers hurt the movie, at least on first viewing.

Figgis has won respect for his previous movies (*The Browning Version* and *Miss Julie*, in which the linear narrative works so well), and he must be respected. His experiments with the medium make him one of the most noteworthy auteurs of our time, but he seems to be fighting a double fight. First, he is expanding the traditional horizons of the medium as some great directors did in the past. Godard, Fellini, and Kurosawa, all experimented with form and with the break-up of the traditional linear narrative. Second, Figgis is battling the Hollywood system and the system's continuing lack of experimentation with the mainstream commercial movie. Hollywood repeats itself, using genre formulas that have worked again and again to please audiences. Such "success," however, will lead to inevitable sterility that will eventually overtake such repetition. Figgis proves that a good movie—even an experimental one—can be made on a minimal budget. He uses non-actors, models, crowds, or locations that suit him when they are available. He achieves superb results with a good photographer, so that even the necessary financial compromises do not show. There is no sign of amateurishness in this movie. This maturing filmmaker has had it with traditional and predetermined formats. He is demonstrating that Hollywood is not only extremely greedy, but also extremely wasteful. Maybe he will succeed in convincing executives to scale down and in the process to upgrade popular taste. After all, he works with movies as a painter does.

Students are advised to see this movie more than once, and possibly to
listen to the commentary on the DVD.

Tango (1998)

Written and directed by Carlos Saura with cinematography by Vittorio
Storaro, music by Lalo Schifrin, and produced by Juan Carlos Codazzi, this is
a Spanish/Argentinian production.

Tango qualifies as film *as film* in a most remarkable way. Its subject is not
an event or a plot or a character or group of characters, although all three of
these ingredients are present. *Tango* highlights a *subject*, in this case the dance
itself. *Tango* is about tango, an Argentinian dance famous since the time of
Rudolph Valentino, the movie star who made it popular in the 1920s with the
film *Four Horsemen of the Apocalypse* (1922). It had been in eclipse lately,
except among ballroom dancers. In Argentina, the tango is a national pastime,
an artistic pursuit, and the soulful self-expression of the individual dancers. In
Argentina people grow up to dance the tango, which is even contained in the
school curriculum. It is not a dance for a single individual, but for couples; "It
takes two to tango," the cliché reminds us. It is a very stylized dance in terms
of body movement, which is confined to the lower half of the body so that
torsos and heads remain straight and almost stiff, as if ignoring what takes
places below the waist. The dancers' faces are expressionless, their eyes riveted
ahead, their heads occasionally snapping at right angles. There are three basic
steps, one to the right or left, and two in the opposite direction, but the variations are endless: The hips swing, the legs intertwine, the feet stretch to create sharp angles or to pirouette. The rhythm is a simple continuous bang-
bang in 2/4 or 4/4 time. It's a serious, even melancholy, dance which suggests absolute control of the body at a moment of erupting passion. A tango
will occasionally end with a symbolic stabbing of the antagonist or lover, the
dancing partner.

And there is the music. Tango songs such as "La Comparsita" have been
popular throughout the world. Well-known classical composers like Igor
Stravinsky have composed tangoes. When Lalo Schifrin agreed to compose
the music for *Tango*, he incorporated traditional strains with broader contemporary themes played by small ensembles—guitar, accordion, piano—
then expanded to polyphonic and symphonic compositions and even to choral
music borrowed from Verdi's "Nabucco." There was a reason for that: The
film is a medley of dances, most performed by couples, but some by mixed
groups of males and females, still others by male or female ensembles. Music
and choreography, movement and rhythm, tune and movement blend harmoniously. Storaro's cinematography has a direct relationship to the music

and dance. After a few establishing shots of Buenos Aires, *Tango* is filmed entirely indoors on a soundstage except for a few numbers done at a restaurant and an apartment. The interior sets give the film its focus and character. To the exclusion of extraneous action or dialogue, the film is a musical consisting entirely of music and dance numbers—nothing more or less than a display of exquisite cinematography, fluid dancing, and lively music.

Tango is, however, much more than that. Among other things it is a love story and an understated political thriller. It raises questions of artistic freedom and of the artist's responsibility to tell the truth. On the surface, *Tango* is about the making of a film called *Tango*. Its director Mario, played by Miguel Angel Sola, agonizes over some of his choices; casting the right female dancer; whether or not to include certain scenes of a political nature that his producers find offensive; whether he can use them but play them down. An auto accident has left him walking with a cane, and he has quarreled with his ex-mistress, accomplished dancer Cecilia Narova. His producer is an Argentine Mafia don who wants him to give the lead to Elena, a young dancer *he* loves. She is played by newcomer Mia Maestro, and she becomes the don's mistress, but she admires Mario and eventually becomes his lover. During their few love scenes—which at first seem intrusions into the dance sequences—he tells her of his troubles, and his confessions comprise the film's two major premises: the imagination is the only "guardrail" against despair, but the artist has a responsibility to remember and incorporate the past. Without the past, we cannot gain full identity as humans. The later dance sequences are choreographed around mass graves where corpses are dumped or groups lined up against a wall to be shot— episodes that no doubt took place during the dictatorships of Juan and Evita Peron. Certain parties in high places ("generals" are mentioned) have vested interests in helping the general populace forget what happened in the past. Here, the artist battles a dilemma that is not confined to the artistic endeavor: Is it better to leave past evil buried or to rake it up and be reminded of it again and again? *Tango* defines art and its social function: there can be no such thing as "pure" entertainment. The artist is obligated to keep a sharp lookout for social ills and to reflect them in his art, even when that art is at its most entertaining. Art's, and film's, social function is to remind us of deeds past while it amuses us. From all possible angles, *Tango* stirs up emotions and memories for all the right reasons.

Suggested Readings and Hypertext Links

Arnheim, Rudolf. *Film as Art*. Berkeley: University of California Press, 1957.
Baudy, Leo, and Marshall Cohen, eds. *Film Theory and Criticism: Introductory Readings*, 5th ed. New York: Oxford University Press, 1998.

Eisenstein, Sergei. *Film Form.* New York: Harcourt Brace, 1949.

Miller, Mark Crispin, ed. *Seeing Through Movies: A Pantheon Guide to Popular Culture.* New York: Pantheon Books, 1990.

Monaco, James. *How to Read Film: The Art, Technology, Language, History and Theory of Film and Media,* 2ⁿᵈ ed. New York: Oxford University Press, 1981.

Perkins, V. F. *Film as Film: Understanding and Judging Movies.* Baltimore: Penguin Books, 1972.

Thomson, David. *A Biographical Dictionary of Film,* 3ʳᵈ ed. New York: Alfred A. Knopf, 1994.

Elizabeth. ClassicHomePage: <http://www.reelclassics.com/Movies/index.htm>

Tango, DVD ed. Sony, 1999. With commentary by producer Juan Carlos Codazzi and leading actress Mia Maestro. <http://www.sonyclassics.com>

Suggested Films for Study

The Battleship Potemkin (or *Potemkin*) (1925), dir. Sergei Eisenstein and Grigori Aleksandrov
The General (1927), dir. Buster Keaton and Clyde Bruckman
Modern Times (1936), dir. Charles Chaplin
La Grande Illusion (1937), dir. Jean Renoir
The Bicycle Thief (1948), dir. Vittorio De Sica
Hamlet (1948), dir. Laurence Olivier
Orpheus (1949), dir. Jean Cocteau
On the Waterfront (1954), dir. Elia Kazan
Pather Panchali (1955), dir. Satyajit Ray
The Searchers (1956), dir. John Ford
Nights of Cabiria (1957), dir. Federico Fellini
La Dolce Vita (1960), dir. Federico Fellini
The Virgin Spring (1960), dir. Ingmar Bergman
Lawrence of Arabia (1962), dir. David Lean
Yojimbo (1962), dir. Akira Kurosawa
2001: A Space Odyssey (1968), dir. Stanley Kubrick
The Wild Bunch (1969), dir. Sam Peckinpah
The Godfather (1972), dir. Francis Ford Coppola
The Trojan Women (1972), dir. Michael Cacoyannis
Dona Flor (1978), dir. Bruno Barreto
Raging Bull (1980), dir. Martin Scorsese
The Natural (1984), dir. Barry Levinson

Fatal Attraction (1987), dir. Adrian Lyne
Dead Poets Society (1989), dir. Peter Weir
The Prince of Tides (1991), dir. Barbra Streisand
The Remains of the Day (1993), dir. James Ivory
Fargo (1996), dir. Joel Coen
L.A. Confidential (1997), dir. Curtis Hanson
American Beauty (1999), dir. Sam Mendes
Boys Don't Cry (1999), dir. Kimberley Pierce

CHAPTER TEN

Responding to Social Themes in Film

How do I respond to social themes in film? This is an important question, since movies are used extensively in college curricula to document, substantiate, and illustrate various social phenomena that film has captured on celluloid. In fact, film has gone far beyond the boundaries of the twentieth century, extending back to show life (albeit fictionally) from prehistoric times, through the classical period of antiquity, medieval times, the Renaissance, and early European and world history. It brings materials to the classroom from every corner of the earth. Through science fiction, film has provided visions of exploration of future frontiers. As a medium of substance, film covers such diverse subjects as philosophy, history, political science, literature, communication, and religion. It touches on social issues: social justice, the environment, the political arena (past and present), war, ethnicity and gender, and many others. Film is a universal medium and as such is uniquely suited to teaching and sometimes inspiring social causes.

Should a Film Contain a Moral?

Students and other viewers who seek social themes in film often ask whether a film should contain a "message" or be simply a means of entertainment.

This is a much debated idea. As in the literary tradition, purists believe that film is simply a form of self-expression whose only purpose is to entertain—that is, to provide a pleasure of purely aesthetic dimensions. Why else go to the movies? What is there to learn from a fictional story projected on a screen? Since antiquity some critics have insisted that any narrative art—the tragedy, epic, novel—loses its organic integrity if a moral is tagged onto it. Others say every story *has* a moral, whether the author intends one or not. Still other critics insist that morality is the business of philosophy, not of art. Aristotle wrote books on both literary criticism and ethics, but in his *Poetics* he never asked critics to consider questions of morality and ethics. His approach to poetry is entirely rhetorical and aesthetic, concerned with problems of language and structure. He asserts that constructing a perfect plot is the major concern of tragedy because tragic action (*mythos*) provides pleasure and effects a catharsis of pity and fear. That was as far as he would go in outlining the purpose of tragic art. Some modern film critics—the Russian Formalists, for instance: Viktor Shklovsky, Fernard Leger, Sergei Eisenstein—insist that art has purely an aesthetic function, with no practical purpose whatsoever (Andrew 80). Moralist critics, on the other hand, beginning with Plato and Horace, insisted that writers teach morality. Any pleasure inherent in art is there to enhance and promote the moral lesson. The debate continued into the Renaissance. Sir Philip Sidney aligned himself with Horace and Plato, insisting that poetry should "teach and delight." Later critics—Samuel Taylor Coleridge among them—held that pleasure remains the immediate end of poetry, though he admitted that the final end" of art should be to teach morality. Henry James responded to Victorian moralist critic Walter Besant, contending that a novelist should not yield to the belief that a novel's purpose is to teach morality. A writer, James claimed, should be completely free to choose a subject and to treat that subject as he likes. His only obligation is to make a "perfect work," and a work that is "interesting" (Kaplan 392).

Film Is Conscious of Moral Behavior

Filmmakers, by and large, have followed Aristotle and Henry James, but not by consciously adhering to aesthetic principles. Hollywood filmmakers place "entertainment values" above everything else. They aim to please audiences without regard for morals or aesthetics. Indeed commercial filmmaking is called the "entertainment industry." High art is not called for here, so, it is not produced. But cinema, like poetry and the novel, has its own theorists. Sergei Eisenstein developed theories on montage that greatly influenced Hollywood filmmakers. French filmmaker Jean Renoir's works have been the basis for André Bazin's theory of realism. Film masters such as Alfred Hitchcock,

Howard Hawks, Akira Kurosawa, and Ingmar Bergman are not theorists in the pure sense, but they have used many cinema techniques to express their views on humanity, society, social and psychological behavior, and a range of other themes. Most of these filmmakers believed that the art and craft of cinema dominated its message; that is, that messages or ideas in a film could be expressed only through meticulous attention to detail and form, complete mastery of the craft of cinema. Structuralist and Poststructuralist critics have by and large followed this same line of reasoning, viewing art as a matter of narrative and language interpretation. The French New Wave added a strain of intellectualism to the filmmaker's purpose, but moralism per se has had few proponents. Filmmakers such as Frank Capra and Stanley Kramer have been considered moralizers, but it is their interpreters who draw conclusions about the points their films are supposed to make. Of the two, Frank Capra is per-

In a typical populist film such as **Mr. Smith Goes to Washington,** *the champion of lost causes wins the day. Here, at the end of a marathon one-man Senate filibuster, the naive honorary appointee Senator Smith nearly despairs when the tide of public opinion seems to turn against him. Moments later, however, the tide will turn against the corrupt political machine he is attempting to overthrow.*

haps more focused on the message. His films express and assert the American values, of optimism, honesty, plainness of manners, and love of truth: *Mr. Smith Goes to Washington* (1939) and *It's a Wonderful Life* (1943), to mention the best known. Stanley Kramer's *On The Beach* (1958) drew directly on human fears of a nuclear holocaust at the height of the Cold War.

Message as Part of a Story

But when message is built into the story, it must be an inseparable part. Kramer, known for his "heavy-on-the-message" style, is a relatively rare specimen among filmmakers. So is Stanley Kubrick, a director and distinguished auteur whose films are persistently antiestablishment: *Spartacus*, set in the Roman empire, or *A Clockwork Orange*, set in a futuristic dictatorship. Generally, however, Kubrick expresses his ideas visually as he does in *Barry Lyndon* and *2001: A Space Odyssey*. Antiwar movies like *Platoon* or *Apocalypse Now* are supposedly made for their messages. The films of Charlie Chaplin are thinly disguised polemics against a technological, materialistic, inhumane twentieth-century society. Yet the best movies are often those whose themes are built into the action and do not cry out for recognition. Analysis of the action includes analysis of characters *in* action and decodification of the film's language—that is, its imagery—through which its themes and subthemes are revealed. Even without a moral, a film can have a moral message which viewers can infer and deduce from what the characters do and say and/or from what the imagery suggests. No film, not even a documentary, can be made without a story involving some moral resolution. Aristotle argued that pity and fear are not produced if a story ends with the villain rising. That does not satisfy the moral sense (33). Even the simplest type of film—indeed, simple films can do this more powerfully—must have a villain punished and a hero rewarded. Children's stories (*A Little Princess* [1939, 1995] or *The Wizard of Oz* [1939]) are paradigmatic and offer strong moral messages.

Using Film Language to Uncover Social Themes

Discovering the message is the job of film interpretation. And the method suggested in this text guide is to read film by identifying film techniques and by searching the film text for axes and nodes. There is no set rule by which imagery should be interpreted to uncover social themes, but it is useful to remember Tzvetan Todorov's suggestions which we introduced in chapter 4, "Film Language": seek points of focalization, strategically placed "axes" and "nodes" which point to thematic development (Kaplan 635). The only obligation

Todorov lays on the reader is not to read *a priori*, based on knowledge of an author's life or technique, but to actually search the text. Todorov is talking about *reading* a text, but his suggestion can easily be transferred to reading a film. Viewers read language, but this language comes to them in images. Reading images is the preferable way to discover a film's themes, subthemes, and meanings. Thus, whatever message a film carries can be decoded by reading the axes and nodes which are the guideposts for readers/viewers. There are other approaches, of course. Viewers can use the historical approach, for instance. In fact, a syllabus can be composed entirely of historical films, films of gender, political films, etc., or the types can be combined. One approach does not exclude the other and several can be used simultaneously. However, a careful reading of the text will yield results useful for any number of purposes.

Reading Imagery in David Lean's Films: *The Bridge on the River Kwai* and *A Passage to India*

Like many great filmmakers, Lean strews his narrative with suggestive, though sometimes unobtrusive, imagery. His imagistic build-up is suggestive of thematic developments. Themes can be revealed through dialogue, camera angles, camera movement, close-ups, montage, and so on, but since film is primarily visual, it is best to search for visual details (axes and nodes) that suggest developing ideas. In David Lean's *The Bridge on the River Kwai* (1957), the flying hawk seen at the beginning and end of the action suggests an Olympian detachment and overview, not unlike that of the gods in *The Iliad*. The swagger stick carried by Colonel Nicholson (the late Alec Guinness) is potentially a thematic image if seen in context. It is first noticed when Nicholson approaches Saito, the Japanese commander of the prison camp, to remind him that officers must not perform manual labor in accordance with the Geneva convention. Nicholson smacks the stick on his thigh as he approaches Saito, asserting the authority he still believes he has. Saito breaks the stick in an outburst of rage, telling him that he is *not* in command. The stick disappears during Nicholson's imprisonment, only to reappear in his hands after Saito is forced to free him in order to get the bridge built. The stick remains in Nicholson's hands until the final moments after the bridge is completed. Then after talking to Saito on the bridge, he accidentally drops it into the river. The swagger stick sums up British military attitudes—arrogance, conceit, contempt for one's opponent, self-assurance, overconfidence, hubris. Shears, the American character, points out with some apprehension that the British have walked to their death clutching it. It is the symbol of the British empire with all its powers and its illusions in its rise, decline, and fall.

In a more recent Lean film, *A Passage to India* (1984), a seemingly insignificant umbrella keeps reappearing. In the first scene, Adela Quested carries an umbrella as she enters a travel bureau. It is a scene of pouring rain, and rain and water in general are key images in this film: "What a terrible river! What a wonderful river!" says Mrs. Moore at the mosque during her encounter with Dr. Aziz, when she is informed that the Ganges contains dead bodies eaten by crocodiles. The umbrella reappears in dry terrain when the British are protecting themselves against the sun, notably when Mrs. Moore and Adela are entertained by Aziz at the first stop at the Marabar caves. No such protection from the sun is afforded Adela when she accompanies Aziz to the second ledge of the caves and suffers her ordeal. The umbrella reappears much later in the hands of Professor Godbole (Alec Guinness) who toys with it, closing it and depositing it outside Fielding's door. He picks it up again a few moments later when he departs and triumphantly snaps it open in Fielding's face, telling him how accurate his predictions were about the outcome of Aziz's trial: "Who would have foretold he would be saved by his enemy?" The umbrella is a weapon in Godbole's hands, a means of protection, a gadget assimilated from western civilization and fastidiously used by the knowing oriental sage. Later Fielding pays a visit to Aziz who is being dressed by his servant for a festival in his honor. The Englishman holds an umbrella which he never opens, even after rain drenches him while he stands outside Aziz's house. If the umbrella is the symbol (or signifier) of protection, it hardly protects Adela Quested from the psychological, moral, and physical torments she suffers after her wish "to see the real India" is satisfied. Fielding self-punishingly refuses to let his protective gadget protect him after his clash with his best Indian friend. Only Godbole, whose knowing wisdom appears to Fielding as apathy and indifference, can use the instrument of protection perfectly. He wields it in protest, to make a point, and to protect himself from the rain.

There is another seemingly insignificant object in the same film: a bicycle. It is a means of conveyance used by Aziz and his friend Mahmout Ali when they are knocked off the road by British officials driving by in their shining new automobiles. Aziz does not use the bicycle when he is abruptly summoned to Major Calendar's house during a dinner with his friends. He takes a tonga instead and ends up being humiliated by a servant. When Adela Quested ventures into the temple and she sees the erotic statues, she has come by bicycle, and so has Godbole when he crosses a bridge to see Aziz near the end of the film. The bicycle is a means of conveyance for the humble underclass Indians, while the conqueror British use carriages and automobiles. It is an image of class transition: Aziz crosses from bicycle to tonga and is punished. Adela crosses from carriage to bicycle and into a "cycle" of adventure. Again, only Godbole uses the gadget correctly, merely as a means of transportation. He is the only character in whom the two cultures, oriental and western, peacefully coexist.

Reading Imagery in Hitchcock Movies

Axes and nodes abound in Hitchcock's works, which have no explicit social message, regardless of specific interpretations viewers may ascribe to them. Of all directors, Hitchcock seems the least socially conscious, oblivious to class and social conflicts, always concentrating on the images projected on the screen to alter an audience's moods and mental states. To that effect, he used MacGuffins, or markers, terms already defined. Hitchcock films can be read from the point of view of a semiotician who interprets freely and at random, with no predetermined point of view about the filmmaker's intentions in making the film. However, Hitchcock developed an existential point of view which is revealed in practically all his protagonists. Nearly all of them are pitted against some mortal danger. They face some hostile force—an adversary, a circumstance, a determined pursuer, an attack from an unexpected source against which they must defend themselves. This crisis often abruptly interrupts an insular existence and subjects the person to severe stress and to a heightened consciousness of peril. Without exception, such an experience enhances the social consciousness. By exposing us to shock—even terror—Hitchcock enables us to deal with the dangers in our environment and the hostility hidden in all of us.

A reading of Hitchcock's social and individual themes requires a reading of axes and nodes because Hitchcock almost always conveys his subtle messages through them. Consider the bottles in Hitchcock's *Notorious* (1946). First a bottle appears in Alicia's hand as she is entertaining guests after her father's trial. Later, Devlin leaves a champagne bottle on his boss's table when he hears of Alicia's assignment. The bottles in Sebastian's palatial home and in his cellar are filled with uranium ore. Later on, a poisoned demitasse is shown at a critical moment. All these containers of liquid—bottles, glasses, cups of coffee, even a glass of milk—reveal things about the protagonists, as well as about the viewers themselves.

The bottle left by Devlin at his boss's office is picked up by the camera for a few seconds, evidently defining the boss's point of view. His eyes rest on it for a few moments to underscore the dramatic point that he knows Devlin is emotionally involved with Alicia. This revelation makes him an all-knowing participant with, perhaps, an omniscient point of view. When the awkward Nazi Emile discovers one of the uranium bottles mistakenly placed on Sebastian's guest table, he pays for that recognition with his life. Devlin, in search of the secret substance in the bottles in Sebastian's cellar, solves the mystery when he accidentally knocks over a "wine" bottle, spilling its contents. The crucial recognition scene, however, the one with the greatest dramatic impact, is Alicia's sudden discovery that the coffee she is drinking is poisoned. Her Nazi physician Dr. Anderson picks up the wrong cup, and both Mrs. Sebastian and Alex very obviously motion to him that he has the wrong cup. Alicia instantly knows. *Strangers on a Train* opens with the image of two pair of feet casually crisscrossed. Viewers see one set of feet briskly approaching the other, and a moment later their owners meet on the train. Meanwhile, other symbols reinforce this casual crossing of the two individuals' paths; for instance, the rail tracks converge at certain points. The meeting, as these symbols suggest, is both casual and fatal. The madman Bruno (Robert Walker) meets Guy (Farley Granger), a famous tennis player whose intimate life is well-known through publicity. Bruno knows Guy's wife refuses to divorce him and supposes Guy must wish his wife dead or out of the way so that he can marry an heiress, Anne Marton (Ruth Roman). Bruno suffers from the usual Hitchcockian Oedipal complex: He hates his tyrannical father and is adored by his daffy mother. He proposes to Guy that he will kill Guy's wife if Guy will kill his father. This way neither killer will have a motive. It will be murder for murder, a perfect exchange. Guy is revolted by the idea, but he doesn't take it seriously at this point. He rejects it as a joke. But when Bruno informs him that he has actually killed Guy's wife, Guy is caught in a web of events that he can hardly control. The film is replete with symbols: Bruno wears a tie on which a lobster with its claws spread suggests Bruno's grasping hands (whose fingers his mad mother has cleanly manicured). Anne's sister Barbara (Patricia Hitchcock) wears thick glasses, exactly the same size and shape as those of Guy's wife Kathy. Kathy's glasses drop to the ground, where they reflect Kathy's death throes while Bruno chokes her. Later, when Bruno sees Barbara at a party and stares at her glasses, he falls into a trance and nearly chokes a female guest to death. He also holds the lighter with Guy's initials which he drops at the park where the murder occurred to implicate him. The key to interpreting these symbols is the idea of the double. Bruno and Guy are each other's doubles. They share a wish for someone else's death, although Guy's wish is unconscious. Kathy and Barbara are also doubles, in Bruno's mind. The lighter, which falls into a sewer and is retrieved by Bruno at a moment of great tension, is the one object that links Bruno to Guy, thus sealing the homosexual relationship that is Bruno's ultimate aim.

Reading Imagery in Steven Spielberg's *Duel*

A movie admired mostly by those who subscribe to French auteur theories, *Duel* is rarely thought of as a movie with a social message. Made for TV audiences in 1971, *Duel* was released theatrically in 1983 and became a hit in Europe, where it is considered an existential masterpiece. It is Spielberg's first full-length movie, and after *Indiana Jones*, *Jurassic Park*, *Schindler's List*, and *Saving Private Ryan*, it may be completely neglected. But when movie history is written and after the dust has settled, it may prove Spielberg's greatest achievement in terms of pure movie-making. It has something that no other Spielberg movie has to the same degree: pure suspense with no obvious social theme. Yet it is a movie in which a message should be sought. It is a thriller and in Henry James's terms, highly "interesting," not to say absorbing. The story is remarkable for its simplicity. A suburban salesman traveling into the California countryside on business is chased by a truck whose driver he never sees. A peaceful man, David Mann (Dennis Weaver) drives to his destination bothered only by minor irritations. He has had a scuffle with his wife the previous evening, and the truck ahead of him on the road is belching smoke. When he tries to pass it, the truck blocks his way, which surprises but does not alarm him. However, when he does move ahead, the truck descends on him at ninety miles an hour. Disconcerted at first, then shattered, he tries to calm himself at a roadside cafe where viewers hear his thoughts in an inner monologue. "Back to the jungle," he mutters to himself. The episode has thrown him off his orbit, obliging him to see how thin the line is between civilized and savage behavior, between aggressive driving and intentional murder. Mann is shaken but he drives on, assuming the brief nightmare is over. Instead, the truck driver, who remains unseen, forces him to accept a duel, to compete for road rights. This is the moment of decision for Mann: a series of quck cuts (a montage) showing close-ups of his face reveals his state of mind: He is no longer a timid suburban salesman but a primitive duelist, reverting to the jungle—no longer fleeing, but determined to fight. He is challenged by the truck driver to fight to the death, and one of them *will die*. Will it be worth it? Today we call it road rage.

The filmmaker uses visual imagery to connect his various themes. A gas station attendant spurting fluid on Mann's window asks if he wants his hose changed, which Mann thinks is another salesman's trick; but when his car stalls going uphill, it nearly costs him his life. The little detail contains a tragic irony: one warning ignored may be one too many. Later at the cafe, he crashes into a fence which may represent the last protective barrier of civilization. He encounters a stalled school bus that needs help to start. Mann's car, a tiny Dodge Valiant that belies its grandiose name, is unable to move the bus and gets caught on the bus's rear. Mann hops frantically on its hood, trying to free his car while schoolchildren stick out their tongues at him through the window. They laugh at his feeble attempts to be man enough (valiant enough?) to help the helpless. A moment later, Mann watches in his rear view mirror as the truck effortlessly pushes the bus. Again, he flees in desperation with the demon truck behind him until he has to stop at a railroad crossing while a train goes endlessly by. Suddenly, a jolt lets him know the demon is pushing him into the train. He is agonized; one more push and the train will drag him to his death. But then the train passes and he dashes on, hardly knowing why or where. He stops at a gas station where a weird woman—she keeps caged snakes and a lone, chained wolf—welcomes him. Reassured, he heads for the outdoor telephone booth so he can call the police. But before he has time to finish his report, the truck demolishes the booth and scatters the cages, letting the rattlers out. One of them is hanging from Mann's sleeve. There is a close-up of the freed reptiles and of the lone wolf, twisting on its chain. The woman throws her arms up, crying, "My snakes! My snakes!" Is civilization coming apart at the seams?

Mann is as peaceful as your next door neighbor, but he has been chased over a cliff, his car half smashed, the relentless truck always pursuing. Now he places his briefcase against the gas pedal and jumps out of his car. The truck driver does not see this and drives over the cliff, smashing the giant truck to pieces. A montage of close-ups shows a wheel still revolving, oil dripping, a fan in the driver's seat still blowing a piece of cloth attached to it. The driver is never shown, but the monster truck is expiring. The Valiant, true to its name at last, has won. Mann hops triumphantly on the hilltop for a few moments, then lapses into a silent gaze at the sunset. He is still sitting there after several hours, tossing pebbles at the wreck, reflecting. Mann can fight when he has to; he can also destroy and kill. What would a jury say at his trial—if there were one?

There is no need to elaborate on the themes here. Henry James, Walter Besant, and Horace would have been satisfied with the outcome. The story, a road thriller without an obvious theme, becomes a parable of the common man in peril, not a story with a moral attached to it, but—something entirely different—a moral tale.

Film and Gender

Gender in film is a complex concept encompassing a great many subtopics in college curricula: women's studies, literature, politics, rhetoric, and history, to mention a few. In film as in the other disciplines, gender is well represented by a considerable number of films and filmmakers who have concentrated on women's issues: patriarchy, equal economic and job status, social biases against women, education of women, women in the military, in the church, in athletics, and so on. Film has done its share in most of these categories, as a reading of film history shows.

Gender concerns in film are not a recent phenomenon. Almost from the outset, relying heavily on female actresses and even on women directors in its early stages (*Reel Models*), film has featured stories with female leads and stories about women, just as literature preceded it with great female characters—Antigone, Medea, Hester Prynne, Anna Karenina, Hedda Gabler. Film has brought to the screen remarkable women played by great actresses: Garbo as Queen Christina, Mata Hari, Anna Christie, and Ninotchka; Bette Davis as Jezebel and Margo Channing; Vivian Leigh as the tempestuous southern belle Scarlett O'Hara; Maria Falconetti as a saintly Joan of Arc; Greer Garson as scientist Madame Marie Curie; Gene Tierney as the mysterious Laura (*Laura* [1944]); Hedy Lamarr as the biblical Delilah (*Samson and Delilah* [1949]); Katharine Hepburn in many distinguished films, including *Adam's Rib* (1949), *The African Queen* (1951), and *Summertime* (1955); Elizabeth Taylor in *Cleopatra* (1963); Faye Dunaway as a gun-toting bank robber in *Bonnie and Clyde* (1967); Meryl Streep as the compassionate Baroness Karen Blixen in *Out of Africa* (1985)—the list is long. More recent examples include Judi Dench and Cate Blanchett, both of whom played Queen Elizabeth, Dench in *Shakespeare in Love* and Blanchett in *Elizabeth*. Most of these characters are more than mere romantic counterparts to male leads. They are persons possessing significant qualities—intelligence, determination, humor, compassion, and understanding.

Chaplin: A Great Filmmaker and Women

Though most of the great filmmakers of the early and middle twentieth century were males, many became known as "women's directors"—Bergman, employing such talented Swedish actresses as Bibi Anderson and Liv Ullmann; Antonioni with Monica Vitti in *L'Avventura* (1960); and Fellini giving significant roles to his wife Gulietta Masina in *La Strada* (1954), *Nights of Cabiria* (1954), and *Juliet of the Spirits* (1964). These directors concentrated not on the battle of the sexes nor a woman's attempts to liberate herself, but on explorations of the woman's psyche, pitting women against each other in the female world as Bergman does in *Persona*. However, most of their works treat female subjects to highlight man's relationship to woman and woman's role in man's fate, for better or worse.

In almost all his feature films, Chaplin has a female character who is a counterpart of the Little Tramp. As a director, Chaplin does not seem to be feminist nor does he make movies *about* women, as Bergman and Antonioni do. In fact, his attention and the viewers' are always absorbed in the persona of the Tramp or the Jewish barber in *The Great Dictator* or Verdoux in *Monsieur Verdoux* or Calvero in *Limelight*—all descendants of the tramp. But the tramp is always saved by the girl—and in turn saves her. In every one of his feature films, starting with *The Gold Rush* (1925) and through *City Lights* (1931), a female figure is unattainable, or life with her is difficult or impossible, or there are other serious obstacles for the hero to surmount. The girl usually likes the tramp at some point in the story. Sometimes she laughs at him; sometimes, she is puzzled by him. In *City Lights*, the blind girl's eyesight is restored because the Tramp steals the money she needs and goes to prison. She laughs at him at the end when, in the store window, she sees a tramp courting her. Later, though, she touches his hand and is shocked to realize that *this* man, not the millionaire she had imagined, gave her the money.

This moment is the tramp's triumph. He is recognized as a benefactor by a beautiful woman whom he loves, though he is worthless. There is the vagabond girl in *Modern Times* and the Jewish Hanna in *The Great Dictator*, both of whom (played by Paulette Goddard) uplift his existence, making him strive for high goals. But the most poignant episode with a woman comes in *Monsieur Verdoux*. He is a killer of rich widows because he needs money to support his invalid wife and their son. Verdoux is experimenting with a poison formula stolen from a friendly chemist, and he is about to "prove" the poison's effectiveness. He will invite a street person—anyone—up to his apartment, give him or her the poison in some wine, and let this victim go back to a hotel where he or she will die of an apparent heart attack. He finds an impoverished young woman in a raincoat lodged in a doorway to protect herself from the rain. He offers to escort her to his apartment where he offers her a meal . . . and a glass of wine. They start a dialogue about love, he taking the cynical view while she assures him that love does exist. Her own story is an example: She loved her dead husband, who was an invalid, so much that she went to prison for him. Verdoux, about to commit murder, suddenly has a change of heart. Pretending he wants to remove a piece of cork from her wine, he cleverly exchanges it with another glass that holds no poison; then he gives her a considerable sum of money. The monster Verdoux who has killed so coldly is struck by the young woman's earnest passion and sincere belief in love's redeeming worth. Though he is eventually apprehended, Verdoux repents when he meets the girl again as a wealthy woman, grateful for his earlier assistance. Telling her he is going to "fulfill his destiny," a phrase he borrows from her, he turns himself in. Soon he marches to the guillotine, but the girl has redeemed him by awakening his dormant conscience.

In *Limelight*, a similar story unfolds: A young woman accidentally crosses the path of an older man in trouble and redeems him. Calvero, an ex-comedian, is old and has fallen on hard times. He returns to his apartment drunk and smells gas coming from a room two floors beneath him. He finds a girl unconscious on a bed, having attempted suicide. He calls a doctor, and the girl is saved. He takes her to his apartment, telling the landlady she is his wife. He is courteous and assures her he has no evil designs. She is grateful but desperate: her legs are paralyzed. The doctor tells Calvero there is nothing wrong with the young woman's legs; she just *thinks* she cannot walk. Unable to find work, Calvero is motivated to help the woman walk again. She does and goes on to become a famous ballerina. Calvero gives her courage, using sometimes harsh but inspirational words, but he is unable to inspire himself and remains in decline. The girl meets a young composer, but she tells Calvero she loves *him* and wants to marry him. He refuses, thinking she is acting out of pity. His efforts to make a comeback as a performer all end in disaster and he ends up in sideshows, passing the hat. Eventually, the girl discovers him (through the young composer) and secures him a last chance to perform before an audience. She convinces him he can still entertain, but the audience has been told to pretend to laugh at his jokes. Finally Calvero, aided by Buster Keaton, comes alive on the stage, giving a dynamic performance, before he dies of a heart attack. He dies, however, knowing he is worthy: The girl has saved him. Woman in Chaplin's movies is equal to man, and even superior to him in moral status.

Noteworthy "Women's" Movies

Thelma and Louise (1991)

Directed by Ridley Scott, *Thelma and Louise* is perceived by many as the ultimate feminist movie. When it premiered in the summer of 1991, there was a seismic explosion among viewers and critics alike. Never before had a movie flouted the predominance of male icons in Hollywood and elsewhere. In came two determined, hard-nosed, colorful, endearing women who took the law into their own hands and fended for themselves. Never before had two heroines been on the road as a team like the male/female (*Bonnie and Clyde*) or male/male (*Butch Cassidy/Sundance Kid*) teams. No pair of women had defied the law in the same manner as these two had. Here came a new Hollywood breed: A woman, attacked and humiliated by a brutal male, finally stands up, a vindictive tigress with claws and teeth, struggling until the very end, preferring death to surrender. The fact that Thelma and Louise leap to their deaths rather than give themselves up to an army of FBI agents and troopers is what gave the movie its special attraction for feminists and underdog-loving audiences in general—because the movie had fanatic male adherents as well. Though Ridley Scott, a man, was the director, Callie Khouri, a woman, wrote the script which Scott followed unhesitatingly and faithfully. There was no doubt among audiences and critics what the message of *this* movie was. The script declared its intentions, and the movie cried out for recognition of its heroines' causes.

Key images throughout the movie underscore its message. Two, in particular, predominate: truck vs car. Oversized eighteen-wheelers fill the screen from the start, while the two women—the housewife Thelma and the waitress Louise—flee Arkansas in a Thunderbird convertible. The open car allows the two women to signal their individuality: they wear sunglasses, their hair flies in the wind, they sing during moments of exhilaration. When tragedy strikes, the roofless car reveals their dejected faces. Even the name Thunderbird fits the tone. This sleek, fast car can drive over paved and country roads and can elude the police cars. Toward the end, the story takes after *Smokey and the Bandit*, another comparatively shallow chase movie in which a male (Burt Reynolds) is at the wheel. Louise drives with aplomb, decisiveness, consummate skill, and defiance. The car is as obedient to her as a horse in a western. In some ways, *Thelma and Louise is* a Western, since it culminates at the Grand Canyon when the two women drive into the chasm rather than give themselves up. No horse would leap to its death, but the Thunderbird obliges.

The other major image, the truck, is a masculine symbol of power and road domination. Trucks appear as soon as the women flee from the parking lot and the inadvertent killing. Leaving a dead Harlan behind them, they swerve in panic as they exit the lot, and a huge truck honks angrily at them as it swerves to avoid a collision. As soon as they stop at a motel and the flight becomes more organized, elongated phallus-shaped trucks hover in the background. From that point on, the movie action is a constant encounter between car and truck. When they reach Arizona, an insolent truck driver sticks his tongue out at them obscenely. "How disgusting," Thelma tells Louise. The truck passes

Thelma and Louise *led popular film audiences down a groundbreaking, liberating road of radical feminism. When the two heroines take the law into their own hands and then choose to die, they prove themselves more than victims of a male-dominated society.*

them, they pass him, and the scene is repeated several times. By this time, the two women have given up any hope of reconciliation with the law. They have locked a trooper who caught them doing 110 miles an hour in his car's trunk, though Thelma shoots airholes so he can breathe. Wearing a baseball cap, her lips pursed in gleeful contempt, Thelma, the most transformed of the two, has no compunctions about wreaking revenge on the offending truck driver. This time the women pretend compliance and lure him onto a side road. There, as he steps out of his rig and swaggers toward them, they ask him to apologize. When he refuses, they shoot holes in his tires and the entire truck explodes while he curses them, "Damn bitches from hell!" They flee the conflagration at top speed, and the final chase begins.

The run-in with the truck driver sums up the essence of the chase. Scorned, pursued, unrepentant, and desperate, they pay arrears with unparalleled gusto and comic touches which ease viewers' anticipation of the tragedy to come. Thelma and Louise decide to deliver a payback blow to their male adversaries. The Thunderbird has beaten the eighteen wheeler—David against Goliath— except this time the driver was Susan Sarandon and not Burt Reynolds.

Music of the Heart (1999)

Directed by Wes Craven, produced by Marianne Maddalena, and written by Pamela Gray, the movie features Meryl Streep, Angela Bassett, Gloria Estefan, and Aidan Quinn. The film was inspired by the documentary "Small Wonders," based on the life of Roberta Guaspari who became a violin teacher in East Harlem in 1980. She taught groups of young children in three elementary schools in a program so successful that it attracted the attention of musical celebrities Isaac Stern and Itzhak Perlman. Eventually, a benefit concert was given under the patronage of these celebrities to continue the music program in the public schools. The documentary promotes the idea that music (fine art) education is not a frill, but a basic need. Therefore, all schools should allow children to cultivate their artistic nature.

Meryl Streep is wonderful again, although the film overdramatizes her character to stress its point. This actress has a way with ordinary people. Here, she fights for the downtrodden, defends the defenseless, and wins. In *Out of Africa*, she fell on her knees before an unworthy British colonial governor in Kenya to plead for a piece of land the conquerors had taken from the displaced Africans. She was heroic.

In *Music of the Heart*, she plays a woman with a runaway husband, two boys, and no job prospects. She convinces a reluctant but admiring principal Janet Williams (Angela Bassett) to let her teach a class of unruly children to play the violin. Bassett gives her her blessing, over the objections of some parents, who think this is a waste of time. Roberta is a feisty disciplinarian, something considered outmoded by many parents, but she learns to cope with these adversities. She leads a double life, coping with trouble at home with her children and facing a hostile environment at school. The movie makes its case for the importance of the arts in human life.

Girl, Interrupted (1999)

Directed by John Mangold, based on the book by Susanna Kaysen, this film relates her experiences in a psychiatric ward in the 1960s. It could be called a docudrama because it is based on a true story. It is also a story of gender, but not in the ordinary sense because it does not pit woman against man or against a man's establishment. Most of the authority figures in it are women. It is a gender story because it features a lone woman struggling to claim her identity.

It is definitely a woman's story, a story about a group of women in a psychiatric institution. The men in the film are almost shadowy figures who stay well out of the main action. In reality, it is *one* woman's story. Susanna Kaysen, played by Winona Ryder, is in every scene, and the story is told from her point of view.

Her career (life) is interrupted by an attempted suicide which she cannot explain, and she admits herself into this psychiatric hospital. She is told that she has "borderline" personality disorder, a vague and ill-defined term that only increases her anxiety. Other, mostly young, women in the ward include Lisa (Angelina Jolie), who has been there eight years and is given to extremely violent and abusive behavior. She forms a strong bond with Susanna, as do several other young women.

Susanna's trip is like a journey to the underworld, an almost dreamlike state in which the line between the sane and the insane is obscured. Upon being admitted, Susanna feels that she is no more insane than those who guard her, but she consents to take her medicines. She submits to the authority of those who guard her and those who treat her, but she becomes aware of the artificial mental and physical barriers between the guards and the guarded. She submits outwardly to a world that she inwardly rejects. Her quest is to find herself, but when she does and realizes that she wants to write, no one believes her. This borderline state is never resolved, so when she is declared sane a year later, she still does not know whether or not she is insane or to what degree.

The ward is full of interesting characters—some inmates and some wardens: Whoopi Goldberg plays a sympathetic character, tough but kind. In two brief cameos, Vanessa Redgrave (looking splendid!) plays the chief warden, sounding academic, theoretical, and somewhat detached, but nevertheless humane.

In his DVD commentary, James Mangold likens this movie to *The Wizard of Oz*—fending off critical comments that he is repeating the classic *One Flew Over the Cuckoo's Nest*. He also invokes some of Hitchcock's tormented female characters—in *Marnie*, for instance. His favorite comment is that

Susanna is like Dorothy in her journey to the land of Oz, from which she returns knowing more about herself. Susanna's trip, however, is more harrowing, real, and revealing, and she gains more knowledge of good and evil. The film's main revelation is its depiction of the uncertainty of mental states: what is the difference between sanity and insanity? What causes each state? Is it genes, environment, events? None of these issues are resolved, but the film succeeds in raising them. In the fullest sense, this is a woman's story about the confirmation of female worthiness under duress.

Film and Social Themes

> *Two roads diverged in a wood, and I—*
> *I took the one less traveled by,*
> *And that has made all the difference.*
> —Robert Frost

Prejudice and Race

Easy Rider (1969)

Directed by Dennis Hopper, *Easy Rider* came at the end of the sixties when antisocial unrest, mainly caused by the Vietnam war, had reached its climax. The movie had some characteristics similar to those of the Western genre, but it was more an "Eastern," since its vagabonds on motorcycles were traveling east in search of freedom. The leads in *Easy Rider*, Dennis Hopper and Peter Fonda, were not as charismatic as the heroes of typical Hollywood Westerns. They were closer by far to the types they represent—harmless peaceniks trying to deal with their alienation by mixing with their own kind, but gradually becoming aware that their isolation is extreme, incurable, and tragic. The graphically violent death at the end is far more sincere moviemaking than the freeze-frame that does not show Newman and Redford's bloodbath in *Butch Cassidy and the Sundance Kid*.

Despite its restricted budget, *Easy Rider* is a rousing, splendidly photographed movie which uses many film techniques—montage, hand-held camera, and many tracking shots, not to mention a soundtrack that admirably catches the tunes and rhythms of the age. It is a simple story: Two young men around thirty are involved in a drug deal and earn some money. With it, they buy two motor bikes and drive from L.A. to Florida, encountering the cumulative American culture along the way. At their first stop somewhere in Arizona or New Mexico (the locales are terrific), they meet the family of a middle-aged white man who doesn't know what L.A. means. He is married to a

Mexican Catholic woman and has a host of kids. The next stop is at a commune of escapees from city life, all young and several of them women. Wyatt (Peter Fonda) and Billy (Hopper) have brief affairs with two of them. A nude swim in a mountain pool is typical of post-Hays-code American movies.

The men drive through magnificent scenery, and viewers can recognize landscapes where John Ford filmed his Westerns. Resuming their trek east, they join a parade in a small town and are arrested and thrown in jail for parading without a license. They are bailed out by a drunk young lawyer (whose father has some pull with the town sheriff) and he joins them on their journey. The young lawyer (Jack Nicholson) is a card-carrying member of the ACLU. He likes whiskey, but he's kind of naïve and they get him to try marijuana. He offers philosophical tirades on extraterrestrial life and explains how the government is hiding the fact that we have already been invaded by aliens. He lectures on freedom and on how this country proclaims individual freedom but denies it to people with long hair on motorbikes.

Later, they enter a local café where some police officers flirting with the girls spot them. The locals follow them to the state or county line where they are all beaten and Nicholson is killed. Before he dies, he has told them about his brother in New Orleans who would get them "meat." The two continue to New Orleans and the "House of Lights." Its décor is heavy—something between a church and an art house. They pick up two convenient prostitutes (Karen Black is one of them) and take them to the Mardi Gras. A montage reveals their experience in hallucinatory fashion—images of past and present, a mixture of the religious and the pornographic, are flashed on the screen.

They continue their trek and cross into Florida. Two rednecks in a pickup truck think longhaired hippies are invading their state so one picks up a shotgun from the rack and shoots Billy. When Wyatt turns to offer help, he is shot too and his bike bursts into flames. In a lingering shot, the camera shows the winding beauty of the St. Johns River.

The film's multiple themes include contrasts among cultures; the tolerant (of hippies) West versus the bigoted Southeast. The arid desert is the eternal refuge for desperadoes, whereas lush vegetation and the good life are reserved for easterners. Locals are portrayed as hostile to invaders, whether from Mars or from big cities. Newcomers from another part of the country are not welcome, especially if they carry hippie culture with them.

America is the main symbol on Wyatt's helmet, and part of his bike is painted like the American flag. What does Wyatt represent? America's freedom, or its rejection of outsiders?

The travelers, first two and then three, are generally happy. They travel, enjoy themselves, exhilarate in the freedom of the road and their rootless existence. But the established order—locals, police, or the capitalist urban centers they left—will not grant their right to exist or to pursue happiness.

The riders are on the whole good people—they are not violent; they are courteous to those they stay with; and they try to avoid trouble when they seek temporary shelter. Of course, they mock local values when they join the parade, but this is an innocent prank.

The movie speaks to the country's lack of tolerance, to the bigotry of some of its inhabitants, to the amorality of others. Religion is subtly disparaged as irrelevant to the lives of those who practice it. Drugs are a way of life to these outcasts. Ultimately, they are rejected on all counts and killed in a paroxysm of hatred.

Fonda and Hopper (and Terry Southern) put together a movie that fully represents the sixties and the counterculture eruption. The movie, however, has some staying power. Do we accept outsiders more tolerantly today? Do we incorporate and allow cultural values other than our own? Are we afraid, in the words of the Nicholson character, that the shock of knowing they exist will be too great for us? Isn't this the ostrich policy?

Snow Falling on Cedars (1999)

Directed by Scott Hicks from a screenplay by Ron Hicks and Scott Hicks, the movie is based on a novel by David Guterson. The time is around 1950, nine years after Pearl Harbor. A fisherman on an unidentified island in the northwest is found drowned. On the island is a colony of Japanese Americans, one of whom is a young man who fought the Nazis and won multiple decorations. He is accused of the murder. There is a lengthy trial in which the biases of the jury and the prosecutor become apparent. The defense attorney (an aging Max Von Sydow) is brilliant in defending humanitarian principles, appealing to idealism rather than to logic. The story is covered by a young journalist, Ishmael (Ethan Hawke), who is a little like the Ishmael in *Moby Dick* and who is also the ex-lover of the accused man's wife. Ishmael eventually discovers that the death of the fisherman was an accident. The jury is dismissed, and the wrongfully accused man freed.

This synopsis does not do justice to the complicated themes and symbolism of the story. Film techniques—long establishing shots, *mise-en-scène*, flashbacks—are used, and the images are suggestive of themes: a lantern at the beginning represents the "shedding of light," as Scott Hicks explains in the DVD director's commentary. In fact, the entire movie is about "revealing," suggesting that "nothing is what it appears to be." The story is an anatomy of bias. In flashbacks, the persecution of Japanese Americans during World War II is depicted. In one scene the entire family of the young girl Ishmael is courting is rounded up; her father is seized for possessing sticks of dynamite (needed in his farming) and taken to a concentration camp. Thus, Americans rounded up Japanese in a reflection—albeit a milder one—of the way Nazis rounded up Jews.

Though the film centers on the trial, it is not a typical courtroom drama.

The scenes alternate between flashbacks to the past and scenes of the present as the story unfolds on several levels. It dwells on personal relationships, thought processes, shocking revelations. The pace is slow, the pieces come together in a ritualistic fashion, and the camera spends as much time on the landscape as on the persons and events the story covers.

Eventually, the film provokes the viewer to think: What is the essence of the evil called racism? Fear, distrust, suspicion? The Japanese are regarded as non-white in this film, and even those who fought for America in the war are not considered patriotic enough. The message is summed up in Max Von Sydow's defense. He appeals to us, not just to the inhabitants of that little island, to be more humane, worthier of being civilized. He has passion and vision, and so does this film.

The Hurricane (1999)

Directed by Norman Jewison, this movie is based on an autobiography by Rubin "Hurricane" Carter and *Lazarus and the Hurricane* by Sam Chaiton and Terry Swinton. The screenplay is by Armyan Bernstein and Dan Gordon, and the music by Christopher Young. Ideally, viewers should see the DVD edition (Universal) with commentary by Norman Jewison.

Denzel Washington gives a strong, very passionate performance as Carter, a prizefighter of the 1960s who was incarcerated for nineteen years for a murder he did not commit. Carter had a history of arrest and incarceration since he was eleven years old, but the film shows why the boy became violent: he attacked a pedophile who was attempting to molest one of his young friends. Carter threw a bottle at the man, who seized him and was about to toss him into the Paterson waterfall when Carter stabbed him. He was placed in a juvenile facility for eight years, then enlisted in the army without revealing his "criminal" record, and was arrested again upon his release. He spent years in prison in his twenties, and that is when he decided to turn his body into a fighting machine. After his prison term he fought several fights in the ring and was about to become world champion when he was arrested for murder.

The film is powerful for many reasons, one of them the performance by Washington himself. The film demonstrates the hatred and bigotry of those responsible for his wrongful conviction, but also the compassion of a group of white Canadians who dedicated their lives to right a wrong. His story unfolds in flashbacks. Some sections are in black and white, including several of his fights—for instance, in Trenton, New Jersey, where he demolished several opponents. But the main thread of the story is told by a black youth, Lezer Martin, who is adopted by some Canadians who want to teach him to read and write so he can go to college. The young man reads Hurricane's biography in the 1980s, writes to Carter, and receives an answer. Soon, the Canadians get involved, become convinced of Carter's innocence, and try to help him. For years they patiently dig up new information and finally present it to a federal

The Hurricane *is not only a moving dramatization of the forces of racial prejudice and hatred but a searching elucidation of the protagonist's transformation into a person of sensitivity and dignity.*

judge who decides to read it instead of sending it back to the state court in New Jersey, where it would have no chance. The judge is played by veteran actor Rod Steiger. He overrules previous court decisions on the grounds of racial prejudice, and Carter is a free man after nineteen years in prison.

This true story happened in the 1960s at the height of the Civil Rights movement. *The Hurricane* is about racial prejudice and hatred, but it is also a story of a man's reformation. In prison, Carter turns toward his inner self, drawing on inner resources to become a free and great man. He is proud and unsubdued, refusing to wear a prison uniform and transforming himself first into a fighter and later into an intellectual and spiritual man. He is capable of change and growth, and that is amply demonstrated by both Washington's performance and Jewison's direction—and by the valuable contributions of all involved in making this film. It is not so much a story of hatred as of the bonds between people of different races and common spirit. Human virtues are highlighted—compassion, vision, dedication, sensitivity—while easy sentimentality and blatant messages are avoided. This is a story of both whites and blacks, not of one race pitted against another. It is a story of the rise of man and woman from the morass of bias to human dignity and freedom.

Suggested Readings and Hypertext Links

Andrew, James Dudley. *The Major Film Theories: An Introduction.* New York: Oxford University Press, 1976.

Black, Gregory D. *Hollywood Censored: Morality Codes, Catholics, and the Movies.* New York: Cambridge University Press, 1994.

Haskell, Molly. *From Reverence to Rape: The treatment of Women in the Movies,* 2nd ed. Chicago: University of Chicago Press, 1987.

James, Henry. "The Art of Fiction." In *Criticism: The Major Statements,* 3rd ed., Charles Kaplan and William Anderson, eds. New York: St. Martin's Press, 1991.

Kael, Pauline. *For Keeps: Thirty Years at the Movies.* New York: Plume, 1996.

Medved, Michael. *Hollywood vs. America: Popular Culture and the War on Traditional Values.* New York: HarperCollins, 1992.

Todorov, Tzvetan. "How to Read." In *Criticism,* op. cit.

The Hurricane, DVD ed. Universal, 2000. With commentary by Norman Jewison.

Music of the Heart, DVD ed. Miramax Collectors' Series, 2000. With commentary by Wes Craven and Marianne Maddalena.

Reel Models: The First Women of Film, based on an article by Doris Carnell. <http://www.AMCTV.com>, 2 January 2001.

Suggested Films for Study

The Blackboard Jungle (1955), dir. Richard Brooks.
The Defiant Ones (1958), dir. Stanley Kramer.
I Want to Live (1958), dir. Robert Wise.
Two Women (1961), dir. Vittorio De Sica.
Lawrence of Arabia (1962), dir. David Lean.
The Organizer (1963), dir. Mario Monicelli.
Guess Who's Coming to Dinner (1967), dir. Stanley Kramer.
The Garden of the Finzi-Continis (1971), dir. Vittorio de Sica.
Reds (1981), dir. Warren Beatty.
Blade Runner (1982), dir. Ridley Scott.
Silkwood (1983), dir. Mike Nichols.
Tender Mercies (1983), dir. Bruce Beresford

The Manhattan Project (1986), dir. Marshall Brickman.
The Mission (1986), dir. Roland Joffé.
Dances with Wolves (1990), dir. Kevin Costner.
A League of Their Own (1992), dir. Penny Marshall.
Leap of Faith (1992), dir. Richard Pearce.
Taste of Cherry (1997), dir. Abbas Kiarostami.
Primary Colors (1998), dir. Mike Nichols.
The Cradle Will Rock (1999), dir. Tim Robbins.

CHAPTER ELEVEN

Responding to Film Violence

How do I respond to film violence? No subject is discussed with more urgency in social, educational, religious, and political circles than violence in the media and its effects on our society. And violence in film (as well as on television) is linked to some degree to violence in streets, schoolyards, and homes, and potentially to terrorism. Violence in film relates to gun control, social conflicts, social tension, and other issues; and it is one of today's most controversial topics. Violence in film merits discussion from a number of points of view. How one responds to film violence depends largely on the point of view one adopts.

Two Facets of Film Violence

Students should consider the subject of film violence as centering on two basic questions: First, to what extent does violence in film have an aesthetic value? That is, what are the legitimate reasons for making violence a component of film art? As soon as one asks this basic question, a series of related questions arise: Is the violence contained in a film an organic part of its aims, themes, and meanings? Does it actually serve a purpose? If so, what is that purpose? Is some violence gratuitous and senseless? Should it, therefore, be eliminated?

Second, to what extent is violence in film related to the specific tastes, interests, or concerns of an audience? That is, is film violence in whatever form harmful or destructive to an audience? Given the social outcry against violence in film, the second question seems by far to outweigh the first. Today, the media are blamed for violence erupting in schoolyards, at home, and in the workplace. This concern over the media's responsibility increases the demand for an explanation of this phenomenon which threatens our society.

A rational debate on this point calls for the examination of both questions. Indeed, they are interrelated and complement each other. Observers can deal with the first in relatively abstract terms, but it is harder to satisfactorily or conclusively answer the second. The second question is borne out in—and may indeed depend on—the first. Without determining what violent acts shown on the screen contribute to a film's total aesthetic effect and deciding what is and what is not an artistic necessity, students cannot begin to estimate or measure the effects of such acts on an audience. If some part of violent action is a necessary component of the film, an argument can be made for its inclusion. In a war movie like *Saving Private Ryan*, the violence is necessary to give the audience a realistic sense of what is happening. The images of young men jumping out of their landing craft into a hail of bullets and sinking under the bloodied water are revolting. Yet without these images viewers would not grasp the horrors of the war. Violence is a necessary component of that film. But what about the violence in thrillers like *The Jackal* and *Lethal Weapon III*, and in epics like *Gladiator* and *The Patriot*. Do audiences need to see sadistic killers, using automatic weapons, swords, or rifles, execute scores of opponents at close range? Are such bloody scenes artistically necessary? Defenders of violence in the media point out that statistics have not proven that on-screen violence is harmful and should be avoided. That does not mean that the argument about violence is over.

The Prevalence of Film Violence

Violence has become a staple of most film genres—drama, melodrama, tragedy, science fiction, thriller, mystery, horror, war movie, western, and so forth. There is no question about the popularity of violence in film. "More than anything else," critic Roger Ebert writes, "the American movie audience loves violence" (Rainer 150). But the reasons for this are far from clear. When most Hollywood filmmakers capitalize on "blood and gore, gunfire and car chases" by offering "new twists on sadistic mayhem" (150), they can offer only surmises about why savagery on screen makes such strong emotional impact. They do not seem overly concerned about the redeeming qualities or artistic merits of their products. For most producers and filmmakers, violence and its partner sex are commodities seen almost exclusively in terms of box-office earnings. If the audience wants violence—and audiences seem to—then violence is what they will get.

Why violence has such attraction for the human psyche is a puzzle not likely to be solved, although journalists, commentators, critics, directors, and occasionally politicians express views on the subject with both zeal and urgency ("Violence" 1). Their conclusions vary according to their political, religious, and/or gender affiliations. Some commentators are outraged (Chavez 1), while some directors and producers offer disclaimers, contending that violence is part of their artistic vision. The protesters, on the other hand, claim that screen violence has gone too far when members of an audience faint or walk out in revulsion (2). Is such violence necessary? they ask. What purpose does it serve? Can film do without it? And so forth. Most of the concerns voiced deal with social ills which may or may not be caused by screen violence, while the question of aesthetic value is ignored. That question, however, in the view of this text guide, is more important. When this question is sufficiently discussed, the question of whether violence is injurious to the public will be placed in proper perspective.

The Historical Perspective on Film Violence

It is useful to remember that violence in literary works, especially in dramas, has been a legitimate critical debate throughout history. Plato and St. Augustine considered violence and the arousing of emotions by theatrical productions in general as injurious to the human soul. Aristotle theorized that tragic action is capable of arousing the emotions of pity and fear, a psychologically healthy catharsis which cleanses the audience. That could be done through "spectacular means"—stage properties and such things—an idea that today translates into special effects of unusual intensity which are often the source of graphic violence in film. The better way, in Aristotle's opinion, was to arouse pity and fear through the plot itself: Anyone who *hears* the story of Oedipus, without ever seeing it on the stage, "will thrill with horror and melt in pity at what takes place" (Kaplan 34). "But to produce this effect," Aristotle continues, "by the mere spectacle is a less artistic method, and dependent on extraneous aids" (34).

Such distinction does not imply a total rejection of visual means by Aristotle, but rather a lesser reliance on them. The plot is what moves an audience, although scenes of suffering can be used to enhance these emotions either through spectacle means or through dialogue. In a similar manner, a filmmaker today evokes such emotions by using plot and visual means according to his or her perception of what is needed. To rely on only one means would not do in most cases. Ancient drama was rife with violent acts—the blinding of Oedipus, the hanging of Jocasta, the death of Antigone in the cave, the slaughter of Agamemnon in his bathtub (or at his dinner table), the butchering of Aigisthos by Orestes—but they all occurred offstage where the audience could not see them. One must remember that Homer's works, which were important educational tools in ancient Greece, contain some of the most graphically violent scenes ever written. Antiquity's major philosophers warned against violent "spectacle." The Roman poet and critic Horace recommends avoidance of grotesque acts on the stage. In the Greek play Medea butchers her children behind the scenes; Atreus cooks human organs in full view (100). Horace in turn is echoed by the English poet John Dryden who recommends delivering violent stage action in a narrative (173). These comments are consistent with the belief of most western critics that pity and fear can be produced through narration without visual aids or spectacular stage properties. The modern question, however, centers not on whether the audience should hear the story or see it projected on the screen—that point has become entirely moot where film is concerned—but on whether the screen story can be told without graphic violence. Can a story that contains violent material be told on film and have an impact on viewers without a graphic depiction of the violence?

From Stage to Movies: Violence Prevails

Despite Aristotle's warnings, however, dramatic production in the western tradition generally adheres to the school of violence created by Seneca and the Romans, who produced bloodbath imitations of Greek drama. Seneca's Oedipus blinds himself with his fingers (how?) while his Jocasta stabs herself in the womb on stage. Renaissance drama was rife with violent acts in the plays of John Webster, John Ford, Thomas Kyd, and William Shakespeare (especially his *King Lear* and *Timon of Athens*). These playwrights were responding to an "appetite for crude bloodshed which was persistent in Elizabethan audiences" (Moody and Lovett, 106). Popular dramatists, in response to this audience demand, defied the conventions of classical drama which had kept violence off the stage (106). But after the Renaissance, violence in western stage productions diminished. In Corneille, Racine, and later Ibsen, violence took place offstage (as in Shaw's *St. Joan*) or was a psychological or mental condition, as in the works of Ibsen, O'Neill, Miller, Williams, and Albee. These authors scripted outbursts of verbal violence, but physical violence was rare. The novel from Stern to Hawthorne to James, including the naturalistic fiction of Zola, remained by and large nonviolent until the advent of Hemingway, in whose works violence is graphically described. From Hemingway and Fitzgerald on, graphic violence becomes routine in modern fiction—Faulkner, Camus, Kazantzakis, Burgess—not to mention in works of commercial fiction where violence is a staple. In film, graphic violence was not an issue under the Hays Code (though it was mostly concerned with sex) until the late 1960s, when it flourished suddenly in the spaghetti Westerns of Sergio Leone, as well as in such worthy films as *Bonnie and Clyde* (1967), and *The Wild Bunch* (1969). This continued in the early '70s with *The Godfather I* and *II, Taxi Driver* (1976), and *Death Wish*, and into the 1980s with such others as the Rambo movies and the Indiana Jones trilogy. The nineties have adopted and accentuated this tradition in *Goodfellas* (1991), *Cape Fear* (1992), *Bram Stoker's Dracula* (1993), *Natural Born Killers* (1994), the notorious, *Pulp Fiction* (1994), and many other films. From the late sixties to the present, the modern tradition of violence in film remains in force and if anything has become more graphic with technological advancement. The sinking of the *Titanic*, though not violent in the ordinary sense, numbs the viewer with the sheer magnitude of human catastrophe.

Whether freedom from the Hays Code alone made both violence and explicit sex in film possible or whether there were other factors is still debated. But it is undeniable that graphic violence in American film erupted in the mid-1960s and has increased. At present violence in film has reached such epidemic proportions as to alarm social, political, and religious institutions. Since the First Amendment protects film expression as freedom of speech, there is no question of returning to a code. After the Columbine massacre in Colorado in the spring of 1999, President Clinton appealed to Hollywood to voluntarily restrain violence in film and television, urging voluntary, rather than a legal, restraint. But each instance of explicit violence must be examined on its own merits. In the current debate right-wing political and religious groups see the advent of uncontrolled violence (along with sex and vulgar language) in film as signs of an unscrupulous, profit-motivated, decadent Hollywood establishment. Despite arguments by such people as Jack Valenti, president of the Motion Picture Industry Association, that the rating system warns parents about the content of violent films, the attacks against Hollywood's unrestrained mayhem in films have intensified.

But the debates don't seem to settle the more theoretical points or to provide more effective restraint. Can people know whether violence is harmful without understanding the rationale of its inclusion in film or in any other narrative art? Violence is one ingredient of the action, a part of the whole which fulfills a certain purpose. When that purpose is clear, the question of whether violence is or is not necessary will also be clear.

Dealing with Violence in Film

Let us, then, return to our opening question: To what extent are violent scenes part of the total vision of a work of art and at what point do they become gratuitous? It is the question of gratuitous violence in dramatic presentation that has drawn the attention of critics since Aristotle. Who determines what proportion of violence is gratuitous? If not a censorship board, then the artist (including all involved in film production) or the audience. Then another question arises: Should the audience try to affect the decisions of the artist (encourage or discourage them by success or failure at the box office)? Or should the artist impose his own vision—whatever that is—on an audience, no matter what the consequence? If the artist thinks that violence is part of the whole work—an ingredient necessary to its purpose—why should an audience or a censorship board object?

It has been argued that the proclivity for violence in the American society of the 1960s was triggered in part by a national consciousness of the spectacle of violence in the Vietnam War. The aesthetics of violence therefore changed during that era. It is not surprising that Hollywood directors—Arthur Penn, Sam Peckinpah, Stanley Kubrick, Francis Ford Coppola—who pioneered screen productions of that era followed suit. Violence arrived on the screen with films such as *Bonnie and Clyde* (1967), the ending of which showed the bullet-riddled bodies of the two protagonists in a ballet-like, slow-motion sequence. Critics cried foul, deploring the movie for its excessive, gratuitous, and socially harmful violence. Similar complaints were later launched against *Natural Born Killers* (1994) and *Pulp Fiction* (1994). Examined by today's standards, however, *Bonnie and Clyde's* violence seems tame. It can be argued that the last scene's graphic violence is totally in tune with the film's aesthetic dimensions. It was entirely appropriate for the filmmaker to show that the lives of his protagonists—bankrobbers, lawbreakers, killers, fugitives—came to a violent and tragic end. The graphic spectacle of the dying criminals entirely captures the irony of the story: The lawman's revenge is bloodier and more cruel than the violent acts perpetrated by the guilty parties. No other rendering could have produced the desired effect (see discussion below).

Such examples demonstrate that it is sometimes difficult to determine what portion of violence is gratuitous and what is not, without considering an audience's specific historic and social orientations. It is the audience, not the critics, who make the aesthetic judgment. If an audience is geared to seeing certain violent acts on film, that audience will react and will judge accordingly. Historical progression is certainly a factor. Hitchcock's *Psycho*, first released in 1960, is said to have caused near-hysteria nationally because of the shower scene. Many Americans who saw the film were afraid to go into a shower for months. Yet Hitchcock's film causes no discomfort for today's audiences who are conditioned by "slasher" movies, some of them imitations of *Psycho*. Comparison with the past is a convenient way to establish certain principles. Graphic violence was not always necessary to produce an emotional response in an audience. Films of emotional violence—*A Streetcar Named Desire, Cat on a Hot Tin Roof, Long Day's Journey into Night* (movies made in the '50s and '60s)—

contained practically no graphic violence of any kind, yet they held the attention of their audiences then and now. Films of epic sweep which would have been extremely violent if made today—*Spartacus, Ben-Hur, Lawrence of Arabia*—contain only minimal violence considering their scope of action. In many westerns of the 1940s and 1950s, only token violence was offered: people fell off horses after they were shot or men clutched their chests when an arrow pierced them—but no blood flowed. Today these scenes would be entirely and routinely graphic. Disney's *Tombstone* (1994) is a far cry from *My Darling Clementine* (1958), though both treat the same subject. *The Gunfighter* (1950) and *High Noon* (1951), two films with violent shootouts, do not show a drop of blood spurting from a wound, but if they were made today, they would be replete with obligatory gore. Yet the emotional impact of those older movies is still intact, at least for older moviegoers. Young persons conditioned to today's standards might find them very tame.

A different example, and a different set of comparisons: Euripides' *Medea* and the film *Fatal Attraction* (1987) bear certain similarities: Both deal with a woman's jealousy and revenge. In both, there is violence with tragic consequences. In *Medea*, however, all the violence is reported. Medea kills her children and causes the agonizing deaths of Jason's future bride and father-in-law (they are burned alive by the poisonous, flammable garments she sent as gifts) offstage. All this action is reported by a messenger in the Greek play, admittedly in graphic terms. It would no doubt be presented in spectacular special effects today. Flammable garments, poison, two people burning and dying in horrible torment, the slashing of the throats of innocent children—this would be Hollywood material. True, in film it would be hard for narration of the event to be effective given just a close-up of the face of the actor who tells the story. Film both demands and justifies visual representation of an event, no matter how gruesome, if it is organic to the story. One can modify violence in film to make it palatable, but to omit it altogether is impossible. Even the tame movies of the 1950s contained minimal visual violence. It is hard to imagine violent scenes reported by a messenger in a film. Seen on the screen, Euripides' play would no doubt contain visual images of the violence, but a stage production of the same story would not and did not require visual violence.

On the other hand, if *Fatal Attraction* were to be produced on the stage, the bathtub scene in which Glenn Close attempts to stab Michael Douglas might be watered down or even eliminated. It could be reported by someone, for it is not possible to render close-ups in a stage play. The violence of that scene and of others in that film would have to be rendered through emotional tensions—voice, gesture, words. But the very nature of a stage play limits, though it does not eliminate, the showing of violent action.

Cinema is the medium of visual representation. Its premises *as a medium* are different from those of other media. Space and time can be expanded or contracted ad infinitum. The larger can be shown as smaller, the longer as shorter; and conversely the short can be lengthened and the small enlarged. A minute hole caused by a bullet entering a face can nearly fill a sixty-foot screen. A fist can explode onto someone's chin, producing a hard, knocking noise that is actually only a sound effect. Augmented by surround sound, the noise can be magnified at will. A knife can scratch the surface of skin, blood spurt or ooze from a wound. Again, the effect on a viewer—judging from the visceral reactions of audiences—is startling. Viewers witness events that they rarely see in real life. A shock is produced and that shock is part of the viewers' total aesthetic experience.

Violence is in a state of evolution, and it has become part of social outlooks and mores that change with changing times. This is seen in the evolution of various cultures since antiquity. Greek plays contained less violence than Roman plays. Scenes of horror abound in the plays of Beaumont and Fletcher, Webster, Ford, and Shakespeare. Today, physical violence, while still muted on the stage, is pandemic on the screen and on the TV screen. It has grown so alarmingly that it is considered a sign of social decline. Are *The Silence of the Lambs* (1991), *Pulp Fiction* (1995), *Natural Born Killers* (1994), *Casino* (1995), and other such films of the nineties signs and specimens of social decadence and a decline in morals? Of excesses by filmmakers unable to control their material who must resort to sensationalism? Or is violence in film, if aesthetically relevant, a vital factor in an audience's reading of visual reality? In that case, realistic depiction of violent events must and will continue. Whether this is a harmful social phenomenon is another question: sugar, alcohol, tobacco, and sunshine can all be harmful depending on their usage. People make choices.

Judging Films with Violent Content

The Wild Bunch (1969)

Directed by Sam Peckinpah, this milestone in the western genre, came at the end of an era when the mild-mannered westerns of the 1940s and '50s were fast becoming extinct. This film marked an abrupt shift in attitude towards the western hero and became notorious mostly for its graphic violence. The classic western featured a cast of heroes pitted against villains, both presented in relatively clear-cut fashion. *The Wild Bunch* features only villains pitted against other villains. The lawbreaker and the law enforcer do not differ from each other. In fact, in this film they interchange roles. A group of outlaws—Pike (William Holden), the brothers Lyle and Tector Gorch (Ben Johnson and Warren Oates), Dutch (Ernest Borgnine), Sykes (Edmond O'Brien), and Angel (Jaime Sanchez)—carry out one robbery after another of the Texas railroad system. They are dogged by a group of bounty hunters led by Thornton (Robert Ryan), who was once part of the Bunch. After being arrested, imprisoned, and tortured, he is released, but only on the condition that he track down and capture Pike and his cohorts. He leads a pack of greedy, nondescript drifters and riffraff, all former inmates whose only alternative to success on this mission is hanging. They are in this for the loot and they strip the possessions from anyone they kill.

The film begins with a robbery and a massacre. Pike and his group prepare to take the railroad office in a small South Texas town, but Thornton has set them up and is waiting in ambush. A montage of freeze frames of the Bunch as they ride in alternates with scenes of children poking two scorpions that are writhing in the middle of an anthill as thousands of red ants devour them. A preacher is shouting Bible quotes to a group of women at a meeting of the Southern Texas Temperance Society while the heist is going on.

In the apocalyptic ending of **The Wild Bunch,** *two of the mortally wounded principals share a last desperate moment of commiseration. This prototypically violent film offers little redemption to its outlaw "heroes" apart from their code of loyalty to one another. In a world changing beyond their power to manipulate it, that code leads to a bloody conclusion.*

A parade complicates Thornton's plan, and when bullets start flying, innocent people are caught in the crossfire. As the criminals are chased out of town, a montage shows the children setting fire to the anthill, scorching both ants and scorpions, and grinning at their triumph. The Bunch's force is reduced, but the main group survives and rides out, only to discover that the sacks of "money" they're carrying are actually filled with steel washers. They've been had by Thornton. The Bunch regroups and crosses into Mexico where they make a deal with General Mapache. He needs American weapons to fight Pancho Villa in the Mexican Civil War of 1913. Mapache is corrupt, pillaging and looting villages to support his troops and, of course, helping himself to their women. One of those women is Angel's former girlfriend. Angel joined the Wild Bunch to get funds to fight men like Mapache. When he sees her in the arms of the general, he shoots and kills her. Angel is arrested, and the Bunch agree to work for Mapache on the condition that he release Angel. With the help of Mapache's German advisors who are there to foil American intervention in Mexico, they mastermind a train robbery, outfoxing Thornton, who is lying in ambush with the federal cavalry. They then cross back into Mexico and sell the stolen boxes of rifles and ammunition to Mapache. The latter sadistically tortures Angel when he discovers one box of rifles missing (Angel has passed it on to his rebel friends). The Bunch takes the gold Mapache has paid them and leaves town—initially. But the men have a change of heart. Pike, especially, is bothered by leaving a loyal friend behind in the hands of a brute. They return to the village—partly to avoid Thornton, who is always on their trail, but mostly to rescue Angel. After a brief bout with village prostitutes, the four men (the word "Bunch" resonates here) march toward their doom, demanding the release of Angel. Mapache has one of his men slit Angel's throat, and the action erupts into the most violent scene ever filmed up to that time. Mapache is killed first, and the four fight valiantly against hundreds of Mexicans, both army and villagers. Lyle Gorch gets hold of a machine gun (a prize weapon they sold to the general) and razes scores of troops. When he is killed, Dutch takes over until he too is killed—though it takes a dozen bullets to do that. Pike, inside a hut, spares a woman he has made love to and she shoots him in the back. He turns, kills her, and joins the expiring Dutch. Almost nobody in the village is left alive, and a boy shoots Pike from behind a window rail. The mass slaughter ends with all four dead and hundreds of corpses strewing the village square, buzzards descending to peck at the dead, ready to feast on carcasses. Thornton and his group arrive too late. After his men pick up all the loot they can—even extracting gold teeth from corpses—they load Pike on a horse and take him back to U.S. territory, an act that will save them from hanging. Thornton surveys the slaughter and takes Pike's gun. He will remain behind, leaning against a wall, until the wounded Sykes shows up with a band of Mexican rebels. He convinces

Thornton to go along on a last venture. "It's not like old times," he spits out, "but it'll do." Thornton joins him, an outlaw again.

The men of the Bunch are portrayed neither as heroes nor villains—or perhaps as villains not totally bereft of heroic qualities. They are gunfighters of the Old West, crusty, hard-boiled, fearless, bold, down on their luck, but perhaps worthy of better things. They have chosen violence as a means to get riches, but they reap the bitter fruits of their endeavors. Violence traps them. Their bravery itself negates their existence. Life has led them nowhere, and they must gun their way out of one tough spot after another. The only code they adhere to is loyalty to each other, and Pike as leader enforces that rule. When one of the Gorch brothers (the true "wild" ones) suggests the elimination of the old and awkward Sykes, Pike stops him: "Once you side with a man, you stay with him." That's what gives the group its strength. Not addicted to violence for its own sake, they use it as a means to an end, knowing the era of the gunslinger on a horse is passing. The automobile Mapache uses to drag Angel through the village streets is itself an emblem of changing times. The machine gun is another. The fast draw, the prime weapon of the nimble-fingered gunfighter, is now worthless. The West with its emphasis on adventure, individual valor, ruggedness, and endurance, has come to an end. "We have to think beyond our guns. These days are closing fast," Pike says in a moment of reflection. Mass killing replaces the honorable duel of the long-running TV series "Gunsmoke." The outdated bandits find that the plains are hard to cross on horseback, the mountains rugged and full of treachery. An aging and arthritic Pike, falling off his horse while trying to climb into the saddle, recognizes the end of his era and seeks one last job before he "backs off." "Back off to what?" Dutch sarcastically responds. This exchange delivers the film's dark message: if there ever were any bright moments, none are left for a life of crime. There is no refuge from the hard-bitten existence of the outlaw, nothing but another tough fight and death. The highly romanticized life of the western hero ended with Peckinpah's movie. Explosive action, somber tone, symbolic setting, tragic mood—these and other attributes of *The Wild Bunch* reduced the rest of the western genre to the status of toy stories. *The Wild Bunch* was the western to end all westerns, *Tombstone* and *Unforgiven* (which came two decades later) notwithstanding.

Psycho (1960)

Hitchcock's famous movie contains only a few violent scenes which became notorious. The shower scene in which Marion Crane (Janet Leigh) is stabbed to death is totally frightening even today, though it contains no actual graphic material. A knife hits Leigh repeatedly—and the audience hears thumps like a watermelon cracking, but never sees the blade penetrating the skin. Blood gurgles down the drain as the dead body slides downward; a hand grabs the

Although celebrated for its violent episodes, **The Godfather** *complements these with equally effective scenes of civilized, businesslike behavior. The result is a balanced and disturbing picture of organized crime that mirrors legitimate corporate America.*

shower curtain and rip its rings off the rod. Leigh's eyes are vacuous, open, gazing into space as the camera zooms in on them. It slowly pans to the bedstead where the money lies folded in the newspaper. By today's standards the scene is mild. Most of what happens is imagined, not shown, but viewers get the point. This is an aesthetically poignant moment which evokes horror, not disgust.

Bonnie and Clyde (1967)

Directed by Arthur Penn, this movie is not really violent by today's standards, until the final scene, which became famous for its choreographed killing of the protagonists. The scene is filmed in slow motion, allowing the viewer to absorb the horrifying sight of two bodies writhing in agony while bullets perforate them. They do not die immediately, as films often suggest, as soon as a single bullet hits. They agonize in convulsions for minutes, as chickens do when farmers chop their heads off with a hatchet, jumping around the yard after the decapitation. Clyde is on the ground, twisting and grunting, while

Bonnie hangs on to the car door until her hand goes limp and dozens of bullets riddle her body. This shattering, aesthetically appropriate scene evokes pity and fear.

The Godfather (1972)

Directed by Francis Ford Coppola, *The Godfather* is celebrated for its subject matter, technique, and gravity. It contains only sporadic violence, which comes swiftly and shockingly and relates to the story development. Examples: The horse's head slipped into a Hollywood executive's bed because he has refused to do a favor for Vito Corleone; Luca Brasi's murder, when his hand, stabbed by a stiletto, is immobilized on the counter while he is choked to death; Michael's point-blank shooting of Sollozzo and McCluskey at the restaurant; Sonny's body strafed by bullets at the toll booth (reminiscent of the ending of *Bonnie and Clyde*); and the ritualistic killings of several gangsters while a baptism takes place. This last example is famous as a unique demonstration of parallel editing.

Natural Born Killers (1994)

Oliver Stone's notorious film opened a can of worms with certain critics who denounced it as the cause of a copycat killing (the murder of John Savage of Hernando, Mississippi, by two youths who had seen Stone's film). John Grisham (French 227–28) accused Stone of indirectly influencing the two. Stone responded with a spirited defense (236) of his movie, decrying the practice of blaming the messenger for his message about society. This exchange is characteristic of the confusion in our society over the effects of movie violence. There is no simple or definitive answer. Violence belongs in a movie if it is an organic part of the larger message.

The Jackal (1998)

Directed by Michael Caton-Jones with Bruce Willis as the Jackal, this film is a remake of *The Day of the Jackal* (1974), directed by Fred Zinnemann and based on the best-selling novel by Frederick Forsyth. In the original movie the Jackal is played convincingly by Edward Fox as a cold, calculating killer, a complete professional—slick, clever, imperturbable, a man pitted against the entire French security system and the French government. None of the characters pursuing him is lovable, and the Jackal not only outfoxes them but also elicits admiration for his clever maneuvers and ability to plan. The movie is utterly lucid, and as soon as its basic premise is laid, everything that happens conforms to it. In the new *Jackal*, the suspense lies in the violent action; the mental game is drenched in blood so frequently that the stomach turns before the brain can grasp what is happening. As in most modern action movies photographed in medium shots and close-ups, there is no aesthetic distance, and viewers are more frequently overwhelmed than satisfied. Bruce Willis's Jackal is a brutal psychopath who kills coldly and sadistically just for the sake of killing. He is not only a pro who works for money, but a man who enjoys bloodshed. This repugnant character has no redeeming trait whatsoever. He is the antithesis of Fox who, though not actually sympathetic, elicits reluctant admiration. Even the puzzle of his existence remains open at the end when he is denounced by all except the man who caught him—who acknowledges an adversary who is his equal in cunning. The two men engaged in a long mental duel and viewers had some fun watching their game. Caton-Jones's *Jackal*, by contrast, is a joyless movie that revels in sadistic torture.

Boys Don't Cry (1999)

Directed and cowritten by Kimberly Pierce, this film contains both emotional and physical violence. *Boys Don't Cry* employs such violence in the fullest sense in the interest of realism, so the film can tell us exactly what happened. Film has the obligation to tell, in the most vivid terms possible, the entire truth, and this film comes close to that goal. The awards it received were well deserved: Best Actress and Best Supporting Actress Golden Globe and Los Angeles Film Critics Association awards for Hilary Swank and Chloe Sevigny, respectively. The movie is based on a real incident in a small Nebraska town. In a seemingly childish prank, a young girl who is undergoing a sexual identity crisis poses as a boy—Teena Brandon becomes Brandon Teena—mixing with a lowlife family and becoming romantically involved with a girl named Lana. The latter is also involved with two unruly young men who eventually find out that Brandon is a girl. They rape her in a scene that is almost unbearable to watch, and then kill her.

Bringing Out the Dead (1999)

Directed by Martin Scorsese with Nicholas Cage, John Goodman, and Patricia Arquette, this film is based on the Joe Connelly novel which, in turn, is based on a real story. Paul Schrader, a veteran of Scorsese movies (*Raging Bull*, *The Last Temptation of Christ*), wrote the script. As with previous films, Scorsese treats violence as part of broader themes. Violence is part and parcel of the action, but it is also ingrained in the concept. There has never been a Scorsese film in which violence is gratuitous. The violence in this film concerns not killing, but dying. The dying suffer, but so do those who see them die and try to save them. In some ways this film is a throwback to *Taxi Driver*. Here again is an underground man, as Pauline Kael called the De Niro character in that film, an alienated person existing on the margin of society. The hero of *Dead*, Cage is not a taxi driver but an ambulance driver and paramedic. Frank Pierce is called to save near-death patients, answer to emergencies, and give aid to all kinds of people—mainly the downtrodden. Fewer than ten percent of these unfortunates will survive, and Pierce himself is near death from exhaustion, fatigue, despair, and disgust.

Here's New York again, still hell on earth thirty years after *Taxi Driver*, according to this movie (if not according to Mayor Giuliani). The dimly-lit streets are replete with prostitutes (some in advanced stages of pregnancy), drug addicts, street punks, grunts, drug dealers, a naked man, homeless persons, "crackheads," more prostitutes, men dying from bullet wounds. For the most part, the calls report cardiac arrests ("What happened to chest pains?" grumbles Pierce), but he ends up finding all sorts of things, including a woman having twins. The driver suffers from haste, heat, neon lights, exhaustion, and more despair.

He's an angel, though, a compassionate man who *wants* to save the nearly dead. He *feels* everything he does; he grieves every time he loses a patient—which is almost always. Bringing out the dead is literally his job: rushing a man shot through the heart to a hospital, and then seeing him die is part of his routine. To save a dying person is his life's work, his obsession. Scorsese captures all this, photographing New York streets from the viewpoint of the hallucinating Pierce. Most of the mood is created through lighting, with 90 percent of the action shot at night. Viewers see a phantasmagoria of changing blimps, spots of glimmer, dark street corners, split images that suggest a mind disintegrating under stress. At one point street pavements burst open and bodies spring out, forming, growing, becoming human again in a scene reminiscent of the tomb openings and the raising of Lazarus in *The Last Temptation of Christ*. In fact, Pierce becomes a Jesus figure. His compassion is intense, and every saved life is to be celebrated as a victory over death. As with all major Scorsese characters, Pierce is in conflict with himself and he needs these victories to sustain him.

The movie offers no comic relief, no relief whatsoever. It does not function as entertainment. Indeed, it's a struggle for viewers to sit through its ugliness, despair, and defeat of the human spirit. But it is honest. Its honesty and hard-boiled toughness are a Scorsese trademark. He creates characters on the brink of collapse, on the very margin of humanity. He is a master of the dark side of human existence, so violent content in his films is fully justified.

The Talented Mr. Ripley (1999)

Directed by Anthony Minghella for Paramount/Miramax, this movie injects violence suddenly, when you least suspect it; so when it comes, it takes a tremendous toll on the sensitive viewer. It is justified by the plot, but is quite brutal. The movie begins entertainingly, promising clever twists, sharp dialogue, lavish Italian locales, great music, and 5.1 Dolby Digital (which makes a sound system worth its cost). Before this movie is half through, though, a shocking murder occurs and upsets everything. One young man murders another on a boat trip, hitting him in the face with an oar. The wound bleeds, half the victim's cheek is cut open, and then he is hit again and again. This looks and sounds like a burst of insanity, the end of the euphoria hitherto present in this movie. Not that viewers don't like twists—or murder, for that matter—but there is no mystery here. We know what the plot is; the suspense arises over the question of whether Tom Ripley (Matt Damon) will get caught. He doesn't, but he goes on to perpetrate another even more savage murder, and then another. In the end, he escapes justice and is known as a murderer only to himself and to the first murdered man's girlfriend, Marge (Gwyneth Paltrow), whom no one believes.

The disappointment in this movie comes from the fact that viewers don't know what to make of the protagonist. Ripley is diabolical, manipulative, deranged, and clever. He eludes suspicion, leaving no trail and carefully laying his plans to enrich himself. At the outset, an American magnate hires Ripley to bring his wandering son back from Italy. Ripley befriends Dickie (Jude Law), a complicated fellow who is enamored of Marge, but has also played around with (and impregnated) an Italian woman. He has vague ambitions to be a jazz musician and maintains a quasi-homosexual relationship with another young American. Ripley is talented at imitating voices and forging letters, and is an accomplished piano performer. He initiates a relationship with Dickie and eventually gets him alone on a small boat. When his overtures are rejected, he murders Dickie, hitting him with an oar. He then assumes the dead man's identity (and the money that goes with it), but he is discovered by Freddie Miles (Philip Seymour Hoffman) and must then murder *him* to avoid arrest. He covers his tracks, though he almost gives himself away when Marge suspects him.

The failure of the movie, as a whole, lies in its failure to win sympathy for the protagonist. Though viewers follow his point of view minutely and want him to escape, the horror of the consecutive murders negates any sympathy. Ripley is obviously a sick man; he has nightmares and suffers some remorse, but never enough. He traps himself in his own manipulations, finding it harder to extricate himself from his own web of lies. It is a classic case of entrapment, but Ripley is not a tragic hero—that would have saved the story. Nor is the film a classic tragedy. The tragic hero is basically a good person, with a character weakness that draws him to an evil act. Nothing we know of Ripley indicates essential goodness. However, he is not a total villain either. He is in hell for hell's sake, and no plot resolution to satisfy the moral sense. There is *peripeteia*, but not *anagnorisis*.

This movie tries hard by presenting splendid photography, astonishing editing, and a straightforward story, which is quite a relief from the recent mania for abandoning sequence. A well-made story is a well-made story. Minghella, whose plotline of *The English Patient* was so convoluted, is superb here, reminding viewers somewhat of the clean plot lines of Hitchcock's *Psycho*. But there the similarities end. At least Norman Bates was both explained and caught.

Still, the movie has merit. It retains a consistent point of view by following the characters and their immediate concerns, rather than taking the usual background tour familiar in movies made in Italy. This concentration on the story gives a sharp focus to the events and to their psychological effects on the main characters.

The sum total: color, beautiful sights and sounds, fast action, crisp dialogue, sharp performances—and the horror of it all: A dark movie in bright colors whose violence is not gratuitous but organically connected to theme and action.

Suggested Readings and Hypertext Links

Aristotle. *Poetics*. W. Hamilton Fyfe, trans. Cambridge, Mass.: Harvard University Press, 1965.

Chavez, Linda, "'Pulp Fiction': Violence as Art." *USA Today*, 18 January 1995, 1.

French, Carl, ed. *Screen Violence*. London: Bloomsbury Publishing, 1996.

Kael, Pauline. *For Keeps: Thirty Years at the Movies*. New York: Plume, 1996.

Kaplan, Charles, and William Anderson, eds. Criticism: *The Major Statements*, 3rd ed. New York: St. Martin's Press, 1991.

Moody, William Vaugh, and Robert Morss Lovett. *A History of English Literature*, rev. by F. B. Millett. New York: Charles Scribner's Sons, 1964.

Rainer, Peter. *Love and Hisses*. San Francisco: Mercury House, 1992.

"Violence as Art." *USA Today*, 26 October 1994, 1.

The Talented Mr. Ripley. DVD ed. Paramount, 1999. With commentary by Anthony Minghella. <http://www.paramount.com/homevideo>

CHAPTER TWELVE

Responding to Film Technology

How do I respond to film technology? Today's viewing experiences are rapidly being complemented by increased technological advancement. The text guide provides guidelines and examples of available tapes, laser discs, and DVDs. The ordinary VCR presents little challenge or profit to the modern film viewer. Its definition is poor (250 lines of resolution), color quality is average at best, while the screen aspect ratio is modified to fit your TV screen, thus eliminating significant portions of the screen space. On the other hand, wide-screen laser disc and DVD provide, in most cases, the original screen aspect ratio of 1.66:1 or 1.85:1, and even the widest screen ratio, 2.35:1. This last was the original anamorphic Cinemascope, Panavision, or other wide-screen option that enabled viewers to appreciate a film's depth of field and *mise-en-scène* as they were intended by the filmmakers. While some VHS tapes include wide-screen editions, those rented in video stores usually do not. Most DVDs offer both the standard (formatted) and wide-screen versions, though some may not be wide enough—for some TV screens This advantage, combined with better resolution, is in itself a sufficient reason to switch from VCR to DVD or laser disc, though the last has increasingly gone out of fashion due to its greater cost and inferior resolution. Other advantages include developments in the technology of film restoration and reproduction, and the upcoming availability of digital TV screens. There is no reason, however, to abandon the 16mm and 35mm classroom screenings which are used at major universities such as UCLA. Student are well advised to keep ahead of developments in the field by visiting the numerous web sites that give information about film-studies programs in the United States and abroad. Several such web sites are listed in the bibliography in this chapter.

The Value of Commentaries

Though the classic mode of classroom screening has used actual 16mm and 35mm film, laser disc and DVD provide additional tools for the study of film, especially of films which have gained considerable critical reputation. Commentaries take several forms, but two are the most useful. First, commentaries by the filmmakers themselves—usually directors and actors—are encoded in the analog track of a laser disc or in the Special Features section of a DVD. The director and actors offer comments, observations, and general remarks on the making of their film, most of their comments coming from memory rather than from prepared notes. A film is thus deconstructed by the very people who participated in making it, and viewers gain valuable insights and learn many details about what went on on a set, what the filmmakers' intentions were, what changes were made, and so forth. Such a commentary on the remaking of *Psycho*, for instance, by director Gus Van Sant and actors Anne Heche and Vince Vaughn explains their motives, methods, and approaches to this project. Similarly, Norman Jewison gives a very insightful commentary on the circumstances, history, and importance of *The Hurricane*. The second type of commentary is offered by a critic, usually long after a movie is made. Such comments are, of course, of a more detached nature. Consider the audio essay by Casper Tybjerg, a Carl Theodor Dreyer scholar from the University of Copenhagen, who gives an informative analysis of the making of *The Passion of Joan of Arc*. The DVD Classical Collection and Criterion Editions are recommended for their scholarly essays, but today nearly every major DVD film edition contains some commentary. To what degree these are valuable, students must judge for themselves. DVDs are for home use only unless permission is granted for other use, but certainly an instructor and students may view these outside a classroom and use them as assignments. Commentaries can also include remarks from musicians, producers, and other participants, which can be adjusted to classroom or individual needs. Photos illustrating certain points in the film are often provided. For instance details of the make-up process that aged Orson Welles in *Citizen Kane*, are given in the laser Criterion Edition of this film. Differences between original restored versions are shown, as in the recently remastered versions of Hitchcock's *Vertigo* and *Psycho*, both available on DVD with added commentaries on the making of the original films and their restored versions. All these materials are excellent aids to instruction, particularly since their use is entirely optional, allowing flexibility for both students and instructors. An instructor might allow the audio track to play either during the first showing, or repeat the showing in its entirety or in portions, to allow the students to absorb the information, depending on the points he wishes to make. Most laser discs and DVDs provide chapter divisions of movies, enabling instructors to switch by remote control to any chapter they choose. These chapter subdivisions are extremely useful in locating the portions of a film one wishes to examine. Potentially, they can also be used in examinations and quizzes, just as an instructor in art history uses slides. In fact, the freeze-mode on the CAV laser disc editions and on all DVDs has the precise function a slide used to have. Stills are very useful for examining *mise-en-scène*. Students can perform most of these functions themselves or follow an instructor's assignments. As DVD players are now components of some computers, libraries can often accommodate these new developments. Since lasers and DVDs have strict copyright laws, students and instructors are advised to check with web sites listed on the jackets of DVDs and lasers, to insure legitimate classroom showings. A student should have no difficulty checking these assignments individually. Some information can also be summarized on information sheets and given to students (see the sample course, page 245ff) or in other formats, again depending on the classroom situation. History-oriented courses might benefit more than courses that stress social themes. Courses in script writing and direction also benefit from these materials. Each of the eleven preceding chapters outlines methods or approaches a course could take. Instructors are, of course, free to choose any approach—the historical, for instance—to format a specific course.

Hypertext and Its Uses

Hypertext is critical material electronically encoded. The material has to be related to a certain text—any narrative, film, play, or written text—which is under critical consideration. These parameters of criticism establish the quality and quantity of hypertext. Students borrow from criticism to enhance their knowledge of a text, and, in today's era of electronic information, students are redirected from the library to the computer and to the CD-ROM, the laser, and the DVD disc, and other digitally encoded materials. Technology has enlarged and complicated this field and the Internet is a vast sea of constantly changing information, some of which may be superfluous and badly written, but nevertheless cannot be ignored. Film benefits particularly from these developments. Only a couple of decades ago, students could watch a film for specific study only by going to a movie theater or to one of the few film societies existing then, or to the classroom (where only a rare film course was offered). The VCR changed this in the 1980s and the laser disc made strides in the 1990s. But the DVD has added the miracle touches with its accessibility (prices of DVD players and discs have tumbled). There are newer and newer editions of both classics and current films, and viewers can obtain optimum audio and video while controlling scene selection, background information, and special features. Video stores have pretty good rental selections that offer both VCR tapes and DVDs.

For the sake of illustration, let us look at several examples from laser and DVD editions, exploring the possibilities for study in the contents of these discs. On the basis of this information, students should compile a discography, a filmography, and a bibliography.

1. *Citizen Kane*, directed by Orson Welles—1941. Considered by many critics the greatest film ever made, mostly because of the introduction or use of many techniques, such as deep focus photography, and because of its powerful story. The laser Criterion Edition contains materials such as storyboard sketches and the make-up process used on Welles. A CAV edition permits extended freeze of image. Chaplin's *The Great Dictator*, *Monsieur Verdoux*, and *Limelight* are available in the same laser editions, and are now coming out on DVD as well.
2. *Beauty and the Beast*, directed by Jean Cocteau—1947. The laser Criterion Edition contains commentary by Arthur Knight which explains many of the techniques used by Cocteau in this film: reverse camera motion; slow motion; special camera tricks; lighting.
3. *L'Avventura*, directed by Michelangelo Antonioni—1961. An analog audio track on the CAV format Criterion Edition contains commentary by Gene Youngblood, who offers various insights and information on Antonioni's filming, discusses casting and the rugged weather conditions during production, and offers other useful facts for students of film literature and film studies. (CAV format of Criterion Edition)
4. *The Seventh Seal*, directed by Ingmar Bergman. The Criterion Collection laser edition of this famous film contains an audio essay by Peter Cowie.
5. *Dr. Strangelove*, directed by Stanley Kubrick—1964. The film is offered in both laser disc and DVD editions.
6. *Amadeus*, directed by Milos Forman—1984. Laser and DVD editions, with commentaries by Peter Shaffer, Carl Corman, Sir Neville Marriner, Tom Hulce, and F. Murray Abraham.
7. *Platoon*, directed by Oliver Stone—1987. Laser disc edition contains commentary by Charles Kiselyak.
8. *Vertigo*, directed by Alfred Hitchcock—1958. The 1998 DVD edition contains "The Making of Vertigo," essays and commentaries on the

restoration of a film that was almost lost. <http://www.universalstudios.com/home>

9. *Psycho*, directed by Alfred Hitchcock—1960. The 1998 DVD edition offers bonus materials: "The Making of *Psycho*," a documentary with Janet Leigh, Hilton Green, Joseph Stefano, and Patricia Hitchcock O'Connell.

10. *Quiz Show*, directed by Rober Redford—1994. Look for the 1996 laser disc edition.

11. *Schindler's List*, directed by Steven Spielberg—1993. Look for the 1995 laser disc edition.

12. *2001: A Space Odyssey*, directed by Stanley Kubrick—1968. The 1998 MGM DVD and laser disc editions include "Special Features," an interview with screenwriter Arthur C. Clarke, and an eight-page booklet featuring production notes and a revealing look at the making of the film. <http://www.mgm.com/dvd>

13. *The Bridge on the River Kwai*, directed by David Lean—1957. Columbia's 2000 DVD edition contains an exclusive documentary on the adaption of Boulle's novel, cast, history of production, score, a USC short film introduced by William Holden, and an appreciation by filmmaker John Milius.

CHAPTER THIRTEEN

A Sample Course

Instructors are of course free to adjust the recommendations in this text guide to the specific needs of their course. A sample course based on the method and materials provided here should contain the following:

- *A syllabus.* Among other necessary items, a syllabus should contain a statement of the purpose and content of a film course. Such a film course can be taught at various levels and made applicable to many majors. It can be an introductory course, or part of a general education program; it can be taught at an intermediate or advanced level as part of a major. Film is a flexible medium comfortable in many disciplines: literature, philosophy, history, rhetoric, social science, religion, and communication. A film syllabus, therefore, is designed on the basis of the specific level and discipline in which film is to be studied. This text guide can accommodate most introductory and intermediate level courses, and instructors can use it as they wish. It is suggested that film be considered as a whole and that attention be paid to all "responses." If, for instance, an instructor decides to use film as part of an art curriculum (painting, music), chapter 1—"Film as Art" will meet the need. "Film as History" is chapter 5, "Foreign Film" is chapter 7, and so forth. But all responses should interlock, and the "Film Techniques" and "Film Language" chapters should be used in all contexts. A philosophy course could benefit from studying "Film as Film," as could literature and social science courses.

- *Information Sheets.* These work well with any class, and several models are provided. Information sheets, prepared and distributed before the viewing of each film, help students understand the instructor's approach in more specific terms.
- *Exercise Sheets.* These can direct the students in very specific terms to what material in this film is useful in studying films, and also to material that may be helpful in a quiz or test. It is left to the instructor's discretion to determine the specific purpose and contents of such sheets.

The Great Dictator (1941): Information Sheet

Charles Chaplin (1889–1977)
Cast: Charles Chaplin, Paulette Goddard, Jack Oakie

Background

Chaplin was a director, producer, writer, musical composer, actor, and editor of his films. He created the Little Tramp persona, the character he played in all his silent films until 1934 and for which he became famous. The Tramp is always at center stage, wearing baggy pants, oversized shoes, a tight coat, and a derby. He is a social outcast, often unemployed and homeless. Though he lives at the margins of society, he maintains his sense of self-worth and dignity. In all the major Chaplin films, a girl casually enters his life and prods him to some heroic act that saves the Tramp and sometimes rights a social wrong.

Mack Sennett (1880–1960) founded Keystone Studios in Hollywood. He produced short films (two-reelers) of silent slapstick comedy, the most vital cinematic form of the 1920s. Such comedy was distinguished for its visual humor, its circus and vaudeville techniques, its burlesque, pantomime, and resemblance to the comic strip.

Chaplin became Sennett's protegé, beginning his career at the Keystone Studios, then leaving for Essenay to develop his own techniques and write his own scripts. In a few years he became the highest paid and most popular film star in the history of American film—and the most recognizable person in the world.

Themes

His films are generally social satires concerned with

- Conflicts between the individual and society
- The dehumanization of the working man in a world run by machines
- Dictatorship and political oppression
- Man-woman relationships
- The pathos of the human condition
- The comedy and tragedy of human life, which often play out together

On Reserve

The Tramp (1915, silent) establishes the persona of the Little Tramp.

The Gold Rush (1925, silent) takes the Little Tramp to Alaska to prospect for gold. He suffers untold miseries from hunger and rejection. See the scene in which he makes a meal of his shoe.

City Lights (1931, silent [see pp. 210–11]) has the Little Tramp fall in love with a blind girl. He tries to raise funds for her eye operation by becoming a boxer and is thrown in prison for stealing money to give her. When he's released he visits the flower shop she now owns. At first she laughs at him, but then she realizes that he—not the rich man she imagined—is her benefactor.

Modern Times (1936, silent) finds the Little Tramp jobless during the Great Depression. He wanders around hungry until he meets a girl and, with her help, becomes a waiter in a restaurant. This savage satire of the machine age ends with them walking into the sunset.

Monsieur Verdoux (1947 [see pp. 210–11]) is a black comedy in which Chaplin plays a debonair serial killer. He murders rich women to support his crippled wife and young son. Eventually he meets an impoverished young woman who nearly saves him from moral collapse. After the 1929 stock market crash, he loses all his money and is finally caught, tried, convicted, and executed. The film was thought scandalous at the time and was withdrawn from theatres after a few weeks, but it has had a critical resurgence.

Exercises

1. *The Great Dictator* is a satire on Hitler and on Nazism in general. How does Chaplin present Hitler? How accurate is this portrayal? Can an

artist make something so horrible into an object of ridicule?

2. When this movie was made, the Holocaust was approaching; but the extent of the Nazi atrocities was not well known. Chaplin said that, had he known what was happening in the concentration camps, he would never had made this film. Would that have been a good thing? Or did this film have a positive effect on its audiences?

3. The duality of the Chaplin character(s) is striking. One side of him skillfully portrays the evil Hynkel, while the other side is the humble, "worthless" Jewish barber. Discuss the irony implied in the barber's decency and heroism.

4. Look at the symbols in the movie: the double cross, the statue of "The Thinker," the balloon globe as Hynkel's dance partner. Find other symbols in the film and offer your interpretations.

5. How plausible is the barber's speech at the end? How convincing is it? Compare it to Hynkel's earlier speech.

6. Chaplin is said to have created *pathos* in his movies, thus evoking certain emotions. Explore this idea.

The Seventh Seal (1956): Information Sheet

Ingmar Bergman (1918–   )
Director of photography: Gunnar Fischer
Music by: Erik Nordgren
Cast: Bibi Andersson, Gunnar Björnstrand, Bengt Ekerot, Nils Poppe, Max Von Sydow

Background

The Seventh Seal was Bergman's sixteenth film, the first to be acknowledged as a masterpiece and to be very popular in the United States. His subsequent films—*Wild Strawberries* (1957), *The Magician* (1958), and *The Virgin Spring* (1960)—catapulted Bergman to international fame and made him the subject of many books and studies of cinematic art. His films are intensely intellectual and visually striking, presenting characters who search for God and the meaning of life. Bergman wrote his own scripts (except for *The Virgin Spring*, which is based on a medieval ballad), which were later published as literary works.

The Seventh Seal can be enjoyed on a realistic level as a representation of life in the Middle Ages, a period in which Bergman is greatly interested. It can also be viewed as an allegory of man's struggle against Death. Knight Antonius Block (Max Von Sydow) returns with his squire Jons (Gunnar Björnstrand) from the Crusades, only to find his land devastated by the plague. To save his life, he engages in a chess game with Death (Bengt Ekerot). If the knight wins—and he believes he can—he will live; if he loses, he will die. Meanwhile, he strikes up a friendship with a band of traveling jugglers among whom are Jof (Nils Poppe) and Mia (Bibi Andersson)—Joseph and Mary— whose lives are saved by Jons. The people of this troubled land are engaged in witch hunts, and a young woman is to be burned at the stake. Block reaches his home to find his wife waiting for him, but happiness is not in the cards. He loses the chess game and is led up a hill by Death, along with his companions, as the jugglers watch. The fear of Death has been conquered, but not Death itself.

Themes

- Revelations 8:1 says, "When the Lamb opened the Seventh Seal, there was silence in heaven for about half an hour." The breaking of the seven seals foreshadows predetermined events or further revelations. The first four release the four horsemen of the Apocalypse: pestilence, war, famine, and death. The fifth reveals Christian martyrs seeking revenge for the torment inflicted on them. The sixth heralds earthquakes and other natural disasters. At the opening of the seventh seal, seven trumpets sound as various plagues descend on the earth.
- On one level, this film can be seen as a parallel between the Middle Ages after the Crusades, when the Black Death was often viewed as the wrath of God, and the McCarthy era with its "witch hunts," Cold War animosities, and fear of nuclear annihilation. This interpretation was favored by many critics, but was emphatically discouraged by Bergman himself.
- The film's universal appeal is based on humanity's natural fear of Death and its efforts to outwit him.
- The divine couple symbolized by Jof and Mia prefigure the salvation of the world.
- A dualism appears in the characters of Block, who is as idealistic as Don Quixote despite his many setbacks, and Jons, his Sancho Panza, whose role is to remind the knight of life's harsh realities.
- The absence or silence of God is a frequent Bergman theme. What Block says in his confession at the chapel expresses this crucial concept.
- The visual aspects of the film—i.e., its *mise-en-scène* and lighting—are impressive. Bergman studied medieval paintings and used them as the basis of some film compositions. This is reflected in groupings of people, forest locations (shot in his studio near Malmo), religious processions, seascapes, the chess game, and the actors' make-up.

On Reserve

Any Bergman film.
John Donner. "*The Seventh Seal: A Director's View.*" In *Ingmar Bergman: Essays in Criticism*, ed. Stuart M. Kasminsky. Oxford, England: Oxford University Press, 1975.

Exercises

1. Compare the historical eras and places which the film reflects: Europe in the Middle Ages after the Crusades and the United States in the McCarthy era of the 1950s. Does anything in the film imply that it refers to the latter period?
2. Study the film's pictorials: lighting, *mise-en-scène*, borrowing from medieval paintings. Find scenes that imitate such paintings. Follow the audio track on the laser edition for more information.
3. Select three or more symbolic scenes in which a grouping of characters has obvious religious or mythical connotations. Interpret these scenes in the context of the movie.
4. Explain dualism. It can be applied to the knight and his squire, but it can also be found elsewhere in the movie.
5. Look for themes in Revelations to see whether and how they correspond to themes in this film.
6. Suggest a theme not touched upon in class. The movie is filled with ideas. Explain some of these in your own words.

Dr. Strangelove, or How I Learned to Stop Worrying and Love the Bomb (1964): Information Sheet

Stanley Kubrick (1928–1999)
Cast: Sterling Hayden, James Earl Jones, Slim Pickens, George C. Scott, Peter Sellers, Keenan Wynn

Background

Based on the novel *Red Alert* by Peter George, this film begins as mad American General Jack D. Ripper (Sterling Hayden) orders a nuclear attack on targets inside Soviet Russia. Pentagon Chief of Staff Buck Turgidson (George C.

Scott) is alerted and in turn alerts President Merkin Muffley (Peter Sellers), who calls an emergency meeting in the Pentagon's War Room. Meanwhile, Texan pilot T. J. "King" Kong (Slim Pickens) is flying his B–52 toward his target, oblivious to efforts by the Pentagon to recall him.

In a desperate attempt to prevent a nuclear war, Muffley has agreed that the Soviets can shoot down the B–52s. Unable to contact Ripper at Burpleson Air Force Base, the military launches an attack on the base and Ripper shoots himself. This leaves his British aide, Group Captain Lionel Mandrake (Peter Sellers), working to decipher the coded attack order to which only Ripper had the key.

When the ex-Nazi Dr. Strangelove (Peter Sellers), who is now the Pentagon's research and development director, explains the Doomsday Machine in the presence of Soviet Ambassador de Sadesky (Peter Bull), the Russian explains that the Soviets already have the device in place. By now Mandrake has decoded the attack order and the planes are returning—except for three already destroyed by Soviet missiles and the one flown by Major Kong. Damage to Kong's plane has rendered its decoding system useless, but it is still flying and delivers its bomb. The Doomsday Machine, thus triggered, will envelop the earth in radioactivity for ninety-three years. Strangelove, however, suggests to his colleagues in the War Room that a sizable number of U.S. citizens can survive in mineshafts for a hundred years, or until the radioactivity wears off.

Themes

- The inevitability of evil caused by human actions. In the 1950s many people—including Kubrick—believed that the hydrogen bomb would inevitably bring about Doomsday.
- The nuclear arms race in particular struck fear in the hearts and minds of many who were convinced it would destroy life on earth.
- Human folly is seen to permeate the human race from top to bottom, but to be especially present in the higher ranks of society, less so in the middle and lower ranks.

On Reserve

Kagan, Norman. "Dr. Strangelove, or How I Learned to Stop Worrying and Love The Bomb." In *The Cinema of Stanley Kubrick*. New York: Continuum Publishing, 1990.

Nelson, Thomas Allen. "The Descent of Man: Dr. Strangelove." In *Kubrick: Inside a Film Artist's Maze*. Bloomington: Indiana University Press, 1982.

Exercises

1. Critics disagree over whether this film is a satire, a black comedy, or a sex allegory. High profile people are satirized in various ways: given ridiculous-sounding names sometimes suggestive of sexual activity or impotence, presented in grotesque make-up, and/or making outrageous statements. The book by Peter George on which the film is based is more serious in tone, but Kubrick thought the film would be more effective as a comedy. Students may want to debate this point.
2. The names of the characters contain a wealth of double-entendres: Jack D. Ripper/Jack the Ripper is incredibly paranoid, convinced the Soviets have been polluting our water since 1946 and diluting our precious "bodily fluids." (He discovers this while having sex.) The grotesque Soviet Ambassador is called de Sadesky/de Sade. The R in Wing Attack Plan R stands for Romeo. The pilot is King Kong: Is he after a girl? One of his bombs features the words, "Hi, there!" and his primary target is Laputa. And so on. Find more examples of suggestive and/or ironic language and of axes and nodes.
3. Compare *Dr. Strangelove* to *The Seventh Seal*. Both are about dread of an impending doomsday. Is the religious theme totally absent from Strangelove? Discuss this point based on your own observations from viewing the film.

Psycho (1960): Information Sheet

Alfred Hitchcock (1899–1980)
Screenplay by: Joseph Stefano, from the Robert Bloch novel based on the life of mass murderer Ed Gein.
Music by: Bernard Hermann
Cast: Martin Balsam, John Gavin, Janet Leigh, Vera Miles, Anthony Perkins

Background

A young woman (Leigh) steals money entrusted to her by her boss and runs away. She intends to use the cash to bolster her own and her boyfriend's finances so they can get married. Haunted by guilt and pursued by police, she stops at the Bates Motel where she is stabbed to death in the shower. Her body is placed in her car which is then submerged in a swamp. Meanwhile, her sister Lila (Miles) alerts Sam (Gavin), the boyfriend, that Marion is missing, and they visit the motel. There, a detective (Balsam) believes he has discovered a clue to the identity and motive of the killer. The detective is killed, but when the murderer attempts to murder Lila, he is caught. A psychologist offers a profile of the murderer, who is said to be suffering from a split personality: He adopted the persona of his mother after killing her. The final scene shows Marion's car being pulled from the swamp.

Hitchcock uses camera movement to make many of his points visually, without the need for dialogue or other explanation. Montage, for instance, is used in the shower scene, which is comprised of over *eighty shots*. These tiny pieces of film were seamed together in the editing process. *Mise-en-scène* is employed in the composition of interior and exterior scenes, such as those set in Bates' office and Mrs. Bates' bedroom.

Themes

- The morality tale presented through imagery and dialogue
- Fate, which allows a bad situation to grow steadily worse
- Freudian psychology, which presents a madman skillfully concealing a dual personality
- The shock value inherent in realizing that your mild-mannered neighbor could be a serial killer

On Reserve

Rebello, Stephen. *Alfred Hitchcock and the Making of Psycho*. New York: St. Martin's Press, 1990.

Spoto, Donald. *The Dark Side of Genius: The Life of Alfred Hitchcock*. New York: Econo-Clad Books, 1987.

Psycho—Collector's Edition, DVD. Includes "The Making of *Psycho*," with remarks by Joseph Stefano, Patricia Hitchcock O'Connell, and Janet Leigh. Universal, 1998.

Exercises

1. Look for axes and nodes in this movie: the mirrors—bathroom, bedroom, and rearview; the stuffed birds; the picture that conceals the peep-

hole. Find others and discuss what these details contribute to particular scenes and to the film as a whole.

2. The musical score has only strings playing during the introduction, the stabbing, and other scenes. Discuss how this enhances the visual elements.

3. After viewing "The Making of Psycho," deconstruct important scenes in the film, such as the shower scene. The principals in the documentary discuss both their own functions in given scenes and the mechanics of putting together such an overwhelming project. Does this deconstruction help you understand the scenes?

4. Study the dialogue and performances. Why does Norman stutter? What effect does this have?

5. Note the camera movement that is the benchmark of Hitchcock's exposition. Find moments when the camera functions as a moralist by panning, zooming, reversing, etc.

6. Observe the themes listed above and look for others. Psycho is above all a moral tale. How is this evident in both imagery and dialogue?

Amadeus (1984): Information Sheet

Milos Forman (1932–   )
Produced by: Saul Zaentz
Screenplay by: Peter Shaffer
Musical direction by: Sir Neville Marriner
Cast: F. Murray Abraham, Elizabeth Berridge, Tom Dotrice, Tom Hulce, and Jeffrey Jones

Background

Amadeus is a collaborative film. Unlike *The Great Dictator* and *Beauty and the Beast*, movies made by auteurs (filmmakers with total control of their productions), *Amadeus* is the work of several individuals, each of whom made a unique contribution. Saul Zaentz, an independent producer from Berkeley, had preserved and catalogued the world's largest jazz collections and had already produced the award-winning *One Flew Over the Cuckoo's Nest* in 1975. Director Milos Forman, the Czech New Wave leader, had fled Czechoslovakia after the Soviet invasion in 1968 and had already collaborated with Zaentz on *Cuckoo's Nest*. Screenwriter Peter Shaffer, a music critic and recognized authority on Mozart, had written the critically acclaimed play *Amadeus*. Sir Neville Marriner, leading world authority on Mozart and conductor of the

Academy of St.-Martin-in-the-Fields, undertook to conduct and supervise the music in the film on the condition that not one note of the original music be altered. Many others also contributed—especially production designer Patricia Brandenstein and actors F. Murray Abraham (Salieri), Tom Hulce (Mozart), Elizabeth Berridge (Constanze), and Jeffrey Jones (Emperor Joseph II).

The story is told in flashbacks as Salieri (F. Murray Abraham) confesses his sins 32 years after Mozart's death. Young Salieri loves music and is talented—but he is not a genius. When he meets Mozart (Tom Hulce) at an archbishop's residence, he is stunned by the boy's vulgarity. The voice of God is in Mozart's music, but he himself speaks like a guttersnipe. Salieri becomes obsessed with his rival and is constantly frustrated by him. Eventually, they both come to the court of the Emperor Joseph (Jeffrey Jones), where they ally themselves with the Italian (Salieri) and German (Mozart) factions. When Salieri tries to catch Mozart unprepared, Amadeus improvises brilliantly. He even wins the heart and hand of the beautiful Constanze (Elizabeth Berridge).

Salieri vows to destroy Mozart, but it often seems as if the latter is determined to destroy himself with his arrogance and irresponsibility. Then he will suddenly defend his work—*The Marriage of Figaro*—with unwonted eloquence or produce the magnificent *Don Giovanni* or the lovely The *Magic Flute*. Eventually, Mozart is commissioned by an anonymous client (the movie suggests Salieri, but it was actually Count Walsegg) to write his own *Requiem*. When Mozart dies deep in debt, Salieri derives no satisfaction because he knows his enemy's music will live on.

Themes

- The *connection between art and politics,* the overriding theme, may be of particular interest to a film literature class. The film offers a look, based on careful research, of patronage of the arts in the eighteenth century. An emperor and his court were uniquely positioned to influence the development of aesthetics and art in many areas, because their patronage was the essential economic base for a striving artist. Indeed, musicians even needed royal permission—granted through the intercession of court composers, opera directors, and Kapellmeisters—to accept pupils, and the teaching might provide the performer's or composer's only source of income.
- Composers were, therefore, encouraged to compose particular kinds of music. *The Marriage of Figaro,* for instance, was considered politically incorrect because it exposed corruption among the aristocracy. Their dependence on such patronage confined the freedom and degraded the

status of the artist, not to mention its effects on personal dignity and standard of living. On the other hand, these necessary connections put artists in close contact with upper-class society and guaranteed them an audience. In that sense, eighteenth-century artists could be more powerful than their modern counterparts. Peter Shaffer made this point clearly in a passage from the stage play that was omitted from the film. Salieri says,

> You, when you come, will be told that we musicians of the eighteenth century were no better than servants: willing slaves of the well-to-do. This is quite true. It is also quite false. Yes, we were servants. But we were *learned* servants. We arrived, each of us, *fully trained,* and we built together—like the masons who built the great cathedrals—a gigantic Palace of Sound, its foundation grounded deep in the Disciplines of Beauty. Lines of strict counterpoint were set to strengthen the spirit; lines of strict harmony stretched to touch the senses. And we said to our so-called Betters, "*Enter*—and we will celebrate your lives."

- Salieri also weaves a Freudian theme into the narrative, comparing Mozart to his father Leopold.

On Reserve

Shaffer, Peter. *Peter Shaffer's Amadeus.* New York: HarperCollins, 1985.

Amadeus, Special Edition Laserdisc. Pioneer, 1995. With analog channel commentary by Milos Forman and Peter Shaffer, photographs, and two music CDs. Also on DVD.

Exercises

1. Look for the Freudian theme and its connection to the music, especially in the excerpts from *Don Giovanni*. Follow Salieri's explanation of this relationship while Mozart conducts the performance.
2. How does the music itself show the contrast between Salieri and Mozart? How does it reflect Mozart's character and mindset?
3. Carefully examine Salieri's motives for wishing to kill Mozart. Does the film—especially in the last scene between Salieri and Mozart—suggest that Salieri actually carried out his plan?
4. Carefully analyze the debate at court between Emperor Joseph and his Italian courtiers regarding the production of *Figaro*. Mozart makes a

spirited defense of his opera and his right to have it produced. Is this politics vs. art debate relevant today?

5. Contrast art patronage in the eighteenth century and art sponsorship by various agents—government, corporations, private—in the late twentieth/early twenty-first century.

Platoon (1986): Information Sheet

Oliver Stone (1946–   )
Screenplay by: Oliver Stone, based on his own experiences in Vietnam
Cast: Tom Berenger, Willem Dafoe, John C. McGinley, Charlie Sheen,
    Forrest Whitaker

Background

The movie was shot in the Philippines, which are at the same latitude as Vietnam, so that foliage, etc., is very similar. The tiny—in Hollywood terms—budget of $6 million mushroomed into gross revenues of $86 million in the United States and $275 million worldwide. The first Vietnam film to be made by an actual Vietnam veteran, *Platoon* was hailed by critics and audiences for its realism. It was nominated for eight Oscars and won four, including Best Director and Best Picture.

Now and for the foreseeable future, this movie will continue to challenge audiences and to raise important ethical questions. Revisiting the Vietnam experience, it presents that war in a microcosm, forcing viewers to seek and analyze the reasons not only for U.S. involvement in the war, but also for the political and social turmoil that surrounded it.

Themes

- Heroism. Although the motives for U.S. involvement in the war were questionable, many young men fought well and bravely under harrowing conditions. They did not receive the credit or honor they deserved for their service.
- The brutality and dehumanization of war. Soldiers are expected to shoot at the enemy, but the killing of civilians raised questions about the legality and ethics of this war. The My Lai massacre in which a whole Vietnamese village was annihilated by U.S. soldiers occurred about the same

time the action of this movie was taking place, so the film touches upon the most controversial aspect of the war.

- Rites of passage/individual growth. Narrator Chris Taylor (Sheen) learns about himself as he faces the horrors of this jungle war. This look into the self can be a cleansing experience, much like the scathing traumas described by Hemingway in the settings of earlier wars.
- Wide range of characters. These men have similar perceptions but widely differing reactions. Consider the psychotic Barnes (Berenger), the saintly Elias (Dafoe), and the cowardly O'Neill (McGinley).

On Reserve

Platoon, Laserdisc. With analog left-channel commentary by Oliver Stone, right-channel commentary by military advisor Captain Dale Dye. Pioneer, 1996. Also on DVD.

Fitzgerald, Frances. *Fire in the Lake: The Vietnamese and Americans in Vietnam.* New York: Vintage, 1989.

Halberstam, David. *The Best and the Brightest. Twentieth Anniversary Edition.* New York: Fawcett, 1993.

O'Brien, Tim. The *Things They Carried.* Econo-Clad Books, 1990.

The Deerhunter (1978), DVD ed. Universal, 1998. With production notes.
Full Metal Jacket (1987), DVD ed. Warner, 1999.

Exercises

1. *Characterization:* Chris Taylor changes from an insecure youth to a hardened fighter to a questionable ethical judge. Examine the content of his letters, delivered in voice-over monologues, and judge them accordingly. Weigh them against his final monologue.
2. Identified the following characters, and determine what they represent: O'Neill, Barnes, Elias, Tex, Gardner, Junior, Big Harold, Crawford, Bunny. Characters here are not stereotypes; they grow and change.
3. *Dehumanization:* This term should he used in conjunction with its opposite—humanization. To a degree war dehumanizes the participants, but may it not have the opposite effect as well? Does fighting not heighten awareness of barbarity? These are questions that apply to the audience. Question Oliver Stone's motives in making the movie. Is it anti-Vietnam, anti-American, anti-military? What do we get out of it? Each viewer could give a different answer.

4. The My Lai massacre occurred in 1968, and resulted in the trial of the officer in charge (find information in the library). Stone says in the audio commentary that he modeled one of his scenes—attack on a Vietnam village—on that episode. What is the message of this particular scene?

5. *Realism/Violence:* Is the "realistic" language necessary? The graphic violence depicted in certain scenes? Read related material in chapter 11 or in other sources. Stone claims that these things were true—or similar— to his recollection of the events he experienced.

6. *Historical background:* In his script, Stone provides the perimeters of the action; that is, the specific space/area where the action on the screen occurs. In this case, a platoon perimeter was about 200 feet wide and equally long; it included a dugout within which the men in the field operated, usually lying in wait in their foxholes to ambush the North vietnamese (NVA) who were infiltrating from Cambodia. As explained by Chris in one of his last voice-overs, Cambodia was only 2000 meters away. Yet the Americans were not allowed to go in and clear out the infiltrating enemy. (When this was finally done under President Nixon early in 1969, the famous Kent State shootings occurred during a protest against that invasion. Many other protests broke out on U.S. campuses.) The film action ends with the ambush of the NVA on the platoon perimeter. It is a holocaust-like ending, with nearly every one of the enemy exterminated and nearly the entire platoons as well—including Barnes. What historical lesson do you learn from studying these details, in the script and in the visual translation?

7. *Music score:* The score for this movie was composed by Georges Delerue, to enhance the action sequences of the movie. Judge how effective this is. Stone explains that he also used Samuel Barber's "Adagio for Strings" in the opening shots, during certain scenes, and at the end, to lend an air of somberness, dignity, and tragedy (which is what the music suggests) to the action. Judge for yourself how effective and appropriate the superimposition of classical music on such a movie is. What mood does it establish? Does it blend with the "lighter" tones of Delerue?

8. *Criticism:* Read Michael Wilmington's, "Platoon," then Pauline Kael's "Platoon," and discuss the contrast of ideas presented. See *Love and Hisses: The National Society of Film Critics Sound Off on the Hottest Movie Controversies.* Peter Rainer, ed., San Francisco: Mercury House, 1992.

Quiz Show (1994): Information Sheet

Robert Redford (1937–   )
Screenplay by: Paul Attanasio
Cast: Ralph Fiennes, Rob Morrow, David Paymer, Paul Scofield, and
    John Turturro

Background

In 1958, Herbie Stempel (Turturro) is the reigning champion of NBC's hit game show *Twenty-One*. When a top executive with Geritol, the show's sponsor, decides that Stempel's on-camera antics might end up lowering the ratings, the producers pressure him to take a dive. They replace him with Columbia English professor Charles Van Doren (Fiennes), the scion of an American intellectual dynasty. In order to keep Van Doren in place, NBC, under the direction of Dan Enright (Paymer), convinces the contestant to accept the answers in advance.

When congressional investigator Dick Goodwin (Morrow) gets the disgruntled Stempel to blow the whistle on this corruption, Van Doren becomes the target. His own scruples, arising from conflicts with his famous father, poet Mark Van Doren, put him at a disadvantage in his confrontations with Goodwin, and he admits his guilt in a confession before a congressional subcommittee. Enright also admits his participation but does not go on to implicate executives of Geritol and NBC.

The reputation of the Van Doren family was severely damaged. The contestant's uncle Carl had been a teacher, biographer, literary historian, and critic, editor of *The Nation*, and a 1938 Pulitzer Prize winner for his biography of Benjamin Franklin. Mark Van Doren was a professor of literature at Columbia from 1942 till 1959, when both he and his son were forced to resign. A Pulitzer Prize winner like his brother, he was a poet, a literary historian, a critic, a novelist, a short story writer, and the editor of several anthologies. Charles Van Doren himself was a writer, editor, TV scriptwriter, and contributor to the Encyclopedia Britannica.

This lofty family position makes the film fit Aristotle's definition of tragedy. Major characters fall (or dive) from heights to depths, and a character of high standing suffers the consequences of his own actions.

The movie is shot primarily indoors (with a few outdoor scenes of sailing on a lake and some social gatherings). Indeed, it becomes primarily a courtroom drama which employs frequent crosscutting to show changes in point of view along with close-ups and medium shots to underscore character and conflict.

Themes

- Moral choice made with full knowledge of the action and its possible consequences
- Deliberately misleading use of language: "What you are doing is good for education."
- Deliberate misuse of a medium—TV—and betrayal of public trust
- "Egregious" agreements among the parties
- Van Doren's betrayal of family values and traditions
- A cover-up by TV network and major corporation
- Goodwin's choice: Become "the Uncle Tom of the Jews"?
- Public infatuation with celebrities; hero worship

On Reserve

"Van Doren, Charles." Microsoft Encarta OnlineEncyclopedia2000 <http://encarta.msn.com>

Exercises

1 *Quiz Show* contains discursive ("heard") axes and nodes that underscore its thematic richness. Study the following, identifying the speaker (or other agent):
- "You are listening to the sound of Sputnik . . . a sound that says . . . all is not well with America."
- "It's the damnedest thing . . . but you've plateau-ed." "Plateau-ed."
- "What the heck is egregious?"
- "Oh, what men dare do, what men may do, what men daily do, now knowing what they do."
- "You are the Uncle Tom of the Jews."

2. Briefly describe the axes and nodes in *Quiz Show*, connecting them to themes:
- The two cars that appear in the movie designated as 300—
- The winding staircases
- Earphones in the booth
- A TV set wrapped in a box
- The Capitol colonnades
- A monkey on the *Today* show

2001: A Space Odyssey (1968): Information Sheet

Stanley Kubrick (1928–1999)
Screenplay by: Arthur C. Clarke and Stanley Kubrick
Cast: Keir Dullea, Gary Lockwood, Daniel Richter, William Sylvester

Background

Kubrick made this film with one specific purpose in mind: To use the medium of cinema to give visual dimension to his belief that intelligent life exists elsewhere in the universe. Widely read on the subject, he was in contact with many scientific authorities, including Arthur C. Clarke. Clarke was a famous science fiction writer and an authority on coral reefs who was then residing in Ceylon (now Sri Lanka). Kubrick wrote to him about making a movie concerning extraterrestrials, and the two men met in 1964 when Clarke was in New York on business. They spent three and a half years collaborating on the project. Clarke coauthored the script and also worked on another treatment which eventually became his novel of the same name, published shortly after the movie's release. Reading the book is not a necessary prerequisite for understanding the film, but it does shed light on some of the complex subjects and aims.

The movie's action is divided into three parts. The first part is set four million years ago, when humans first appeared on earth. Moon Watcher (Richter) is near starvation after a prolonged drought when he discovers a monolith. The strange object inspires him to use an animal bone to kill another animal and thus to satisfy his hunger.

Part two occurs four million years later in "the present"—that is, in the year 2000. A spaceship is hurrying to a space station near the moon, carrying a lone passenger—Dr. Heywood Floyd (Sylvester), Chairman of the National Council of Astronautics. He has been summoned to study an anomalous object found on the moon, which is now colonized by humans. The object is buried in the crater Tycho, and Heywood interprets the loud shriek it emits as a signal directed to the planet Jupiter.

In part three, set eighteen months later, an expedition sets out for Jupiter. Its mission is so secret that it is unknown not only to the crew of the spaceship Discovery, but even to its commander Dr. Dave Bowman (Dullea) and his assistant Frank Poole (Lockwood). Aboard the Discovery, only the ship's computer HAL 9000 is fully aware of the mission. The secret is also known, however, to three hibernating astronauts who will be awakened when the ship approaches its destination. Inexplicably, HAL rebels and kills both Poole and the sleeping astronauts. When Bowman arrives on Jupiter, he is mysteriously transformed into an old man and then into an infant.

The movie is scientifically and technologically accurate. In addition to his own extensive reading, Kubrick consulted U.S. and British scientists from academic, military, and industrial institutions. Nuclear scientists, astronomers, geophysicists, and cores of technicians offered input and expertise in memos and letters. With this help, the spacecrafts were designed and constructed with absolute scientific accuracy. Harry Lang and Frederick Ordway III of NASA's Marshall Space Flight Center in Huntsville, Alabama, were hired by Kubrick to assist in this effort. Work at the design stage was done at the Polaris Production Center in New York; then for construction and filming, crews moved to MGM British Studios in Borehamwood, England.

The entire musical score is taken from classical compositions, and Kubrick choreographs action—both inside and outside the spacecraft—*to* that music. That adds an aesthetic influence that, as always, affects the meaning of the action. The music used most prominently comes from Richard Strauss's *Thus Spake Zarathustra*; Johann Strauss's *The Blue Danube*; and György Ligeti's *Atmospherics, Lux Aeterna*, and *Requiem*.

Themes

- The existence of intelligent life elsewhere in the universe. The film offers scant evidence to support Kubrick's belief.
- The evolution of technology and of spiritual man. The movie takes viewers from bones as tools/weapons to spacecraft, to time warp, and on to rebirth and immortality.
- Man vs. machine: Who is in charge?
- The lure of the stars and of the far reaches of space.

On Reserve

Clarke, Arthur C. *2001: A Space Odyssey.* New York: New American Library, 1968.

Nelson, Thomas Allen. *Kubrick: Inside a Film Artist's Maze.* Bloomington: Indiana University Press, 1982.

Exercises

1. In terms of cause and effect, summarize the action of "The Dawn of Man," the first part of this movie. How does this reading enhance your understanding of the film's action?

2. In terms of film continuity, what is the connecting link between Heywood Floyd's mission and the action summarized above?
3. Briefly compare the ape-man and Bowman. In what specific ways do they remind you of each other?
4. Make one or two specific references to the two vehicles (indicate which one) flying through space to the tunes of Strauss music. What does the music add to the action?
5. Dying HAL sings a song. What is the song? Why was the song programmed for this particular moment? What emotion does this song evoke? Is your opinion of HAL affected by it?
6. The film shows you Bowman's arrival at Jupiter in montage sequences. Describe the most memorable of those sequences. How relevant are these to your understanding of space travel?
7. Describe the architectural decor when Bowman is *on* Jupiter, and offer opinions about its meaning. Of what other film by Kubrick (or any other filmmaker) does this remind you?
8. The film is rich in axes and nodes. When Bowman has his meal as he sits at the table in the Jupiter mansion, his wineglass falls and breaks. Interpret this incident as one of these nodes.
9. The monolith is the most important axis in the movie. Account for all its appearances, and offer an interpretation of each.
10. A critic called Bowman's adventure "journey to freedom." What would be a cogent interpretation of this idea, based on film facts?

A Passage to India (1984): Information Sheet

Sir David Lean (1908–1991)
Screenplay adapted from: E. M. Forster's 1924 novel
Cast: Peggy Ashcroft, Victor Banerjee, Michael Culver, Judy Davis, James Fox, Alec Guinness, Nigel Havers, Saeed Jaffrey, Art Malik, Antonia Pemberton, Clive Swift, Richard Wilson

Background

India, a subcontinent of Asia, is the most populous country in the world next to China. It is at once the world's largest democracy and one of its poorest nations. Its political history is complex, but it was subjected to British rule for nearly two hundred years. The Mughal Empire lasted from 1526 till 1857, but the British effectively governed India from 1761 till Gandhi succeeded in driving them out in 1947. Before the British arrived, however, India had a rich and fascinating history (see Part II of the novel, pp. 123–24, for the geological and mythological history of the Marabar Caves).

The film is set in the early 1920s in Chandrapore, which is probably based on Patna, an administrative post of one of the Indian states with a population of about forty thousand. It is well described in chapter one of the novel.

India's complexity carries over into its religious makeup. In 1941, there were 254,000,000 Hindus; 92,000,000 Muslims; 5,000,000 Sikhs (a Muslim sect); 6,000,000 Christians; 115,000 Parsees; and 233,000 Buddhists. Clearly, the Hindu faith predominated. That religion's sacred books are the *Vedas* (*Books of Faith*) and the *Upanishads* (epic tales of the Hindu gods), though many other texts are revered by various branches of Hinduism. The highest Hindu rank is that of Brahmin (from *brahma—being*), one who understands the Reality infused in all things.

Muslims have their own holy book, *the Koran*, which declares that there is only one God. Many Muslims are descended from the Mughal conquerors who took over India in the twelfth century. Those invaders were followed by the Portuguese, who came to trade for pepper, spices, fruit, and silk from 1497 to 1600. They were displaced by the Dutch from 1600 to 1758. The British arrived only a year after the Portuguese and established the East India Company which traded for spices and built factories. The British settled in Bengal, Bombay (driving out the Portuguese in 1611), and Calcutta (founded in 1688). In 1757 the British victory at the Battle of Plassey captured Bengal and secured English dominance in India. The defeat at Plassey is still being mourned by Muslim Indians like Dr. Aziz (Banerjee) in the 1920s.

The movie conveys something of the Indians' resentment of the British, the resentment of the conquered toward the conqueror. This is not hatred based on skin color, but hostility toward people of a different nationality.

The film's characters reflect this profound complexity. Young Indian intellectuals are feared by the English. Aziz, the young Indian doctor accused of raping Adela (Davis), is defended by his lawyer friends Hamidullah (Jaffrey) and Mahmoud Ali (Malik). They resent European encroachment on their civilization. Finally, the Brahmin Narayan Godbole (Guinness) is an Indian who harmonizes East with West.

The Europeans are equally uncomfortable. Some are fascinated by the Indians they meet, others are repelled. Mrs. Moore (Ashcroft) and Adela resolutely ignore the unwritten rules about crosscultural associations, especially when they go off to the caves with Aziz. Yet it is Adela who accuses Aziz. The Turtons (Pemberton and Wilson), Ronny Heaslop (Havers), Richard Fielding (Fox), Major Callendar (Swift), and McBryde (Culver) all embody various responses to life in a foreign place. The overall English reaction is to deny its foreignness and proceed with tea or lawn tennis or whatever as if they were on the outskirts of London.

Themes

- The conflict between East and West; self-knowledge; view of the universe
- Brotherhood of man
- Colonialism: the Anglo-Indian British Raj vs. native India
- "Only connect": Failure to communicate
- Good vs. evil: Hindu version, Muslim version, Western version

On Reserve

Brownlow, Kevin. *David Lean: A Biography.* New York: St. Martin's Press, 1996.
Forster, E. M. *A Passage to India.* New York: Harcourt Brace, 1976.
Silverman, Stephen M. *David Lean.* New York: Harry N. Abrams, Inc., 1992.
Silver, Allain, and James Ursini *David Lean and His Films.* Los Angels: Silman-James Press, 1991.

Exercises

1. The film begins with long shots, or establishing shots, as Adela Quested and Mrs. Moore arrive in India—a parade, a crowded harbor, a train over a bridge. Why are these used? What information do they convey to the viewer?
2. Long shots alternate with close-ups, or medium shots—the train, for instance, and those sitting inside conversing. What is the effect produced by these alternating shots?
3. Lean is a specialist in reaction shots (explained in chapter 3). Study several: Aziz looking at Mrs. Moore after their encounter in the mosque; Adela looking at the statues in the ruined temple; Mrs. Moore in the cave; Fielding at Aziz after their fight. Explain what the shot reveals about the mental state of each of these characters in these particular scenes.
4. *Visual symbolism:* Notice how Lean carefully and deliberately juxtaposes images in key scenes throughout the film. Study several for their symbolic significance, including the following: the picture of the Marabar Caves when Adela enters the travel bureau in London; the hawk flying over the caves (also a node); the numerous pools in the story and water symbolism in general; the domes of mosques and temples; drops falling on the glass roof after the trial. Discover some more and tie these to the

various themes in the story: the mystery of India; self-knowledge in main characters, especially Adela and Mrs. Moore; catharsis of pity and fear; loss of friendship.

5. *Musical strains.* Maurice Jarre's musical score is quite unobtrusive but comes in at key moments in the action, as, for instance, during Adela's visit to the temples and later before she goes to sleep during the storm. Analyze those scenes (and others) and comment on their emotional impact.

6. *Lean's editing.* David Lean's editing is clipped, establishing a fast pace in a lengthy and complicated story that extends over several months. Study the effects of pacing: condensing information in transitional shots, as, for instance, the Marabar train climbing uphill, the elephant's bells, the empire's flag on Turton's automobile. Discover more of these nodes and comment on their effect on the narrative flow.

7. *Comparing and contrasting the film to the book.* Lean changed the beginning of Forster's novel and also the ending. He eliminated minor characters but lengthened two major scenes: the Marabar adventure and Aziz's trial. Study these changes and write an essay highlighting the most important. Does the film measure up to the book? Is the message different? Does the time difference between book and film (1924, 1984) make a difference?

8. Is there a common theme? Despite their differences, the book and the film share the same story; the major episodes are approximately the same. Study the similarities or common themes. Write an essay outlining the similarities.

9. "Only connect" was the same motto of one of Forster's other books, *Howard's End.* Does the same motto apply to *A Passage to India?* Study both the book and the film for the same answer. Write a brief essay analyzing this idea in the context of both book and film.

10. *Ensemble acting.* Lean is famous for casting groups of major actors instead of leads in most of his films. These groupings reflect on the themes and relationships developed: friendship (Aziz-Fielding, Aziz-Mrs. Moore), enmity (Aziz-Adela), mystical communion (Godbole-Mrs. Moore), lack of communion (Adela-Ronny, Ronny-Mrs. Moore). Study these relationships and write an essay outlining the differences between this type of film and the leading man/leading lady type.

Schindler's List (1993): Information Sheet

Steven Spielberg (1946–   )
Screenplay by: Steven Zaillian, based on the fact-based novel by Thomas Keneally

Musical score by: John Williams, with violin solos by Itzhak Perlman
Cast: Embeth Davidtz, Ralph Fiennes, Ben Kingsley, Liam Neeson

Background

Spielberg said, "I made *Schindler's List* as a document to the memory of the 6,000,000 Jews and millions of other men, women, and children who died during the Holocaust."

The movie won seven Oscars, including Best Picture and Best Director; seven British Academy awards; a New York Film Critics Best Picture Award; a National Society of Film Critics award; a Producer's Guild award; a Los Angeles Film Critics award; Chicago, Boston, and Dallas Film Critics awards; the Hollywood Foreign Press Association Golden Globe Award; and a Directors Guild of America Award for Spielberg.

It tells the story of Oskar Schindler (Neeson), a Catholic German-Czech industrialist who freely associates with Nazi officers and party officials. At the start of the movie, he is an ambiguous character—a drinker, womanizer, and war profiteer who may simply be trying to protect himself from charges of war crimes should the Allies win. By the end, however, he is an heroic (if not saintly) character, transformed by the horrors he has confronted. By employing Polish Jews in his factory (which produces crockery for the German army), he saves them from the ovens.

The character of Amon Goeth (Fiennes), on the other hand, is unequivocal: He is a monster—"the Butcher of Plaszow"—and the actor gives insights into his twisted psyche.

The film is shot in black and white because of the "darkness" of its subject matter, but symbolic flashes of color occasionally appear. Although it is well over three hours in length, the rapidity of its crosscutting gives it a breathless pace that enhances its dramatic impact.

By focusing on the Jews of Kracow who lived in the Plaszow concentration camp, the film attains a narrative and thematic unity while still delivering its universal message. Hitler's name is never mentioned, and there are few references to the war.

Themes

- *The Holocaust.* Despite focusing on the Jews Schindler saves, the movie concerns all the Jews and other victims of the Nazis.
- *Ambiguity of Schindler's character.* Historians disagree as to his original motives for involvement.
- *Life-and-death situations.* The movie presents a harrowing picture of what it means to fight for your very life on a daily basis. The cruelty and inhuman brutality of the camps are rendered very directly.
- *Good vs. evil.* Spielberg says, "The Nazis were evil Everybody knows that. But the fact that good also existed must also be known."
- *Ethical choices.* Characters make crucial decisions at several points in the film. Consider both Itzhak Stern (Kinglsey), Schindler's accountant, and Helen Hirsch (Davidtz).

On Reserve

Feinberg, Steven. "Steven Spielberg: The Holocaust." *Social Education,* October 1995.
Keneally, Thomas. *Schindler's List.* New York: A Touchstone Book, 1993.
Schickel, Richard. "Holocaust: Heart of Darkness." *Time,* 13 December 1993.

Exercises

1. Study materials on the Holocaust, from whatever sources you can. Consult articles on reserve, particularly Keneally's book on the subject. Write a short essay comparing the book to the film.
2. Draw thematic/chronological/historical parallels between *Schindler's List, The Great Dictator,* and *Life Is Beautiful.* Write an essay highlighting these parallels.
3. Study the major characters in *Schindler's List* and pair them accordingly: Schindler-Stern, Schindler-Goeth, Goeth-Hirsch, Schindler-Hirsch. How do these relationships develop through the film?
4. Spielberg used black-and-white photography for this film. Does this technique affect the theme and style or the movie? Spot the scenes where color is used. Is there a justification for it?
5. Despite its length (over three hours), *Schindler's List* seems to move rapidly. What specific technique does Spielberg use to achieve that effect?

6. *Montage.* Study the use of this technique in the first ten minutes of the film and outline its effectiveness.
7. *Axes and nodes.* The film is rich in suggestive imagery: swastikas, cuf-flinks, money clips, inkstands, jewelry, extracted teeth, etc. Study the thematic implications of the use of such images.

The English Patient (1996): Information Sheet

Anthony Minghella (1954–   )
Produced by: Saul Zaentz
Screenplay based on the novel by: Michael Ondaatje
Musical score by: Gabriel Jared, including music by Irving Berlin, Benny Goodman, and Johann Sebastian Bach
Cast: Naveen Andrews, Juliette Binoche, Willem Dafoe, Ralph Fiennes, Colin Firth, Kristin Scott Thomas, Julian Wadham

Background

Like the novel, the movie begins at the end of the story, then unravels the mysterious past of its central character, the horrifically burned English patient whose identity remains an enigma. Eschewing the book's leisurely presenta-tion of characters, the movie turns immediately to the story of Katherine (Thomas) and Almasy (Fiennes), which is the focus of the film.

Thus, the scope of the film is narrower, playing on the two love stories, placing Hana and Kip's in the background while Katherine and Almasy's takes over the screen. The triangle to come is foreshadowed in Herodotus's fable of the Lydian king Candaules who exposed his wife to his bodyguard Gyges, thereby losing both his wife and his throne. Almasy even warns Clifton (Firth), who ignores him. The tragedy evolves from that refusal to listen, which eventually leads to Clifton's attempt to murder Katherine and Almasy and kill himself.

Almasy's decision to turn over the maps to the Germans in order to save Katherine leads, in turn, to Caravaggio's maiming.

The desert scenery and the imagery of the swimmers, borrowed from the book, become striking subtexts in the film. The music adds an operatic ele-ment, enhancing the emotional impact of certain scenes. The blend of mod-ern popular tunes and traditional Hungarian melodies adds multilayered dimensions to the movie.

Themes

- *War.* It surrounds the story but is not the entire story, which is told in the context of the African invasion by the Germans and the invasion of Italy by the Allies. War shapes the major characters' destinies.
- *Betrayal.* This theme runs through the story in several lines. Katherine Clifton has an affair with the amoral Count Almasy, thus betraying her husband. Almasy hands over secret documents and photographs of the desert to Germans, thus betraying the Allied cause. And their betrayal of humanity in general with the erosion of such values as fidelity, loyalty, and historical consciousness (the last being more evident in the book than in the film).
- *Identity.* The film, taking most of its cues from the book, dwells on the fragmentation of identity. The major character Almasy, presented as the English patient, remains mysterious as his story of love and betrayal slowly unravels. The clues as to who he really is come from his recollections as Hana listens to him read from a tattered copy of Herodotus, and as Caravaggio, Almasy's nemesis, fills in the fragments of the narrative
- *History.* This theme ties up with the previous one. Just as Almasy's identity is an enigma, so the identities of lost desert civilizations remain mysteries. Their existence is a fleeting memory, documented by the ancient historian Herodotus who told tales resembling science fiction more than actual events.
- *The Desert.* In a sense, the dominant character in the film. A group of cartographers endeavors to discover its secrets through elaborate expeditions, but it seems that most of the secrets of the desert will remain hidden forever from the human eye. The book offers more elaborate data about those expeditions by the Geographical Society of London than does the film, which of necessity only alludes to the actual discoveries by some of its members, including Almasy and Madox.

On Reserve

Ondaatje, Michael. *The English Patient.* New York: Vintage Books, 1993.
Herodotus. *The Histories.* Walter Blanco and Jennifer Tolbert Roberts, eds. Walter Blanco, trans. A Norton Critical Edition. New York: W.W. Norton, 1992.
The Talented Mr. Ripley (1999) directed by Anthony Minghella.

Exercises

1. Visual axes and nodes: The film photographed by John Seale, A.C.S., is a virtual bonanza of striking imagery, all of which has a direct or indirect bearing on the multiple subtexts of the story. Study such significant axes as the desert itself or the cave drawings of swimmers, and see how these are related to the themes. Discover more of these.
2. Musical axes and nodes: Minghella's film relies on music for its total emotional impact. Study the musical score by Gabriel Jared in its relation to the action. Relate the appropriateness of the jazz music (songs by Irving Berlin) in the spots in which it is inserted and also of the Hungarian love song and the classical music of Bach.
3. The moral of the story: Determine whether the story has a moral. When Katherine reads the tale of the foolish husband Candaules, is this not a warning to her own husband? Yet he ignores the warning and leaves his wife behind with a group of men. Write an essay drawing a parallel between the two stories, using references from the book if necessary. Does the film contain other moral points on different levels?
4. Book vs. film: Given the great complexity of the book, does the film do well to stand on its own, or do you find it necessary to consult the book to get the full story? Find one element of the book that was omitted from the film to the disadvantage of the latter, and one element in the film missing from the book but enriching your perception of the whole story. Write an essay exploring these contrasts.

Subject Index

Accelerated montage, 60–61
Action, believability, 179–81
Action shots
    hand-held camera, 67
    multicamera, 67
Aesthetic transaction, 3
American Cinema, 18
American Film Institute, 41
American Movie Classics, 134
Antiwar messages, 49
Architecture in film, 14
Art
    film as, 11–13
    in *Great Dictator,* 24
    in relation to film, 13–14
Art form, 15–16
Art-house films, 134
Art of Fiction (James), 3
Audience diversity, 2
Auditory imagery
    axes and nodes, 79–85
    combined with visual imagery,
        85–87
    in comedy, 87–89
    in *Goldfinger,* 81–83

Auteur theory, 18–19, 21–22
Axes and nodes, 79–85, 79–98
    in comedy, 87–89
    in *Goldfinger,* 81–83
    in *Lolita,* 83–85
    sound track, 90–91

Beauty-Beast archetype, 46
Biograph, 131
Black-and-white films
    appeal of, 116–17
    Celebrity, 126–28
    classics, 119–19
    current, 126–28
    and *Psycho* remake, 123–26
    reasons for endurance of, 119–21
    through 1960s and beyond, 121–23
Box office success or failure, 16
Bravo channel, 73, 134

Cable TV channels, 134, 178
Cahiers du Cinema, 18
Camera movement, 57–59
Camera shots, 62–69
    close-up, 65

Camera shots (continued)
  crane shot, 68
  establishing shot, 67
  hand-held camera, 67
  jump shot, 65–66
  long shots, 63–65
  master shot, 67
  medium shot, 65–66
  multicamera action shots, 69
  overhead shots, 68–69
  reaction shot, 65–66
  static shot, 68
Candlelight, 71
CD-ROM, 93
Cinderella myth, 46
Cinema, 11–12
Cinema art
  classic film as, 22–25
  modern film as, 25–27
Cinemascope, 34, 63, 116, 240
Cinematography, 11–12, 57
  and film viewer, 72–73
  camera movement, 57–59
  camera shots, 63–69
  of *Citizen Kane*, 41–42
  deep focus photography,
    59–60
  lighting, 69–72
  mise-en-scène, 62–63
  montage, 60–62
  Oscar nominations, 57
  sound effects, 71–72
Cinemax, 134
Cinerama, 34, 116
Civil Rights movement, 111–12
Classic film as cinema art, 22–25
Close-up shots, 65
Code, 76–79
Codification, 76–79
Cold War, 100–101
Color films
  advance over black-and-white,
    121–23
  remake of *Psycho*, 123–26
Colorization, 117–19

Comedy
  in black-and-white films, 119
  language of, 87–89
Comic genre, 30–32, 45–48
  romantic archetype, 45–48
Commercial art, 14–16
Communication
  in *Great Dictator,* 25
  via film, 16–18
Confessions (St. Augustine), 91
Crane shot, 68
Criterion Edition, 187, 241
Critical response, 2–3

Dance, in *Great Dictator,* 24
Day of the Jackal (Forsyth), 235
D-Day invasion, 108–109
Deep focus photography, 59–60
Diffuse light, 71
Digital technology, 92–94
Director
  as *auteur,* 18–19, 21–22
  and cinematography, 57
  intent of, 2–3
  Neo-Realist, 131
  New Wave, 131, 152, 181, 202
Disney Studios, 49
Dolby (Digital), 72
Drama, 30–32, 36–40
  in black-and-white films, 119–21
  commercial, 15
  role of music in, 91
DVD, 240, 241–42
DVD Classic Collection, 241
DVD editions, 243–45
DVD players, 93
  sound quality, 72
DVD Universal Home Video, 122–23

Entertainment Weekly, 135
Epic genre, 30–32
  modern epics, 32–35
  precursor to modern epics, 48
Establishing shot, 67
Extracontextual technique, 77

Fast-action shots, 57
Fiction, 180–81
Film. *See also* Foreign films
   aesthetic transaction, 3
   affinity with literature, 13
   as art, 11–13, 15–16
   centering and decentering, 4
   as cinema art, 22–27
   as commercial art, 14–16
   as communication, 16–18
   contrasting color and black-and-
      white, 123–26
   critical response, 2–3
   distinctiveness from literature,
      181–82
   experience of viewing, 4–8
   fragility and restoration of, 178
   greater than sum of its parts,
      183–84
   individual response, 1–2
   legitimacy of all responses, 304
   liking or not liking, 4–5
   as literary art, 21–22
   literary response to, 9
   and literary tradition, 149–51
   moral versus aesthetic functions,
      200–201
   narrative form, 9, 22
   poor literary adaptations, 152–53
   rating system, 133
   realism, 17
   reasons for persistence of black-and-
      white, 119–21
   in relation to other arts, 13–14
   slow or fast-paced, 5
   social themes, 216–18
   and star power, 184–87
   tragic genre, 40–45
   uniqueness of, 177–78
   universal visual medium, 17
   as visual reality, 182–83
Film as film
   *Butch Cassidy and the Sundance
      Kid,* 190–91
   Citizen Kane, 188

   Loss of Sexual Innocence, 193–98
   Passion of Joan of Arc, 187–88
   Quiz Show, 191–93
   Tango, 196–97
   Testament of Orpheus, 188
   World of Apu, 189–90
Film as history
   Bridge Too Far, 103–105
   context, 97–99
   Elizabeth, 101–103
   Gladiator, 109–11
   Midway, 103–105
   new historicism, 111–12
   Patton, 105–108
   reasons for studying, 100–12
   responding to, 96–97
   Saving Private Ryan, 108–109
   social issues, 112–13
   war movies as biography,
      105–108
   war movies as history, 103–105
Film collaborative effort, 18
Film courses, 22
   sample, 245–72
Film equivalents of classics, 156–74
   Death in Venice, 156–58
   Emma, 166–67
   English Patient, 164–66
   Hamlet, 167–68
   Howard's End, 160–63
   Last Temptation of Christ, 159–60
   Miss Julie, 168–70
   Passage to India, 158–59
   Sense and Sensibility, 166–67
   Zorba the Greek, 171–74
Film festivals, 140
Film genres, 22
   comedy, 45–48, 87–89
   derivatives and subgenres, 48–51
   drama and melodrama, 36–40
   modern epics, 32–35
   musicals, 48–49, 92
   origin of, 30–32
   and seasonal changes, 50
   westerns, 35–36

Film language, 54–55
    codes and codification, 76–79
    combining visual and auditory
        imagery, 85–87
    in comedy, 87–89
    definition, 75–76
    digital technology, 92–94
    in *Goldfinger,* 81–83
    hypertext, 92–94
    in *Lolita,* 83–85
    music, 91–92
    thematic development, 203–204
Filmmaker(s)
    as *auteur,* 18–19
    intent of, 2–3
    of 20th century, 15–16
Film nationality classification, 22
Film noir, 48–49, 118
Film seminars, 16
Film stars, 17; *see also* Star power
Film syllabus, 245
Film techniques
    and film viewer, 72–73
    attractions of color, 116–17
    camera movement, 57–59
    camera shots, 62–69
    cinematography, 57
    colorization, 117–19
    deep focus photography, 59–60
    evolution of, 73
    extracontextual, 77
    interrelation of, 55–56
    learning, 54–55
    lighting, 68–72
    mise-en-scène, 62–63
    montage, 60–62
    sound effects, 71–72
Film technology
    advances in, 240–41
    hypertext, 242–44
    value of commentaries, 241–42
Film violence
    aspects of, 223–24
    Bonnie and Clyde, 234–35
    Boys Don't Cry, 236
    Bringing Out the Dead, 236–37

    dealing with, 227–30
    evolution of, 230
    Godfather series, 235
    historical perspective, 225–26
    Jackal, The, 235–36
    Natural Born Killers, 235
    prevalence of, 224–25
    Psycho, 233–34
    from stage to movies, 226–27
    Talented Mr. Ripley, 237–39
    Wild Bunch, 230–33
Financing, 14–15
First Amendment, 227
Foreign films
    in art houses, 134
    Claire's Knee, 137–38
    contrasts with domestic films,
        135–36
    decline of, 132–33
    Eternity and a Day, 140–44
    heyday of, 133–34
    negative responses by American
        students, 132
    origin of, 130–32
    Pierrot le Fou, 138–40
    poor literary adaptations, 152–53
    slow, 5
    star power, 186
    for study, 140–44
Fox Lorber, 136

Gangster movies, 49
Gender in film, 209–16
    Chaplin's movies, 210–12
    Girl, Interrupted, 215–16
    Music of the Heart, 214–15
    Thelma and Louise, 212–14
Genres. *see* Film genres
German Expressionism, 131
Golden Era of Hollywood, 37
Grammar of film, 76
Great Depression, 97
Greek comedy, 45

Hand-held camera action shots, 67
Hard light, 71

Hays Code, 133, 155, 226–27
HBO, 134
Hinduism, 264–65
History; *see* Film as history
Hitchcock films, 206–207
Hollywood
    golden era of, 37
    poor literary adaptations,
        151–53
    silent era, 71
    and star power, 184–87
    studio era, 184
Holocaust, 99
Home theater systems, 72
Horror films, 48–49
Hypertext, 92–94, 242–44

Imagery
    Bridge on the River Kwai, 204–205
    Duel, 207–209
    in Hitchcock films, 206–207
    Passage to India, 204–205
    by thematic development,
        203–204
Imaging, 72
Impressionist painters, 69–70
India, 264–65
Individual response, 1–2
Information sheet
    Amadeus, 254–56
    Dr. Strangelove, 250–52
    English Patient, 270–72
    Great Dictator, 246–47
    Passage to India, 264–67
    Platoon, 257–59
    Psycho, 252–54
    Quiz Show, 260–61
    Schindler's List, 267–70
    Seventh Seal, 248–50
    2001: A Space Odyssey, 262–64
Inside lighting, 71
International cinema, 130–32
Intratextual superposition, 87
Italy, Neo-Realist movement, 3

Jump shot, 65–66

Keystone Studio, 131, 246
Kinetograph, 131

Legion of Decency, 133, 155
Lighting, 69–71
Literary adaptations
    A Clockwork Orange, 155–56
    Death in Venice, 156–58
    Emma, 166–67
    English Patient, 164–66
    foreign mediocrity, 152–53
    Hamlet, 167–68
    Hollywood mediocrity, 151–52
    Howard's End, 160–63
    Last Temptation of Christ,
        159–60
    Lolita, 155–56
    Miss Julie, 168–70
    origins and limitations, 148–49
    Passage to India, 158–59
    Sense and Sensibility, 166–67
    Zorba the Greek, 171–74
Literary art, 21–22
Literary genres, 22
Literary source
    adaptation problems, 153–54
    measuring up to, 147–49
    mediocre adaptations, 151–53
    origins and limitations, 148–49
    poor literary adaptations,
        152–53
Literary tradition, 149–51
Literature
    affinity of film with, 13
    distinctiveness from film, 181–82
    prevalence of violence in, 225–26
Location, camera shots, 67
Long shots, 63–65

MacGuffin, 77, 206
Mack Sennett Company, 131
Master shot, 67
McCarthy era, 111–12
Medium shot, 65–66
Melodrama, 31–32, 36–40
Merchant/Ivory productions, 134

Message
    moral behavior, 201–203
    as part of story, 203
    by thematic development, 203–204
    uncovering social themes, 203–204
MGM, 15, 131, 184
Middle Ages, 100
Mise-en-scène, 62–63, 76, 182, 240,
    242
Modern epics, 32–35
Montage, 60–62
Montage by attraction, 60, 61–62
Monument Valley, Arizona, 63–65
Moral behavior, 201–203
Moral message, 200–201
Motion Picture Association of
    America, 133
Motion Picture Industry Association,
    227
Motion Picture Producers and
    Distributors of America,
    133
Motion pictures, invention of, 11–13
Multicamera action shot, 69
Music
    in film, 14, 91–92
    in Great Dictator, 24
    missing from sound track, 90–91
    on sound track, 90
Musicals, 48–49, 92

Narrative form, 22
National Association of the Motion
    Picture Industry, 133
National Society of Film Critics, 137
Neo-Realist directors, 131
Neo-Realist movement, Italy, 3
New Comedy, 45
New historicism, 111–12
New Wave directors, 131, 152, 181,
    202
Nodes. see Axes and nodes

Odyssey (Homer), 149
Old Comedy, 45
Opera, 12

Otto Rank productions, 134
Overhead shot, 68–69

Painting
    in film, 14
    and film lighting techniques, 69–70
Panavision, 240
Parallel montage, 60–61
Paramount studios, 131
Patton: Ordeal and Triumph (Farago),
    106
Pay TV channels, 134
Picaresque films, 60–61
Poetics (Aristotle), 30, 75, 201
Postimpressionist painters, 70
Poststructuralist critics, 202
Prejudice and race
    Easy Rider, 216–18
    Hurricane, The, 219–21
    Snow Falling on Cedars, 218–19
Production Code Administration, 133
Prologic, 72
Pygmalion myth, 46

Race; see Prejudice and race
Rating system, 133
Reaction shot, 65–66
Realism, 179–81
Red Alert (George), 250
Republic (Plato), 91
RKO Studios, 184
Romantic comedies, 45–48
    examples, 46–48
Romantic poets, 143
Russian Formalists, 201

Science fiction, 48–49
Screenwriter
    as artist, 19–21
    distinct role of, 20–21
Sculpture in film, 14
Semiotics, 76–79
Seven Pillars of Wisdom (Lawrence),
    114
Showtime channel, 155
Silent era, 71

Silent-era stars, 17
Slapstick comedies, 48–49
Slow-action shots, 57
Social themes, 112–13, 203–204
  prejudice and race, 216–18
Soft light, 71
Sound effects, 71–72
Sound track, 72
Soundtrack
  components, 90
  without music, 90–91
Spy thrillers, 48–49
Stage theater, 12
Star power, 37–40, 184–87
  actresses, 187, 209–210
Static shot, 68
Structuralist critics, 202
Studio era, 184
Subgenres, 48–51
Surround Sound, 72
Syllabus, 245

Tableaux-vivants, 70
Technicolor, 34
Technology and uniqueness of film,
  177–78
Thematic development, 203–204
  Bridge on the River Kwai, 203–205
  Duel, 207–209
  in Hitchcock films, 206–207
Tragedy, Aristotle on, 201
Tragic genre
  audience response to, 41
  basic requirement of, 41

Citizen Kane, 40–43
  drama and melodrama, 36–40
  examples, 43–45
Tragic hero/heroine, 41–43
Turner Classic Movies, 134

United Artists, 22–23
Universal Studios, 131
Upanishads, 254

VCRs, 240
Vedas, 264–65
Vietnam-era films, 228
Vietnam War, 97
Villains, 37–39
Visual imagery
  codes and codification, 76–79
  combined with auditory imagery,
    85–87
  in comedy, 87–89
  in Goldfinger, 81–83
  in Lolita, 83–85
Visual realism, 179–81, 182–83

War Department, 49
War movies, 48–49
  as biography, 105–108
  as history, 103–105
Warner Brothers, 131, 184
Westerns, 35–36
  Monument Valley, Arizona,
    63–65
Women, as evildoers, 39–40
World War II films, 103–109

Name Index

Abraham, F. Murray, 243, 254–55
Aeschylus, 175
Albee, Edward, 13, 226
Aldrich, Robert, 35
Aleksandrov, Grigori, 198
Allen, Woody, 66, 77, 119, 122,
    126–28, 129, 141, 175, 188
Almodóvar, Pedro, 53, 146
Altman, Robert, 18, 52
Anderson, Judith, 39
Andersson, Bibi, 210, 248
Andrew, James Dudley, 51, 73, 221
Angelopoulos, Theo, 29, 132, 141,
    142–44, 146
Antonioni, Michelangelo, 4–6, 8, 14,
    15, 18, 21, 29, 79, 91, 144,
    145, 210, 243
Aristophanes, 45
Aristotle, 13, 30, 35, 41, 75, 91, 94,
    113, 144, 158, 180, 201,
    203, 225, 226, 227, 239,
    260
Arnheim, Rudolf, 2, 51, 55, 197
Arnold, Matthew, 158

Arquette, Patricia, 236
Arvanitis, Yiorgos, 142
Ashcroft, Peggy, 158, 163, 264
Asquith, Anthony, 47, 151
Astaire, Fred, 92
Attanasio, Paul, 260
Attenborough, Richard, 102, 105, 115
August, Bille, 146
Augustine, St., 91, 225
Austen, Jane, 13, 45, 48, 86, 149,
    151, 161, 166–67, 175, 176
Auteuil, Daniel, 136
Axel, Gabriel, 146

Bacall, Lauren, 38
Bach, Johann Sebastian, 270, 271
Bacharach, Burt, 190
Ball, Lucille, 32
Ballhaus, Michael, 57
Balsam, Martin, 252
Banerjee, Victor, 264
Banerji, Bibhutibhushan, 189
Barber, Samuel, 14, 259
Bardot, Brigitte, 133

Barreto, Bruno, 198
Barry, Raymond, 8
Barrymore, Drew, 136
Barrymore, Lionel, 38
Bassett, Angela, 214
Baxter, Anne, 20, 39
Bazin, André, 10, 12, 18, 60, 73, 131,
    150, 177, 201
Beatty, Warren, 221
Beaumont, Francis, 230
Beaumont, Jeanne-Marie Leprince de,
    45
Beaumarchais, Pierre Augustin Caron
    de, 9
Beckett, Samuel, 13, 31
Beethoven, Ludwig von, 92, 179
Belmondo, Jean-Paul, 138–39
Benigni, Roberto, 25–27, 99, 141,
    150
Berenger, Tom, 257
Beresford, Bruce, 221
Bergman, Ingmar, 13, 15, 18, 19, 21,
    28, 29, 55–56, 57, 65, 70,
    100–101, 119–20, 129, 131,
    133, 141, 145, 181–82, 183,
    184, 186, 198, 202, 210,
    243, 248–50
Bergman, Ingrid, 21, 37, 39, 77, 117,
    118, 151, 184, 185
Berlin, Irving, 270, 272
Bernstein, Armyan, 219
Bernstein, Elmer, 191
Berri, Claude, 141
Berridge, Elizabeth, 254–55
Bertolucci, Bernardo, 52, 141, 146
Besant, Walter, 201
Biddle, Adrian, 57
Binoche, Juliette, 270
Björnstrand, Gunnar, 248
Black, Karen, 217
Blanchett, Cate, 210
Blixen, Karen, 210
Bloch, Robert, 252
Bogarde, Dirk, 104, 157
Bogart, Humphrey, 21, 37–39, 117
Bogdanovich, Peter, 122

Bolt, Robert, 21, 115
Borgnine, Ernest, 35, 230
Bowman, David, 48
Bradley, Omar, 107
Brahms, Johannes, 24
Branagh, Kenneth, 28, 95, 126–27,
    154, 167–68, 176
Brandenstein, Patricia, 255
Brando, Marlon, 164, 171, 234
Brickman, Marshall, 222
Brooks, Mel, 122
Brooks, Richard, 20, 38, 221
Brosnan, Pierce, 187
Buñuel, Louis, 15, 141, 145
Burgess, Anthony, 156, 226
Burrows, Saffron, 168
Byron, George Gordon, Lord, 143,
    174

Caan, James, 104
Cacoyannis, Michael, 122, 134, 172,
    198
Cage, Nicholas, 236
Cagney, James, 35
Caine, Michael, 186
Cameron, James, 179–80
Campion, Jane, 21
Camus, Albert, 15–16, 31, 174, 226
Camus, Marcel, 145
Capra, Frank, 17, 19, 202–203
Carrey, Jim, 32
Carter, Helena Bonham, 163
Carter, Rubin "Hurricane," 219
Caton-Jones, Michael, 235
Cezanne, Paul, 70
Chabrol, Claude, 18, 131, 152–53
Chaiton, Sam, 219
Chaplin, Charles, 14, 17, 19, 22–25,
    26, 27, 29, 32, 60, 98–99,
    130, 150, 181–82, 183, 198,
    203, 210–12, 243, 246–48
Chavez, Linda, 225, 239
Chen, Kaige, 141
Christie, Julie, 186
Clancy, Tom, 148
Clark, Tom C., 133

Clarke, Arthur C., 19, 94, 244, 262–64
Clayton, Jack, 151
Clinton, Bill, 113, 227
Clooney, George, 185
Close, Glenn, 229
Clouzot, Henri-Georges, 133–34
Cocteau, Jean, 14, 28, 29, 46, 63, 118, 129, 131, 182, 188, 198, 243
Codazzi, Juan Carlos, 196, 198
Coen, Joel, 199
Coleman, Ronald, 185, 186
Coleridge, Samuel Taylor, 17, 174, 182, 183, 201
Collins, Joan, 40
Connelly, Joe, 236
Connery, Sean, 104, 186
Conrad, Joseph, 34, 164
Cooper, Gary, 21, 35–36, 61, 68, 151, 184, 185, 186
Coppola, Francis Ford, 18, 19, 26, 44, 95, 105, 152, 164, 183, 198, 228, 235
Corman, Carl, 243
Corneille, Pierre, 226
Costa-Gavras, Constantin, 115
Costner, Kevin, 222
Cowie, Peter, 243
Craven, Wes, 214, 221
Crawford, Joan, 184
Crowe, Russell, 109, 111
Cruise, Tom, 7–8, 136, 187
Crystal, Billy, 167
Cukor, George, 53
Culver, Michael, 264
Curtiz, Michael, 28, 36, 37

Dafoe, Willem, 94, 176, 257, 270
Dali, Salvador, 188
Damon, Matt, 238
Dante, 149
Dardenne, Jean-Pierre, 67
Dardenne, Luc, 67, 141
Dassin, Jules, 47, 133, 142
Davidtz, Embeth, 268

Da Vinci, Leonardo, 12
Davis, Bette, 20, 21, 39, 184, 185, 210
Davis, Judy, 65, 126–27, 264
De Gaulle, Charles, 37
De Laurentis, Dino, 139
De Niro, Robert, 236
De Sica, Vittorio, 131, 146, 198, 221
Delerue, Georges, 259
Delhomme, Benoit, 169, 193–98, 195
Demi, Jacques, 18
DeMille, Cecil B., 52
Dench, Judi, 210
Deneuve, Catherine, 136
Depardieu, Gerard, 168
Dern, Bruce, 152
Derrida, Jacques, 4, 174
DiCaprio, Leonardo, 127, 135
Dickens, Charles, 13, 148, 149, 151, 153
Dixon, Thomas E., 19
Donner, John, 250
Dostoevsky, Fyodor, 9, 153
Dotrice, Tom, 254
Douglas, Kirk, 149
Douglas, Michael, 184, 186, 229
Doyle, Patrick, 91, 92
Dreiser, Theodore, 153
Dreyer, Carl Theodor, 128, 146, 187, 241
Dryden, John, 226
Dryden, Wheeler, 23
Dukakis, Michael, 172
Dullea, Keir, 8, 262
Dunaway, Faye, 210
Durbin, Deanna, 21
Duvall, Robert, 92
Dye, Dale, 258

Earp, Wyatt, 49
Eastwood, Clint, 185, 186
Ebert, Roger, 136, 224
Eccleston, Christopher, 102
Edeson, Arthur, 118
Edison, Thomas A., 12, 131
Edwards, Blake, 53

Einhorn, Richard, 187
Eisenhower, Dwight D., 105
Eisenstein, Sergei, 2, 15, 19, 60, 131,
    145, 184, 198, 201
Ekerot, Bengt, 248
Eliot, George, 149
Eliot, T. S., 128, 144, 175
Elizabeth I, 100
Emmerich, Roland, 52
Enright, Dan, 260
Ephron, Nora, 95
Estefan, Gloria, 214
Euripides, 13, 51, 229

Fairbanks, Douglas, 17, 130, 184
Fairbanks, Douglas, Jr., 184
Falconetti, Maria, 187, 210
Farago, Ladislas, 106–107
Farrow, Mia, 126, 152
Fassbinder, Rainer Werner, 146
Faulkner, William, 153, 226
Fellini, Federico, 2–3, 15, 18, 19, 21,
    26, 29, 56, 94, 127, 129,
    131, 133, 134, 136, 141,
    174, 183, 186, 195, 198
Fiennes, Ralph, 102, 165, 192–93,
    260, 268, 270
Figgis, Mike, 95, 154, 168–70,
    176192–98
Firth, Colin, 165, 270
Fischer, Gunnar, 248
Fitzgerald, F. Scott, 77, 152, 226
Fitzgerald, Frances, 258
Flaubert, Gustave, 152–53, 176
Fleming, Victor, 18, 28, 114
Fletcher, John, 230
Flynn, Errol, 123, 184, 185, 186
Fonda, Henry, 35, 104, 153, 185
Fonda, Jane, 184
Fonda, Peter, 216–18
Ford, Glenn, 104
Ford, Harrison, 50, 184, 187
Ford, John, 2–3, 18, 19, 56, 61, 94,
    114, 118, 153, 175, 198,
    217, 226, 230
Foreman, Carl, 20

Forman, Milos, 18, 146, 176, 243,
    254–56
Forster, E. M., 148, 158, 161, 176,
    182, 264–67
Forsyth, Frederick, 235–36
Foscolo, Ugo, 143
Foundas, Giorgos, 172
Fox, Edward, 104
Fox, James, 264
Frankenheimer, John, 19
Freedman, Al, 193
Frost, Robert, 216
Frye, Northrup, 50, 51

Gable, Clark, 21, 185
Gabriel, Peter, 160
Gandhi, Mohandas, 115
Ganz, Bruno, 144
Garbo, Greta, 184, 185, 210
Garson, Greer, 210
Gavin, John, 252
Gein, Ed, 252
George, Peter, 250, 252
Gere, Richard, 138
Giannetti, Louis, 113, 175
Gibson, Mel, 186
Girard, François, 29, 141
Gish, Lillian, 151
Giuliani, Rudolph, 237
Godard, Jean-Luc, 18, 29, 77, 129,
    134, 136, 138–40, 141, 145,
    152, 181, 188, 195
Goddard, Paulette, 211, 246
Goldberg, Whoopi, 215
Goldman, William, 190
Goodman, Benny, 270
Goodman, John, 236
Goodwin, Dick, 260
Gordon, Dan, 219
Gould, Elliott, 104
Granger, Farley, 61, 207
Granger, Stewart, 186
Grant, Cary, 39, 77, 184
Grant, Hugh, 186
Gray, Pamela, 214
Green, Hilton, 244

Griffith, D. W., 1, 15, 19, 32, 52, 60, 131
Griffith, Melanie, 156
Grisham, John, 148, 235
Guaspari, Roberta, 214
Guinness, Alec, 69, 158, 204–205, 264
Guterson, David, 218

Hackman, Gene, 104
Hanks, Tom, 48
Hardy, Oliver, 32, 89
Harris, James B., 155
Harris, Richard, 111
Havers, Nigel, 264
Hawke, Ethan, 218
Hawkins, Jack, 69
Hawks, Howard, 18, 19, 28, 52, 56, 92, 202
Hawthorne, Nathaniel, 153, 226
Hayakawa, Sessue, 69
Hayden, Sterling, 250
Haydn, Franz Joseph, 184
Hayes, John Michael, 20
Hayworth, Rita, 184
Haze, Charlotte, 84–85, 155
Heche, Anne, 124–25, 241
Hecht, Ben, 20
Heller, Joseph, 176
Hemingway, Ernest, 15, 114, 151, 176, 226
Hepburn, Audrey, 184
Hepburn, Katherine, 185, 210
Hermann, Bernard, 14, 91, 123, 252
Herodotus, 165–66, 271
Herzog, Werner, 146
Heston, Charlton, 104, 110, 167
Hicks, Ron, 218
Hicks, Scott, 79, 218
Hildyard, Jack, 69
Hill, George Roy, 176, 190–91
Hitchcock, Alfred, 15, 16, 18, 19, 20, 21, 28, 39, 47–48, 55, 58, 61, 63, 66, 68, 74, 77, 90, 93, 121, 122, 123–26, 128, 154, 170, 181, 183, 188, 201,

206–207, 215, 228, 232–34, 239, 241, 243, 244, 252–54
Hitler, Adolf, 17, 24, 26, 98–99, 166, 247–48
Hoffman, Dustin, 51
Hoffman, Philip Seymour, 238
Holden, William, 69, 185, 230, 231, 244
Holliday, Doc, 49
Homer, 35, 48, 49, 51, 102, 149, 180
Hopkins, Anthony, 104, 162, 163, 186
Hopper, Dennis, 115, 216–18
Horace, 201, 226
Horne, Geoffrey, 69
Housman, A. E., 174
Hugo, Victor, 143
Hulce, Tom, 243, 254–55
Huston, Angelica, 136
Huston, John, 38

Ibsen, Henrik, 13, 31, 36, 50, 170, 226
Ionesco, Eugene, 31
Irons, Jeremy, 156
Ishiguro, Kazuo, 161, 164, 176
Ives, Charles, 195
Ivory, James, 154, 160–63, 176, 199

Jacobi, Derek, 167
Jaffrey, Saeed, 264
James, Dan, 23
James, Henry, 3, 113, 180, 201, 208, 221
James, William, 226
Jared, Gabriel, 270, 271
Jarre, Maurice, 267
Jewison, Norman, 53, 219, 221, 241
Jhabvala, Ruth Prawer, 160–61
Joffé, Roland, 222
Johnson, Ben, 230
Jolie, Angelina, 215
Jones, James Earl, 250
Jones, Jeffrey, 254–55

Kael, Pauline, 158, 163, 236, 259
Kafka, Franz, 57, 122

Kaige, Chen, 141
Kaminsky, Janusz, 126
Kaplan, Charles, 51, 94, 201, 221,
        225, 239
Kapur, Shekhar, 68–69, 102–103
Karaindrou, Eleni, 142
Karina, Anna, 139
Kasdan, Lawrence, 21
Kasminsky, Stuart M., 250
Kaye, Danny, 24, 32
Kaysen, Susanna, 215
Kazan, Elia, 19, 29, 198
Kazantzakis, Nikos, 58, 159–60, 172,
        174, 226
Keaton, Buster, 32, 130, 198
Keaton, Diane, 126
Kedrova, Lila, 172
Keitel, Harvey, 143
Kelly, Gene, 92
Keneally, Thomas, 150, 267, 269
Kennedy, Maria Doyle, 168
Khouri, Callie, 21, 212
Kiarostami, Abbas, 141, 146, 222
Kidman, Nicole, 6–7
King, Larry, 162
King, Stephen, 148
Kingsley, Ben, 268
Kiselyak, Charles, 243
Knight, Arthur, 243
Konstantin, Leopoldine, 39
Kramer, Stanley, 18, 19, 29, 101,
        202–203, 221
Krasker, Robert, 57, 119
Kruger, Hardy, 104
Kubrick, Stanley, 6–8, 14, 18, 19, 28,
        29, 52, 67, 71, 83–85,
        86–87, 93, 95, 114, 119,
        122, 137, 154, 155–56, 160,
        179, 183, 198, 203, 228,
        243, 244, 250–52, 262–64
Kurosawa, Akira, 14, 15–16, 18, 19,
        21, 29, 49, 52, 65, 70, 79,
        95, 129, 131, 141, 144, 146,
        183, 186, 195, 198, 202
Kusturica, Emir, 141
Kyd, Thomas, 50, 226

Ladd, Alan, 151
Lamarr, Hedy, 210
Lamartine, Alphonse de, 143
La Motta, Jake, 122
Lancaster, Burt, 35, 185
Langella, Frank, 156
Lardner, Ring, Jr., 20
Lassally, Walter, 172, 173
Laurel, Stan, 32, 89
Law, Jude, 238
Lawrence, T. E., 43, 114
Lean, David, 28, 34, 43, 65, 66, 69,
        71, 114, 126, 151, 152, 154,
        157–59, 160, 163, 182, 198,
        204–205, 221, 244, 264–67,
        267
Lee, Ang, 166–67
Leger, Fernard, 201
Leigh, Janet, 125, 232–34, 244, 252,
        253
Leigh, Vivian, 210
Leone, Sergio, 52, 185, 186
Levine, Joseph E., 105
Levinson, Barry, 51, 198
Lewinsky, Monica, 113
Lewis, Jerry, 24, 32
Ligeti, György, 263
Livius, Titus, 111
Lockwood, Gary, 262
Lorre, Peter, 37
Loy, Myrna, 184
Lucas, George, 21, 92
Lumière, Auguste, 11–12, 131
Lumière, Louis, 11–12, 131
Lyne, Adrian, 132, 137-38, 155–56,
        199
Lyon, Sue, 155

MacMurray, Fred, 43, 119, 120
Maddalena, Marianne, 214, 221
Maestro, Mia, 198
Mahler, Gustav, 157
Malick, Terrence, 52
Malik, Art, 264
Malle, Louis, 19, 146
Mangano, Sylvana, 149

Mangold, John, 215
Mankiewicz, Herman J., 20
Mankiewicz, Joseph L., 19
Mann, Michael, 52, 156–57
Mann, Thomas, 15
Marceau, Marcel, 24, 32
Marlowe, Christopher, 175
Marriner, Sir Neville, 243, 254
Marshall, Garry, 47, 53
Marshall, Penny, 222
Martin, Steve, 32
Marvin, Lee, 36, 186
Marx Brothers, 87–89
    Marx, Chico, 88–89
    Marx, Groucho, 87–89
Mason, James, 155–56, 186
Massina, Gulietta, 186, 210
Mastroianni, Marcello, 186
Maté, Rudolph, 187
McCarthy, Frank, 105
McCarthy, Joseph R., 100
McGinley, John C., 257
McGrath, Douglas, 53, 166–67
McQueen, Steve, 61, 153, 185
Méliès, Georges, 12, 131, 148
Meltzer, Bob, 23
Menander, 24, 45, 49
Mendes, Sam, 18, 19, 52, 199
Merchant, Ismail, 160, 164
Mercouri, Melina, 133, 142
Merman, Ethel, 32
Messter, Oskar, 12
Mifune, Toshiro, 104, 186
Miles, Vera, 252
Milius, John, 21, 164, 244
Miller, Arthur, 50
Minghella, Anthony, 19, 95, 154,
    164–66, 237, 239, 270–72,
    271–72
Minnelli, Vincent, 176
Mirren, Helen, 40
Mitchum, Robert, 104
Mizoguchi, Kenji, 131
Monet, Claude, 14, 70
Monicelli, Mario, 221
Monroe, Marilyn, 47, 184

Montenegro, Fernanda, 136
Montgomery, Bernard L., 105, 107
Moore, Julianne, 124
Moore, Roger, 186
Morrow, Rob, 193, 260
Mozart, Wolfgang Amadeus, 9, 92,
    184, 254–55
Mullan, Peter, 168
Murnau, Friedrich, 131
Mussolini, Benito, 26, 27

Nabokov, Vladimir, 138, 155
Neeson, Liam, 268
Newman, Paul, 190–91, 216
Nichols, Mike, 52, 176, 221
Nicholson, Jack, 217
Nielsen, Connie, 109
Nietzsche, Friedrich, 174
Nordgren, Erik, 248
Norman, Marc, 21
Norris, Frank, 175
North, Edmund H., 105
Northam, Jeremy, 166
Nykvist, Sven, 57, 128

O'Brien, Edmond, 230
O'Connell, Patricia Hitchcock, 207,
    244, 253
O'Connor, Flannery, 149
O'Neal, Ryan, 104
O'Neill, Eugene, 13, 31, 50, 226
O'Toole, Peter, 71
Oakie, Jack, 246
Oates, Warren, 230
Offenbach, Jacques, 14
Olivier, Laurence, 39, 47, 104, 168,
    198
Ondaatje, Michael, 164–65, 270, 271

Pacino, Al, 44, 61
Paltrow, Gwyneth, 166–67, 184, 187,
    238
Pappas, Irene, 172, 173
Pasolini, Pier Paolo, 146
Pasternak, Boris, 114
Pasztor, Beatrix Aruna, 125

Patton, George, 32, 106–108
Paxinou, Katina, 151
Paymer, David, 260
Peck, Gregory, 185
Peckinpah, Sam, 198, 228, 230–33
Pemberton, Antonia, 264
Penn, Arthur, 228, 234
Pericles, 16
Perkins, Anthony, 124, 252
Perlman, Itzhak, 214, 268
Petersen, Wolfgang, 146
Petronius, 174
Phoenix, Joaquin, 109
Picasso, Pablo, 15, 16
Pickens, Slim, 250
Pickford, Mary, 185
Pierce, Kimberley, 21, 199, 236
Piovani, Nicola, 26
Pirandello, 31
Pitt, Brad, 187
Plato, 17, 91, 201, 225
Plautus, 24, 45
Polanski, Roman, 146
Pollack, Sydney, 52
Poppe, Nils, 248
Porter, Edwin S., 131, 148
Potente, Franka, 136
Power, Tyrone, 184, 185
Puccini, Giacomo, 14
Pudovkin, Vsevolod, 184
Purcell, Henry, 35
Puzo, Mario, 19

Quinn, Aidan, 214
Quinn, Anthony, 122, 171–74

Raboch, Alfred, 52
Racine, Jean, 31, 50, 226
Rains, Claude, 37, 39, 202
Rathbone, Basil, 123
Ravel, Maurice, 90
Ray, Satyajit, 15, 18, 19, 129, 131,
     136, 189, 198
Rebello, Stephen, 253
Redford, Robert, 52, 95, 104, 152,
     190–91, 193, 216, 244,

260–61
Redgrave, Vanessa, 163, 186, 215
Reed, Carol, 52, 55
Reed, Oliver, 110
Reisz, Karel, 134
Renoir, Jean, 29, 131, 145, 198, 201
Renoir, Pierre-Auguste, 70
Resnais, Alain, 14, 29, 129, 131, 141,
     146
Reynolds, Burt, 213, 214
Richard, Edmond, 57, 122
Richardson, Tony, 134
Richter, Daniel, 262
Riefenstahl, Leni, 17
Robbins, Tim, 222
Roberts, Julia, 50, 135, 184, 187
Robinson, Edward G., 38, 43, 120
Rodin, Auguste, 24
Roget, Peter Mark, 12
Rohmer, Eric, 19, 137–38, 141
Roman, Ruth, 207
Roosevelt, Franklin D., 49, 99
Rossellini, Roberto, 131, 133, 186
Rota, Nino, 26, 94
Royko, Mike, 172
Rush, Geoffrey, 103
Ryan, Meg, 48
Ryan, Robert, 231
Ryder, Wynona, 127, 215

Salles, Walter, 29
Sanchez, Jaime, 230
Sanders, George, 40
Sandrich, Mark, 128
Sands, Julie, 194
Sarandon, Susan, 214
Saura, Carlos, 196
Sautet, Claude, 141
Sayles, John, 19, 52, 71, 74
Scacchi, Greta, 166
Schaffner, Franklin J., 105
Schell, Maximilian, 104
Schifrin, Lalo, 196
Schindler, Oskar, 268
Schrader, Paul, 21, 52, 159, 176, 236
Schroeder, Paul, 94

Schubert, Franz, 14
Scofield, Paul, 193, 260
Scorsese, Martin, 18, 19, 52, 58, 94,
        122, 128, 129, 134, 154,
        156, 159–60, 176, 198,
        236–37
Sorvino, Mira, 193
Scott, George C., 106–107, 250
Scott, Ridley, 18, 29, 34, 109, 110,
        212–14, 221
Seale, John, 272
Seberg, Jean, 77
Sellers, Peter, 24, 155–56, 186, 250
Selznick, David O., 18, 185
Seneca, 111, 226
Sennett, Mack, 131, 246
Sevigny, Chloe, 236
Shaffer, Peter, 9, 176, 243, 254, 256
Shakespeare, William, 13, 24, 31, 36,
        45, 50, 149, 151, 168, 176,
        226, 230
Shankar, Ravi, 190
Sharif, Omar, 65
Shaw, George Bernard, 13, 226
Sheen, Charlie, 257, 258
Sheen, Martin, 164
Shelley, Percy B., 143
Sheridan, Jim, 52
Shklovsky, Viktor, 201
Shyamalan, M. Night, 21
Sidney, Philip, 201
Sinatra, Frank, 42, 185
Sirk, Douglas, 52
Siskel, Gene, 136
Skelton, Red, 24, 32
Skjoldbjaerg, Erik, 146
Sluizer, George, 146
Smight, Jack, 104
Sola, Miguel Angel, 197
Sophocles, 9
Spiegel, Sam, 185
Spielberg, Steven, 18, 19, 29, 34, 50,
        62, 66, 99, 108–109, 122,
        126, 179, 183, 207–209,
        244, 267–70
Stallone, Sylvester, 21, 111, 112

Stanwyck, Barbara, 119, 184, 185
Stefano, Joseph, 123, 125, 244, 252,
        253
Steiger, Rod, 220
Steinbeck, John, 153, 175
Stempel, Herb, 192–93, 260
Stern, Isaac, 214
Stern, Lawrence, 226
Sternberg, Joseph von, 153
Stevens, George, 52
Stevenson, Robert, 52
Stewart, James, 21, 36, 202
Stone, Oliver, 14, 21, 29, 97, 179,
        235, 243, 257–59
Stoppard, Tom, 21
Storaro, Vittorio, 196
Strauss, Johann, 263
Strauss, Richard, 14, 263
Stravinsky, Igor, 15, 196
Streep, Meryl, 184, 187, 210, 214
Streisand, Barbra, 184, 199
Strindberg, August, 168, 176176
Stroheim, Erich von, 131, 175
Suetonius, 111
Swain, Dominique, 155, 182
Swank, Hilary, 236
Swift, Clive, 264
Swift, Jonathan, 87, 149
Swinton, Terry, 219
Sydow, Max von, 121, 186, 218, 248
Sylvester, William, 262
Szabo, Istvan, 146

Tacitus, 50, 111
Tandy, Jessica, 66
Tavernier, Bernard, 74
Taylor, Elizabeth, 210
Terrence, 45
Teshigahara, Hiroshi, 146
Tetzlaff, Ted, 118
Thackeray, William Makepeace, 19,
        149, 156
Theodorakis, Mikis, 172
Thomas, Kristin Scott, 165, 270
Thomas, Nicholas, 145
Thompson, Emma, 92, 151, 166

Tierney, Gene, 39, 185, 210
Todorov, Tzvetan, 79–81, 86, 90, 92, 203–204
Toland, Gregg, 57
Tolstoy, Leo, 13, 31, 149, 153, 179
Tomlin, Lily, 32
Townsend, Percy, 23
Tracy, Spencer, 185
Travolta, John, 185
Trevor, Claire, 38
Truffaut, François, 18, 131, 141, 145, 152, 181, 195
Turner, Lana, 185
Turturro, John, 192–93, 260
Twain, Mark, 24, 51
Tybjerg, Casper, 28, 241
Tykwer, Tom, 29, 92–93

Ullmann, Liv, 104, 186, 210
Uris, Leon M., 20
Uys, Jamie, 146

Vadim, Roger, 133
Valenti, Jack, 227
Valentino, Rudolph, 17, 196
Van Doren, Charles, 95, 192–93, 260
Van Doren, Mark, 193, 260
Van Gogh, Vincent, 14, 65, 70
Van Sant, Gus, 123–26, 241
Vaughn, Vince, 241
Veidt, Conrad, 37
Verdi, Giuseppe, 14, 196
Verne, Jules, 148
Vigo, Jean, 128
Virgil, 35, 49
Visconti, Luchino, 14, 28, 70, 146, 154, 156–58, 160
Vitti, Monica, 210
Vonnegut, Kurt, Jr., 149, 176

Wadham, Julian, 270
Wagner, Richard, 24, 94

Wagner, Robert, 61
Walker, Robert, 207
Washington, Denzel, 219
Waterston, Sam, 152
Wayne, John, 2–3, 35, 36, 49, 184
Weaver, Dennis, 66, 208
Webster, John, 226, 230
Weir, Peter, 146, 199
Welles, Orson, 15, 18, 20, 41, 55, 57, 60, 62, 118, 122, 128, 129, 183, 241, 243
Wenders, Wim, 146
Wertheimer, Max, 12
Wertmüller, Lina, 136, 141, 146
Whitaker, Forrest, 257
Wilder, Billy, 18, 28, 43, 53, 119
Williams, John, 268
Williams, Robin, 32, 185
Williams, Tennessee, 13, 20, 31, 36, 50, 226
Willis, Bruce, 186, 187, 235–36
Wilmington, Michael, 259
Wilson, Meredith, 23
Wilson, Michael, 20
Wilson, Richard, 264
Winslet, Kate, 168
Wise, Robert, 221
Woods, Sam, 114
Wyler, William, 52, 53, 60, 128
Wynn, Keenan, 250

Young, Christopher, 219
Youngblood, Gene, 243

Zaentz, Saul, 254, 270
Zaillian, Steven, 267
Zinnemann, Fred, 68, 115, 154, 176, 235–36
Zola, Emile, 226
Zorba, Alexis, 172

Movie Title Index

8½, 29, 94, 129, 141
Absence of Malice, 52
Adam's Rib, 53, 210
Affliction, 52
African Queen, 210
Agamemnon, 175
Age of Innocence, The, 57
Aguirre, the Wrath of God, 146
Air Force One, 50, 187
Akira Kurosawa's Dreams, 29, 95
Alexander Nevsky, 19
Alexander the Great, 142
All About Eve, 19, 20, 39, 67
All About My Mother, 146
Alphaville, 129, 136
Amadeus, 9, 13, 14, 34, 92, 176
    film course material, 254–56
    laser-DVD edition, 243
Amarcord, 136
America, America, 19
American Beauty, 52, 199
Anastasia, 118, 186
And God Created Woman, 133
Anna Karenina, 165

Annie Hall, 77
Antigone, 41
Aparujito, 131
Apocalypse Now, 21, 44, 49, 108, 164,
    203
Apostle, The, 92
Autumn Sonata, 29, 141, 186

Babette's Feast, 146
Barry Lyndon, 8, 14, 67, 70, 71, 95,
    156, 203
Bataan, 49
Battle Cry, 20
Battleship Potemkin, The, 19, 60, 131,
    145, 198
Beauty and the Beast, 29, 63, 118, 131,
    188, 254
    analysis of, 46–47
    laser-DVD edition, 243
Be Big, 89
Beekeeper, The, 142
Belle de Jour, 141
Ben-Hur, 32, 34, 52, 92, 110, 136,
    148, 229

Bicycle Thief, 131, 198
Big Sleep, The, 118
Billy Liar, 134
Birds, The, 55, 63, 66, 74, 90, 91, 180, 181
Birth of a Nation, The, 19, 32, 52, 60
Blackboard Jungle, The, 221
Black Cat, The, 141
Black Orpheus, 145
Blazing Saddles, 49
Blood of a Poet, 188
Blow Up, 8
Bonnie and Clyde, 50, 139, 140, 191, 210, 212, 227, 228
   analysis of, 234–35
Boys Don't Cry, 21, 45, 199
   analysis of, 236
Bram Stoker's Dracula, 227
Breakfast at Tiffany's, 53
Breathless, 77, 134, 138–40, 140, 141, 145
Bridge on the River Kwai, The, 20, 34, 65, 66, 69, 185
   analysis of, 204–205
   laser-DVD edition, 244
Bridge Too Far, A, 34
   analysis of, 103–105
   DVD edition, 113
Bringing Out the Dead, 236–37
Browning Version, The, 168, 175
Butch Cassidy and the Sundance Kid, 50, 212, 216
   analysis of, 190–91

Camelot, 92, 186
Cape Fear, 52, 227
Casablanca, 22, 39, 49, 117, 118, 185
   analysis of, 37–38
Casino, 230
Catch-22, 41, 119, 176
Cat on a Hot Tin Roof, 20, 228
Celebrity, 119
   analysis of, 126–28
Central Station, 29, 136
China Syndrome, The, 186
Chloe in the Afternoon, 137, 141

Citizen Kane, 20, 55, 56, 57, 59–60, 61, 62, 74, 118, 174, 183, 241
   analysis of, 40–43, 188
   laser-DVD edition, 243
City Lights, 14, 181–82, 210–11, 247
Claire's Knee, analysis of, 137–38
Cleopatra, 34, 154, 210
Clockwork Orange, A, 13, 203
   analysis of, 155–56
Clueless, 166
Coeur en Hiver, 141
Comancheros, The, 36
Coming Home, 49
Confidence, 146
Count of Monte Cristo, The, 148
Cradle Will Rock, The, 222
Crime and Punishment, 153

Dances with Wolves, 222
Das Boot, 146
Dead Poets Society, 199
Death in Venice, 14, 70
   analysis of, 156–58
Death Wish, 112, 227
Deconstructing Harry, 66, 77, 141, 188
Deerhunter The, 258
Defiant Ones, The, 221
Diabolique, 134
Dial M for Murder, 121, 154
Die Hard, 186
Die Hard with a Vengeance, 112
Dirty Harry, 21
Divine Comedy, The, 51, 150
Dona Flor, 198
Don Juan de Marco, 174
Don Quixote, 149
Double Indemnity, 22, 43, 118, 119, 120
Dr. Jekyll and Mr. Hyde, 118
Dr. Strangelove, 29, 87, 119, 122
   film course material, 250–52
   laser-DVD edition, 243
Dr. Zhivago, 21, 65, 114–15, 154, 165
Dracula, 148

Dreams, 14, 65, 70, 141
Duel, 65, 66
  analysis of, 207–209

Easy Rider, 50, 115
  analysis of, 216–18
El Cid, 34
Elizabeth, 68, 100, 210
  analysis of, 101–103
  DVD edition, 114
Emma, 53, 71, 187
  analysis of, 166–67
English Patient, The, 48, 95, 192, 193,
      238–29
  analysis of, 164–66
  film course material, 270–72
Erin Brockovich, 187
Eternity and a Day, 29, 141, 146
  analysis of, 142–44
Ever After, 46, 136
Eyes Wide Shut, analysis of, 6–8

Fall of Babylon, The, 32
Fall of the Roman Empire, The, 92
Farewell, My Concubine, 141
Farewell to Arms, A, 151
Fargo, 72, 199
Fatal Attraction, 199, 229
Fistful of Dollars, A, 49, 185
For a Few Dollars More, 185
Fort Apache, 94
For Whom the Bell Tolls, 114, 151
Four Horsemen of the Apocalypse, The,
      196
Frankenstein, 148
Franz Kafka's The Trial, 122
French Lieutenant's Woman, The, 187
Full Metal Jacket, 19, 49, 258

Gandhi, 34, 115
Garden of the Finzi-Continis, The, 146,
      221
General, The, 198
Gertrud, 146
Ghare Babire, 136
Giant, The, 52

Girl, Interrupted
  analysis of, 215–16
Gladiator, The, 34, 63, 151, 224
  analysis of, 109–111
Godfather films, 32, 44, 61, 112, 154,
      198, 227, 234
  Godfather I, The, 95
    analysis of, 235
  Godfather II, The, 95
Gods Must Be Crazy, The, 146
Goldfinger
  analysis of, 81–83
  laser disc, 94
Gold Rush, 210, 247
Gone With the Wind, 18, 20, 22, 114,
      118–19, 119, 148, 188
Goodfellas, 49, 112, 227
Gospel According to St. Matthew, 146
Graduate, The, 52
Grand Illusion, The, 131
Grapes of Wrath, The, 97, 114, 153,
      175
Great Dictator, The, 14, 17, 19, 26,
      27, 29, 60, 98, 150, 210,
      211, 254, 269
  analysis of, 22–25
  film course material, 246–48
  laser-DVD edition, 243
Great Escape, The, 34
Greatest Story Ever Told, The, 186
Great Expectations, 151, 152, 187
Great Gatsby, The, 2, 77, 148, 151
Great Train Robbery, The, 131
Greed, 131, 175
Guess Who's Coming to Dinner, 221
Gulliver's Travels, 87
Gunfight at the OK Corral, 49
Gunfighter, The, 229
Gunga Din, 20
Guns of Navarone, 20, 142, 185

Hamlet, 41, 149, 198
  analysis of, 167–68
Heart of Darkness, 164
Heat, 49
Hell in the Pacific, 186

Hell's Angels, 117
Helpmates, 89
High Noon, 61, 68, 111, 170, 186,
   229
Hiroshima, Mon Amour, 141
Hitchcock films
   analysis of, 206–207
Horse Soldiers, The, 36
Howard's End, 148, 160–63, 164, 267
Huckleberry Finn, 51, 150
Hunters, The, 142
Hurricane, The, 241
   analysis of, 219–21

Iliad, 102, 204–205
Immortal Beloved, 14, 92
Il Conformists, 146
Indiana Jones, 207, 227
Informer, The, 118
Insider, The, 52
Insomnia, 146
Intervista, 136
In the Name of the Father, 52
Intolerance, 32, 52
It's a Wonderful Life, 203
I Want to Live, 221

Jackal, The, 224, 235–36
James Bond films, 40, 81–83
Jane Eyre, 52, 151, 170
Jaws, 40
Jean de Florette, 141
Jezebel, 39
Johnny Stecchino, 141
Jules and Jim, 141, 145, 195
Juliet of the Spirits, 210
Jurassic Park, 207

Key Largo, 37–38
   analysis of, 38–39
Killers, The, 118
King Lear, 226
Klansman, The, 19
Knife in the Water, 146
Kramer vs. Kramer, 187
Kreutzer Sonata, The, 179

L. A. Confidential, 199
La Dolce Vita, 127, 129, 133, 186,
   198
La Grande Illusion, 198
La Guerre Est Finie, 146
Land of the Pharaohs, 52, 92
Landscape in the Mist, 142
La Notte, 145
Last Emperor, The, 141
Last Man Standing, 49
Last Picture Show, The, 122
La Strada, 129, 172, 186, 210
Last Tango in Paris, 52
Last Temptation of Christ, The, 21, 58,
   159–60, 176, 236, 237
   DVD-laser disc, 94
Last Year at Marienbad, 14, 29, 129,
   141, 188
L'Atalante, 128
Laura, 210
L'Avventura, 14, 29, 65, 79, 91, 136,
   183
   analysis of, 4–6
   laser-DVD edition, 243
Lawrence of Arabia, 21, 34, 43, 65,
   71, 114, 154, 171, 198, 221,
   229
League of Their Own, A, 222
Leap of Faith, 222
Leave Her to Heaven, 39
Leaving Las Vegas, 169
Leopard, The, 146
Lethal Weapon, 186
Lethal Weapon III, 224
Lifeboat, 20
Life Is Beautiful, 14, 99, 141, 150,
   269
   analysis of, 25–27
Limbo, 19, 52
Limelight, 211–12
   laser-DVD edition, 243
Little Caesar, 49
Little Princess, A, 203
Lolita, 52, 132, 137, 182
   analysis of, 83–85, 155–56
   laser disc, 94

Loneliness of the Long Distance Runner,
    The, 134
Long Day's Journey into Night, 228
Long Hot Summer, The, 153
Lord Jim, 34
Loss of Sexual Innocence, The, 95,
    193–98
Love and Death, 175
Love's Labour's Lost, 45
Loves of A Blonde, 146
Lumière Brothers' First Films, 74
Lust for Life, 171

Macbeth, 150
Madame Bovary, 152–53, 176
Magic Flute, 255
Magician, The, 248
Magic Mountain, 149
Magnificent Ambersons, 128
Magnificent Obsession, 52
Magnificent Seven, The, 191
Magnolia, 136
Mahler, 14
Maltese Falcon, 118
Manchurian Candidate, 19, 111, 123,
    185
    DVD edition, 114
Man For All Seasons, A, 21, 115
Manhattan, 129
Manhattan Project, The, 222
Manon of the Spring, 141
Mansfield Park, 71
Man Who Knew Too Much, The, 121
Man Who Shot Liberty Valance, The, 36
Man Who Would Be King, The, 48, 186
Marnie, 215
Marriage of Figaro, The, 255
Marriage of Maria Braun, The, 146
Mash, 20, 119
Maurice, 148, 164
Medea, 229
Mephisto, 146
Midsummer Night's Dream, A., 45
Midway
    analysis of, 103–105
    DVD edition, 114

Miracle, The, 133
Mission, The, 222
Mission Impossible, 187
Miss Julie, 176
    analysis of, 168–70
Mist, 142
Moby Dick, 150, 218
Modern Times, 198, 211, 247
Monkey Business, 20
Monsieur Verdoux, 60, 210, 211, 247
    laser-DVD edition, 243
Moonraker, 40
Moonstruck, 14, 53
Mr. Smith Goes to Washington, 202,
    203
Much Ado About Nothing, 13, 40, 45,
    92, 95, 127, 176
Music of the Heart, analysis of, 214–15
My Best Friend's Wedding, 50
My Darling Clementine, 49, 229
My Fair Lady, 46, 92
My Favorite Season, 136

Napoleon, 32
Natural, The, 198
Natural Born Killers, 112, 227, 228,
    230
    analysis of, 235
Never On Sunday, 133, 142
    analysis of, 47
Night at Maud's, A, 137
Night at the Opera, A
    analysis of, 87–89
Nights of Cabiria, 134, 135, 186, 198,
    210
Nine Months, 186
North by Northwest, 14, 154, 165
Nosferatu, 131
Notorious, 20, 39, 68, 77, 118, 185,
    206
    analysis of, 47–48
Notting Hill, 135

Odyssey, The, 149
Oklahoma, 92
Old Man and the Sea, The, 176

Oliver Twist, 151
Once Upon a Time in America, 52
One, Two, Three, 119
One Flew Over the Cuckoo's Nest, 40,
        215, 254
Only You, 14, 53
On the Beach, 29, 101, 203
On the Waterfront, 29, 198
Organizer, The, 221
Orpheus, 198
Orphic Trilogy, 188
Out of Africa, 174, 210, 214

Passage to India, A, 17, 34, 65, 126,
        136, 148, 163, 182
    analysis of, 158–59, 204–205
    film course material, 264–67
Passion of Joan of Arc, The, 128, 241
    analysis of, 187–88
Pather Panchali, 131, 189, 198
Paths of Glory, 111
Patriot, The, 52, 63, 151, 224
Patton
    analysis of, 105–108
    DVD edition, 114
Pelle the Conqueror, 146
Perfect Murder, A., 187
Persona, 57, 65, 129, 141, 186, 210
Persuasion, 166, 176
Piano, The, 21
Picnic at Hanging Rock, 146
Pierrot le Fou, 29, 77, 136, 188
    analysis of, 138–40
Pink Panther, The, 186
Place in the Sun, A, 52
Platoon, 14, 21, 29, 49, 97, 98, 108,
        203
    film course material, 257–59
    laser-DVD edition, 243
Player, The, 52
Prelude to War, 49
Pretty Woman, 14, 67, 187
    analysis of, 47
Pride and Prejudice, 45–46, 161, 175
    analysis of, 86
Primary Colors, 222

Prince and the Showgirl, The, analysis
        of, 47
Prince of Tides, The, 199
Prisoner of Zenda, The, 186
Psycho, 14, 21, 55, 60, 65, 78, 90,
        122–23, 128, 154, 228, 239,
        241
    analysis of, 58–59, 123–26, 233–34
    film course material, 252–54
    laser-DVD edition, 244
Public Enemy, 49, 112
Pulp Fiction, 49, 112, 227, 228, 230
Pygmalion, 46, 151
    analysis of, 47

Quiz Show, 44, 52, 95, 112
    analysis of, 191–93
    film course material, 260–61
    laser-DVD edition, 244
Quo Vadis, 33

Raging Bull, 21, 52, 122, 129, 198,
        236
Raiders of the Lost Ark, 21

Rambo films, 111, 112, 227
Ran, 14, 52, 141, 146
Rashomon, 129, 131, 186
Rear Window, 20, 55, 58, 63, 67, 121,
        154
Reconstruction, 142
Red Alert (George), 250
Reds, 221
Red Violin, The, 29, 141
Reivers, The, 153
Remains of the Day, 161, 164, 176,
        199
Road to Rio, 50
Robe, The, 33, 159–60
Rocky, 21, 112
Roma, 136
Roman Holiday, 53
Romeo and Juliet, 175
Room With a View, A, 148, 164, 176
Rope, 20, 170
Rosetta, 67, 141

Rules of the Game, The, 29, 131, 145
Run, Lola, Run, 29, 92, 136
Runaway Bride, The, 53

Sabrina, 53
Samson and Delilah, 210
Sanjuro, 186
Saturday Night and Sunday Morning, 134
Satyricon, 174
Saving Private Ryan, 34, 49, 50, 72, 207, 224
   analysis of, 108–109
   DVD edition, 114
Scarface, 20, 49
Scarlet Letter, The, 148, 150, 151, 153
Schindler's List, 29, 34, 49, 62, 99, 108–109, 112, 126, 150, 154, 164, 183, 192, 207
   film course material, 267–70
   laser-DVD edition, 244
Searchers, The, 198
Secret of Roan Inish, The, 71, 74
Sense and Sensibility, 71, 91, 151, 168
   analysis of, 166–67
Senses of Cinema, 74
Seven Beauties, 136, 141, 146
Seven Samurai, The, 52, 78, 79, 129, 186
Seventh Seal, The, 100, 101, 131, 174, 183, 186
   film course material, 248–50
   laser-DVD edition, 243
Shakespeare In Love, 21, 174, 187, 210
Shine, 14
Shoes of the Fisherman, The, 171
Shogun, 186
Silence of the Lambs, The, 162, 186, 230
Silkwood, 221
Sister Carrie, 153
Sixth Sense, The, 21
Slaughterhouse Five, 149, 176
Smokey and the Bandit, 213
Snow Falling on Cedars, 79
   analysis of, 218–19
Sophie's Choice, 187

Sound and the Fury, The, 153
South Pacific, 92
Spanish Tragedy, The, 50
Spartacus, 33–34, 63, 114, 136, 229
Spellbound, 185, 188
St. Joan, 226
Stagecoach, 61, 63–65
Star Wars, 21, 32, 92
Stella, 142
Strangers on a Train, 61, 78, 207
Streetcar Named Desire, The, 154, 228
Summertime, 210
Sun Also Rises, The, 176
Swept Away, 136

Talented Mr. Ripley, 187, 239, 271
   analysis of, 237–39
Tango, analysis of, 196–97
Taste of Cherry, The, 141, 146, 222
Taste of Honey, 134
Taxi Driver, 14, 21, 134, 236–37
Teaching Mrs. Tingle, 40
Tempest, The, 10, 40, 53
Ten Commandments, The, 32, 33, 52, 92, 117, 136
Tender Mercies, 221
Terminator, The, 186
Testament of Orpheus, The, 14, 129
   analysis of, 188
Thelma and Louise, 21, 29, 50, 57, 65, 86
   analysis of, 212–14
Thin Red Line, The, 49, 52
Third Man, The, 52, 55, 57, 119
Thomas Crown Affair, The, 14
Three Musketeers, The, 148
Through a Glass Darkly, 145
Thunderball, 40
Timon of Athens, 226
Titanic, 33, 34, 63, 92, 100, 136, 180
To Catch a Thief, 121
Tombstone, 49, 229, 233
Tom Jones, 50
Tomorrow Never Dies, 40
Tom Sawyer, 150
Top Hat, 128

Tora, Tora, Tora, 104
Touch of Evil, A, 118, 129
Tramp, The, 247
Traveling Players, 142
Trial, The, 57, 122, 129
Trip to Kythira, 142
Trip to the Moon, A, 131, 148
Trojan Women, 198
Trouble with Harry, The, 121
True Grit, 49
Two Gentlemen of Verona, 45
2001: A Space Odyssey, 8, 14, 19, 32,
        40, 48, 86–87, 198, 203
    DVD edition, 94
    film course material, 262–64
    laser-DVD edition, 244
Two Women, 221

Ulysses' Gaze, 132, 142, 143, 144
Uncle Tom's Cabin, 148
Underworld, The, 49
Unforgiven, The, 233

Vanishing, The, 146
Vanity Fair, 148, 176
Vanya on 42nd Street, 146
Vera Cruz, 35
Vertigo, 90, 188, 241–42
    laser-DVD edition, 243–44
Virgin Spring, 13, 56, 70, 119–20,
        186, 198, 248
Viridiana, 145
Viva Zapata, 171
Voices of Light, 187

Wages of Fear, 133
Wag the Dog, 113
War and Peace, 153
White Cat, The, 141
Who's Afraid of Virginia Woolf?, 13
Wild Blood, 149
Wild Bunch, The, 112, 198, 227
    analysis of, 230–33
Wild Strawberries, 131, 141, 248
Wings of Desire, 146
Winter Light, 129
Wise Blood, 149
Wizard of Oz, The, 203, 215
Woman in the Dunes, 146
*Women on the Verge of a Nervous
        Breakdown,* 53
Workers Leaving the Lumière Factory,
        131
World Is Not Enough, The, 82
World of Apu, 129
    analysis of, 189–90
Wrong Man, The, 121, 125
Wuthering Heights, 52, 128, 151
Wyatt Earp, 154

Yojimbo, 49, 186, 198
Young Frankenstein, 122
You've Got Mail, 95, 175
    analysis of, 48

Z, 115
Zorba the Greek, 122, 134, 142,
        172
    analysis of, 171–74